MARK MILLS

Crafting the Very Short Story: An Anthology of 100 Masterpieces

Prentice
Hall

Upper Saddle River, New Jersey 07458

Library of Congress Cataloging-in-Publication Data

Crafting the very short story: an anthology of 100 masterpieces/[compiled by] Mark Mills.
  p.; cm.
 ISBN 0-13-086762-4
  1. Short stories. 2. Short story—Authorship. I. Mills, Mark.

PN6120.2.C73 2003
808.3'1—dc21   2002019741

Senior Acquisitions Editor: Carrie Brandon
Editorial Assistant: Jennifer Migueis
Production Editor: Maureen Benicasa
Prepress and Manufacturing Buyer: Sherry Lewis
Marketing Manager: Rachel Falk
Marketing Assistant: Christine Moodie
Text Permissions Specialist: Katie Huha
Cover Designer: Robert Farrar-Wagner
Cover Art: "Near the Sea," oil canvas painting by Steven Kennedy, 18"x24", courtesy of Left
Bank Gallery, Wellfleet, MA.

This book was set in 10/12 Palatino by Lithokraft II
and was printed and bound by Courier Companies, Inc.
The cover was printed by Phoenix Color Corp.

For permission to use copyrighted material, grateful
acknowledgment is made to the copyright holders
on pages 441-444, which are considered an extension
of this copyright page.

 © 2003 by Pearson Education, Inc.
Upper Saddle River, New Jersey 07458

Printed in the United States of America
10 9 8 7 6 5 4 3

ISBN 0-13-086762-4

Pearson Education LTD., London
Pearson Education Australia PTY, Limited, Sydney
Pearson Education Singapore, Pte. Ltd
Pearson Education North Asia Ltd, Hong Kong
Pearson Education Canada, Ltd, Toronto
Pearson Educación de Mexico, S.A. de C.V.
Pearson Education—Japan, Tokyo
Pearson Education Malaysia, Pte. Ltd
Pearson Education, Upper Saddle River, New Jersey

For Halina, my heaven on earth

Contents

Stylistic Table of Contents

VOICE

Preface

This first edition of *Crafting the Very Short Story* comprises five parts. The first section is composed of 100 stories and 26 critical essays. The stories are organized alphabetically by author. The narratives represent diverse types of fiction ranging from antiquity to the present, such as Luke's parable, Galeano's fable, Calvino's folktale, Wilde's prose poem, Mann's sketch, Theroux's humor, Maupassant's satire, Moore's realism, S. L. Wisenberg's naturalism, García Márquez's magical realism, Frame's fantasy, Le Guin's allegory, Bukowski's dramatic monologue, Woolf's experimental prose, Lispector's stream of consciousness, and Poe's gothic horror. Among the internationally acclaimed authors are Pulitzer Prize winner Eudora Welty, James Joyce, and Nobel laureate Naguib Mafouz, as well as three of the finest writers of this relatively new genre: Yasunari Kawabata, H. H. Munro, and Amy Hemple. Many of the stories will serve as engaging introductions to the authors' longer works. For example, there are pieces by Alice Walker, Marcel Proust, Vladimir Nabokov, Fyodor Dostoevsky, and Herman Melville. The rich diversity of excellent literature is designed to provide a global array of choices that peak your students' imagination and desire to write creatively.

The first-person and commentary essays by distinguished writers and scholars appear immediately after their corresponding stories. In many cases, these essays explicate the writers' motivation and stylistic choices, enabling students to better understand how stylistic elements—such as character, dialogue, and mood—work seamlessly with the governing pattern of the whole to engage the reader and achieve the writer's predetermined goal.

You may want to direct students' attention to how the writers dispense with impedimenta to craft lean subtle prose, how they pare the narrative down to its most salient details, thereby achieving economy and grace.

The second section is a stylistic table of contents listing each story by one of the three stylistic devices that dominate this often quickly paced form: voice, point of view, and setting. The section that follows is a Top Ten, if you will, of guidelines for crafting a very short story. More suggestive than prescriptive, it is meant to stimulate thought about stylistic choices as students embark on the creative process. The fourth section comprises 20 exercises that will challenge students' ability to craft succinct narratives that balance emotional pitch and intellectual power.

The above-mentioned literary terms, as well as others, can be found in the glossary, the text's last section.

I must thank certain individuals whose sage counsel has been invaluable throughout the development of *Crafting*, from its embryonic form to its final proofing: Halina Makowska, whose tact, incisiveness, and translation services were without peer; the exemplary design and edit staff at Prentice Hall, Pearson Education, from Thomas DeMarco and Carrie L. Brandon to Katie Huha and Maureen Benicasa; educators and writers Siobhan Benet, Edwidge Danticat, Barbara McFarlane, Luz Tellez, Kay-Ann Boswell, Beth Coleman, Lisa Jones, Meg O'Rourke, Helen Schulman, Philip Lopate, Mary Gordon, Hemie Kim, Heather Malloy, Ras Baraka, Kevin Powell, and Richard Goldstein; and the following reviewers: Marvin Diognes, University of Arizona; Loren C. Gruber, Missouri Valley College; Frederico Moramarco, San Diego State University; Scott Odom, Loyola Marymount University; and Christopher Trogan, John Jay College of Criminal Justice.

Introduction

"I suspect," critic Charles Baxter has said, "that [the very short story] appeals to readers so much now because they are on so many thresholds. They are between poetry and fiction, the short story and the sketch, prophecy and reminiscence, the personal and the crowd. . . . We find in them a depth of intensity and penetration into human life that is a luminous difference in kind from the novel or the larger story."

Indeed. Whereas the novel illustrates the triumph of the human spirit, the very short story concerns illumination and enlightenment. The masterful stories selected for this text illuminate the human condition by dramatizing universal aspects of human nature. Consider, for example, the ways in which our actions betray our thoughts, whether we are in Welty's Mississippi in the 1970s or Parker's Spain during World War II. Each narrative starts with the scene most critical to fully understanding the story. There is no "vamping until ready," to quote Mary Gordon. The pace of this succinct genre is swift yet unhurried, its uncommon voice supplemented by inventive design. The writers pare their narratives down to the most salient details, achieving efficiency and grace with the barest of essentials. They dispense with impedimenta to craft lean subtle prose, as if seeking to explore the lyrical resonance of their dominant ideas. These compelling artistic works engage the heart and mind, and linger. The end result is evocative structural design, extremely pure sentences, and radiant distillations of light upon the soul.

"Less," as architect Mies van der Rohe once noted, "is more." Like Mies's signature buildings, the stories in this text are ostensibly simple in appearance, yet complex and precise in detail. The writers deftly employ the tools of fiction to maximize each story's power while minimizing length. The authors exercise restraint and discretion to produce the perfect visceral and intellectual pitch. Each detail works in concert with the whole to realize the author's desired effect (see Poe's essay on the single unifying effect). The cohesiveness between facade and foundation is achieved with an unseen interplay between the text's smooth surface and the veiled infrastructure below it. This invisible design comprises an intricate lattice of fictional devices, such as *structure* (the specific placement of events and details, which in this case, may deviate from the standard construction of crisis, climax, and resolution); *dialogue*, which propels a story forward and reveals character; *symbolism* (a detail that underscores a story's theme, e.g., an image of a worm-riddled apple in a narrative about innocence lost or the title of Ann Beattie's story "Janus"), *imagery* (figurative language that summons in the reader's mind a picture related to one of the five senses, such as the aroma from a steaming cup of hot chocolate); *conflict* (both internal and external); and *suspense*, which engenders in the reader an anxiousness to know what is going to occur next or at the end of a story.

The very short story's primary stylistic features are voice, point of view, and setting (character is typically only a glanced symbol; plot—the sequence of what happens in a story—is a slim shadow of the larger and more important structure). Voice—sentence construction, word choice, and emotional tone—acts as a musical instrument in the fine art of crafting the very short story. It has the primary responsibility of seducing the reader, because its rhythm and tone function in much the same way as a ballad's harmony and mood (see Baraka's and Le Guin's essays on this feature of form). Point of view is the perspective of the narrator. First-person point of view (*I lifted his bullet-riddled body and. . . .*) conveys a sense of urgency and lacks comprehensive knowledge of the characters and events in the story. Third-person point of view (*They didn't realize he was still alive because. . . .*) is usually objective and omniscient (read Le Guin's detailed essay on the topic). Setting (time and place) influences the story in the same way that cultural environment and heritage impacts personality (see Welty's essay on the subject). For example, coming of age in turbulent 1960s America will create a person much different from one who comes of age at the dawn of the new millennium in Bolivia. The common bond is that both share human characteristics.

The first person and text analysis essays by distinguished writers and scholars will enable you to understand how these fictional devices work seamlessly with the governing pattern of the whole to engage the reader and achieve the writer's predetermined goal. For example, in Petronius's tale, the author hooks the reader into the story with a familiar yet controversial subject. He then proceeds to reveal universal truths regarding human desires and frailties with simple syntax and poetic diction while simultaneously juxtaposing a macabre setting with romantically charged events. Most importantly, Petronius links carefully paced surprises to an unexpected climax while delicately emphasizing the most important attribute of humanity.

As exemplified by Petronius's "The Widow of Ephesus," *Crafting* comprises international voices and diverse fiction types ranging from antiquity to the present, including Luke's parable, Galeano's fable, Calvino's folktale, Wilde's prose poem, Mann's sketch, Theroux's humor, Maupassant's satire, Moore's realism, Wisenberg's naturalism, García Márquez's magical realism, Frame's fantasy, Le Guin's allegory, Bukowski's dramatic monologue, Woolf's experimental prose, Lispector's stream of consciousness, and Poe's gothic horror. Also included are three of the finest writers of the genre: Yasunari Kawabata (*The Palm-of-the-Hand Stories*), H. H. Munro (*The Collected Short Stories of Saki*), and Amy Hemple (*Tumble Home*).

You will find that all of the artists distill the complexities of human emotion with economy and accuracy, rapidly disclosing what we sense is happening, but are often too busy to fully acknowledge or completely comprehend. The writers give shape and meaning to the chaos of life. Predominant in their works are the themes of truthful expression of form and the search for a higher sense of order.

It is my hope that this garland of stories will provoke thought and discussion about our place in the development of the human race, prompting a renewed look at vital questions regarding humanity, the price of unconditional love and total commitment, the role of information technology, modernity, the necessity of internal and external conflict, the notion of home, and the self.

Jonis Agee

Cata 1, 2, and 3

Cata #1 Something Early

My mother got short and fat at the end, thick from bottom to top. I couldn't understand for years except that there finally wasn't a man around to make her stop. It must have surprised her too, the way her body thickened up like tapioca. She had this little black dog with a short thick body, thin scrambling legs, skinny worried tail. Big patches of hair kept falling out where he'd scratch himself. At night when everything in the house was dark, I'd hear him in the next room at the foot of Mama's bed, lapping at the spots, slopping them raw with his rough pink tongue. And I'd hear her too, sucking her teeth, even in her sleep, like there was something caught in them, some last little bit of food

Cata #2 Inheritance

There is a fury that rides the reticulated hills, that buries her teeth in the neck of a running horse, that wants nothing more than the metal salt of blood on her tongue, hair as coarse as rope in her teeth.

I am the dark hedge shears, I add the odd geometry, square the wild stalky shoots, circumcise the thick joints of old wood. You can't say I have my father's magic. In my hands is my own—the same my mother had, rubbing his back, making him soft and fluid beneath her. When he was dying, I rubbed the pain from place to place, his back breaking with every step he took. I could put it straight, I could weld the bones back together, when I wanted, when he let me. Magic in my hands. Dark, molding magic.

One day he lined up the rings he'd saved. Five in all. *These are for you,* he said. I didn't want any of them. The sick yellow diamond, the bloody ruby, the blue idiot blink of the sapphire. I felt them like little prisons wanting to cuff my hands. He lined them up and they judged his life. I don't think he felt it, but I did. The indifferent cuts they made, letting the velvet benches wet.

One for the master, one for the dame, one for the little girl who lives down the lane. I remember the rhyme. There is so much pride in uselessness. He put one on each of his fingers and held them up. They rested like angry beetles biting the tips while he irrigated them with light.

As if he had done it all for me. That's what I was supposed to feel. His little hedge of velvet caskets, the battered indifference of platinum and gold. I hid my hands from their eyes. Give me something valueless. A piece of quartz or tourmaline. Turquoise. A bead of sand you've soaked and sucked in your mouth, Father. But I said nothing, and he respected my offer. Let me rub the rings of pain from his shoulders, up his neck, out the crown of his skull.

When he died, I buried them deep in the red moroccan leather bag and hung them in the back of my closet. I hear them fighting even now. Calling like the jingle horse outside, bringing the other close in, *Come sister, come to us.* But I have my own magic. In my hands, without the cruel splintered green of that emerald or the diamond teeth fierce for my skin. Certain things you feel, you must obey. Or blacken your mouth like licorice with their damage.

Cata #3 The First Hunger

Once I went into the chicken house by myself, after I was told not to. I wanted what was there. In the winter, after the blizzard, I was the first one to push through the waist and shoulder-high drifts. Sometimes I burrowed like a rabbit through and under them. The cold hot on my face, I opened my mouth and ate as much as I could, letting the snow turn my inside white and hard. I took off my mittens to watch my red fingers stiffen, and used my teeth to pull the leather strap holding the door.

The first burst of ammonia, then dry heaving straw and feathers, was like a cloud of water I had to plunge into. The chickens began to roar, running toward me for food. It'd been a week since we could reach them. I walked slowly, giving them time to get out of the way, letting my hands warm in the heat.

I knew where to look. In the nest boxes where the shattered eggs spilled their yolks, smearing the straw with shit and yellow, then strands of blood where the fertile ones had broken. In the summer I watched for the big bull snakes that curled around the eggs before they swallowed them whole. Now, it was the dark glinting eye, the swift pointed beak that almost took a wedge of my finger.

The chickens were bodying up to my legs, pecking the snow from my pants and boots for water. Their feathers rose clattering against the roosts along the wall, where the gray pyramids of shit rested delicate as ash beneath them. I waited patiently, bending my knees slowly, so they couldn't catch me growing down to meet them. They ran and squawked and pulled hungrily at my jacket threads.

Scrambling over the empty waterers, the big flat pans for corn and mash, filled with watery shit, they dove at each other, drove each other off, as if I held in some secret palm of my hand the last food on earth. I put my hands out, willing to take the bites, until one stood too long between them and I grabbed its thick feathered body and drew it to my face. What I wanted, the licey skin, red and sweet beneath the down, that special throbbing heat of the racing bird heart, the slick oily feathers as it flapped its wings in my face, plunging uselessly to get away. I loved the sour breeze that churned up as it fought my grip, the stringy muscles taped around the wing bones I embraced, and the screeching outrage as it tried to bite itself loose, just before I let go.

In the dark corner, away from the dim overhead light bulbs and the dirty windows. That was where it waited, what I'd come for. The helpless leg stretched gray yellow, the long toenails reaching out, pushing away. A mound of torn feathers, dilapidated, the body dismantled and reshaped, guts and flesh torn away, stumps of stringy arteries and nerves stranded among shattered skin, broken bones. And the head, the eyelid itself so thin and papery it made me want to cry. The dislocated head, in the beak an open slit of dark, nose holes crusted dots of blood, comb dried brown and hopeless. The back of the head raw pink and pimply where the feathers had been pulled, day after day, hour after hour, until the bird took refuge in the corner, and began to weaken.

I didn't hate the chickens because of that. It was something I wanted to know: the hungry eye that waits, the patience hidden in the beak and claws. When I undressed that afternoon, I held up a hand mirror to watch the pale lice crawling on my arm. Then I licked them off, closing my cruel eye as if I could taste them on the back of my slivered little tongue. *Cata*, I whispered to them. *Cata*.

SHERWOOD ANDERSON

Hands

Upon the half decayed veranda of a small frame house that stood near the edge of a ravine near the town of Winesburg, Ohio, a fat little old man walked nervously up and down. Across a long field that had been seeded for clover but that had produced only a dense crop of yellow mustard weeds, he could see the public highway along which went a wagon filled with berry pickers returning from the fields. The berry pickers, youths and maidens, laughed and shouted boisterously. A boy clad in a blue shirt leaped from the wagon and attempted to drag after him one of the maidens who screamed and protested shrilly. The feet of the boy in the road kicked up a cloud of dust that floated across the face of the departing sun. Over the long field came a thin girlish voice. "Oh, you Wing Biddlebaum, comb your hair, it's falling into your eyes," commanded the voice to the man, who was bald and whose nervous little hands fiddled about the bare white forehead as though arranging a mass of tangled locks.

Wing Biddlebaum, forever frightened and beset by a ghostly band of doubts, did not think of himself as in any way a part of the life of the town where he had lived for twenty years. Among all the people of Winesburg but one had come close to him. With George Willard, son of Tom Willard, the proprietor of the new Willard House, he had formed something like a friendship. George Willard was the reporter on the *Winesburg Eagle* and sometimes in the evenings he walked out along the highway to Wing Biddlebaum's house. Now as the old man walked up and down on the veranda, his hands moving nervously about, he was hoping that George Willard would come and spend the evening with him. After the wagon containing the berry pickers had passed, he went across the field through the tall

4

mustard weeds and climbing a rail fence peered anxiously along the road to the town. For a moment he stood thus, rubbing his hands together and looking up and down the road, and then, fear overcoming him, ran back to walk again upon the porch of his own house.

In the presence of George Willard, Wing Biddlebaum, who for twenty years had been the town mystery, lost something of his timidity, and his shadowy personality, submerged in a sea of doubts, came forth to look at the world. With the young reporter at his side, he ventured in the light of day into Main Street or strode up and down on the rickety front porch of his own house, talking excitedly. The voice that had been low and trembling became shrill and loud. The bent figure straightened. With a kind of wriggle, like a fish returned to the brook by the fisherman, Biddlebaum the silent began to talk, striving to put into words the ideas that had been accumulated by his mind during long years of silence.

Wing Biddlebaum talked much with his hands. The slender expressive fingers, forever active, forever striving to conceal themselves in his pockets or behind his back, came forth and became the piston rods of his machinery of expression.

The story of Wing Biddlebaum is a story of hands. Their restless activity, like unto the beating of the wings of an imprisoned bird, had given him his name. Some obscure poet of the town had thought of it. The hands alarmed their owner. He wanted to keep them hidden away and looked with amazement at the quiet inexpressive hands of other men who worked beside him in the fields, or passed, driving sleepy teams on country roads.

When he talked to George Willard, Wing Biddlebaum closed his fists and beat with them upon a table or on the walls of his house. The action made him more comfortable. If the desire to talk came to him when the two were walking in the fields, he sought out a stump or the top board of a fence and with his hands pounding busily talked with renewed ease.

The story of Wing Biddlebaum's hands is worth a book itself. Sympathetically set forth it would tap many strange, beautiful qualities in obscure men. It is a job for a poet. In Winesburg the hands had attracted attention merely because of their activity. With them Wing Biddlebaum had picked as high as a hundred and forty quarts of strawberries in a day. They became his distinguishing feature, the source of his fame. Also they made more grotesque an already grotesque and elusive individuality. Winesburg was proud of the hands of Wing Biddlebaum in the same spirit in which it was proud of Banker White's new stone house and Wesley Moyer's bay stallion, Tony Tip, that had won the two-fifteen trot at the fall races in Cleveland.

As for George Willard, he had many times wanted to ask about the hands. At times an almost overwhelming curiosity had taken hold of him. He felt that there must be a reason for their strange activity and their inclination to keep hidden away and only a growing respect for Wing Biddlebaum kept him from blurting out the questions that were often in his mind.

Once he had been on the point of asking. The two were walking in the fields on a summer afternoon and had stopped to sit upon a grassy bank. All afternoon Wing Biddlebaum had talked as one inspired. By a fence he had stopped and beating like a giant woodpecker upon the top board had shouted at George Willard, condemning his tendency to be too much influenced by the people about him. "You are destroying yourself," he cried.

"You have the inclination to be alone and to dream and you are afraid of dreams. You want to be like others in town here. You hear them talk and you try to imitate them."

On the grassy bank Wing Biddlebaum had tried again to drive his point home. His voice became soft and reminiscent, and with a sigh of contentment he launched into a long rambling talk, speaking as one lost in a dream.

Out of the dream Wing Biddlebaum made a picture for George Willard. In the picture men lived again in a kind of pastoral golden age. Across a green open country came clean-limbed young men, some afoot, some mounted upon horses. In crowds the young men came to gather about the feet of an old man who sat beneath a tree in a tiny garden and who talked to them.

Wing Biddlebaum became wholly inspired. For once he forgot the hands. Slowly they stole forth and lay upon George Willard's shoulders. Something new and bold came into the voice that talked. "You must try to forget all you have learned," said the old man. "You must begin to dream. From this time on you must shut your ears to the roaring of the voices."

Pausing in his speech, Wing Biddlebaum looked long and earnestly at George Willard. His eyes glowed. Again he raised the hands to caress the boy and then a look of horror swept over his face.

With a convulsive movement of his body, Wing Biddlebaum sprang to his feet and thrust his hands deep into his trousers pockets. Tears came to his eyes. "I must be getting along home. I can talk no more with you," he said nervously.

Without looking back, the old man had hurried down the hillside and across a meadow, leaving George Willard perplexed and frightened upon the grassy slope. With a shiver of dread the boy arose and went along the road toward town. "I'll not ask him about his hands," he thought, touched by the memory of the terror he had seen in the man's eyes. "There's something wrong, but I don't want to know what it is. His hands have something to do with his fear of me and of everyone."

And George Willard was right. Let us look briefly into the story of the hands. Perhaps our talking of them will arouse the poet who will tell the hidden wonder story of the influence for which the hands were but fluttering pennants of promise.

In his youth Wing Biddlebaum had been a school teacher in a town in Pennsylvania. He was not then known as Wing Biddlebaum, but went by the less euphonic name of Adolph Myers. As Adolph Myers he was much loved by the boys of his school.

Adolph Myers was meant by nature to be a rare teacher of youth. He was one of those rare, little-understood men who rule by a power so gentle that it passes as a lovable weakness. In their feeling for the boys under their charge such men are not unlike the finer sort of women in their love of men.

And yet that is but crudely stated. It needs the poet there. With the boys of his school, Adolph Myers had walked in the evening or had sat talking until dusk upon the schoolhouse steps lost in a kind of dream. Here and there went his hands, caressing the shoulders of the boys, playing about the tousled heads. As he talked his voice became soft and musical. There was a caress in that also. In a way the voice and the hands, the stroking of the shoulders and the touching of the hair was a part of the schoolmaster's effort to carry a dream into the young minds. By the caress that was in his fingers he expressed himself. He was one of those men in whom the force that creates life is diffused, not centralized. Under the caress of his hands doubt and disbelief went out of the minds of the boys and they began also to dream.

And then the tragedy. A half-witted boy of the school became enamored of the young master. In his bed at night he imagined unspeakable things and in the morning went forth to tell his dreams as facts. Strange, hideous accusations fell from his loose-hung lips. Through the Pennsylvania town went a shiver. Hidden, shadowy doubts that had been in men's minds concerning Adolph Myers were galvanized into beliefs.

The tragedy did not linger. Trembling lads were jerked out of bed and questioned. "He put his arms about me," said one. "His fingers were always playing in my hair," said another.

One afternoon a man of the town, Henry Bradford, who kept a saloon, came to the schoolhouse door. Calling Adolph Myers into the school yard he began to beat him with his fists. As his hard knuckles beat down into the frightened face of the schoolmaster, his wrath became more and more terrible. Screaming with dismay, the children ran here and there like disturbed insects. "I'll teach you to put your hands on my boy, you beast," roared the saloon keeper, who, tired of beating the master, had begun to kick him about the yard.

Adolph Myers was driven from the Pennsylvania town in the night. With lanterns in their hands a dozen men came to the door of the house where he lived alone and commanded that he dress and come forth. It was raining and one of the men had a rope in his hands. They had intended to hang the schoolmaster, but something in his figure, so small, white, and pitiful, touched their hearts and they let him escape. As he ran away into the darkness they repented of their weakness and ran after him, swearing and throwing sticks and great balls of soft mud at the figure that screamed and ran faster and faster into the darkness.

For twenty years Adolph Myers had lived alone in Winesburg. He was but forty but looked sixty-five. The name Biddlebaum he got from a box of goods seen at a freight station as he hurried through an eastern Ohio town. He had an aunt in Winesburg, a black-toothed old woman who raised chickens, and with her he lived until she died. He had been ill for a year after the experience in Pennsylvania, and after his recovery worked as a day laborer in the fields, going timidly about and striving to conceal his hands. Although he did not understand what had happened he felt that the hands must be to blame. Again and again the fathers of the boys had talked of the hands. "Keep your hands to yourself," the saloon keeper had roared, dancing with fury in the schoolhouse yard.

Upon the veranda of his house by the ravine, Wing Biddlebaum continued to walk up and down until the sun had disappeared and the road beyond the field was lost in the grey shadows. Going into his house he cut slices of bread and spread honey upon them. When the rumble of the evening train that took away the express cars loaded with the day's harvest of berries had passed and restored the silence of the summer night, he went again to walk upon the veranda. In the darkness he could not see the hands and they became quiet. Although he still hungered for the presence of the boy, who was the medium through which he expressed his love of man, the hunger became again a part of his loneliness and his waiting. Lighting a lamp, Wing Biddlebaum washed the few dishes soiled by his simple meal and, setting up a folding cot by the screen door that led to the porch, prepared to undress for the night. A few stray white bread crumbs lay on the cleanly washed floor by the table; putting the lamp upon a low stool he began to pick up the crumbs, carrying them to his mouth one by one with unbelievable rapidity. In the dense blotch of light beneath the table, the kneeling figure looked like a priest engaged in some service of his church. The nervous expressive fingers, flashing in and out of the light, might well have been mistaken for the fingers of the devotee going swiftly through decade after decade of his rosary.

First Person: Sherwood Anderson on "Writing Stories"

I have seldom written a story, long or short, that I did not have to write and rewrite. There are single short stories of mine that have taken me ten or twelve years to get written. It isn't that I have lingered over sentences, being one of the sort of writers who say . . . "Oh, to write the perfect sentence." It is true that Gertrude Stein once declared I was one of the few American writers who could write a sentence. Very well. I am always pleased with any sort of flattery. I love it. I eat it up. For years I have had my wife go over all criticisms of my work. "I can make myself miserable enough," I have said to her. "I do not want others to make me miserable about my work." I have asked her to show me only the more favorable criticisms. There are enough days of misery, of black gloom.

However this has leaked through to me. There is the general notion, among those who make a business of literary criticism and who have done me the honor to follow me more or less closely in my efforts, that I am best at the short story.

And I do not refer here to those who constantly come to me saying, "*Winesburg* contains your best work," and who, when questioned, admit they have never read anything else. I refer instead to the opinion that is no doubt sound.

The short story is the result of a sudden passion. It is an idea grasped whole as one would pick an apple in an orchard. All of my own short stories have been written at one sitting, many of them under strange enough circumstances. There are these glorious moments, these pregnant hours and I remember such hours as a man remembers the first kiss got from a woman loved.

I was in the little town of Harrodsburg in Kentucky . . . this when I was still a writer of advertisements. It was evening and I was at a railroad station—a tiny station as I remember it and all day had been writing advertisements of farm implements. A hunch had come to me and I had bought a yellow tablet of paper at a drug store as I walked to the station. I began writing on a truck on the station platform . . . I stood by the truck writing. There were men standing about and they stared at me.

It did not matter. The great passion had come upon me and the men standing about, small town men, loitering about the station, now and then walking past me . . . the train must have been late but it was a summer night and the light lasted. . . .

There were crates of live chickens at the other end of the truck on which I rested my tablet. There is this curious absorption that at the same time permits a great awareness. You are, as you are not at other times, aware of all going on about you, of the color and shapes of the clouds in the sky, of happenings along a street, of people passing, the expression of faces, clothes people wear . . . all of your senses curiously awake. . . .

At the same time an intense concentration on the matter in hand.

Oh that I could live all of my life so. Once I wrote a poem about a strange land few of us ever enter. I called it the land of the Now.

How rapidly they march. How the words and sentences flow, how they march.

It is strange, but, now that I try to remember which of my stories I began, standing by the truck at the little railroad station at Harrodsburg, Kentucky, and finished riding in the day coach of the train on my way to Louisville, I can remember only the station, each board of the station wall, the places where the boards of the station wall had pulled loose, nails pulled half out. The tail feather of a rooster stuck out of one of the crates. Once later I made love to a woman in the moonlight in a field. We had gone into the field for that purpose. There were some white flowers, field daisies, and she plucked one of them. "I am going to keep it to remember this moment," she said.

So also did I pluck a feather from the tail of a rooster at the railroad station at Harrodsburg. I put it in my hat. "I will wear it for this moment, for this glorious peep I am having into the land of Now," I said to myself. I do not remember which of my stories I wrote that evening but I remember a young girl sitting on the porch of a house across a roadway.

She also was wondering what I was up to. She kept looking across at me. When I raised my eyes from the paper on which I wrote so rapidly, she smiled at me. The girl . . . she couldn't have been more than sixteen . . . was something of a flirt. She had on a soiled yellow dress. She had thick red hair. In such moments as I am here trying to describe the eyes see more clearly. They see everything. The ears hear every little sound. The very smell of the roots, of seeds and grass buried down under the earth, seem to come up into your nostrils.

The girl sitting on the porch of the house across the road from the railroad station, had heavy sleepy blue eyes. She was full of sensuality. "She would be a pushover," I thought. "If I were not writing this story I could walk over to her.

"Come," I could say to her. "What woman could resist such a man as I am now, at this moment?"

I am trying to give, in this broken way, an impression of a man, a writer in one of the rich moments of his life. I am trying to sing in these words, put down here the more glorious moments in a writer's life.

My mind moves on to other such moments. I was in a big business office, surrounded by many people. Clerks and other fellow workers in the office where I was employed walked up and down past my desk.

They stopped to speak to me. They gave me orders, discussed with me the work in which I was engaged, or rather the work in which I was presumed to be engaged.

I had been for days in a blue funk. I had been drinking. "Here I am condemned day after day to write advertising. I am sick of it." I had been filled with self-pity. No one would buy the stories I wrote. "I will have to spend all of my life in some such place as this. I am a man of talent and they will not let me practice the art I love." I had begun hating the men and women about me, my fellow employees. I hated my work. I had been on a drunk. For several days I stayed half drunk.

I sat at my desk in the crowded busy place and wrote the story, "I'm a Fool." It is a very beautiful story. Can it be possible that I am right, that the thoughts I now am having, looking back upon the two or three hours when I wrote this story in that crowded busy place, have any foundation in fact? It seems to me, looking back, on that particular morning as I sat at my desk in a long room where there were many other desks, that a curious hush fell over the place, that the men and women engaged in the writing of advertisements in the room, advertisements of patent medicines, of toilet soaps, of farm tractors, that they all suddenly began to speak with lowered voices, that men passing in and out of the room walked more softly. There was a man who came to my desk to speak to me about some work I was to do, a series of advertisements to be written, but he did not speak.

He stood before me for a moment. He began speaking. He stopped. He went silently away.

Do I just imagine all of this? Is it but a fairy tale I am telling myself? The moments, the hours in a writer's life of which I am here trying to speak, seem very real to me. I am, to be sure, speaking only of the writing of short stories. The writing of the long story, the novel, is another matter. I had intended when I began to write to speak of the great gulf that separates the two arts, but I have been carried away by this remembering of the glorious times in the life of the writer of short tales.

There was the day, in New York City, when I was walking in a street and the passion came upon me. I have spoken of how long it sometimes takes to really write a story. You have the theme, you try and try but it does not come off.

And then, one day, at some unexpected moment it comes clearly and sweetly. It is in your brain, in your arms, your legs, your whole body.

I was in a street in New York City and, as it happened, was near the apartment of a friend.

The friend was Stark Young and I rang his bell.

It was in the early morning and he was going out.

"May I sit in your place?"

I tried to explain to him. "I have had a seizure." I tried to tell him something of my story.

"There is this tale, Stark, that I have for years been trying to write. At the moment it seems quite clear in my mind. I want to write. Give me paper and ink and go away."

He did go away. He seemed to understand. "Here is paper. And here is a bottle."

He must have left with me a bottle of whiskey for I remember that as I wrote that day, hour after hour, sitting by a window, very conscious of everything going on in the street below, of a little cigar store on a corner, men going on in and coming out, feeling all the time that, were I not at the moment engaged with a particular story I could write a story of any man or woman who went along the city street, feeling half a god who knew all, felt all, saw all . . . I remember that, as I wrote hour after hour in Mr. Young's apartment, when my hand began to tremble from weariness, I drank from the bottle.

It was a long short story. It was a story I called "The Man's Story." For three, four, five years I had been trying to write it. I wrote until the bottle before me was empty. The drink had no effect upon me until I had finished the story.

That was in the late afternoon and I staggered to a bed. When I had finished the story, I went and threw myself on the bed. There were sheets of my story thrown about the room. Fortunately I had numbered the pages. There were sheets under the bed, in the bedroom into which I went, blown there by a wind from the open window by which I had been sitting. There were sheets in Mr. Young's kitchen.

I am trying as I have said to give an impression of moments that bring glory into the life of the writer. What nonsense to mourn that we do not grow rich, get fame. Do we not have these moments, these hours? It is time something is said of such times. I have long been wanting to write of these moments, of these visits a writer sometimes makes into the land of the Now.

On the particular occasion here spoken of I was on the bed in Stark Young's apartment when in the late afternoon he came home.

He had brought a friend with him and the two men stood beside the bed on which I lay. It may have been that I was pale. Stark may have thought that I was ill. He began pulling at my coat. He aroused me.

"What has happened?" he asked.

"I have just written a beautiful, a significant story and now I am drunk," I replied.

As it happens I have not re-read the story for years. But I have a kind of faith that something of the half mystic wonder of my day in that apartment still lingers in it.

Commentary: Robert Allen Papinchak on "Anderson's Prose Style"

Anderson's new short-story form, new themes, and new concept of character and incident are well represented in the story that begins *Winesburg, Ohio* (1919), "Hands." But the new style he developed is particularly transparent in this story, and what follows is an analysis of what could be termed Anderson's representative stylistic technique.

Writing about "Hands," Waldo Frank recognized "the tragic ambivalence of hands, which is the fate of all the characters of Winesburg," and, indeed, the fate of all Anderson's characters. At the turn of the twentieth century, hands "were making machines, making all sorts of things; making the world that was unmaking the tender, sensitive, intimate lives of the folk in their villages and farms. Hands are made for loving; but hands making mechanical things grow callous, preoccupied . . . fail at love."

This is precisely the dilemma that confronts Wing Biddlebaum in "Hands." At the school where he taught when he had his real name, Adolph Myers, a "half-witted boy . . . became enamored of the young master [and] imagined unspeakable things and [then] in the morning went forth to tell his dreams as facts." Biddlebaum was driven from the Pennsylvania town he had been teaching in. Though he has now lived in Winesburg for 20 years, he does not "think of himself as in any way a part of the life of the town" and is friends only with George Willard, with whom he attempts "to put into words the ideas that had been accumulated by his mind during long years of silence." The story relies on the title image as it details Biddlebaum's isolation and loneliness. Because the story is "concretely, poetically realized, its symbolism is true . . . not intellectualized, not schematized."

The words *hand* and *hands* occur 30 times in a story of just over 2,350 words. Hands are more than simply a symbol of Biddlebaum's perplexity;

besides giving the caresses that led to his expulsion from the Pennsylvania town, hands are also characterized as dragging, beating, picking berries, and caressing.

But the repetition of a symbol is not the most significant stylistic technique Anderson brought to the short-story genre. His prose is cleaner, more pristine and clipped, less cluttered with lengthy sentences and multisyllabic words, than that of Irving, Hawthorne, Poe, and other American writers to that time. Instead, Anderson used short, direct sentences, frequent modifications of nouns, series of prepositional phrases, and the repetition of phrases and ideas, which often depend on a structural circularity.

The opening sentence of "Hands" is a complex sentence whose subordinate clause comprises a series of prepositional phrases and an adjectival phrase. The independent clause introduces Wing Biddlebaum with a noun modified by several adjectives: "Upon the half decayed veranda of a small frame house that stood near the edge of a ravine near the town of Winesburg, Ohio, a fat little old man walked nervously up and down." Stripped to its bare essentials, the sentence would read, "A man walked." Here we see Anderson's use of prepositional phrases to define and develop details about a character and his setting. It is important to recognize, however, that Anderson relied on prepositional phrases not to lengthen a sentence but to clarify its sense and give fuller meaning to his subject.

When he modified a noun, it was generally to the same end. The description of Wing Biddlebaum as "fat," "little," and "old" emphasizes both his physical and mental conditions, which the remainder of the story will elaborate. The "half decayed" veranda of the "small frame" house he occupies is a metaphorical extension of the wasteland he occupies and defines Biddlebaum's dejection and his blighted predicament.

The opening paragraph of "Hands" also introduces Anderson's use of repetition for emphasis and impact. The image of hands and Biddlebaum's nervous habit of walking up and down on the veranda of the house immediately recur in the second paragraph, which ends with Biddlebaum "rubbing his hands together and looking up and down the road" as he "walked up and down on the veranda, his hands moving nervously about." These details appear one last time in the story's closing paragraph, which exemplifies all of Anderson's stylistic techniques—the series of prepositional phrases, the modified nouns, the direct sentences, and the repetitions. "Upon the veranda of his house by the ravine Wing Biddlebaum continued to walk up and down until the sun disappeared and the road beyond the field was lost in the grey shadows."

The concluding paragraph also intensifies the central meaning of the story by circling back to an image established in the fifth paragraph. Wing Biddlebaum's story is "a story of hands. Their restless activity, like unto the beating of the wings of an imprisoned bird, had given him his name." ("The name of Biddlebaum he got from a box of goods seen at a freight station as he hurried through an eastern Ohio town.")

As the story closes, Wing Biddlebaum, in "his loneliness and his waiting," prepares to go to sleep and notices a "few stray white bread crumbs . . . on the cleanly washed floor by the table; putting the lamp upon a low stool he began to pick up the crumbs, carrying them to his mouth one by one with unbelievable rapidity." This is the quick, frustrated motion of hands that, with their "slender expressive fingers," Wing Biddlebaum is "forever striving to conceal . . . in his pockets or behind his back" in order to not betray his loneliness and his waiting. The story ends still resonating with the poignancy and clarity created by Anderson's prose style.

MARGARET ATWOOD

Happy Endings

John and Mary meet.
What happens next?
If you want a happy ending, try A.

A

John and Mary fall in love and get married. They both have worthwhile and remunerative jobs which they find stimulating and challenging. They buy a charming house. Real estate values go up. Eventually, when they can afford live-in help, they have two children, to whom they are devoted. The children turn out well. John and Mary have a stimulating and challenging sex life and worthwhile friends. They go on fun vacations together. They retire. They both have hobbies which they find stimulating and challenging. Eventually they die. This is the end of the story.

B

Mary falls in love with John but John doesn't fall in love with Mary. He merely uses her body for selfish pleasure and ego gratification of a tepid kind. He comes to her apartment twice a week and she cooks him dinner, you'll notice that he doesn't even consider her worth the price of a dinner out, and after he's eaten the dinner he fucks her and after that he falls asleep, while she does the dishes so he won't think she's untidy, having all those dirty dishes lying around, and puts on fresh lipstick so she'll look good when he wakes up, but when he wakes up he doesn't even notice, he puts on his socks and his shorts and his pants and his shirt and his tie and his shoes, the reverse order from the one in which he took them off. He doesn't take off Mary's clothes, she takes them off herself, she acts as if she's dying for it every time, not because she likes sex exactly, she doesn't, but she wants John to think she does because if they do it often enough surely he'll get used to her, he'll come to depend on her and they will get married, but John goes out the door with hardly so much as a good-night and three days later he turns up at six o'clock and they do the whole thing over again.

Mary gets run-down. Crying is bad for your face, everyone knows that and so does Mary but she can't stop. People at work notice. Her friends tell her John is a rat, a pig, a dog, he isn't good enough for her, but she can't believe it. Inside John, she thinks, is another John, who is much nicer. This other John will emerge like a butterfly from a cocoon, a Jack from a box, a pit from a prune, if the first John is only squeezed enough.

One evening John complains about the food. He has never complained about the food before. Mary is hurt.

Her friends tell her they've seen him in a restaurant with another woman, whose name is Madge. It's not even Madge that finally gets to Mary: it's the restaurant. John has never taken Mary to a restaurant. Mary collects all the sleeping pills and aspirins she can find, and takes them and a half a bottle of sherry. You can see what kind of a woman she is by the fact that it's not even whiskey. She leaves a note for John. She hopes he'll discover her and get her to the hospital in time and repent and then they can get married, but this fails to happen and she dies.

John marries Madge and everything continues as in A.

C

John, who is an older man, falls in love with Mary, and Mary, who is only twenty-two, feels sorry for him because he's worried about his hair falling out. She sleeps with him even though she's not in love with him. She met him at work. She's in love with someone called James, who is twenty-two also and not yet ready to settle down.

John on the contrary settled down long ago: this is what is bothering him. John has a steady, respectable job and is getting ahead in his field, but Mary isn't impressed by him, she's impressed by James, who has a motorcycle and a fabulous record collection. But James is often away on his motorcycle, being free. Freedom isn't the same for girls, so in the meantime Mary spends Thursday evenings with John. Thursdays are the only days John can get away.

John is married to a woman called Madge and they have two children, a charming house which they bought just before the real estate values went up, and hobbies which they find stimulating and challenging, when they have the time. John tells Mary how important she is to him, but of course he can't leave his wife because a commitment is a commitment. He goes on about this more than is necessary and Mary finds it boring, but older men can keep it up longer so on the whole she has a fairly good time.

One day James breezes in on his motorcycle with some top-grade California hybrid and James and Mary get higher than you'd believe possible and they climb into bed. Everything becomes very underwater, but along comes John, who has a key to Mary's apartment. He finds them stoned and entwined. He's hardly in any position to be jealous, considering Madge, but nevertheless he's overcome with despair. Finally he's middle-aged, in two years he'll be bald as an egg and he can't stand it. He purchases a handgun, saying he needs it for target practice—this is the thin part of the plot, but it can be dealt with later—and shoots the two of them and himself.

Madge, after a suitable period of mourning, marries an understanding man called Fred and everything continues as in A, but under different names.

D

Fred and Madge have no problems. They get along exceptionally well and are good at working out any little difficulties that may arise. But their charming house is by the seashore and one day a giant tidal wave approaches. Real estate values go down. The rest of the story is about what caused the tidal wave and how they escape from it. They do, though thousands drown, but Fred and Madge are virtuous and lucky. Finally on high ground they clasp each other, wet and dripping and grateful, and continue as in A.

E

Yes, but Fred has a bad heart. The rest of the story is about how kind and understanding they both are until Fred dies. Then Madge devotes herself to charity work until the end of A. If you like, it can be "Madge," "cancer," "guilty and confused," and "bird watching."

F

If you think this is all too bourgeois, make John a revolutionary and Mary a counterespionage agent and see how far that gets you. Remember, this is Canada. You'll still end up with A, though in between you may get a lustful brawling saga of passionate involvement, a chronicle of our times, sort of.

You'll have to face it, the endings are the same however you slice it. Don't be deluded by any other endings, they're all fake, either deliberately fake, with malicious intent to deceive, or just motivated by excessive optimism if not by downright sentimentality.

The only authentic ending is the one provided here:
John and Mary die. John and Mary die. John and Mary die.

So much for endings. Beginnings are always more fun. True connoisseurs, however, are known to favor the stretch in between, since it's the hardest to do anything with.

That's about all that can be said for plots, which anyway are just one thing after another, a what and a what and a what.

Now try How and Why.

ISAAC BABEL

My First Goose

Savitsky, Commander of the VI Division, rose when he saw me, and I wondered at the beauty of his giant's body. He rose, the purple of his riding breeches and the crimson of his little tilted cap and the decorations stuck on his chest cleaving the hut as a standard cleaves the sky. A smell of scent and the sickly sweet freshness of soap emanated from him. His long legs were like girls sheathed to the neck in shining riding boots.

He smiled at me, struck his riding whip on the table, and drew toward him an order that the Chief of Staff had just finished dictating. It was an order for Ivan Chesnokov to advance on Chugunov-Dobryvodka with the regiment entrusted to him, to make contact with the enemy and destroy the same.

"For which destruction," the Commander began to write, smearing the whole sheet, "I make this same Chesnokov entirely responsible, up to and including the supreme penalty, and will if necessary strike him down on the spot; which you, Chesnokov, who have been working with me at the front for some months now, cannot doubt."

The Commander signed the order with a flourish, tossed it to his orderlies and turned upon me gray eyes that danced with merriment.

I handed him a paper with my appointment to the Staff of the Division.

"Put it down in the Order of the Day," said the Commander. "Put him down for every satisfaction save the front one. Can you read and write?"

"Yes, I can read and write," I replied, envying the flower and iron of that youthfulness. "I graduated in law from St. Petersburg University."

"Oh, are you one of those grinds?" he laughed. "Specs on your nose, too! What a nasty little object! They've sent you along without making any enquiries; and this is a hot place for specs. Think you'll get on with us?"

"I'll get on all right," I answered, and went off to the village with the quartermaster to find a billet for the night.

The quartermaster carried my trunk on his shoulder. Before us stretched the village street. The dying sun, round and yellow as a pumpkin, was giving up its roseate ghost to the skies.

We went up to a hut painted over with garlands. The quartermaster stopped, and said suddenly, with a guilty smile:

"Nuisance with specs. Can't do anything to stop it, either. Not a life for the brainy type here. But you go and mess up a lady, and a good lady too, and you'll have the boys patting you on the back."

He hesitated, my little trunk on his shoulder; then he came quite close to me, only to dart away again despairingly and run to the nearest yard. Cossacks were sitting there, shaving one another.

"Here, you soldiers," said the quartermaster, setting my little trunk down on the ground. "Comrade Savitsky's orders are that you're to take this chap in your billets, so no nonsense about it, because the chap's been through a lot in the learning line."

The quartermaster, purple in the face, left us without looking back. I raised my hand to my cap and saluted the Cossacks. A lad with long straight flaxen hair and the handsome face of the Ryazan Cossacks went over to my little trunk and tossed it out at the gate. Then he turned his back on me and with remarkable skill emitted a series of shameful noises.

"To your guns—number double-zero!" an older Cossack shouted at him, and burst out laughing. "Running fire!"

His guileless art exhausted, the lad made off. Then, crawling over the ground, I began to gather together the manuscript and tattered garments that had fallen out of the trunk. I gathered them up and carried them to the other end of the yard. Near the hut, on a brick stove, stood a cauldron in which pork was cooking. The steam that rose from it was like the far-off smoke of home in the village, and it mingled hunger with desperate loneliness in my head. Then I covered my little broken trunk with hay, turning it into a pillow, and lay down on the ground to read in *Pravda* Lenin's speech at the Second Congress of the Comintern. The sun fell upon me from behind the toothed hillocks, the Cossacks trod on my feet, the lad made fun of me untiringly, the beloved lines came toward me along a thorny path and could not reach me. Then I put aside the paper and went out to the landlady, who was spinning on the porch.

"Landlady," I said, "I've got to eat."

The old woman raised to me the diffused whites of her purblind eyes and lowered them again.

"Comrade," she said, after a pause, "what with all this going on, I want to go and hang myself."

"Christ!" I muttered, and pushed the old woman in the chest with my fist. "You don't suppose I'm going to go into explanations with you, do you?"

And turning around I saw somebody's sword lying within reach. A severe-looking goose was waddling about the yard, inoffensively preening its feathers. I overtook it and pressed it to the ground. Its head cracked beneath my boot, cracked and emptied itself. The white neck lay stretched out in the dung, the wings twitched.

"Christ!" I said, digging into the goose with my sword. "Go and cook it for me, landlady."

Her blind eyes and glasses glistening, the old woman picked up the slaughtered bird, wrapped it in her apron, and started to bear it off toward the kitchen.

"Comrade," she said to me, after a while, "I want to go and hang myself." And she closed the door behind her.

The Cossacks in the yard were already sitting around their cauldron. They sat motionless, stiff as heathen priests at a sacrifice, and had not looked at the goose.

"The lad's all right," one of them said, winking and scooping up the cabbage soup with his spoon.

The Cossacks commenced their supper with all the elegance and restraint of peasants who respect one another. And I wiped the sword with sand, went out at the gate, and came in again, depressed. Already the moon hung above the yard like a cheap earring.

"Hey, you," suddenly said Surovkov, an older Cossack. "Sit down and feed with us till your goose is done."

He produced a spare spoon from his boot and handed it to me. We supped up the cabbage soup they had made, and ate the pork.

"What's in the newspaper?" asked the flaxen-haired lad, making room for me.

"Lenin writes in the paper," I said, pulling out *Pravda*. "Lenin writes that there's a shortage of everything."

And loudly, like a triumphant man hard of hearing, I read Lenin's speech out to the Cossacks.

Evening wrapped about me the quickening moisture of its twilight sheets; evening laid a mother's hand upon my burning forehead. I read on and rejoiced, spying out exultingly the secret curve of Lenin's straight line.

"Truth tickles everyone's nostrils," said Surovkov, when I had come to the end. "The question is, how's it to be pulled from the heap. But he goes and strikes at it straight off like a hen pecking at a grain!"

This remark about Lenin was made by Surovkov, platoon commander of the Staff Squadron; after which we lay down to sleep in the hayloft. We slept, all six of us, beneath a wooden roof that let in the stars, warming one another, our legs intermingled. I dreamed: and in my dreams saw women. But my heart, stained with bloodshed, grated and brimmed over.

Amiri Baraka

Words

Now that the old world has crashed around me, and it's raining in early summer. I live in Harlem with a baby shrew and suffer for my decadence which kept me away so long. When I walk in the streets, the streets don't yet claim me, and people look at me, knowing the strangeness of my manner, and the objective stance from which I attempt to "love" them. It was always predicted this way. This is what my body told me always. When the child leaves, and the window goes on looking out on empty walls, you will sit and dream of old things, and things that could never happen. You will be alone, and ponder on your learning. You will think of old facts, and sudden seeings which made you more than you had bargained for, yet a coward on the earth, unless you claim it, unless you step upon it with your heavy feet, and feel actual hardness.

Last night in a bar a plump black girl sd, "O.K., be intellectual, go write some more of them jivey books," and it could have been anywhere, a thousand years ago, she sd "Why're you so cold," and I wasn't even thinking coldness. Just tired and a little weary of myself. Not even wanting to hear me thinking up things to say.

But the attention. To be always looking, and thinking. To be always under so many things' gaze, the pressure of such attention. I wanted something, want it now. But don't know what it is, except words. I cd say anything. But what would be left, what would I have made? Who would love me for it? Nothing. No one. Alone, I will sit and watch the sun die, the moon fly out in space, the earth wither, and dead men stand in line, to rot away and never exist.

Finally, to have passed away, and be an old hermit in love with silence. To have the thing I left, and found. To be older than I am, and with the young animals marching through the trees. To want what is natural, and strong.

Today is more of the same. In the closed circle I have fashioned. In the alien language of another tribe. I make these documents for some heart who will recognize me truthfully. Who will know what I am and what I wanted beneath the maze of meanings and attitudes that shape the reality of everything. Beneath the necessity of talking or the necessity for being angry or beneath the actual core of life we make reference to digging deep into some young woman, and listening to her come.

Selves fly away in madness. Liquid self shoots out of the joint. Lives which are salty and sticky. Why does everyone live in a closet, and hope no one will understand how badly they need to grow? How many errors they canonize or justify, or kill behind? I need to be an old monk and not feel sorry or happy for people. I need to be a billion years old with a white beard and all of ASIA to walk around.

The purpose of myself, has not yet been fulfilled. Perhaps it will never be. Just these stammerings and poses. Just this need to reach into myself, and feel something wince and love to be touched.

The dialogue exists. Magic and ghosts are a dialogue, and the body bodies of material, invisible sound vibrations, humming in emptyness, and ideas less than humming, humming, images collide in empty ness, and we build our emotions into blank invisible structures which never exist, and are not there, and are illusion and pain and madness. Dead whiteness.

We turn white when we are afraid.
We are going to try to be happy.
We do not need to be fucked with.
We can be quiet and think and love the silence.
We need to look at trees more closely.
We need to listen.

First Person: Amiri Baraka on "Voice and Beginnings"

The beginnings—words as notes and beats. My writing came out of me without too much formal grunting and extrapolation of the dry. I was first more interested in music naturally enough. African-American life is rhythm-wrapped. Its social context, its history, the living rooms and kitchens and churches and street corners pushing sweet blues afternoon and evening. We are abundantly chorded, and our syncopated walks harmonize us to the blue future like laughter from the only thing bigger and warmer than our hearts—our soul. I'd taken all kinds of music lessons, too. Thrice pianistic, trumpet, drums, plus drawing and painting classes, too. I guess our mama wanted us to be close to or well acquainted with art instead of not. I had bands, sang in choruses, hung out all night traveling light in and out of joints to hear Larry Darnell, Ruth Brown, the Orioles, Ravens, Little Esther, Lynn

Hope, Bullmoose Jackson, Louis Jordan, Nat King Cole, Tuesday mambos at Lloyd's Manor, and later Bird, Diz, Kenton, Miles and his Monkness, Thelonius, Billy, and Ella. My parents always played plus my grandparents loved old blues. We had concerts of spirituals. Mama and my grandmama, Nana, put together a gospel chorus for the middle-class negroes at Bethany Baptist each and every Sunday. My grandfather used to promise me a silver dollar to memorize Weldon Johnson's "The Creation," and the slim volume with the fantastic Aaron Douglas woodcuts has always sat heavy in the breakfasts of my poetic sensibility. My mother, on the other hand, got me to memorize Lincoln's "Gettysburg Address," which I recited on his birthday annually for years in a Boy Scout suit.

But then, all of a sudden, it was college-going-away-time and, after being the fly in the proverbial buttermilk at Rutgers, I found Howard and lifelong friends and Sterling Brown, who taught me the music as history and analysis and, you know what? I put my trumpet down. Although for sure there is nothing I love so much or identify my very soul so deeply with as music word, make no mistake. And even the first formal verse I loved was in the music, the blues, city and country. I used to walk down the halls of my high school reciting Larry Darnell quietly at the top of my voice—"YOU'RE RIGHT UP ON TOP NOW, YOU WANT TO BE FREE, WHY YOU FOOL, YOU POOR SAD WORTHLESS FOOLISH FOOL." It was poetry; the form and feeling of the blues that first moved me wordwise, like, [sung] "If you don't love me, tell me so, Don't tell other people, I'm the one to know," or "It's rainin' teardrops from my eyes," or "Yoooou made me lose my happy hoooome, You stole my love and now you're gooooone," or [dialogue] "You way out in the forest fighting the big old grizzly bear. How come you ain't out in the forest? I'm a lady. They got lady bears out there."

And with them add the Langston poems and *The Defender*, a copy of *The Rubaiyat* they sent my mother from the Book-of-the-Month Club, where I also got *Black Boy, Native Son, The Collected Poe*, and Frank Yerby. In grammar school I had a short-lived comic strip with a feature called "The Crime Wave." In my senior year, I took the only creative-writing course I ever had hanging out with two friends of mine who also wanted to be writers and imitating Poe and Yerby, terrified by Wright. Now, suddenly, I was writing some little jive sonnets and cellophane love jingles after Herrick and Shakespeare and Suckling. And then reading Joyce and Pound and Eliot and Stein, etc. An old high-school buddy, Alan Polite, I ran track with, a real hero athlete I looked up to and longed to know, to imitate, had gotten out of school and gone to the Village to live. Somehow he summoned me/us over to his all-white-with-yellow-trim Bedford Street apartment. He was a writer now, he said. I looked at the neat piles of legal pads, the walls of books, the smiling graceful woman his wife, now the writer Charlene Polite, and seeing that life and that look in his eyes and already idealizing him, I knew that's where I was headed. Yeah, that's where I wanted to go. And the music? Did I leave it? Hell, no. Check the writing, any of it. Music's still got me going.

ANN BEATTIE

Janus

The bowl was perfect. Perhaps it was not what you'd select if you faced a shelf of bowls, and not the sort of thing that would inevitably attract a lot of attention at a crafts fair, yet it had real presence. It was as predictably admired as a mutt who has no reason to suspect he might be funny. Just such a dog, in fact, was often brought out (and in) along with the bowl.

Andrea was a real-estate agent, and when she thought that some prospective buyers might be dog lovers, she would drop off her dog at the same time she placed the bowl in the house that was up for sale. She would put a dish of water in the kitchen for Mondo, take his squeaking plastic frog out of her purse and drop it on the floor. He would pounce delightedly, just as he did every day at home, batting around his favorite toy. The bowl usually sat on a coffee table, though recently she had displayed it on top of a pine blanket chest and on a lacquered table. It was once placed on a cherry table beneath a Bonnard still life, where it held its own.

Everyone who has purchased a house or who has wanted to sell a house must be familiar with some of the tricks used to convince a buyer that the house is quite special: a fire in the fireplace in early evening; jonquils in a pitcher on the kitchen counter, where no one ordinarily has space to put flowers; perhaps the slight aroma of spring, made by a single drop of scent vaporizing from a lamp bulb.

The wonderful thing about the bowl, Andrea thought, was that it was both subtle and noticeable—a paradox of a bowl. Its glaze was the color of cream and seemed to glow no matter what light it was placed in. There were a few bits of color in it—tiny geometric flashes—and some of these were tinged with flecks of silver. They were as mysterious as cells seen under a microscope; it was difficult not to study them, because they shimmered, flashing for a split second, and then resumed their shape. Something about the colors and their random placement suggested motion. People who liked country furniture always commented on the bowl, but then it turned out that people who felt comfortable with Biedermeier loved it just as much. But the bowl was not at all ostentatious, or even so noticeable that anyone would suspect that it had been put in place deliberately. They might notice the height of the ceiling on first entering a room, and only when their eye moved down from that, or away from the refraction of sunlight on a pale wall, would they see the bowl. Then they would go immediately to it and comment. Yet they always faltered when they tried to say something. Perhaps it was because they were in the house for a serious reason, not to notice some object.

Once Andrea got a call from a woman who had not put in an offer on a house she had shown her. That bowl, she said—would it be possible to find out where the owners had bought that beautiful bowl? Andrea pretended that she did not know what the woman was referring to. A bowl, somewhere in the house? Oh, on a table under the window. Yes, she would ask, of course. She let a couple of days pass, then called back to say that the bowl had been a present and the people did not know where it had been purchased.

When the bowl was not being taken from house to house, it sat on Andrea's coffee table at home. She didn't keep it carefully wrapped (although she transported it that way, in a box); she kept it on the table, because she liked to see it. It was large enough so that it didn't seem fragile or particularly vulnerable if anyone sideswiped the table or Mondo blundered into it at play. She had asked her husband to please not drop his house key in it. It was meant to be empty.

When her husband first noticed the bowl, he had peered into it and smiled briefly. He always urged her to buy things she liked. In recent years, both of them had acquired many things to make up for all the lean years when they were graduate students, but now that they had been comfortable for quite a while, the pleasure of new possessions dwindled. Her husband had pronounced the bowl "pretty," and he had turned away without picking it up to examine it. He had no more interest in the bowl than she had in his new Leica.

She was sure that the bowl brought her luck. Bids were often put in on houses where she had displayed the bowl. Sometimes the owners, who were always asked to be away or to step outside when the house was being shown, didn't even know that the bowl had been in their house. Once—she could not imagine how—she left it behind, and then she was so afraid that something might have happened to it that she rushed back to the house and sighed with relief when the woman owner opened the door. The bowl, Andrea explained—she had purchased a bowl and set it on the chest for safekeeping while she toured the house with the prospective buyers, and she . . . She felt like rushing past the frowning woman and seizing her bowl.

The owner stepped aside, and it was only when Andrea ran to the chest that the lady glanced at her a little strangely. In the few seconds before Andrea picked up the bowl, she realized that the owner must have just seen that it had been perfectly placed, that the sunlight struck the bluer part of it. Her pitcher had been moved to the far side of the chest, and the bowl predominated. All the way home, Andrea wondered how she could have left the bowl behind. It was like leaving a friend at an outing—just walking off. Sometimes there were stories in the paper about families forgetting a child somewhere and driving to the next city. Andrea had only gone a mile down the road before she remembered.

In time, she dreamed of the bowl. Twice, in a waking dream—early in the morning, between sleep and a last nap before rising—she had a clear vision of it. It came into sharp focus and startled her for a moment—the same bowl she looked at every day.

She had a very profitable year selling real estate. Word spread, and she had more clients than she felt comfortable with. She had the foolish thought that if only the bowl were an animate object she could thank it. There were times when she wanted to talk to her husband about the bowl. He was a stockbroker, and sometimes told people that he was fortunate to be married to a woman who had such a fine aesthetic sense and yet could also function in the real world. They were a lot alike, really—they had agreed on that. They were both quiet people—reflective, slow to make value judgments, but almost intractable once they had come to a conclusion. They both liked details, but while ironies attracted her, he was more impatient and dismissive when matters became many-sided or unclear. They both knew this, and it was the kind of thing they could talk about when they were alone in the car together, coming home from a party or after a weekend with friends. But she never talked to him about the bowl. When they were at dinner, exchanging their news of the day, or while they lay in bed at night listening to the stereo and murmuring sleepy disconnections, she was often tempted to come right out and say that she thought that the bowl in the living room, the cream-colored bowl, was responsible for her success. But she didn't say it. She couldn't begin to explain it. Sometimes in the morning, she would look at him and feel guilty that she had such a constant secret.

Could it be that she had some deeper connection with the bowl—a relationship of some kind? She corrected her thinking: how could she imagine such a thing, when she was a human being and it was a bowl? It was ridiculous. Just think of how people lived together and loved each other . . . But was that always so clear, always a relationship? She was confused by these thoughts, but they remained in her mind. There was something within her now, something real, that she never talked about.

The bowl was a mystery, even to her. It was frustrating, because her involvement with the bowl contained a steady sense of unrequited good fortune; it would have been easier to respond if some sort of demand were made in return. But that only happened in fairy tales. The bowl was just a bowl. She did not believe that for one second. What she believed was that it was something she loved.

In the past, she had sometimes talked to her husband about a new property she was about to buy or sell—confiding some clever strategy she had devised to persuade owners who seemed ready to sell. Now she stopped doing that, for all her strategies involved the bowl. She became more deliberate with the bowl, and more possessive. She put it in houses only when no one was there, and removed it when she left the house. Instead of just moving a pitcher or a dish, she would remove all the other objects from a table. She had to force herself to handle them carefully, because she didn't really care about them. She just wanted them out of sight.

She wondered how the situation would end. As with a lover, there was no exact scenario of how matters would come to a close. Anxiety became the operative force. It would be irrelevant if the lover rushed into someone else's arms, or wrote her a note and departed to another city. The horror was the possibility of the disappearance. That was what mattered.

She would get up at night and look at the bowl. It never occurred to her that she might break it. She washed and dried it without anxiety, and she moved it often, from coffee table to mahogany corner table or wherever, without fearing an accident. It was clear that she would not be the one who would do anything to the bowl. The bowl was only handled by her, set safely on one surface or another; it was not very likely that anyone would break it. A bowl was a poor conductor of electricity: it would not be hit by lightning. Yet the idea of damage persisted. She did not think beyond that— to what her life would be without the bowl. She only continued to fear that some accident would happen. Why not, in a world where people set plants where they did not belong, so that visitors touring a house would be fooled into thinking that dark corners got sunlight—a world full of tricks?

She had first seen the bowl several years earlier, at a crafts fair she had visited half in secret, with her lover. He had urged her to buy the bowl. She didn't *need* any more things, she told him. But she had been drawn to the bowl, and they had lingered near it. Then she went on to the next booth, and he came up behind her, tapping the rim against her shoulder as she ran her fingers over a wood carving. "You're still insisting that I buy that?" she said. "No," he said. "I bought it for you." He had bought her other things before this—things she liked more, at first—the child's ebony-and-turquoise ring that fitted her little finger; the wooden box, long and thin, beautifully dovetailed, that she used to hold paper clips; the soft gray sweater with a pouch pocket. It was his idea that when he could not be there to hold her hand she could hold her own—clasp her hands inside the lone pocket that stretched across the front. But in time she became more attached to the bowl than to any of his other presents. She tried to talk herself out of it. She owned other things that were more striking or valuable. It wasn't an object whose beauty jumped out at you; a lot of people must have passed it by before the two of them saw it that day.

Her lover had said that she was always too slow to know what she really loved. Why continue with her life the way it was? Why be two-faced, he asked her. He had made the first move toward her. When she would not decide in his favor, would not change her life and come to him, he asked her what made her think she could have it both ways. And then he made the last move and left. It was a decision meant to break her will, to shatter her intransigent ideas about honoring previous commitments.

Time passed. Alone in the living room at night, she often looked at the bowl sitting on the table, still and safe, unilluminated. In its way, it was perfect: the world cut in half, deep and smoothly empty. Near the rim, even in dim light, the eye moved toward one small flash of blue, a vanishing point on the horizon.

Giovanni Boccaccio

The Pot of Basil

In Messina, there once lived three brothers, all of them merchants who had been left very rich after the death of their father, whose native town was San Gimignano. They had a sister called Lisabetta, but for some reason or other they had failed to bestow her in marriage, despite the fact that she was uncommonly gracious and beautiful.

In one of their trading establishments, the three brothers employed a young Pisan named Lorenzo, who planned and directed all their operations, and who, being rather dashing and handsomely proportioned, had often attracted the gaze of Lisabetta. Having noticed more than once that she had grown exceedingly fond of him, Lorenzo abandoned all his other amours and began in like fashion to set his own heart on winning Lisabetta. And since they were equally in love with each other, before very long they gratified their dearest wishes, taking care not to be discovered.

In this way, their love continued to prosper, much to their common enjoyment and pleasure. They did everything they could to keep the affair a secret, but one night, as Lisabetta was making her way to Lorenzo's sleeping-quarters, she was observed, without knowing it, by her eldest brother. The discovery greatly distressed him, but being a young man of some intelligence, and not wishing to do anything that would bring discredit upon his family, he neither spoke nor made a move, but spent the whole of the night applying his mind to various sides of the matter.

Next morning he described to his brothers what he had seen of Lisabetta and Lorenzo the night before, and the three of them talked the thing over at considerable length. Being determined that the affair should leave no stain upon the reputation either of themselves or of their sister, he decided that they must pass it over in silence and pretend to have neither seen nor heard anything until such time as it was safe and convenient for them to rid themselves of this ignominy before it got out of hand.

Abiding by this decision, the three brothers jested and chatted with Lorenzo in their usual manner, until one day they pretended they were all going off on a pleasure-trip to the country, and took Lorenzo with them. They bided their time, and on reaching a very remote and lonely spot, they took Lorenzo off his guard, murdered him, and buried his corpse. No one had witnessed the deed, and on their return to Messina they put it about that they had sent Lorenzo away on a trading assignment, being all the more readily believed as they had done this so often before.

Lorenzo's continued absence weighed heavily upon Lisabetta, who kept asking her brothers, in anxious tones, what had become of him, and eventually her questioning became so persistent that one of her brothers rounded on her, and said:

'What is the meaning of this? What business do you have with Lorenzo, that you should be asking so many questions about him? If you go on pestering us, we shall give you the answer you deserve.'

From then on, the young woman, who was sad and miserable and full of strange forebodings, refrained from asking questions. But at night she would repeatedly utter his name in a heart-rending voice and beseech him to come to her, and from time to time she would burst into tears because of his failure to return. Nothing would restore her spirits, and meanwhile she simply went on waiting.

One night, however, after crying so much over Lorenzo's absence that she eventually cried herself off to sleep, he appeared to her in a dream, pallid-looking and all dishevelled, his clothes tattered and decaying, and it seemed to her that he said:

'Ah, Lisabetta, you do nothing but call to me and bemoan my long absence, and you cruelly reprove me with your tears. Hence I must tell you that I can never return, because on the day that you saw me for the last time, I was murdered by your brothers.'

He then described the place where they had buried him, told her not to call to him or wait for him any longer, and disappeared.

Having woken up, believing that what she had seen was true, the young woman wept bitterly. And when she arose next morning, she resolved to go to the place and seek confirmation of what she had seen in her sleep. She dared not mention the apparition to her brothers, but obtained their permission to make a brief trip to the country for pleasure, taking with her a maidservant who had once acted as her go-between and was privy to all her affairs. She immediately set out, and on reaching the spot, swept aside some dead leaves and started to excavate a section of the ground that appeared to have been disturbed. Nor did she have to dig very deep before she uncovered her poor lover's body, which, showing no sign as yet of decomposition or decay, proved all too clearly that her vision had been true. She was the saddest woman alive, but knowing that this was no time for weeping, and seeing that it was impossible for her to take away his whole body (as she would dearly have wished), she laid it to rest in a more appropriate spot, then severed the head from the shoulders as best she could and enveloped it in a towel. This she handed into her maidservant's keeping whilst she covered over the remainder of the corpse with soil, and then they returned home, having completed the whole of their task unobserved.

Taking the head to her room, she locked herself in and cried bitterly, weeping so profusely that she saturated it with her tears, at the same time implanting a thousand kisses upon it. Then she wrapped the head in a piece of rich cloth, and laid it in a large and elegant pot, of the sort in which basil or marjoram is grown. She next covered it with soil, in which she planted several sprigs of the finest Salernitan basil, and never watered them except with essence of roses or orange-blossom, or with her own teardrops. She took to sitting permanently beside this pot and gazing lovingly at it, concentrating the whole of her desire upon it because it was where her beloved Lorenzo lay concealed. And after gazing raptly for a long while upon it, she would bend over it and begin to cry, and her weeping never ceased until the whole of the basil was wet with her tears.

Because of the long and unceasing care that was lavished upon it, and also because the soil was enriched by the decomposing head inside the pot, the basil grew very thick and exceedingly fragrant. The young woman constantly followed this same routine, and from time to time she attracted the attention of her neighbours. And as they had heard her brothers expressing their concern at the decline in her good looks and the way in which her eyes appeared to have sunk into their sockets, they told them what they had seen, adding:

'We have noticed that she follows the same routine every day.'

The brothers discovered for themselves that this was so, and having reproached her once or twice without the slightest effect, they caused the pot to be secretly removed from her room. When she found that it was missing, she kept asking for it over and over again, and because they would not restore it to her she sobbed and cried without a pause until eventually she fell seriously ill. And from her bed of sickness she would call for nothing else except her pot of basil.

The young men were astonished by the persistence of her entreaties, and decided to examine its contents. Having shaken out the soil, they saw the cloth and found the decomposing head inside it, still sufficiently intact for them to recognize it as Lorenzo's from the curls of his hair. This discovery greatly amazed them, and they were afraid lest people should come to know what had happened. So they buried the head, and without breathing a word to anyone, having wound up their affairs in Messina, they left the city and went to live in Naples.

The girl went on weeping and demanding her pot of basil, until eventually she cried herself to death, thus bringing her ill-fated love to an end.

But after due process of time, many people came to know of the affair, and one of them composed the song which can still be heard to this day:

> Whoever it was,
> Whoever the villain
> That stole my pot of herbs, etc.

JORGE LUIS BORGES

The Book of Sand

Translated by Norman Thomas Di Giovanni

> Thy rope of sands . . .
> —George Herbert

The line is made up of an infinite number of points; the plane of an infinite number of lines; the volume of an infinite number of planes; the hyper-volume of an infinite number of volumes. . . . No, unquestionably this is not—*more geometrico*—the best way of beginning my story. To claim that it is true is nowadays the convention of every made-up story. Mine, however, *is* true.

I live alone in a fourth-floor apartment on Belgrano Street, in Buenos Aires. Late one evening, a few months back, I heard a knock at my door. I opened it and a stranger stood there. He was a tall man, with nondescript features—or perhaps it was my myopia that made them seem that way. Dressed in gray and carrying a gray suitcase in his hand, he had an unassuming look about him. I saw at once that he was a foreigner. At first, he struck me as old; only later did I realize that I had been misled by his thin blond hair, which was, in a Scandinavian sort of way, almost white. During the course of our conversation, which was not to last an hour, I found out that he came from the Orkneys.

I invited him in, pointing to a chair. He paused awhile before speaking. A kind of gloom emanated from him—as it does now from me.

"I sell Bibles," he said.

Somewhat pedantically, I replied, "In this house are several English Bibles, including the first—John Wiclif's. I also have Cipriano de Valera's, Luther's—which, from a literary viewpoint, is the worst—and a Latin copy of the Vulgate. As you see, it's not exactly Bibles I stand in need of."

After a few moments of silence, he said, "I don't only sell Bibles. I can show you a holy book I came across on the outskirts of Bikaner. It may interest you."

He opened the suitcase and laid the book on a table. It was an octavo volume, bound in cloth. There was no doubt that it had passed through many hands. Examining it, I was surprised by its unusual weight. On the spine were the words "Holy Writ" and, below them, "Bombay."

"Nineteenth century, probably," I remarked.

"I don't know," he said. "I've never found out."

I opened the book at random. The script was strange to me. The pages, which were worn and typographically poor, were laid out in double columns, as in a Bible. The text was closely printed, and it was ordered in versicles. In the upper corners of the pages were Arabic numbers. I noticed that one left-hand page bore the number (let us say) 40,514 and the facing right-hand page 999. I turned the leaf; it was numbered with eight digits. It also bore a small illustration, like the kind used in dictionaries—an anchor drawn with pen and ink, as if by a schoolboy's clumsy hand.

It was at this point that the stranger said, "Look at the illustration closely. You'll never see it again."

I noted my place and closed the book. At once, I reopened it. Page by page, in vain, I looked for the illustration of the anchor. "It seems to be a version of Scriptures in some Indian language, is it not?" I said to hide my dismay.

"No," he replied. Then, as if confiding a secret, he lowered his voice. "I acquired the book in a town out on the plain in exchange for a handful of rupees and a Bible. Its owner did not know how to read. I suspect that he saw the Book of Books as a talisman. He was of the lowest caste; nobody but other untouchables could tread his shadow without contamination. He told me his book was called the Book of Sand, because neither the book nor the sand has any beginning or end."

The stranger asked me to find the first page.

I laid my left hand on the cover and, trying to put my thumb on the flyleaf, I opened the book. It was useless. Every time I tried, a number of pages came between the cover and my thumb. It was as if they kept growing from the book.

"Now find the last page."

Again I failed. In a voice that was not mine, I barely managed to stammer, "This can't be."

Still speaking in a low voice, the stranger said, "It can't be, but it is. The number of pages in this book is no more or less than infinite. None is the first page, none the last. I don't know why they're numbered in this arbitrary way. Perhaps to suggest that the terms of an infinite series admit any number."

Then, as if he were thinking aloud, he said, "If space is infinite, we may be at any point in space. If time is infinite, we may be at any point in time."

His speculations irritated me. "You are religious, no doubt?" I asked him.

"Yes, I'm a Presbyterian. My conscience is clear. I am reasonably sure of not having cheated the native when I gave him the Word of God in exchange for his devilish book."

I assured him that he had nothing to reproach himself for, and I asked if he were just passing through this part of the world. He replied that he planned to return to his country in a few days. It was then that I learned that he was a Scot from the Orkney Islands. I told him I had a great personal affection for Scotland, through my love of Stevenson and Hume.

"You mean Stevenson and Robbie Burns," he corrected.

While we spoke, I kept exploring the infinite book. With feigned indifference, I asked, "Do you intend to offer this curiosity to the British Museum?"

"No. I'm offering it to you," he said, and he stipulated a rather high sum for the book.

I answered, in all truthfulness, that such a sum was out of my reach, and I began thinking. After a minute or two, I came up with a scheme.

"I propose a swap," I said. "You got this book for a handful of rupees and a copy of the Bible. I'll offer you the amount of my pension check, which I've just collected, and my black-letter Wiclif Bible. I inherited it from my ancestors."

"A black-letter Wiclif!" he murmured.

I went to my bedroom and brought him the money and the book. He turned the leaves and studied the title page with all the fervor of a true bibliophile.

"It's a deal," he said.

It amazed me that he did not haggle. Only later was I to realize that he had entered my house with his mind made up to sell the book. Without counting the money, he put it away.

We talked about India, about Orkney, and about the Norwegian jarls who once ruled it. It was night when the man left. I have not seen him again, nor do I know his name.

I thought of keeping the Book of Sand in the space left on the shelf by the Wiclif, but in the end I decided to hide it behind the volumes of a broken set of The Thousand and One Nights. I went to bed and did not sleep. At three or four in the morning, I turned on the light. I got down the impossible book and leafed through its pages. On one of them I saw engraved a mask. The upper corner of the page carried a number, which I no longer recall, elevated to the ninth power.

I showed no one my treasure. To the luck of owning it was added the fear of having it stolen, and then the misgiving that it might not truly be infinite. These twin preoccupations intensified my old misanthropy. I had only a few friends left; I now stopped seeing even them. A prisoner of the book, I almost never went out anymore. After studying its frayed spine and covers with a magnifying glass, I rejected the possibility of a contrivance of any sort. The small illustrations, I verified, came two thousand pages apart. I set about listing them alphabetically in a notebook, which I was not long in filling up. Never once was an illustration repeated. At night, in the meager intervals my insomnia granted, I dreamed of the book.

Summer came and went, and I realized that the book was monstrous. What good did it do me to think that I, who looked upon the volume with my eyes, who held it in my hands, was any less monstrous? I felt that the book was a nightmarish object, an obscene thing that affronted and tainted reality itself.

I thought of fire, but I feared that the burning of an infinite book might likewise prove infinite and suffocate the planet with smoke. Somewhere I recalled reading that the best place to hide a leaf is in a forest. Before retirement, I worked on Mexico Street, at the Argentine National Library, which contains nine hundred thousand volumes. I knew that to the right of the entrance a curved staircase leads down into the basement, where books and maps and periodicals are kept. One day I went there and, slipping past a member of the staff and trying not to notice at what height or distance from the door, I lost the Book of Sand on one of the basement's musty shelves.

Kay Boyle

The Astronomer's Wife

There is an evil moment on awakening when all things seem to pause. But for women, they only falter and may be set in action by a single move: a lifted hand and the pendulum will swing, or the voice raised and through every room the pulse takes up its beating. The astronomer's wife felt the interval gaping and at once filled it to the brim. She fetched up her gentle voice and sent it warily down the stairs for coffee, swung her feet out upon the oval mat, and hailed the morning with her bare arms' quivering flesh drawn taut in rhythmic exercise: left, left, left my wife and fourteen children, right, right, right in the middle of the dusty road.

The day would proceed from this, beat by beat, without reflection, like every other day. The astronomer was still asleep, or feigning it, and she, once out of bed, had come into her own possession. Although scarcely ever out of sight of the impenetrable silence of his brow, she would be absent from him all the day in being clean, busy, kind. He was a man of other things, a dreamer. At times he lay still for hours, at others he sat upon the roof behind his telescope, or wandered down the pathway to the road and out across the mountains. This day, like any other, would go on from the removal of the spot left there from dinner on the astronomer's vest to the severe thrashing of the mayonnaise for lunch. That man might be each time the new arching wave, and woman the undertow that sucked him back, were things she had been told by his silence were so.

In spite of the earliness of the hour, the girl had heard her mistress's voice and was coming up the stairs. At the threshold of the bedroom she paused, and said: "Madame, the plumber is here."

The astronomer's wife put on her white and scarlet smock very quickly and buttoned it at the neck. Then she stepped carefully around the motionless spread of water in the hall.

"Tell him to come right up," she said. She laid her hands on the bannisters and stood looking down the wooden stairway. "Ah, I am Mrs. Ames," she said softly as she saw him mounting. "I am Mrs. Ames," she said softly, softly down the flight of stairs. "I am Mrs. Ames," spoken soft as a willow weeping. "The professor is still sleeping. Just step this way."

The plumber himself looked up and saw Mrs. Ames with her voice hushed, speaking to him. She was a youngish woman, but this she had forgotten. The mystery and silence of her husband's mind lay like a chiding finger on her lips. Her eyes were gray, for the light had been extinguished in them. The strange dim halo of her yellow hair was still uncombed and sideways on her head.

For all of his heavy boots, the plumber quieted the sound of his feet, and together they went down the hall, picking their way around the still lake of water that spread as far as the landing and lay docile there. The plumber was a tough, hardy man; but he took off his hat when he spoke to her and looked her fully, almost insolently in the eye.

"Does it come from the wash-basin," he said, "or from the other . . .?"

"Oh, from the other," said Mrs. Ames without hesitation.

In this place the villas were scattered out few and primitive, and although beauty lay without there was no reflection of her face within. Here all was awkward and unfit; a sense of wrestling with uncouth forces gave everything an austere countenance. Even the plumber, dealing as does a woman with matters under hand, was grave and stately. The mountains round about seemed to have cast them into the shadow of great dignity.

Mrs. Ames began speaking of their arrival that summer in the little villa, mourning each event as it followed on the other.

"Then, just before going to bed last night," she said, "I noticed something was unusual."

The plumber cast down a folded square of sack-cloth on the brimming floor and laid his leather apron on it. Then he stepped boldly onto the heart of the island it shaped and looked long into the overflowing bowl.

"The water should be stopped from the meter in the garden," he said at last.

"Oh, I did that," said Mrs. Ames, "the very first thing last night. I turned it off at once, in my nightgown, as soon as I saw what was happening. But all this had already run in."

The plumber looked for a moment at her red kid slippers. She was standing just at the edge of the clear, pure-seeming tide.

"It's no doubt the soil lines," he said severely. "It may be that something has stopped them, but my opinion is that the water seals aren't working. That's the trouble often enough in such cases. If you had a valve you wouldn't be caught like this."

Mrs. Ames did not know how to meet this rebuke. She stood, swaying a little, looking into the plumber's blue relentless eye.

"I'm sorry—I'm sorry that my husband," she said, "is still—resting and cannot go into this with you. I'm sure it must be very interesting. . . ."

"You'll probably have to have the traps sealed," said the plumber grimly, and at the sound of this Mrs. Ames' hand flew in dismay to the side of her face. The plumber made no move, but the set of his mouth as he looked at her seemed to soften. "Anyway, I'll have a look from the garden end," he said.

"Oh, do," said the astronomer's wife in relief. Here was a man who spoke of action and object as simply as women did! But however hushed her voice had been, it carried clearly to Professor Ames who lay, dreaming and solitary, upon his bed. He heard their footsteps come down the hall, pause, and skip across the pool of overflow.

"Katherine!" said the astronomer in a ringing tone. "There's a problem worthy of your mettle!"

Mrs. Ames did not turn her head, but led the plumber swiftly down the stairs. When the sun in the garden struck her face, he saw there was a wave of color in it, but this may have been anything but shame.

"You see how it is," said the plumber, as if leading her mind away. "The drains run from these houses right down the hill, big enough for a man to stand upright in them, and clean as a whistle too." There they stood in the garden with the vegetation flowering in disorder all about. The plumber looked at the astronomer's wife. "They come out at the torrent on the other side of the forest beyond there," he said.

But the words the astronomer had spoken still sounded in her in despair. The mind of man, she knew, made steep and sprightly flights, pursued illusion, took foothold in the nameless things that cannot pass between the thumb and finger. But whenever the astronomer gave voice to the thoughts that soared within him, she returned in gratitude to the long expanses of his silence. Desert-like they stretched behind and before the articulation of his scorn.

Life, life is an open sea, she sought to explain it in sorrow, and to survive women cling to the floating debris on the tide. But the plumber had suddenly fallen upon his knees in the grass and had crooked his fingers through the ring of the drains' trap-door. When she looked down she saw that he was looking up into her face, and she saw too that his hair was as light as gold.

"Perhaps Mr. Ames," he said rather bitterly, "would like to come down with me and have a look around?"

"Down?" said Mrs. Ames in wonder.

"Into the drains," said the plumber brutally. "They're a study for a man who likes to know what's what."

"Oh, Mr. Ames," said Mrs. Ames in confusion. "He's still—still in bed, you see."

The plumber lifted his strong, weathered face and looked curiously at her. Surely it seemed to him strange for a man to linger in bed, with the sun pouring yellow as wine all over the place. The astronomer's wife saw his lean cheeks, his high, rugged bones, and the deep seams in his brow. His flesh was as firm and clean as wood, stained richly tan with the climate's rigor. His fingers were blunt, but comprehensible to her, gripped in the ring and holding the iron door wide. The backs of his hands were bound round and round with ripe blue veins of blood.

"At any rate," said the astronomer's wife, and the thought of it moved her lips to smile a little, "Mr. Ames would never go down there alive. He likes going up," she said. And she, in her turn, pointed, but impudently, towards the heavens. "On the roof. Or on the mountains. He's been up on the tops of them many times."

"It's a matter of habit," said the plumber, and suddenly he went down the trap. Mrs. Ames saw a bright little piece of his hair still shining, like a star, long after the rest of him had gone. Out of the depths, his voice, hollow and dark with foreboding, returned to her. "I think something has stopped the elbow," was what he said.

This was speech that touched her flesh and bone and made her wonder. When her husband spoke of height, having no sense of it, she could not picture it nor hear. Depth or magic passed her by unless a name were given. But madness in a daily shape, as elbow stopped, she saw clearly and well. She sat down on the grasses, bewildered that it should be a man who had spoken to her so.

She saw the weeds springing up, and she did not move to tear them up from life. She sat powerless, her senses veiled, with no action taking shape beneath her hands. In this way some men sat for hours on end, she knew, tracking a single thought back to its origin. The mind of man could balance and divide, weed out, destroy. She sat on the full, burdened grasses, seeking to think, and dimly waiting for the plumber to return.

Whereas her husband had always gone up, as the dead go, she knew now that there were others who went down, like the corporeal being of the dead. That men were then divided into two bodies now seemed clear to Mrs. Ames. This knowledge stunned her with its simplicity and took the uneasy motion from her limbs. She could not stir, but sat facing the mountains' rocky flanks, and harking in silence to lucidity. Her husband was the mind, this other man the meat, of all mankind.

After a little, the plumber emerged from the earth: first the light top of his head, then the burnt brow, and then the blue eyes fringed with whitest lash. He braced his thick hands flat on the pavings of the garden-path and swung himself completely from the pit.

"It's the soil lines," he said pleasantly. "The gases," he said as he looked down upon her lifted face, "are backing up the drains."

"What in the world are we going to do?" said the astronomer's wife softly. There was a young and strange delight in putting questions to which true answers would be given. Everything the astronomer had ever said to her was a continuous query to which there could be no response.

"Ah, come, now," said the plumber, looking down and smiling. "There's a remedy for every ill, you know. Sometimes it may be that," he said as if speaking to a child, "or sometimes the other thing. But there's always a help for everything amiss."

Things come out of herbs and make you young again, he might have been saying to her; or the first good rain will quench any drought; or time of itself will put a broken bone together.

"I'm going to follow the ground pipe out right to the torrent," the plumber was saying. "The trouble's between here and there and I'll find it on the way. There's nothing at all that can't be done over for the caring," he was saying, and his eyes were fastened on her face in insolence, or gentleness, or love.

The astronomer's wife stood up, fixed a pin in her hair, and turned around towards the kitchen. Even while she was calling the servant's name, the plumber began speaking again.

"I once had a cow that lost her cud," the plumber was saying. The girl came out on the kitchen-step and Mrs. Ames stood smiling at her in the sun.

"The trouble is very serious, very serious," she said across the garden. "When Mr. Ames gets up, please tell him I've gone down."

She pointed briefly to the open door in the pathway, and the plumber hoisted his kit on his arm and put out his hand to help her down.

"But I made her another in no time," he was saying, "out of flowers and things and what-not."

"Oh," said the astronomer's wife in wonder as she stepped into the heart of the earth. She took his arm, knowing that what he said was true.

Bertolt Brecht

The Monster

Just how many constructions can be put on a man's behaviour was shown recently by an incident at the Russian Mezhrabpom film studios. It may have been insignificant and it had no consequence, but there was something horrible about it. While *The White Eagle*—a film about the pre-war pogroms in south Russia, which pilloried the attitude of the police at the time—was being shot in the studio, an old man turned up and asked for a job. He forced his way into the porter's box at the street entrance and told the porter he would like to take the liberty of drawing the company's attention to his extraordinary resemblance to the notorious governor Muratov. (Muratov had instigated the blood bath at the time. His was the leading role in the aforesaid film.)

The porter laughed in his face, but since he was an old man he did not eject him straight away, and that is how the long, thin fellow came to be standing, hat in hand, with a faraway look amid the hubbub of extras and studio technicians, seemingly still nursing a faint hope of earning bread and shelter for a couple of days on the strength of his resemblance to the notorious killer.

For almost an hour he stood there, constantly stepping aside to let people go by until he ended up hemmed in behind a desk, and there he was at last suddenly noticed. There was a break in the shooting and the actors headed for the canteen or stood around chatting. Kochalov, the famous Moscow actor playing Muratov, went into the porter's box to make a phone call. As he stood by the phone he was nudged by the grinning gatekeeper and when he turned he saw the man behind the desk, whereupon peals of laughter rang out all around him. Kochalov's make-up was based on historical photo-graphs, and the extraordinary resemblance that the old man behind the desk had been telling them about was obvious to everybody.

Half an hour later the old man was sitting with the directors and cam-eramen like the twelve-year-old Jesus in the temple, discussing his contract with them. The negotiations were greatly facilitated by the fact that Kochalov had from the outset not been very keen to risk his popularity by playing an out and out monster. He was all for giving the 'double' a screen test.

It was not unusual for the studios to cast historical figures with suitable types rather than actors. The directors have special methods for handling these people: they simply outlined to the new Muratov the bald historical facts of the incident being enacted and asked him to play the said Muratov for the tests just as he imagined him. It was hoped that his manner would match his physical resemblance to the real Muratov.

They chose the scene in which Muratov receives a deputation of Jews who implore him to call a halt to the murders. (Page 17 of the script: 'Depu-tation waits. Enter Muratov. Hangs cap and sabre on a peg on the wall. Goes to his desk. Glances through the morning paper', etc.) Lightly made up, wearing the uniform of an Imperial Governor, the 'double' stepped on to the set, part of which was an authentic historical mock-up of the office in the governor's palace, where he proceeded to play Muratov 'as he imagined him' to the entire production team. He played him as follows:

('Deputation waits. Enter Muratov.') The 'double' came in quickly at the door. Hands forward in his pockets, bad, drooping posture. ('Hangs cap and sabre on a peg on the wall.') The 'double' had apparently forgotten this stage direction. He sat down at the desk straight away without taking off his cap or sabre. ('Glances through the morning paper.') The 'double' did this quite absent-mindedly. ('Opens the hearing.') He did not even look at the bowing Jews. He put the paper aside hesitantly, seemingly unsure just how to switch his attention to the business with the Jews. Simply froze and cast an agonized look at the team of directors.

The team of directors laughed. One of the assistants stood up with a grin, sauntered on to the set with his hands in his pockets, sat down beside the 'double' at the desk and tried to help him along.

'Now comes eating the apple', he said encouragingly. 'Muratov's apple-eating was famous. His governorship, apart from his bloodthirsty de-crees, consisted mainly of eating apples. He kept his apples in this drawer. Look, here are the apples.' He opened the drawer to the left of the 'double.' 'The deputation now approaches and as soon as the first man opens his mouth you eat your apple, my lad.'

The 'double' had listened to the young man with the keenest attention. The apples seemed to have made a big impression on him.

When shooting resumed Muratov did in fact slowly take an apple out of the drawer with his left hand, and as he began to scrawl characters on some paper with his right he ate the apple, not with any great zest, but more out of habit as it were. By the time the deputation came to the point he was wholly engrossed in the apple. After a short time, during which he had not listened to a word, he made a casual gesture with his right hand to a Jew in mid-sentence and brought the matter to an instant end.

Then the 'double' turned enquiringly to the directors and muttered, 'Who is going to see them out?'

The head director stayed in his seat. 'Have you finished, then?'

'Yes, I thought they would be taken away now.'

The head director looked around with a grin and said: 'With monsters it's not that simple. You'll have to try a little harder.' At that he stood up and began to run through the scene again.

'No monster ever behaves like that,' he said, 'That is how a little clerk behaves. You see, you have to think about it. You can't do it without giving it some thought. You have to try to imagine this killer for yourself. You have to get right into his skin. Now come back on.'

He began to construct the scene anew on dramatic principles. He built up details and developed the characterisation. The 'double's' efforts were not without skill. He did all that they told him, and not at all badly either. He seemed just as capable of acting the monster as anybody else. All he lacked, it seemed, was a little imagination of his own. After they had worked on it for half an hour the scene looked like this:

('Enter Muratov.') Shoulders back, chest out, jerky movements of the head. As he came in at the door he cast a hawk-like look at the deeply bow- ing Jews. ('Hangs his cap and sabre on the peg on the wall.') His coat fell as he did this and he left it lying. ('Goes to the desk. Glances through the morn- ing paper.') He looked for the theatre notices on the arts page. He tapped the rhythm of a hit song with his hand. ('Opens the hearing.') Meanwhile he moved the Jews back three metres with an unceremonious gesture with the back of his hand.

'You won't understand, but what you are doing there won't do,' said the head director. 'It's just ham acting. A villain of the old school, my dear chap, is not how we picture a monster in this day and age. That's not Muratov.'

The team of directors stood up and addressed themselves to Kochalov who had been watching it all. They were all talking at the same time. They broke up into groups, exploring the nature of the monster.

On General Muratov's authentic chair the 'double' sat clumsily slumped forward, staring into space but listening nonetheless. He followed each conversation closely. He made great efforts to grasp the situation. The actors playing the Jewish deputation also took part in the discussion. At one point everybody listened to two extras, both Old Jews from the city who had been members of that deputation at the time. These old men had been taken on to give the film character and authenticity. Curiously enough they found the way the 'double' had played the part at the outset had not been bad at all. They could not say how it affected others, people who had not been in- volved, but at the time it was precisely the routine, bureaucratic way in which everything was done that made the experience so terrifying. The 'double' had got this side of it pretty accurately. And the way he ate the apple during the first take, quite mechanically—during their interview, by the way, Muratov had not eaten an apple. The assistant director could not accept this. 'Muratov always ate apples,' he said sharply. 'Are you sure you were really there?'

The Jews, who had no wish to be suspected of not being among the candidates for execution at the time, took fright at this and conceded that Muratov might perhaps have eaten an apple just before or just after he received them.

At this point there was a movement in the group around Kochalov and the head director. The 'double' had pushed his way through the group till he was face to face with the director. He began to talk insistently to him with an avid, hasty look on his gaunt physiognomy. He seemed to have understood what people wanted of him and the fear of losing his bread and butter had brought illumination to him—now he wanted to make a suggestion.

'I think I know what you have in mind. He is supposed to be a monster. Look, I tell you what we can do with the apples. Just try to imagine: I take an apple, and I hold it right in front of a Jew's nose. "Eat", I say. And while he'— 'now, you listen to this,' he said, turning to the actor playing the spokesman of the deputation—'while you are eating the apple you have to remember, you must realise, that the fear of death naturally makes it stick in your throat, and yet you have to eat the apple if I, the governor, give it to you. It's a friendly gesture on my part towards you, is it not?' and he turned to the director, 'Then I could just sign the death warrant, quite offhand. And the man eating the apple sees me do it.'

The head director stared at him raptly for a moment. The old man stood stooping before him, thin, excited and yet burnt-out, a full head taller than himself, so that he could see over his shoulder; and for a moment the director thought the old man was mocking him, for he seemed to detect a passing, almost intangible scorn, something quite contemptuous and un-seemly in his flashing eyes.

Kochalov had listened avidly to the apple scene suggested by the 'dou-ble', and it had sparked off his artistic imagination. Pushing the 'double' aside with a brutal movement of the arm he said to the team, 'Brilliant. This is what he means.' And he began to act the scene in a fashion that froze the blood in your veins. The entire studio burst into applause as Kochalov, sweat streaming down his face, signed the death warrant.

The lights were rigged. The Jews were told what was to happen. The cameras were set up. The take began. Kochalov played Muratov. It had been shown yet again that mere physical resemblance to a killer means nothing, and that it takes art to convey an authentically monstrous impression.

Former Imperial Governor Muratov collected his cap from the porter's box, said a humble farewell to the porter and dragged himself off into the cold October day towards the town, where he disappeared into the slum quarters. That day he had managed to eat two apples and lay his hands on a little money, enough for a bed for the night.

My Madness

There are degrees of madness, and the madder you are the more obvi-ous it will be to other people. Most of my life I have hidden my madness within myself but it is there. For instance, some person will be speaking to me of this or that and while this person is boring me with their stale general-ities, I will imagine this person with his or her head resting on the block of the guillotine, or I will imagine them in a huge frying pan frying away, as they look at me with their frightened eyes. In actual situations such as these, I would most probably attempt a rescue, but while they are speaking to me I can't help imagining them thus. Or, in a milder mood, I might envision them on a bicycle riding swiftly away from me. I simply have problems with human beings. Animals, I love. They do not lie and seldom attempt to attack you. At times they may be crafty but this is allowable. Why?

Most of my young and middle-aged life was spent in tiny rooms, hud-dled there, staring at the walls, the torn shades, the knobs on dresser draw-ers. I was aware of the female and desired her but I didn't want to jump through all the hoops to get to her. I was aware of money, but again, like with the female, I didn't want to do the things needed to get it. All I wanted was enough for a room and for something to drink. I drank alone, usually on the bed, with all the shades pulled. At times I went to the bars to check out the species but the species remained the same—not much and often far less than that.

In all the cities, I checked out the libraries. Book after book. Few of the books said anything to me. They were mostly dust in my mouth, sand in my mind. None of it related to me or how I felt: where I was—nowhere—what I had—nothing—and what I wanted—nothing. The books of the centuries only compounded the mystery of having name, a body, walking around, talking, doing things. Nobody seemed stuck with my particular madness.

In some of the bars I became violent, there were alley fights, many of which I lost. But I wasn't fighting anybody in particular, I wasn't angry, I just couldn't understand people, what they were, what they did, how they looked. I was in and out of jail, I was evicted from my rooms. I slept on park benches, in graveyards. I was confused but I wasn't unhappy. I wasn't vicious. I just couldn't make anything out of what there was. My violence was against the obvious trap, I was screaming and they didn't understand. And even in the most violent fights I would look at my opponent and think, why is he angry? He wants to kill me. Then I'd have to throw punches to get the beast off me. People have no sense of humor, they are so fucking serious about themselves.

Somewhere along the way, and I have no idea where it came from, I got to thinking, maybe I should be a writer. Maybe I can put down the words that I haven't read, maybe by doing that I can get this tiger off my back. And so I started and decades rolled by without much luck. Now I was a mad writer. More rooms, more cities. I sunk lower and lower. Freezing one time in Atlanta in a tar paper shack, living on one dollar and a quarter a week. No plumbing, no light, no heat. I sat freezing in my California shirt. One morning I found a small pencil stub and I began writing poems in the margins of old newspapers on the floor.

Finally, at the age of 40, my first book appeared, a small chapbook of poems, *Flower, Fist and Bestial Wail.* The package of books had arrived in the mail and I opened the package and here were the little chapbooks. They spilled on the sidewalk, all the little books and I knelt down among them, I was on my knees and I picked up a *Flower Fist* and I kissed it. That was 30 years ago.

I'm still writing. In the first four months this year I have written 250 poems. I still feel the madness rushing through me, but I still haven't gotten the word down the way I want it, the tiger is still on my back. I will die with that son-of-a-bitch on my back but I've given him a fight. And if there is anybody out there who feels crazy enough to want to become a writer, I'd say go ahead, spit in the eye of the sun, hit those keys, it's the best madness going, the centuries need help, the species cry for light and gamble and laughter. Give it to them. There are enough words for all of us.

ITALO CALVINO

The Tale of the Cats

A woman had a daughter and a stepdaughter, and she treated the step-daughter like a servant. One day she sent her out to pick chicory. The girl walked and walked, but instead of chicory, she found a cauliflower, a nice big cauliflower. She tugged and tugged, and when the plant finally came up, it left a hole the size of a well in the earth. There was a ladder, and she climbed down it.

She found a house full of cats, all very busy. One of them was doing the wash, another drawing water from a well, another sewing, another cleaning house, another baking bread. The girl took a broom from one cat and helped with the sweeping, from another she took soiled linen and helped with the washing; then she helped draw water from the well, and also helped a cat put loaves of bread into the oven.

At noon, out came a large kitty, the mamma of all the cats, and rang the bell. "Ding-a-ling! Ding-a-ling! Whoever has worked, come and eat! Whoever hasn't worked, come and look on!"

The cats replied, "Mamma, every one of us worked, but this maiden worked more than we did."

"Good girl!" said the cat. "Come and eat with us." The two sat down to the table, the girl in the middle of the cats, and Mamma Cat served her meat, macaroni, and roast chicken; but she offered her children only beans. It made the maiden unhappy, however, to be the only one eating and, noticing the cats were hungry, she shared with them everything Mamma Cat gave her. When they got up, the girl cleared the table, washed the cats' plates, swept the room, and put everything in order. Then she said to Mamma Cat, "Dear cat, I must now be on my way, or my mother will scold me."

"One moment, my daughter," replied the cat. "I want to give you something." Downstairs was a large storeroom, stacked on one side with silk goods, from dresses to pumps, and on the other side with homemade things like skirts, blouses, aprons, cotton handkerchiefs, and cowhide shoes. The cat said, "Pick out what you want."

The poor girl, who was barefooted and dressed in rags, replied, "Give me a homemade dress, a pair of cowhide shoes, and a neckerchief."

"No," answered the cat, "you were good to my little ones, and I shall give you a nice present." She picked out the finest silk gown, a large and delicately worked handkerchief, and a pair of satin slippers. She dressed her and said, "Now when you go out, you will see a few little holes in the wall. Push your fingers into them, then look up."

When she went out, the girl thrust her fingers into those holes and drew them out ringed with the most beautiful rings you ever saw. She lifted her head, and a star fell on her brow. Then she went home adorned like a bride.

Her stepmother asked, "And who gave you all this finery?"

"Mamma, I met up with some little cats that I helped with their chores, and they gave me a few presents." She told how it had all come about. Mother could hardly wait to send her own idle daughter out next day, saying to her, "Go, daughter dear, so you too will be blessed like your sister."

"I don't want to," she replied, ill-mannered girl that she was. "I don't feel like walking. It's cold, and I'm going to stay by the fire."

But her mother took a stick and drove her out. A good way away the lazy creature found the cauliflower, pulled it up, and went down to the cats' dwelling. The first one she saw got its tail pulled, the second one its ears, the third one had its whiskers snatched out, the one sewing had its needle unthreaded, the one drawing water had its bucket overturned. In short, she worried the life out of them all morning, and how they did meow!

At noon, out came Mamma Cat with the bell. "Ding-a-ling! Ding-a-ling! Whoever has worked, come and eat! Whoever hasn't worked, come and look on!"

"Mamma," said the cats, "we wanted to work, but this girl pulled us by the tail and tormented the life out of us, so we got nothing done!"

"All right," replied Mamma Cat, "let's move up to the table." She offered the girl a barley cake soaked in vinegar, and her little ones macaroni and meat. But throughout the meal the girl filched food from the cats. When they got up from the table, heedless of clearing away the dishes or cleaning up, she said to Mamma Cat, "Give me the stuff now you gave my sister."

So Mamma Cat showed her into the storeroom and asked her what she wanted. "That dress there, the nicest! Those pumps with the highest heels!"

"All right," replied the cat, "undress and put on these greasy woolen togs and these hobnailed shoes worn down completely at the heels." She tied a ragged neckerchief around her and dismissed her, saying, "Off with you, and when you go out, stick your fingers in the holes and look up."

The girl went out, thrust her fingers into the holes, and countless worms wrapped around them. The harder she tried to free her fingers, the tighter the worms gripped them. She looked up, and a blood sausage fell on her face and hung over her mouth, and she had to nibble it constantly so it would get no longer. When she arrived home in that attire, uglier than a witch, her mother was so angry she died. And from eating blood sausage day in, day out, the girl died too. But the good and industrious stepsister married a handsome youth.

> A pair so handsome and happy
> We are ever happy to see;
> Listen, and more will I tell to thee.

First Person: Italo Calvino on "Economy of Expression"

Translated by Patrick Creagh

I do not wish to say that quickness is a value in itself. Narrative time can also be delaying, cyclic, or motionless. In any case, a story is an operation carried out on the length of time involved, an enchantment that acts on the passing of time, either contracting or dilating it. Sicilian storytellers use the formula "lu cuntu nun mette tempu" (time takes no time in a story) when they want to leave out links or indicate gaps of months or even years. The technique of oral narration in the popular tradition follows functional criteria. It leaves out unnecessary details but stresses repetition: for example, when the tale consists of a series of the same obstacles to be overcome by different people. A child's pleasure in listening to stories lies partly in waiting for things he expects to be repeated: situations, phrases, formulas. Just as in poems and songs the rhymes help to create the rhythm, so in prose narrative there are events that rhyme. The Charlemagne legend is highly effective narrative because it is a series of events that echo each other as rhymes do in a poem.

If during a certain period of my career as a writer I was attracted by folktales and fairytales, this was not the result of loyalty to an ethnic tradition (seeing that my roots are planted in an entirely modern and cosmopolitan Italy), nor the result of nostalgia for things I read as a child (in my family, a child could read only educational books, particularly those with some scientific basis). It was rather because of my interest in style and structure, in the economy, rhythm, and hard logic with which they are told. In working on my transcription of Italian folktales as recorded by scholars of the last century, I found most enjoyment when the original text was extremely laconic. This I tried to convey, respecting the conciseness and at the same time trying to obtain the greatest possible narrative force. See, for instance, number 57 in *Italian Folktales (Fiabe italiane):*

> A king fell ill and was told by his doctors "Majesty, if you want to get well, you'll have to obtain one of the ogre's feathers. That will not be easy, since the ogre eats every human he sees."

> The king passed the word on to everybody, but no one was willing to go to the ogre. Then he asked one of his most loyal and courageous attendants, who said, "I will go."
>
> The man was shown the road and told, "On a mountaintop are seven caves, in one of which lives the ogre."
>
> The man set out and walked until dark, when he stopped at an inn . . .

Not a word is said about what illness the king was suffering from, or why on earth an ogre should have feathers, or what those caves were like. But everything mentioned has a necessary function in the plot. The very first characteristic of a folktale is economy of expression. The most outlandish adventures are recounted with an eye fixed on the bare essentials. There is always a battle against time, against the obstacles that prevent or delay the fulfillment of a desire or the repossession of something cherished but lost. Or time can stop altogether, as in the castle of Sleeping Beauty. To bring this about, Charles Perrault has only to write: "Les broches mâmes qui étaient au feu toutes pleines de perdrix et de faisans s'endormirent, et le feu aussi. Tout cela se fit en un moment; les Fées n'étaient pas longues à leur besogne" (Even the spits on the fire, all laden with partridges and pheasants, went to sleep, and the fire along with them. All this happened in a moment: the fairies were not long at their work).

The relativity of time is the subject of a folktale known almost everywhere: a journey to another world is made by someone who thinks it has lasted only a few hours, though when he returns, his village is unrecognizable because years and years have gone by. In early American literature, of course, this was the theme of Washington Irving's "Rip Van Winkle," which acquired the status of a foundation myth for your ever-changing society.

This motif can also be interpreted as an allegory of narrative time and the way in which it cannot be measured against real time. And the same significance can be seen in the reverse operation, in the expanding of time by the internal proliferations from one story to another, which is a feature of oriental storytelling. Scheherazade tells a story in which someone tells a story in which someone tells a story, and so forth. The art that enables Scheherazade to save her life every night consists of knowing how to join one story to another, breaking off at just the right moment—two ways of manipulating the continuity and discontinuity of time. It is a secret of rhythm, a way of capturing time that we can recognize from the very beginning: in the epic by means of the metrical effects of the verse, in prose narrative by those effects that make us eager to know what comes next.

Everybody knows the discomfort felt when someone sets out to tell a joke without being good at it and gets everything wrong, by which I mean, above all, the links and the rhythms. This feeling is evoked in one of Boccaccio's novellas (VI.1), which is in fact devoted to the art of storytelling.

A jovial company of ladies and gentlemen, guests of a Florentine lady in her country house, go for an after-lunch outing to another pleasant place in the neighborhood. To cheer them on their way, one of the men offers to tell a story.

> "Mistress Oretta, if you please, I shall carry you a great part of the way we have to go on horseback, with one of the best stories in the world." "Sir," she replied, "I pray you to do so; that will be most agreeable." Hearing this, master cavalier, who perhaps fared no better with sword at side than with tale on tongue, began his story, which was indeed a very fine one. But what with his repeating of the same word three or four or six times over, his recapitulations, his "I didn't say that right," his erring in putting one name for another, he spoiled it dreadfully. Also his delivery was very poor, quite out of keeping with the circumstances and the quality of his persons. Mistress Oretta, hearing him, was many times taken with a sweat and a sinking of the heart, as if she were sick and about to die. At last, unable to endure the torment any longer and seeing that the gentleman was entangled in a maze of his own making, she said pleasantly: "Sir, this horse of yours has too hard a trot, and I pray you to set me on my feet again."

The novella is a horse, a means of transport with its own pace, a trot or a gallop according to the distance and the ground it has to travel over; but the speed Boccaccio is talking about is a mental speed. The listed defects of the clumsy storyteller are above all offenses against rhythm, as well as being defects of style, because he does not use the expressions appropriate either to the characters or to the events. In other words, even correctness of style is a question of quick adjustment, of agility of both thought and expression. . . .

Angela Carter

The Werewolf

It is a northern country; they have cold weather, they have cold hearts.

Cold; tempest; wild beasts in the forest. It is a hard life. Their houses are built of logs, dark and smoky within. There will be a crude icon of the virgin behind a guttering candle, the leg of a pig hung up to cure, a string of drying mushrooms. A bed, a stool, a table. Harsh, brief, poor lives.

To these upland woodsmen, the Devil is as real as you or I. More so; they have not seen us nor even know that we exist, but the Devil they glimpse often in the graveyards, those bleak and touching townships of the dead where the graves are marked with portraits of the deceased in the naïf style and there are no flowers to put in front of them, no flowers grow there, so they put out small, votive offerings, little loaves, sometimes a cake that the bears come lumbering from the margins of the forest to snatch away. At midnight especially on Walpurgisnacht, the Devil holds picnics in the graveyards and invites the witches; then they dig up fresh corpses, and eat them. Anyone will tell you that.

Wreaths of garlic on the doors keep out the vampires. A blue-eyed child born feet first on the night of St John's Eve will have second sight. When they discover a witch—some old woman whose cheeses ripen when her neighbour's do not, another old woman whose black cat, oh, sinister! *follows her about all the time*, they strip the crone, search her for marks, for the supernumary nipple her familiar sucks. They soon find it. Then they stone her to death.

Winter and cold weather.

Go and visit grandmother, who has been sick. Take her the oatcakes I've baked for her on the hearthstone and a little pot of butter.

The good child does as her mother bids—five miles' trudge through the forest; do not leave the path because of the bears, the wild boar, the starving wolves. Here, take your father's hunting knife; you know how to use it.

The child had a scabby coat of sheepskin to keep out the cold, she knew the forest too well to fear it but she must always be on her guard. When she heard that freezing howl of a wolf, she dropped her gifts, seized her knife and turned on the beast.

It was a huge one, with red eyes and running, grizzled chops; any but a mountaineer's child would have died of fright at the sight of it. It went for her throat, as wolves do, but she made a great swipe at it with her father's knife and slashed off its right forepaw.

The wolf let out a gulp, almost a sob, when she saw what had happened to it; wolves are less brave than they seem. It went lolloping off disconsolately between the trees as well as it could on three legs, leaving a trail of blood behind it. The child wiped the blade of her knife clean on her apron, wrapped up the wolf's paw in the cloth in which her mother had packed the oatcakes and went on towards her grandmother's house. Soon it came on to snow so thickly that the path and any footsteps, track or spoor that might have been upon it were obscured.

She found her grandmother was so sick she had taken to her bed and fallen into a fretful sleep, moaning and shaking so that the child guessed she had a fever. She felt the forehead, it burned. She shook out the cloth from her basket, to use it to make the old woman a cold compress, and the wolf's paw fell to the floor.

But it was no longer a wolf's paw. It was a hand, chopped off at the wrist, a hand toughened with work and freckled with age. There was a wedding ring on the third finger and a wart on the index finger. By the wart, she knew it for her grandmother's hand.

She pulled back the sheet but the old woman woke up, at that, and began to struggle, squawking, and shrieking like a thing possessed. But the child was strong, and armed with her father's hunting knife; she managed to hold her grandmother down long enough to see the cause of her fever. There was a bloody stump where her right hand should have been, festering already.

The child crossed herself and cried out so loud the neighbours heard her and came rushing in. They knew the wart on the hand at once for a witch's nipple; they drove the old woman, in her shift as she was, out into the snow with sticks, beating her old carcass as far as the edge of the forest, and pelted her with stones until she fell down dead.

Now the child lived in her grandmother's house; she prospered.

RAYMOND CARVER

Popular Mechanics

Early that day the weather turned and the snow was melting into dirty water. Streaks of it ran down from the little shoulder-high window that faced the backyard. Cars slushed by on the street outside, where it was getting dark. But it was getting dark on the inside too.

He was in the bedroom pushing clothes into a suitcase when she came to the door.

I'm glad you're leaving! I'm glad you're leaving! she said. Do you hear?

He kept on putting his things into the suitcase.

Son of a bitch! I'm so glad you're leaving! She began to cry. You can't even look me in the face, can you?

Then she noticed the baby's picture on the bed and picked it up.

He looked at her and she wiped her eyes and stared at him before turning and going back to the living room.

Bring that back, he said.

Just get your things and get out, she said.

He did not answer. He fastened the suitcase, put on his coat, looked around the bedroom before turning off the light. Then he went out to the living room.

She stood in the doorway of the little kitchen, holding the baby.

I want the baby, he said.

Are you crazy?

No, but I want the baby. I'll get someone to come by for his things.

You're not touching this baby, she said.

The baby had begun to cry and she uncovered the blanket from around his head.

Oh, oh, she said, looking at the baby.

He moved toward her.

For God's sake! she said. She took a step back into the kitchen.

I want the baby.

Get out of here!

She turned and tried to hold the baby over in a corner behind the stove.

But he came up. He reached across the stove and tightened his hands on the baby.

Let go of him, he said.

Get away, get away! she cried.

The baby was red-faced and screaming. In the scuffle they knocked down a flowerpot that hung behind the stove.

He crowded her into the wall then, trying to break her grip. He held on to the baby and pushed with all his weight.

Let go of him, he said.

Don't, she said. You're hurting the baby, she said.

I'm not hurting the baby, he said.

The kitchen window gave no light. In the near-dark he worked on her fisted fingers with one hand and with the other hand he gripped the screaming baby up under an arm near the shoulder.

She felt her fingers being forced open. She felt the baby going from her.

No! she screamed just as her hands came loose.

She would have it, this baby. She grabbed for the baby's other arm. She caught the baby around the wrist and leaned back.

But he would not let go. He felt the baby slipping out of his hands and he pulled back very hard.

In this manner, the issue was decided.

First Person: Raymond Carver, "On Writing"

Back in the mid-1960s, I found I was having trouble concentrating my attention on long narrative fiction. For a time I experienced difficulty in trying to read it as well as in attempting to write it. My attention span had gone out on me; I no longer had the patience to try to write novels. It's an involved story, too tedious to talk about here. But I know it has much to do now with why I write poems and short stories. Get in, get out. Don't linger. Go on. It could be that I lost any great ambitions at about the same time, in my late twenties. If I did, I think it was good it happened. Ambition and a little luck are good things for a writer to have going for him. Too much ambition and bad luck, or no luck at all, can be killing. There has to be talent.

Some writers have a bunch of talent; I don't know any writers who are without it. But a unique and exact way of looking at things, and finding the right context for expressing that way of looking, that's something else. *The World According to Garp* is, of course, the marvelous world according to John Irving. There is another world according to Flannery O'Connor, and others according to William Faulkner and Ernest Hemingway. There are worlds according to Cheever, Updike, Singer, Stanley Elkin, Ann Beattie, Cynthia Ozick, Donald Barthelme, Mary Robison, William Kittredge, Barry Hannah, Ursula K. Le Guin. Every great or even every very good writer makes the world over according to his own specifications.

It's akin to style, what I'm talking about, but it isn't style alone. It is the writer's particular and unmistakable signature on everything he writes. It is his world and no other. This is one of the things that distinguishes one writer from another. Not talent. There's plenty of that around. But a writer who has some special way of looking at things and who gives artistic expression to that way of looking: that writer may be around for a time.

Isak Dinesen said that she wrote a little every day, without hope and without despair. Someday I'll put that on a three-by-five card and tape it to the wall beside my desk. I have some three-by-five cards on the wall now. "Fundamental accuracy of statement is the ONE sole morality of writing." Ezra Pound. It is not everything by ANY means, but if a writer has "fundamental accuracy of statement" going for him, he's at least on the right track.

I have a three-by-five up there with this fragment of a sentence from a story by Chekov: ". . . and suddenly everything became clear to him." I find these words filled with wonder and possibility. I love their simple clarity, and the hint of revelation that's implied. There is mystery, too. What has been unclear before? Why is it just now becoming clear? What's happened? Most of all—what now? There are consequences as a result of such sudden awakenings. I feel a sharp sense of relief—and anticipation.

I overheard the writer Geoffrey Wolff say "No cheap tricks" to a group of writing students. That should go on a three-by-five card. I'd amend it a little to "No tricks." Period. I hate tricks. At the first sign of a trick or a gimmick in a piece of fiction, a cheap trick or even an elaborate trick, I tend to look for cover. Tricks are ultimately boring, and I get bored easily, which may go along with my not having much of an attention span. But extremely clever chi-chi writing, or just plain tomfoolery writing, puts me to sleep. Writers don't need tricks or gimmicks or even necessarily need to be the smartest fellows on the block. At the risk of appearing foolish, a writer sometimes needs to be able to just stand and gape at this or that thing—a sunset or an old shoe—in absolute and simple amazement.

Some months back, in the *New York Times Book Review*, John Barth said that ten years ago most of the students in his fiction writing seminar were interested in "formal innovation," and this no longer seems to be the case. He's a little worried that writers are going to start writing mom and pop novels in the 1980s. He worries that experimentation may be on the way out, along with liberalism. I get a little nervous if I find myself within earshot of somber discussions about "formal innovation" in fiction writing. Too often "experimentation" is a license to be careless, silly or imitative in the writing. Even worse, a license to try to brutalize or alienate the reader. Too often such writing gives us no news of the world, or else describes a desert landscape and that's all—a few dunes and lizards here and there, but no people; a place uninhabited by anything recognizably human, a place of interest only to a few scientific specialists.

It should be noted that real experiment in fiction is original, hard-earned and cause for rejoicing. But someone else's way of looking at things—Barthelme's, for instance—should not be chased after by other writers. It won't work. There is only one Barthelme, and for another writer to try to appropriate Barthelme's peculiar sensibility or *mise en scène* under the rubric of innovation is for that writer to mess around with chaos and disaster and, worse, self-deception. The real experimenters have to Make It New, as Pound urged, and in the process have to find things out for themselves. But if writers haven't taken leave of their senses, they also want to stay in touch with us, they want to carry news from their world to ours.

It's possible, in a poem or a short story, to write about commonplace things and objects using commonplace but precise language, and to endow those things—a chair, a window curtain, a fork, a stone, a woman's earring—with immense, even startling power. It is possible to write a line of seemingly innocuous dialogue and have it send a chill along the reader's spine—the source of artistic delight, as Nabokov would have it. That's the kind of writing that most interests me. I hate sloppy or haphazard writing whether it flies under the banner of experimentation or else is just clumsily rendered realism. In Isaac Babel's wonderful short story, "Guy de Maupassant," the narrator has this to say about the writing of fiction: "No iron can pierce the heart with such force as a period put just at the right place." This too ought to go on a three-by-five.

Evan Connell said once that he knew he was finished with a short story when he found himself going through it and taking out commas and then going through the story again and putting commas back in the same places. I like that way of working on something. I respect that kind of care for what is being done. That's all we have, finally, the words, and they had better be the right ones, with the punctuation in the right places so that they can best say what they are meant to say. If the words are heavy with the writer's own unbridled emotions, or if they are imprecise and inaccurate for some other reason—if the words are in any way blurred—the reader's eyes will slide right over them and nothing will be achieved. The reader's own artistic sense will simply not be engaged. Henry James called this sort of hapless writing "weak specification."

I have friends who've told me they had to hurry a book because they needed the money, their editor or their wife was leaning on them or leaving them—something, some apology for the writing not being very good. "It would have been better if I'd taken the time." I was dumbfounded when I heard a novelist friend say this. I still am, if I think about it, which I don't. It's none of my business. But if the writing can't be made as good as it is within us to make it, then why do it? In the end, the satisfaction of having done our best, and the proof of that labor, is the one thing we can take into the grave. I wanted to say to my friend, for heaven's sake go do something else. There have to be easier and maybe more honest ways to try and earn a living. Or else just do it to the best of your abilities, your talents, and then don't justify or make excuses. Don't complain, don't explain.

In an essay called, simply enough, "Writing Short Stories," Flannery O'Connor talks about writing as an act of discovery. O'Connor says she most often did not know where she was going when she sat down to work on a short story. She says she doubts that many writers know where they are going when they begin something. She uses "Good Country People" as an example of how she put together a short story whose ending she could not even guess at until she was nearly there:

> When I started writing that story, I didn't know there was going to be a Ph.D. with a wooden leg in it. I merely found myself one morning writing a description of two women I knew something about, and before I realized it, I had equipped one of them with a daughter with a wooden leg. I brought in the Bible salesman, but I had no idea what I was going to do with him. I didn't know he was going to steal that wooden leg until ten or twelve lines before he did it, but when I found out that this was what was going to happen, I realized it was inevitable.

When I read this some years ago it came as a shock that she, or anyone for that matter, wrote stories in this fashion. I thought this was my uncomfortable secret, and I was a little uneasy with it. For sure I thought this way of working on a short story somehow revealed my own shortcomings. I remember being tremendously heartened by reading what she had to say on the subject.

I once sat down to write what turned out to be a pretty good story, though only the first sentence of the story had offered itself to me when I began it. For several days I'd been going around with this sentence in my head: "He was running the vacuum cleaner when the telephone rang." I knew a story was there and that it wanted telling. I felt it in my bones, that a story belonged with that beginning, if I could just have the time to write it. I found the time, an entire day—twelve, fifteen hours even—if I wanted to make use of it. I did, and I sat down in the morning and wrote the first sentence, and other sentences promptly began to attach themselves. I made the story just as I'd make a poem; one line and then the next, and the next. Pretty soon I could see a story, and I knew it was my story, the one I'd been wanting to write.

I like it when there is some feeling of threat or sense of menace in short stories. I think a little menace is fine to have in a story. For one thing, it's good for the circulation. There has to be tension, a sense that something is imminent, that certain things are in relentless motion, or else, most often, there simply won't be a story. What creates tension in a piece of fiction is partly the way the concrete words are linked together to make up the visible action of the story. But it's also the things that are left out, that are implied, the landscape just under the smooth (but sometimes broken and unsettled) surface of things.

V. S. Pritchett's definition of a short story is "something glimpsed from the corner of the eye, in passing." Notice the "glimpse" part of this. First the glimpse. Then the glimpse given life, turned into something that illuminates the moment and may, if we're lucky—that word again—have even further-ranging consequences and meaning. The short story writer's task is to invest the glimpse with all that is in his power. He'll bring his intelligence and literary skill to bear (his talent), his sense of proportion and sense of the fitness of things: of how things out there really are and how he sees those things—like no one else sees them. And this is done through the use of clear and specific language, language used so as to bring to life the details that will light up the story for the reader. For the details to be concrete and convey meaning, the language must be accurate and precisely given. The words can be so precise they may even sound flat, but they can still carry; if used right, they can hit all the notes.

GEOFFREY CHAUCER

The Physician's Tale

Here follows the physician's tale: Once there was a knight, as Livy tells us, named Virginius, very honorable and worthy, with many friends, and very wealthy. This knight and his wife had one daughter, but no other children, during their lives. This girl surpassed all others in exceptional beauty, for Nature, with sovereign care, had endowed her with supreme excellence, as if to say: "See, I, Nature, can create and adorn a creature thus when I so desire. Who can counterfeit my work? Not Pygmalion, even if he forged and beat, or engraved, or painted forever. And I dare say that Appelles and Zeuxis would also work in vain at their engraving, painting, forging, or beating, if they presumed to counterfeit my work. For He who is the Chief Creator has made me his Vicar General, to form and paint earthly creatures just as I wish, and everything under the waxing and waning moon is in my care. And in my own work I do not need to ask anyone's advice; my Lord and I are in complete agreement. I created this girl out of worship for my Lord, just as I do with all my other creatures, whatever their complexions or figures." It seems to me that Nature would speak in this fashion.

This girl in whom Nature took such delight was fourteen years old. Just as Nature can paint a lily white or a rose red, so she had painted the lovely body of this noble girl before birth, wherever such colors were appropriate, while Phoebus had dyed her long hair so that it resembled his burnished sunbeams. And if her beauty was extraordinary, a thousand times more so was her virtue. In her there was lacking no quality which deserves praise for discretion. She was chaste in spirit as well as in body, and she grew into a virgin, humble, abstinent, temperate, patient, and moderate both in manner and dress. She was always discreet in answering; though I'll venture that she was as wise as Pallas, and her eloquence was always womanly and plain, she used no counterfeit terms to appear wise, but spoke in accordance with her station, and all her words, great and small, were proper and courteous. She was modest with a maiden's modesty, constant in affection, and always industrious to avoid idleness. Bacchus had no power at all over her mouth; wine given to the young increases Venus' influence, just as when people feed a fire with oil or grease. Because of her natural purity, she frequently pretended to be ill in order to avoid company where there was likely to be talk of folly, as is the case at feasts, revels, and dances, which are the occasions for wantonness. Such things make children become ripe and bold too early, as anyone can see—a thing that has always been very dangerous. For a girl learns about boldness all too soon, when she becomes a woman.

You governesses, who in your old age have supervision over the daughters of lords, do not take offense at my words. Remember, you are placed in charge of the daughters of lords for one of only two reasons: either because you have retained your virtue, or else because you have fallen into such frailty that you are very familiar with the old dance and have decided to give up such misconduct forever. Therefore, for the sake of Christ, be sure that you are not lax in teaching virtue to your charges. A man who has stolen venison, but has given up all his evil ways and his old trade, can guard a forest better than any other man. Now guard your charges well, for you can do it if you want to. See that you do not countenance any kind of vice, or you will be damned for your wicked intentions; for whoever does so is surely a traitor. And take heed of what I say: of all betrayals the most evil occurs when a man betrays an innocent.

You fathers and you mothers, also; whether you have one child or more, their supervision is your full responsibility while they are under your control. Beware that they do not perish because of the poor example you set them or because of your negligence in scolding them; for I dare say that if they die you shall pay dearly for it. Under a soft and negligent shepherd, many a sheep and lamb have been devoured by the wolf. Let this one example suffice for the present, for I must turn again to my story.

This girl, who is the subject of this tale, so conducted herself that she needed no governess; for she was so prudent and generous that in her manner of living all girls could read, as in a book, every good word or deed which befits a virtuous maiden. As a result, the fame of both her beauty and her excellence spread far and wide. Everyone who admired virtue in that land, except Envy, who regrets anyone else's prosperity and rejoices in his woes and misfortunes (so St. Augustine describes it), sang her praises.

One day this girl went to a temple in the town with her dear mother, as is the custom for young girls. Now there was then a judge in this town who was governor of that region. And it so happened that this judge cast his eyes upon the girl, appraising her rapidly as she passed by where he stood. At once his heart and his feelings changed, he was so taken by her beauty, and he said quietly to himself, "This girl must be mine, in spite of any man!"

At once the devil ran into his heart and taught him quickly that be could win the girl to his purpose by trickery. For, truly, it seemed to the judge that he would be unable to accomplish his purpose either by force or bribery, for she had many powerful friends, and also she was confirmed in such steadfast righteousness that he knew he could never persuade her to bodily sin. Therefore, after great deliberation, he sent for a fellow in town whom he knew to be cunning and bold. The judge told his tale to this fellow secretly, and made him swear to tell no one, under the penalty of losing his head. When the wicked plan was agreed to, the judge was happy and treated the fellow generously, giving him many precious and expensive gifts.

When the conspiracy had been planned point by point, to the end that the judge's lust should be subtly satisfied, as you shall soon hear fully, the fellow, who was named Claudius, went home. The false judge, whose name was Appius (that was his name, for this is no fable; rather, it is widely known as a recognized historical fact; the moral of it is true beyond doubt)—this false judge bestirred himself to hasten his pleasure as much as possible. So, it happened one day soon afterwards, so the story says, that this false judge was sitting in his court, as was his custom, giving his decision on various cases.

The wicked fellow came rushing in and said: "Lord, if it be your will, give me justice in this pitiful complaint which I make against Virginius; and if he says it is not so, I will prove by reliable witnesses that what my bill of complaint sets forth is true."

"In the absence of Virginius," the judge answered, "I cannot give a definite decision on this matter. Have him called, and I shall gladly hear the case. You shall have only justice here; no partiality."

Virginius came to learn why the judge wanted him, and the cursed complaint was immediately read. Its contents were as you shall hear: "To you, my dear lord Appius, your poor servant Claudius wishes to show how a knight named Virginius, against the law, against all equity, and directly against my wishes, holds my servant, who is my rightful slave, and who was stolen from my house one night when she was very young. I will prove this by witnesses, lord, so that you will have no doubts. She is not his daughter, no matter what he says. Therefore, I pray you, my lord judge, give back my servant to me, if that is your will." See, this was the complete text of the complaint.

Virginius began to stare at the fellow before he had even finished his complaint. He would have contested the case as a knight should, showing by many witnesses that everything claimed by his opponent was false, but the accursed judge would not wait at all, or hear a single word from Virginius. He immediately handed down his decision, saying. "I now decree that this fellow shall have his servant; you shall no longer keep her in your house. Go bring her here and put her into our keeping. This fellow shall have his servant; that is my judgment."

When the worthy knight, Virginius, had been ordered by the decision of the judge, Appius, to give up his dear daughter to the judge to live in lechery, he went home, sat down in his hall, and immediately sent for his beloved daughter. Then, with a face as deathlike as cold ashes, he gazed upon her humble face. A father's pity struck through his heart, but he would not swerve from his purpose.

"Daughter," he said, "Virginia to call you by name, there are two ways that you may take; death or dishonor. Alas, that I was born! For never have you deserved to die by knife or sword. Oh, dear daughter, beloved of my life, in whose raising I have taken such pleasure that you were never out of my thoughts! Oh, daughter, who are my final joy in life, and my final woe; oh, gem of chastity, take your death in patience, for that is my decision. For love and not for hate, you must die; my poor hand must cut off your head. Alas, that ever Appius saw you! His false judgment today was because of that"—and he told her the whole story, as you heard it before; there is no need to repeat it.

"Oh, mercy, dear father!" the girl said, and with these words put both arms around his neck, as was her custom. The tears rushed from her eyes, and she said: "Good father, must I die? Is there no mercy? Is there no remedy?"

"No, verily, my dear daughter," he said.

"Then give me time, dear father," she said, "to lament my death a little while. For indeed, Jeptha gave his daughter time to lament before he killed her, alas! And, God knows, her sin was only that she was the first to run to meet her father and welcome him fittingly." With these words she immediately fainted. When she had recovered, she rose and said to her father: "God be thanked that I shall die a virgin! Kill me before I am dishonored. Do your will with your child, in God's name!"

After these words she begged many times that he would smite gently with his sword; then she fell down in a swoon. Her father, with a very sorrowful heart and spirit, cut off her head. He grasped it by the hair and took it to the judge, who still sat in judgment in the court. When the judge saw the head, so the story says, he commanded that Virginius be taken and hanged at once. But, immediately, a thousand people burst in to save the knight, out of pity, for the wicked treachery was known. Because of the manner of the fellow's complaint, the people had quickly suspected that Appius had conspired in this case, for they knew very well that he was lecherous. Therefore, they took him into custody and cast him into prison, where he killed himself. And Claudius, who was Appius' servant, was condemned to be hanged from a tree, but Virginius, out of pity, begged that he be exiled instead, for he had truly been misguided. The others who were involved in this wickedness, great and small, were hanged.

From this story, you can see how sin is repaid. Beware, for no one knows what man of any rank God will smite, or in what way the worm of conscience will show the terror of a wicked life, even though it is kept so secret that no one knows of it but him and God. For no matter whether he is an ignorant man or a learned man, he does not know how soon he shall be brought to fear. Therefore, I advise you to accept this counsel: forsake sin, before sin destroys you. Here ends the physician's tale.

The Worm in the Apple

The Crutchmans were so very, very happy and so temperate in all their habits and so pleased with everything that came their way that one was bound to suspect a worm in their rosy apple and that the extraordinary rosiness of the fruit was only meant to conceal the gravity and the depth of the infection. Their house, for instance, on Hill Street with all those big glass windows. Who but someone suffering from a guilt complex would want so much light to pour into their rooms? And all the wall-to-wall carpeting as if an inch of bare floor (there was none) would touch on some deep memory of unrequition and loneliness. And there was a certain necrophilic ardor to their gardening. Why be so intense about digging holes and planting seeds and watching them come up? Why this morbid concern with the earth? She was a pretty woman with that striking pallor you so often find in nymphomaniacs. Larry was a big man who used to garden without a shirt, which may have shown a tendency to infantile exhibitionism.

They moved happily out to Shady Hill after the war. Larry had served in the Navy. They had two happy children: Rachel and Tom. But there were already some clouds on their horizon. Larry's ship had been sunk in the war and he had spent four days on a raft in the Mediterranean and surely this experience would make him skeptical about the comforts and songbirds of Shady Hill and leave him with some racking nightmares. But what was perhaps more serious was the fact that Helen was rich. She was the only daughter of old Charlie Simpson—one of the last of the industrial buccaneers —who had left her with a larger income than Larry would ever take away from his job at Melcher & Thaw. The dangers in this situation are well known. Since Larry did not have to make a living—since he lacked any incentive—he might take it easy, spend too much time on the golf links, and always have a glass in his hand. Helen would confuse financial with emotional independence and damage the delicate balances within their marriage. But Larry seemed to have no nightmares and Helen spread her income among the charities and lived a comfortable but a modest life. Larry went to his job each morning with such enthusiasm that you might think he was trying to escape from something. His participation in the life of the community was so vigorous that he must have been left with almost no time for self-examination. He was everywhere: he was at the communion rail, the fifty-yard line, he played the oboe with the Chamber Music Club, drove the fire truck, served on the school board, and rode the 8:03 into New York every morning. What was the sorrow that drove him?

He may have wanted a larger family. Why did they only have two children? Why not three or four? Was there perhaps some breakdown in their relationship after the birth of Tom? Rachel, the oldest, was terribly fat when she was a girl and quite aggressive in a mercenary way. Every spring she would drag an old dressing table out of the garage and set it up on the sidewalk with a sign saying: FReSH LEMonADE. 15¢. Tom had pneumonia when he was six and nearly died, but he recovered and there were no visible complications. The children may have felt rebellious about the conformity of their parents, for they were exacting conformists. Two cars? Yes. Did they go to church? Every single Sunday they got to their knees and prayed with ardor. Clothing? They couldn't have been more punctilious in their observance of the sumptuary laws. Book clubs, local art and music lover associations, athletics and cards—they were up to their necks in everything. But if the children were rebellious they concealed their rebellion and seemed happily to love their parents and happily to be loved in return, but perhaps there was in this love the ruefulness of some deep disappointment. Perhaps he was impotent. Perhaps she was frigid—but hardly, with that pallor. Everyone in the community with wandering hands had given them both a try but they had all been put off. What was the source of this constancy? Were they frightened? Were they prudish? Were they monogamous? What was at the bottom of this appearance of happiness?

As their children grew one might look to them for the worm in the apple. They would be rich, they would inherit Helen's fortune, and we might see here, moving over them, the shadow that so often falls upon children who can count on a lifetime of financial security. And anyhow Helen loved her son too much. She bought him everything he wanted. Driving him to dancing school in his first blue serge suit she was so entranced by the manly figure he cut as he climbed the stairs that she drove the car straight into an elm tree. Such an infatuation was bound to lead to trouble. And if she favored her son she was bound to discriminate against her daughter. Listen to her. "Rachel's feet," she says, "are immense, simply immense. I can never get shoes for her." Now perhaps we see the worm. Like most beautiful women she is jealous; she is jealous of her own daughter! She cannot brook competition. She will dress the girl in hideous clothing, have her hair curled in some unbecoming way, and keep talking about the size of her feet until the poor girl will refuse to go to the dances or if she is forced to go she will sulk in the ladies' room, staring at her monstrous feet. She will become so wretched and so lonely that in order to express herself she will fall in love with an unstable poet and fly with him to Rome, where they will live out a miserable and a boozy exile. But when the girl enters the room she is pretty and prettily dressed and she smiles at her mother with perfect love. Her feet are quite large, to be sure, but so is her front. Perhaps we should look to the son to find our trouble.

And there is trouble. He fails his junior year in high school and has to repeat and as a result of having to repeat he feels alienated from the members of his class and is put, by chance, at a desk next to Carrie Witchell, who is the most conspicuous dish in Shady Hill. Everyone knows about the Witchells and their pretty, high-spirited daughter. They drink too much and live in one of those frame houses in Maple Dell. The girl is really beautiful and everyone knows how her shrewd old parents are planning to climb out of Maple Dell on the strength of her white, white skin. What a perfect situation! They will know about Helen's wealth. In the darkness of their bedroom they will calculate the settlement they can demand and in the malodorous kitchen where they take all their meals they will tell their pretty daughter to let the boy go as far as he wants. But Tom fell out of love with Carrie as swiftly as he fell into it and after that he fell in love with Karen Strawbridge and Susie Morris and Anna Macken and you might think he was unstable, but in his second year in college he announced his engagement to Elizabeth Trustman and they were married after his graduation and since he then had to serve his time in the Army she followed him to his post in Germany, where they studied and learned the language and befriended the people and were a credit to their country.

Rachel's way was not so easy. When she lost her fat she became very pretty and quite fast. She smoked and drank and probably fornicated and the abyss that opens up before a pretty and an intemperate young woman is unfathomable. What, but chance, was there to keep her from ending up as a hostess at a Times Square dance hall? And what would her poor father think, seeing the face of his daughter, her breasts lightly covered with gauze, gazing mutely at him on a rainy morning from one of those showcases? What she did was to fall in love with the son of the Farquarsons' German gardener. He had come with his family to the United States on the Displaced Persons quota after the war. His name was Eric Reiner and to be fair about it he was an exceptional young man who looked on the United States as a truly New World. The Crutchmans must have been sad about Rachel's choice—not to say heartbroken—but they concealed their feelings. The Reiners did not. This hard-working German couple thought the marriage hopeless and improper. At one point the father beat his son over the head with a stick of firewood. But the young couple continued to see each other and presently they eloped. They had to. Rachel was three months pregnant. Eric was then a freshman at Tufts, where he had a scholarship. Helen's money came in handy here and she was able to rent an apartment in Boston for the young couple and pay their expenses. That their first grandchild was premature did not seem to bother the Crutchmans. When Eric graduated from college he got a fellowship at M.I.T. and took his Ph.D. in physics and was taken on as an associate in the department. He could have gone into industry at a higher salary but he liked to teach and Rachel was happy in Cambridge, where they remained.

With their own dear children gone away the Crutchmans might be expected to suffer the celebrated spiritual destitution of their age and their kind—the worm in the apple would at last be laid bare—although watching this charming couple as they entertained their friends or read the books they enjoyed one might wonder if the worm was not in the eye of the observer who, through timidity or moral cowardice, could not embrace the broad range of their natural enthusiasms and would not grant that, while Larry played neither Bach nor football very well, his pleasure in both was genuine. You might at least expect to see in them the usual destructiveness of time, but either through luck or as a result of their temperate and healthy lives they had lost neither their teeth nor their hair. The touchstone of their euphoria remained potent, and while Larry gave up the fire truck he could still be seen at the communion rail, the fifty-yard line, the 8:03, and the Chamber Music Club, and through the prudence and shrewdness of Helen's broker they got richer and richer and richer and lived happily, happily, happily, happily.

ANTON CHEKHOV

The Huntsman

It is midday, hot and close. Not a puff of cloud in the sky . . . The sun-parched grass looks at you sullenly, despairingly: even a downpour won't turn it green now . . . The forest stands there silent and still, as if gazing somewhere with the tops of its trees, or waiting for something.

Along the edge of the scrub ambles a tall, narrow-shouldered man of about forty with a lazy, rolling gait and wearing a red shirt, patched trousers that were his master's cast-offs, and big boots. He is ambling along the road. To his right is the green of the scrub, to his left a golden sea of ripe rye stretching to the very horizon . . . He is red in the face and sweating. Perched jauntily on his handsome, flaxen head is a small white cap with a stiff jockey peak to it—evidently a present from some young gentleman in a fit of generosity. He has a shooting-bag over his shoulder, with a rumpled black grouse hanging out of it. The man is holding a cocked twelve-bore in his hands and keeping a weather eye on his lean old dog, who has run ahead and is sniffing round the bushes. All is completely quiet, not a sound in the air . . . Every living thing has hidden away from the heat.

'Yegor Vlasych!' the sportsman suddenly hears a soft voice say.

He starts, looks round, and frowns. Right beside him, as though she had just sprung out of the ground, stands a pale-faced peasant woman of about thirty, with a sickle in her hand. She tries to look into his face, and smiles at him bashfully.

'Oh, it's you, Pelageya!' says the sportsman, stopping and slowly uncocking his gun. 'Hm! . . . What brings you to these parts?'

'The girls from our village are working here, so I've come over with them . . . As a labourer, Yegor Vlasych.'

'Uhuh . . .' grunts Yegor Vlasych, and slowly continues on his way.

Pelageya follows him. They walk about twenty paces in silence.

'It's a long time since I saw you last, Yegor Vlasych . . .' says Pelageya, looking fondly at the rippling motion of his shoulders. 'Not since you came into our hut for a drink of water at Eastertide—that was the last time we saw you . . . Yes, you came inside for a minute at Easter, and Lord knows the state you were in—under the influence, you were . . . You just swore at us, beat me and went off again . . . And I've been waiting and waiting—I've worn my eyes out looking for you to come . . . Ah, Yegor Vlasych, Yegor Vlasych! You could have called in once, just once!'

'To do what?'

'Not to do anything, of course, but . . . it is your household, after all . . . Just to see how everything is . . . You are the head . . . Oh, you've shot a little grouse. Ye-gor Vlasych! Why not sit down and have a rest—'

As she says all this, Pelageya keeps laughing like a simpleton and looking up at Yegor's face . . . Her own face positively breathes happiness . . .

'All right, I'll sit down for a bit . . .' Yegor says nonchalantly, choosing a spot between two fir-trees growing side by side. 'What are you standing up for? You sit down too!'

Pelageya sits a little way off in the sun and, ashamed to show how happy she is, keeps covering her smiling mouth with her hand. A couple of minutes pass in silence.

'You could have called in just once,' Pelageya says quietly.

'What for?' sighs Yegor, taking off his cap and mopping his ruddy brow with his sleeve. 'What's the point? Calling in for an hour or two's just a bother, it just gets you worked up, and as for living in the village all the time—my soul couldn't take it . . . You know yourself I've been mollycoddled . . . I need a bed to sleep in, good tea to drink, fine conversations . . . I need everything to be just right . . . and all you've got there in the village is poverty and grime . . . I couldn't stick it for a day. Supposing they even made a decree, saying I had to live with thee come what may, I'd either burn the hut down, or I'd lay hands on myself. I've loved the easy life since I was a kid, you won't change me.'

'And where are you living nowadays?'

'At the master's, Dmitry Ivanych's, as one of his shooters. I provide game for his table, but really . . . he just likes having me around.'

'It's not a proper way of life, that, Yegor Vlasych . . . For other people that's their leisure, but it's as though you've made it your trade . . . like a real job . . .'

'You're stupid, you don't understand anything,' says Yegor, gazing dreamily at the sky. 'Never in all your born days have you understood what kind of a man I am, nor will you . . . You think I'm crazy, I've ruined my life, but to those as knows, I'm the top shot in the whole district. The gents know that all right, and they've even written about me in a magazine. There's not a man can compare with me when it comes to hunting . . . And I don't despise your village jobs because I'm spoilt or proud. You know I never done anything else since I was small than shooting and keeping a dog, don't you? If they took my gun away, I'd use my line, if they took my line away, I'd catch things with my hands. I did a bit of horse-dealing, too, I went the round of the fairs when I had money, and you know yourself that once a peasant's joined the huntsmen and horse-dealers, it's goodbye to the plough. Once that free spirit's got into a man, there's no winkling it out. Just like when a gent goes off with the players, or one of them other arts, he can't work in an office or be a squire again. You're a woman, you don't understand, but you got to.'

'I do understand, Yegor Vlasych . . .'

'You can't do, if you're going to cry about it . . .'

'I—I'm not crying . . .' says Pelageya, turning away. 'It's a sin, Yegor Vlasych! You could at least have some pity and spend a day with me. It's twelve years now since I married you, and . . . and there's never once been *love* between us! . . . I'm not crying . . .'

'Love . . .' mumbles Yegor, scratching the back of his hand. 'There can't be any love. We're man and wife in name only, we're not really, are we? To you I'm a wild man, and to me you're just a simple girl who doesn't understand anything. Call that a match? I'm free, I'm mollycoddled. I come and go as I please, and you're a working-girl, you trudge around in bast shoes all day, you live in dirt, your back's always bent. The way I see myself, when it comes to hunting I'm number one, but when you look at me you just feel pity . . . What kind of a match is that?'

'But we were married in church, Yegor Vlasych!' Pelageya sobs loudly.

'Not freely we weren't . . . You haven't forgotten, have you? You can thank the Count, Sergey Pavlych, for that—and yourself. Because he was so jealous I could shoot better'n him, the Count got me drunk on wine for a month, and when a man's drunk you can make him change his religion, never mind get married. He went and married me off drunk to you, to get his own back . . . A huntsman to a cowherd! You could see I was drunk, so why did you marry me? You're not a serf, you could have gone against his will! 'Course, it's a great thing for a cowherd, marrying a huntsman, but why didn't you stop and think first? Now it's nothing but tears and tribulation. The Count has his laugh, and you're left crying . . . hanging your head against a wall . . .'

They fall silent. Three mallard fly in above the scrub. Yegor looks up and stares after them until they turn into three barely visible points, and come down far beyond the forest.

'What do you do for money?' he asks, turning back to Pelageya.

'Nowadays I work in the fields, but in winter I take in a little baby from the orphanage and feed him with a bottle. I get a rouble and a half a month for it.'

'Uhuh . . .'

Once more there is silence. Over in the cut rye, someone begins softly singing, but breaks off almost immediately. It's too hot to sing . . .

'I hear you've put up a new hut for Akulina,' says Pelageya.

Yegor does not reply.

'So she must be to your liking.'

'That's how it is, such is life!' says the sportsman, stretching. 'Have patience, orphan. I must be going, though, I've been chatting too long . . . I've got to be in Boltovo by nightfall . . .'

Yegor rises, stretches again, and slings his gun over his shoulder. Pelageya stands up.

'So when will you be coming to the village?' she asks quietly.

'No point. I'll never come sober, and a drunk's not much use to you. I get mad when I'm drunk . . . Goodbye, then!'

'Goodbye, Yegor Vlasych . . .'

Yegor sticks his cap on the back of his head, calls his dog over with a tweet of the lips, and continues on his way. Pelageya stays where she is and watches him go . . . She can see his shoulder-blades rippling, the rakish set of his cap, his lazy, casual walk, and her eyes fill with sadness and a deep tenderness . . . Her gaze runs all over the slim, tall figure of her husband and caresses and strokes him . . . He stops, as if feeling this gaze, and looks round . . . He says nothing, but from his face and hunched-up shoulders, Pelageya can tell that he wants to say something to her. She goes up timidly to him and looks at him with pleading eyes.

'Here!' he says, turning aside.

He hands her a very worn rouble note and moves quickly away.

'Goodbye, Yegor Vlasych!' she says, mechanically taking the rouble.

He walks off down the road, which is as long and straight as a taut thong . . . Pale and still, she stands there like a statue, and her eyes devour every stride he takes. But now the red of his shirt merges with the dark of his trousers, his strides become invisible, his dog cannot be distinguished from his boots. Only his little cap can be seen, then . . . Suddenly Yegor turns off sharply to the right into the scrub and his cap disappears among the green.

'Goodbye, Yegor Vlasych!' whispers Pelageya, and rises on tiptoe to try and catch a last glimpse of his little white cap.

Commentary: Vladimir Nabokov on "Chekhov's Prose"

Chekhov's books are sad books for humorous people; that is, only a reader with a sense of humor can really appreciate their sadness. There exist writers that sound like something between a titter and a yawn—many of these are professional humorists, for instance. There are others that are something between a chuckle and a sob—Dickens was one of these. There is also that dreadful kind of humor that is consciously introduced by an author in order to give a purely technical relief after a good tragic scene—but this is a trick remote from true literature. Chekhov's humor belonged to none of these types; it was purely Chekhovian. Things for him were funny and sad at the same time, but you would not see their sadness if you did not see their fun, because both were linked up.

Russian critics have noted that Chekhov's style, his choice of words and so on, did not reveal any of those special artistic preoccupations that obsessed, for instance, Gogol or Flaubert or Henry James. His dictionary is poor, his combination of words almost trivial—the purple patch, the juicy verb, the hothouse adjective, the crème-de-menthe epithet, brought in on a silver tray, these were foreign to him. He was not a verbal inventor in the sense that Gogol was; his literary style goes to parties clad in its everyday suit. Thus Chekhov is a good example to give when one tries to explain that a writer may be a perfect artist without being exceptionally vivid in his verbal technique or exceptionally preoccupied with the way his sentences curve. When Turgenev sits down to discuss a landscape, you notice that he is concerned with the trouser-crease of his phrase; he crosses his legs with an eye upon the color of his socks. Chekhov does not mind, not because these matters are not important—for some writers they are naturally and very beautifully important when the right temperament is there—but Chekhov does not mind because his temperament is quite foreign to verbal inventiveness. Even a bit of bad grammar or a slack newspaperish sentence left him unconcerned. The magical part of it is that in spite of his tolerating flaws which a bright beginner would have avoided, in spite of his being quite satisfied with the man-in-the-street among words, the word-in-the-street, so to say, Chekhov managed to convey an impression of artistic beauty far surpassing that of many writers who thought they knew what rich beautiful prose was. He did it by keeping all his words in the same dim light and of the same exact tint of gray, a tint between the color of an old fence and that of a low cloud. The variety of his moods, the flicker of his charming wit, the deeply artistic economy of characterization, the vivid detail, and the fade-out of human life—all the peculiar Chekhovian features—are enhanced by being suffused and surrounded by a faintly iridescent verbal haziness.

KATE CHOPIN

Caline

The sun was just far enough in the west to send inviting shadows. In the centre of a small field, and in the shade of a haystack which was there, a girl lay sleeping. She had slept long and soundly, when something awoke her as suddenly as if it had been a blow. She opened her eyes and stared a moment up in the cloudless sky. She yawned and stretched her long brown legs and arms, lazily. Then she arose, never minding the bits of straw that clung to her black hair, to her red bodice, and the blue cotonade skirt that did not reach her naked ankles.

The log cabin in which she dwelt with her parents was just outside the enclosure in which she had been sleeping. Beyond was a small clearing that did duty as a cotton field. All else was dense wood, except the long stretch that curved round the brow of the hill, and in which glittered the steel rails of the Texas and Pacific road.

When Caline emerged from the shadow she saw a long train of passenger coaches standing in view, where they must have stopped abruptly. It was that sudden stopping which had awakened her; for such a thing had not happened before within her recollection, and she looked stupid, at first, with astonishment. There seemed to be something wrong with the engine; and some of the passengers who dismounted went forward to investigate the trouble. Others came strolling along in the direction of the cabin, where Caline stood under an old gnarled mulberry tree, staring. Her father had halted his mule at the end of the cotton row, and stood staring also, leaning upon his plow.

There were ladies in the party. They walked awkwardly in their high-heeled boots over the rough, uneven ground, and held up their skirts

mincingly. They twirled parasols over their shoulders, and laughed im-
moderately at the funny things which their masculine companions were
saying.

They tried to talk to Caline, but could not understand the French patois
with which she answered them.

One of the men—a pleasant-faced youngster—drew a sketch book
from his pocket and began to make a picture of the girl. She stayed
motionless, her hands behind her, and her wide eyes fixed earnestly upon
him.

Before he had finished there was a summons from the train; and all
went scampering hurriedly away. The engine screeched, it sent a few lazy
puffs into the still air, and in another moment or two had vanished, bearing
its human cargo with it.

Caline could not feel the same after that. She looked with new and
strange interest upon the trains of cars that passed so swiftly back and forth
across her vision, each day; and wondered whence these people came, and
whither they were going.

Her mother and father could not tell her, except to say that they came
from "loin là bas," and were going "Djieu sait é où."

One day she walked miles down the track to talk with the old flagman, who stayed down there by the big water tank. Yes, he knew. Those
people came from the great cities in the north, and were going to the city
in the south. He knew all about the city; it was a grand place. He had lived
there once. His sister lived there now; and she would be glad enough to
have so fine a girl as Caline to help her cook and scrub, and tend the
babies. And he thought Caline might earn as much as five dollars a
month, in the city.

So she went; in a new cotonade, and her Sunday shoes; with a
sacredly guarded scrawl that the flagman sent to his sister.

The woman lived in a tiny, stuccoed house, with green blinds, and
three wooden steps leading down to the banquette. There seemed to be
hundreds like it along the street. Over the house tops loomed the tall
masts of ships, and the hum of the French market could be heard on a still
morning.

Caline was at first bewildered. She had to readjust all her preconcep-
tions to fit the reality of it. The flagman's sister was a kind and gentle task-
mistress. At the end of a week or two she wanted to know how the girl liked
it all. Caline liked it very well, for it was pleasant, on Sunday afternoons, to
stroll with the children under the great, solemn sugar sheds; or to sit upon
the compressed cotton bales, watching the stately steamers, the graceful
boats, and noisy little tugs that plied the waters of the Mississippi. And it
filled her with agreeable excitement to go to the French market, where the
handsome Gascon butchers were eager to present their compliments and little Sunday bouquets to the pretty Acadian girl; and to throw fistfuls of
lagniappe into her basket.

When the woman asked her again after another week if she were still pleased, she was not so sure. And again when she questioned Caline the girl turned away, and went to sit behind the big, yellow cistern, to cry unobserved. For she knew now that it was not the great city and its crowds of people she had so eagerly sought; but the pleasant-faced boy, who had made her picture that day under the mulberry tree.

SANDRA CISNEROS

My Name

In English my name means hope. In Spanish it means too many letters. It means sadness, it means waiting. It is like the number nine. A muddy color. It is the Mexican records my father plays on Sunday mornings when he is shaving, songs like sobbing.

It was my great-grandmother's name and now it is mine. She was a horse woman too, born like me in the Chinese year of the horse—which is supposed to be bad luck if you're born female—but I think this is a Chinese lie because the Chinese, like the Mexicans, don't like their women strong.

My great-grandmother. I would've liked to have known her, a wild horse of a woman, so wild she wouldn't marry. Until my great-grandfather threw a sack over her head and carried her off. Just like that, as if she were a fancy chandelier. That's the way he did it.

And the story goes she never forgave him. She looked out the window her whole life, the way so many women sit their sadness on an elbow. I wonder if she made the best with what she got or was she sorry because she couldn't be all the things she wanted to be. Esperanza. I have inherited her name, but I don't want to inherit her place by the window.

At school they say my name funny as if the syllables were made out of tin and hurt the roof of your mouth. But in Spanish my name is made out of a softer something, like silver, not quite as thick as sister's name— Magdalena—which is uglier than mine. Magdalena who at least can come home and become Nenny. But I am always Esperanza.

I would like to baptize myself under a new name, a name more like the real me, the one nobody sees. Esperanza as Lisandra or Maritza or Zeze the X. Yes. Something like Zeze the X will do.

Bygone Spring

Translated by Una Vicenzo Troubridge and Enid McLeed

The beak of a pruning shears goes clicking all down the rose-bordered paths. Another clicks in answer from the orchard. Presently the soil in the rose garden will be strewn with tender shoots, dawn-red at the tips but green and juicy at the base. In the orchard the stiff, severed twigs of the apricot trees will keep their little flames of flower alight for another hour before they die, and the bees will see to it that none of them is wasted.

The hillside is dotted with white plum trees like puffs of smoke, each of them filmy and dappled as a round cloud. At half past five in the morning, under the dew and the slanting rays of sunrise, the young wheat is incontestably blue, the earth rust-red, and the white plum trees coppery pink. It is only for a moment, a magic delusion of light that fades with the first hour of day. Everything grows with miraculous speed. Even the tiniest plant thrusts upward with all its strength. The peony, in the flush of its first month's growth, shoots up at such a pace that its scapes and scarcely unfolded leaves, pushing through the earth, carry with them the upper covering of it so that it hangs suspended like a roof burst asunder.

The peasants shake their heads. "April will bring us plenty of surprises." They bend wise brows over this folly, this annual imprudence of leaf and flower. They grow old, borne helplessly along in the wake of a terrible pupil who learns nothing from their experience. In the tilled valley, still crisscrossed with parallel rivulets, lines of green emerge above the inundation. Nothing can now delay the mole-like ascent of the asparagus, or extinguish the torch of the purple iris. The furious breaking of bonds infects birds, lizards, and insects. Greenfinch, goldfinch, sparrow, and chaffinch behave in the morning like farmyard fowl gorged with brandy-soaked grain. Ritual dances and mock battles, to the accompaniment of exaggerated cries, are renewed perpetually under our eyes, almost under our very hands. Flocks of birds and mating gray lizards share the same sun-warmed flagstones, and when the children, wild with excitement, run aimlessly hither and thither, clouds of mayfly rise and hover around their heads.

Everything rushes onward, and I stay where I am. Do I not already feel more pleasure in comparing this spring with others that are past than in welcoming it? The torpor is blissful enough, but too aware of its own weight. And though my ecstasy is genuine and spontaneous, it no longer finds expression. "Oh, look at those yellow cowslips! And the soapwort! And the unicorn tips of the lords and ladies are showing! . . ." But the cowslip, that wild primula, is a humble flower, and how can the uncertain mauve of the watery soapwort compare with a glowing peach tree? Its value for me lies in the stream that watered it between my tenth and fifteenth years. The slender cowslip, all stalk and rudimentary in blossom, still clings by a frail root to the meadow where I used to gather hundreds to straddle them along a string and then tie them into round balls, cool projectiles that struck the check like a rough, wet kiss.

I take good care nowadays not to pick cowslips and crush them into a greenish ball. I know the risk I should run if I did. Poor rustic enchantment, almost evaporated now. I cannot even bequeath you to another me. "Look, Bel-Gazou, like this and then like that; first you straddle them on the string and then you draw it tight." "Yes, I see," says Bel-Gazou. "But it doesn't bounce; I'd rather have my India-rubber ball."

The shears click their beaks in the gardens. Shut me into a dark room and that sound will still bring in to me April sunshine, stinging the skin and treacherous as wine without a bouquet. With it comes the bee scent of the pruned apricot trees, and a certain anguish, the uneasiness of one of those slight preadolescent indispositions that develop, hang about for a time, improve, are cured one morning, and reappear at night. I was ten or eleven years old but, in the company of my foster-mother, who had become our cook, I still indulged in nursling whims. A grown girl in the dining room, I would run to the kitchen to lick the vinegar off the salad leaves on the plate of Mélie, my faithful watchdog, my fair-haired, fair-skinned slave. One April morning I called out to her, "Come along, Mélie, let's go and pick up the clippings from the apricot trees. Milien's at the espaliers."

She followed me, and the young housemaid, well named Marie-la-Rose, came too, though I had not invited her. Milien, the day laborer, a handsome, crafty youth, was finishing his job, silently and without haste.

"Mélie, hold out your apron and let me put the clippings in it."

I was on my knees collecting the shoots starred with blossom. As though in play, Mélie went "Hou!" at me and, flinging her apron over my head, folded me up in it and rolled me gently over. I laughed, thoroughly enjoying making myself small and silly. But I began to stifle and came out from under it so suddenly that Milien and Marie-la-Rose, in the act of kissing, had not time to spring apart, nor Mélie to hide her guilty face.

Click of the shears, harsh chatter of hard-billed birds! They tell of blossoming, of early sunshine, of sunburn on the forehead, of chilly shade, of uncomprehended repulsion, of childish trust betrayed, of suspicion, and of brooding sadness.

Julio Cortázar

Continuity of Parks

He had begun to read the novel a few days before. He had put it down because of some urgent business conferences, opened it again on his way back to the estate by train; he permitted himself a slowly growing interest in the plot, in the characterizations. That afternoon, after writing a letter giving his power of attorney and discussing a matter of joint ownership with the manager of his estate, he returned to the book in the tranquillity of his study which looked out upon the park with its oaks. Sprawled in his favorite arm-chair, its back toward the door—even the possibility of an intrusion would have irritated him, had he thought of it—he let his left hand caress repeatedly the green velvet upholstery and set to reading the final chapters. He remembered effortlessly the names and his mental image of the characters; the novel spread its glamour over him almost at once. He tasted the almost per-verse pleasure of disengaging himself line by line from the things around him, and at the same time feeling his head rest comfortably on the green vel-vet of the chair with its high back, sensing that the cigarettes rested within reach of his hand, that beyond the great windows the air of afternoon danced under the oak trees in the park. Word by word, licked up by the sor-did dilemma of the hero and heroine, letting himself be absorbed to the point where the images settled down and took on color and movement, he was witness to the final encounter in the mountain cabin. The woman arrived first, apprehensive; now the lover came in, his face cut by the backlash of a branch. Admirably, she stanched the blood with her kisses, but he rebuffed her caresses, he had not come to perform again the ceremonies of a secret passion, protected by a world of dry leaves and furtive paths through the forest. The dagger warmed itself against his chest, and underneath liberty pounded, hidden close. A lustful, panting dialogue raced down the pages like a rivulet of snakes, and one felt it had all been decided from eternity. Even to those caresses which writhed about the lover's body, as though wishing to keep him there, to dissuade him from it; they sketched abominably the frame of that other body it was necessary to destroy. Nothing had been forgotten: alibis, unforeseen hazards, possible mistakes. From this hour on, each instant had its use minutely assigned. The cold-blooded, twice-gone-over reexamination of the details was barely broken off so that a hand could caress a cheek. It was beginning to get dark.

Not looking at one another now, rigidly fixed upon the task which awaited them, they separated at the cabin door. She was to follow the trail that led north. On the path leading in the opposite direction, he turned for a moment to watch her running, her hair loosened and flying. He ran in turn, crouching among the trees and hedges until, in the yellowish fog of dusk, he could distinguish the avenue of trees which led up to the house. The dogs were not supposed to bark, they did not bark. The estate manager would not be there at this hour, and he was not there. He went up the three porch steps and entered. The woman's words reached him over the thudding of blood in his cars: first a blue chamber, then a hall, then a carpeted stairway. At the top, two doors. No one in the first room, no one in the second. The door of the salon, and then, the knife in hand, the light from the great windows, the high back of an armchair covered in green velvet, the head of the man in the chair reading a novel.

STEPHEN CRANE

An Episode of War

The lieutenant's rubber blanket lay on the ground, and upon it he had poured the company's supply of coffee. Corporals and other representatives of the grimy and hot-throated men who lined the breastwork had come for each squad's portion.

The lieutenant was frowning and serious at this task of division. His lips pursed as he drew with his sword various crevices in the heap, until brown squares of coffee, astoundingly equal in size, appeared on the blanket. He was on the verge of a great triumph in mathematics, and the corporals were thronging forward, each to reap a little square, when suddenly the lieutenant cried out and looked quickly at a man near him as if he suspected it was a case of personal assault. The others cried out also when they saw blood upon the lieutenant's sleeve.

He had winced like a man stung, swayed dangerously, and then straightened. The sound of his hoarse breathing was plainly audible. He looked sadly, mystically, over the breastwork at the green face of a wood, where now were many little puffs of white smoke. During this moment the men about him gazed statue-like and silent, astonished and awed by this catastrophe which happened when catastrophes were not expected—when they had leisure to observe it.

As the lieutenant stared at the wood, they too swung their heads, so that for another instant all hands, still silent, contemplated the distant forest as if their minds were fixed upon the mystery of a bullet's journey.

The officer had, of course, been compelled to take his sword into his left hand. He did not hold it by the hilt. He gripped it at the middle of the blade, awkwardly. Turning his eyes from the hostile wood, he looked at the sword as he held it there, and seemed puzzled as to what to do with it, where to put it. In short, this weapon had of a sudden become a strange thing to him. He looked at it in a kind of stupefaction, as if he had been endowed with a trident, a scepter, or a spade.

Finally he tried to sheathe it. To sheathe a sword held by the left hand, at the middle of the blade, in a scabbard hung at the left hip, is a feat worthy of a sawdust ring. This wounded officer engaged in a desperate struggle with the sword and the wobbling scabbard, and during the time of it he breathed like a wrestler.

But at this instant the men, the spectators, awoke from their stone-like poses and crowded forward sympathetically. The orderly-sergeant took the sword and tenderly placed it in the scabbard. At the time, he leaned nervously backward, and did not allow even his finger to brush the body of the lieutenant. A wound gives strange dignity to him who bears it. Well men shy from this new and terrible majesty. It is as if the wounded man's hand is upon the curtain which hangs before the revelations of all existence—the meaning of ants, potentates, wars, cities, sunshine, snow, a feather dropped from a bird's wing; and the power of it sheds radiance upon a bloody form, and makes the other men understand sometimes that they are little. His comrades look at him with large eyes thoughtfully. Moreover, they fear vaguely that the weight of a finger upon him might send him headlong, precipitate the tragedy, hurt him at once into the dim, gray unknown. And so the orderly-sergeant, while sheathing the sword, leaned nervously backward.

There were others who proffered assistance. One timidly presented his shoulder and asked the lieutenant if he cared to lean upon it, but the latter waved him away mournfully. He wore the look of one who knows he is the victim of a terrible disease and understands his helplessness. He again stared over the breastwork at the forest, and then, turning, went slowly rearward. He held his right wrist tenderly in his left hand as if the wounded arm was made of very brittle glass.

And the men in silence stared at the wood, then at the departing lieutenant; then at the wood, then at the lieutenant.

As the wounded officer passed from the line of battle, he was enabled to see many things which as a participant in the fight were unknown to him. He saw a general on a black horse gazing over the lines of blue infantry at the green woods which veiled his problems. An aide galloped furiously, dragged his horse suddenly to a halt, saluted, and presented a paper. It was, for a wonder, precisely like a historical painting.

To the rear of the general and his staff a group, composed of a bugler, two or three orderlies, and the bearer of the corps standard, all upon maniacal horses, were working like slaves to hold their ground, preserve their respectful interval, while the shells boomed in the air about them, and caused their chargers to make furious quivering leaps.

A battery, a tumultuous and shining mass, was swirling toward the right. The wild thud of hoofs, the cries of the riders shouting blame and praise, menace and encouragement, and, last, the roar of the wheels, the slant of the glistening guns, brought the lieutenant to an intent pause. The battery swept in curves that stirred the heart; it made halts as dramatic as the crash of a wave on the rocks, and when it fled onward this aggregation of wheels, levers, motors had a beautiful unity, as if it were a missile. The sound of it was a war chorus that reached into the depths of man's emotion.

The lieutenant, still holding his arm as if it were of glass, stood watching this battery until all detail of it was lost, save the figures of the riders, which rose and fell and waved lashes over the black mass.

Later, he turned his eyes toward the battle, where the shooting sometimes crackled like bush-fires, sometimes sputtered with exasperating irregularity, and sometimes reverberated like the thunder. He saw the smoke rolling upward and saw crowds of men who ran and cheered, or stood and blazed away at the inscrutable distance.

He came upon some stragglers, and they told him how to find the field hospital. They described its exact location. In fact, these men, no longer having part in the battle, knew more of it than others. They told the performance of every corps, every division, the opinion of every general. The lieutenant, carrying his wounded arm rearward, looked upon them with wonder.

At the roadside a brigade was making coffee and buzzing with talk like a girls' boarding school. Several officers came out to him and inquired concerning things of which he knew nothing. One, seeing his arm, began to scold. "Why, man, that's no way to do. You want to fix that thing." He appropriated the lieutenant and the lieutenant's wound. He cut the sleeve and laid bare the arm, every nerve of which softly fluttered under his touch. He bound his handkerchief over the wound, scolding away in the meantime. His tone allowed one to think that he was in the habit of being wounded every day. The lieutenant hung his head, feeling, in this presence, that he did not know how to be correctly wounded.

The low white tents of the hospital were grouped around an old schoolhouse. There was here a singular commotion. In the foreground two ambulances interlocked wheels in the deep mud. The drivers were tossing the blame of it back and forth, gesticulating and berating, while from the ambulances, both crammed with wounded, there came an occasional groan. An interminable crowd of bandaged men were coming and going. Great numbers sat under the trees nursing heads or arms or legs. There was a dispute of some kind raging on the steps of the schoolhouse. Sitting with his back against a tree a man with a face as gray as a new army blanket was serenely smoking a corncob pipe. The lieutenant wished to rush forward and inform him that he was dying.

A busy surgeon was passing near the lieutenant. "Good morning," he said, with a friendly smile. Then he caught sight of the lieutenant's arm, and his face at once changed. "Well, let's have a look at it." He seemed possessed suddenly of a great contempt for the lieutenant. This wound evidently placed the latter on a very low social plane. The doctor cried out impatiently:

"What mutton-head had tied it up that way anyhow?" The lieutenant answered, "Oh, a man."

When the wound was disclosed the doctor fingered it disdainfully. "Humph," he said. "You come along with me and I'll 'tend to you." His voice contained the same scorn as if he were saying: "You will have to go to jail."

The lieutenant had been very meek, but now his face flushed, and he looked into the doctor's eyes. "I guess I won't have it amputated," he said.

"Nonsense, man! Nonsense! Nonsense!" cried the doctor. "Come along, now. I won't amputate it. Come along. Don't be a baby."

"Let go of me," said the lieutenant, holding back wrathfully, his glance fixed upon the door of the old schoolhouse, as sinister to him as the portals of death.

And this is the story of how the lieutenant lost his arm. When he reached home, his sisters, his mother, his wife, sobbed for a long time at the sight of the flat sleeve. "Oh, well," he said, standing shamefaced amid these tears, "I don't suppose it matters so much as all that."

EDWIDGE DANTICAT

Night Women

I cringe from the heat of the night on my face. I feel as bare as open flesh. Tonight I am much older than the twenty-five years that I have lived. The night is the time I dread most in my life. Yet if I am to live, I must depend on it.

Shadows shrink and spread over the lace curtain as my son slips into bed. I watch as he stretches from a little boy into the broom-size of a man, his height mounting the innocent fabric that splits our one-room house into two spaces, two mats, two worlds.

For a brief second, I almost mistake him for the ghost of his father, an old lover who disappeared with the night's shadows a long time ago. My son's bed stays nestled against the corner, far from the peeking jalousies. I watch as he digs furrows in the pillow with his head. He shifts his small body carefully so as not to crease his Sunday clothes. He wraps my long blood-red scarf around his neck, the one I wear myself during the day to tempt my suitors. I let him have it at night, so that he always has something of mine when my face is out of sight.

I watch his shadow resting still on the curtain. My eyes are drawn to him, like the stars peeking through the small holes in the roof that none of my suitors will fix for me, because they like to watch a scrap of the sky while lying on their naked backs on my mat.

A firefly buzzes around the room, finding him and not me. Perhaps it is a mosquito that has learned the gift of lighting itself. He always slaps the mosquitoes dead on his face without even waking. In the morning, he will have tiny blood spots on his forehead, as though he had spent the whole night kissing a woman with wide-open flesh wounds on her face.

In his sleep he squirms and groans as though he's already discovered that there is pleasure in touching himself. We have never talked about love. What would he need to know? Love is one of those lessons that you grow to learn, the way one learns that one shoe is made to fit a certain foot, lest it cause discomfort.

There are two kinds of women: day women and night women. I am stuck between the day and night in a golden amber bronze. My eyes are the color of dirt, almost copper if I am standing in the sun. I want to wear my matted tresses in braids as soon as I learn to do my whole head without numbing my arms.

Most nights, I hear a slight whisper. My body freezes as I wonder how long it would take for him to cross the curtain and find me.

He says, "Mommy."

I say, "*Darling.*"

Somehow in the night, he always calls me in whispers. I hear the buzz of his transistor radio. It is shaped like a can of cola. One of my suitors gave it to him to plug into his ears so he can stay asleep while Mommy *works*.

There is a place in Ville Rose where ghost women ride the crests of waves while brushing the stars out of their hair. There they woo strollers and leave the stars on the path for them. There are nights that I believe that those ghost women are with me. As much as I know that there are women who sit up through the night and undo patches of cloth that they have spent the whole day weaving. These women, they destroy their toil so that they will always have more to do. And as long as there's work, they will not have to lie next to the lifeless soul of a man whose scent still lingers in another woman's bed.

The way my son reacts to my lips stroking his cheeks decides for me if he's asleep. He is like a butterfly fluttering on a rock that stands out naked in the middle of a stream. Sometimes I see in the folds of his eyes a longing for something that's bigger than myself. We are like faraway lovers, lying to one another, under different moons.

When my smallest finger caresses the narrow cleft beneath his nose, sometimes his tongue slips out of his mouth and he licks my fingernail. He moans and turns away, perhaps thinking that this too is a part of the dream.

I whisper my mountain stories in his ear, stories of the ghost women and the stars in their hair. I tell him of the deadly snakes lying at one end of a rainbow and the hat full of gold lying at the other end. I tell him that if I cross a stream of glass-clear hibiscus, I can make myself a goddess. I blow on his long eyelashes to see if he's truly asleep. My fingers coil themselves into visions of birds on his nose. I want him to forget that we live in a place where nothing lasts.

I know that sometimes he wonders why I take such painstaking care. Why do I draw half-moons on my sweaty forehead and spread crimson powders on the rise of my cheeks. We put on his ruffled Sunday suit and I tell him that we are expecting a sweet angel and where angels tread the hosts must be as beautiful as floating hibiscus.

In his sleep, his fingers tug his shirt ruffles loose. He licks his lips from the last piece of sugar candy stolen from my purse.

No more, no more, or your teeth will turn black. I have forgotten to make him brush the mint leaves against his teeth. He does not know that one day a woman like his mother may judge him by the whiteness of his teeth.

It doesn't take long before he is snoring softly. I listen for the shy laughter of his most pleasant dreams. Dreams of angels skipping over his head and occasionally resting their pink heels on his nose.

First Person: Edwidge Danticat on "Writing 'Night Women'"

I wrote "Night Women" one night when I had trouble sleeping. I was lying in bed when I began to imagine that I was waiting for someone to come home. That's when the idea for the story came to me.

At first the nameless character, a mother who had just put her young son to bed, was a wife waiting for her husband. Where was this husband? I wondered. With another woman, I decided. And that other woman was a prostitute.

The focus of the story then shifted from the wife to the prostitute. She was a mother who had just put her son to bed and was waiting for a visit from a client, a married man.

Once my main character was in place, I wondered how she would explain her "work" to her son. I decided to put the son in the same cramped living and "working" quarters with the mother, which would make an explanation that much harder to produce. It then became obvious that the mother would have to wait for her son to go to sleep before doing her "job," and that if her son caught her at it, she would have to "make up stories" about what she was actually doing. These "stories" became the legends at the heart of "Night Women," fictions about the son's missing father returning home, about angels visiting them for a while, about ghost women with stars in their hair, and about rainbows with snakes at one end and a pot of gold at the other. In the same way that we sometimes use myths, legends, and folktales to explain the creation of the earth, sun, moon, and stars, this woman uses these bedtime legends to protect her son's uncomplicated view of the world and to assure herself that in spite of their unusual circumstances, he still has a childhood filled with fantastical and beautiful notions.

While writing "Night Women," I thought of Penelope from *The Odyssey*. Penelope is a wife who waits for twenty years for her husband, Odysseus, to come home from war. As she waits, Penelope wards off suitors by spending her days weaving a shroud that she unravels each night, only to begin her task again the next day. The stories that this prostitute tells her son becomes her own shroud, her way of mourning the life she could have had, had her husband not disappeared. The legends also become beacons of hope for the son, a way for him to overlook a painful reality and find alternate truths.

I used the first person point of view in this story because I wanted the reader to feel very close to this character, to hear the intimate thoughts directly, in her own voice. I also wanted to avoid any unintentional judgement on my part, removing my voice from the situation all together. I did not want to cast any judgements, just as the character casts no judgements on herself. The only possible "judge" is the son, who the mother is so desperately trying to protect with these tales.

Some readers have asked me whether or not the son is aware of the fact that his mother is a prostitute. The answer is yes. He knows. And perhaps the mother also realizes that he knows. However, because she loves him so much, she feels it is her duty to shield him from this.

Many readers have also asked me whether or not I consider this woman a liar. The answer to this question is not as simple. It is my opinion—and readers are allowed to have differing opinions since the story becomes as much theirs as mine once it is out in the world—it is my opinion that this woman is simply weaving tales in response to a difficult situation, much like some fiction writers invent stories, concoct sometimes beautiful and sometimes painful tales, for their readers.

Lydia Davis

The Sock

My husband is married to a different woman now, shorter than I am, about five feet tall, solidly built, and of course he looks taller than he used to and narrower, and his head looks smaller. Next to her I feel bony and awkward and she is too short for me to look her in the eye, though I try to stand or sit at the right angle to do that. I once had a clear idea of the sort of woman he should marry when he married again, but none of his girlfriends was quite what I had in mind and this one least of all.

They came out here last summer for a few weeks to see my son, who is his and mine. There were some touchy moments, but there were also some good times, though of course even the good times were a little uneasy. The two of them seemed to expect a lot of accommodation from me, maybe because she was sick—she was in pain and sulky, with circles under her eyes. They used my phone and other things in my house. They would walk up slowly from the beach to my house and shower there, and later walk away clean in the evening with my son between them, hand in hand. I gave a party, and they came and danced with each other, impressed my friends and stayed till the end. I went out of my way for them, mostly because of our boy. I thought we should all get along for his sake. By the end of their visit I was tired.

The night before they went, we had a plan to eat out in a Vietnamese restaurant with his mother. His mother was flying in from another city, and then the three of them were going off together the next day, to the Midwest. His wife's parents were giving them a big wedding party so that all the people she had grown up with, the stout farmers and their families, could meet him.

When I went into the city that night to where they were staying, I took what they had left in my house that I had found so far: a book, next to the closet door, and somewhere else a sock of his. I drove up to the building, and I saw my husband out on the sidewalk flagging me down. He wanted to talk to me before I went inside. He told me his mother was in bad shape and couldn't stay with them, and he asked me if I would please take her home with me later. Without thinking I said I would. I was forgetting the way she would look at the inside of my house and how I would clean the worst of it while she watched.

In the lobby, they were sitting across from each other in two armchairs, these two small women, both beautiful in different ways, both wearing lipstick, different shades, both frail, I thought later, in different ways. The reason they were sitting here was that his mother was afraid to go upstairs. It didn't bother her to fly in an airplane, but she couldn't go up more than one story in an apartment building. It was worse now than it had been. In the old days she could be on the eighth floor if she had to, as long as the windows were tightly shut.

Before we went out to dinner my husband took the book up to the apartment, but he had stuck the sock in his back pocket without thinking when I gave it to him out on the street and it stayed there during the meal in the restaurant, where his mother sat in her black clothes at the end of the table opposite an empty chair, sometimes playing with my son, with his cars, and sometimes asking my husband and then me and then his wife questions about the peppercorns and other strong spices that might be in her food. Then after we all left the restaurant and were standing in the parking lot he pulled the sock out of his pocket and looked at it, wondering how it had got there.

It was a small thing, but later I couldn't forget the sock, because here was this one sock in his back pocket in a strange neighborhood way out in the eastern part of the city in a Vietnamese ghetto, by the massage parlors, and none of us really knew this city but we were all here together and it was odd, because I still felt as though he and I were partners, we had been partners a long time, and I couldn't help thinking of all the other socks of his I had picked up, stiff with his sweat and threadbare on the sole, in all our life together from place to place, and then of his feet in those socks, how the skin shone through at the ball of the foot and the heel where the weave was worn down; how he would lie reading on his back on the bed with his feet crossed at the ankles so that his toes pointed at different corners of the room; how he would then turn on his side with his feet together like two halves of a fruit; how, still reading, he would reach down and pull off his socks and drop them in little balls on the floor and reach down again and pick at his toes while he read; sometimes he shared with me what he was reading and thinking, and sometimes he didn't know whether I was there in the room or somewhere else.

I couldn't forget it later, even though after they were gone I found a few other things they had left or rather his wife had left them in the pocket of a jacket of mine—a red comb, a red lipstick, and a bottle of pills. For a while these things sat around in a little group of three on one counter of the kitchen and then another, while I thought I'd send them to her, because I thought maybe the medicine was important, but I kept forgetting to ask, until finally I put them away in a drawer to give her when they came out again, because by then it wasn't going to be long, and it made me tired all over again just to think of it.

CHARLES DICKENS

The Child's Story

Once upon a time, a good many years ago, there was a traveller, and he set out upon a journey. It was a magic journey, and was to seem very long when he began it, and very short when he got half way through.

He travelled along a rather dark path for some little time, without meeting anything, until at last he came to a beautiful child. So he said to the child, "What do you do here?" And the child said, "I am always at play. Come and play with me!"

So, he played with that child, the whole day long, and they were very merry. The sky was so blue, the sun was so bright, the water was so sparkling, the leaves were so green, the flowers were so lovely, and they heard such singing-birds and saw so many butterflies, that everything was beautiful. This was in fine weather. When it rained, they loved to watch the falling drops, and to smell the fresh scents. When it blew, it was delightful to listen to the wind, and fancy what it said, as it came rushing from its home—where was that, they wondered!—whistling and howling, driving the clouds before it, bending the trees, rumbling in the chimneys, shaking the house, and making the sea roar in fury. But, when it snowed, that was best of all; for, they liked nothing so well as to look up at the white flakes falling fast and thick, like down from the breasts of millions of white birds; and to see how smooth and deep the drift was; and to listen to the hush upon the paths and roads.

They had plenty of the finest toys in the world, and the most astonishing picture-books: all about scimitars and slippers and turbans, and dwarfs and giants and genii and fairies, and blue-beards and bean-stalks and riches and caverns and forests and Valentines and Orsons: and all new and all true.

But, one day, of a sudden, the traveller lost the child. He called to him over and over again, but got no answer. So, he went upon his road, and went on for a little while without meeting anything, until at last he came to a handsome boy. So, he said to the boy, "What do you do here?" And the boy said, "I am always learning. Come and learn with me."

So he learned with that boy about Jupiter and Juno, and the Greeks and the Romans, and I don't know what, and learned more than I could tell—or he either, for he soon forgot a great deal of it. But, they were not always learning; they had the merriest games that ever were played. They rowed upon the river in summer, and skated on the ice in winter; they were active afoot, and active on horseback; at cricket, and all games at ball; at prisoners' base, hare and hounds, follow my leader, and more sports than I can think of; nobody could beat them. They had holidays too, and Twelfth cakes, and parties where they danced till midnight, and real Theatres where they saw palaces of real gold and silver rise out of the real earth, and saw all the wonders of the world at once. As to friends, they had such dear friends and so many of them, that I want the time to reckon them up. They were all young, like the handsome boy, and were never to be strange to one another all their lives through.

Still, one day, in the midst of all these pleasures, the traveller lost the boy as he had lost the child, and, after calling to him in vain, went on upon his journey. So he went on for a little while without seeing anything, until at last he came to a young man. So, he said to the young man, "What do you do here?" And the young man said, "I am always in love. Come and love with me."

So, he went away with that young man, and presently they came to one of the prettiest girls that ever was seen—just like Fanny in the corner there—and she had eyes like Fanny, and hair like Fanny, and dimples like Fanny's, and she laughed and coloured just as Fanny does while I am talking about her. So, the young man fell in love directly—just as Somebody I won't mention, the first time he came here, did with Fanny. Well! he was teased sometimes—just as Somebody used to be by Fanny; and they quarrelled sometimes—just as Somebody and Fanny used to quarrel; and they made it up, and sat in the dark, and wrote letters every day, and never were happy asunder, and were always looking out for one another and pretending not to, and were engaged at Christmas-time, and sat close to one another by the fire, and were going to be married very soon—all exactly like Somebody I won't mention, and Fanny!

But, the traveller lost them one day, as he had lost the rest of his friends, and, after calling to them to come back, which they never did, went on upon his journey. So, he went on for a little while without seeing anything, until at last he came to a middle-aged gentleman. So, he said to the gentleman, "What are you doing here?" And his answer was, "I am always busy. Come and be busy with me!"

So, he began to be very busy with that gentleman, and they went on through the wood together. The whole journey was through a wood only it had been open and green at first, like a wood in spring; and now began to be thick and dark, like a wood in summer; some of the little trees that had come out earliest, were even turning brown. The gentleman was not alone, but had a lady of about the same age with him, who was his Wife; and they had children, who were with them too. So, they all went on together through the wood, cutting down the trees, and making a path through the branches and the fallen leaves, and carrying burdens, and working hard.

Sometimes, they came to a long green avenue that opened into deeper woods. Then they would hear a very little distant voice crying, "Father, father, I am another child! Stop for me!" And presently they would see a very little figure, growing larger as it came along, running to join them. When it came up, they all crowded round it, and kissed and welcomed it; and then they all went on together.

Sometimes, they came to several avenues at once, and then they all stood still, and one of the children said, "Father, I am going to sea," and another said, "Father, I am going to India," and another, "Father, I am going to seek my fortune where I can," and another, "Father, I am going to Heaven!" So, with many tears at parting, they went, solitary, down those avenues, each child upon its way; and the child who went to Heaven, rose into the golden air and vanished.

Whenever these partings happened, the traveller looked at the gentleman, and saw him glance up at the sky above the trees, where the day was beginning to decline, and the sunset to come on. He saw, too, that his hair was turning grey. But, they never could rest long, for they had their journey to perform, and it was necessary for them to be always busy.

At last, there had been so many partings that there were no children left, and only the traveller, the gentleman, and the lady, went upon their way in company. And now the wood was yellow; and now brown; and the leaves, even of the forest trees, began to fall.

So, they came to an avenue that was darker than the rest, and were pressing forward on their journey without looking down it when the lady stopped.

"My husband," said the lady. "I am called."

They listened, and they heard a voice a long way down the avenue, say, "Mother, mother!"

It was the voice of the first child who had said, "I am going to Heaven!" and the father said, "I pray not yet. The sunset is very near. I pray not yet!"

But, the voice cried, "Mother, mother!" without minding him, though his hair was now quite white, and tears were on his face.

Then, the mother, who was already drawn into the shade of the dark avenue and moving away with her arms still round his neck, kissed him, and said, "My dearest, I am summoned, and I go!" And she was gone. And the traveller and he were left alone together.

And they went on and on together, until they came to very near the end of the wood: so near, that they could see the sunset shining red before them through the trees.

Yet, once more, while he broke his way among the branches, the traveller lost his friend. He called and called, but there was no reply, and when he passed out of the wood, and saw the peaceful sun going down upon a wide purple prospect, he came to an old man sitting on a fallen tree. So, he said to the old man, "What do you do here?" And the old man said with a calm smile, "I am always remembering. Come and remember with me!"

So the traveller sat down by the side of that old man, face to face with the serene sunset; and all his friends came softly back and stood around him. The beautiful child, the handsome boy, the young man in love, the father, mother, and children: every one of them was there, and he had lost nothing. So, he loved them all, and was kind and forbearing with them all, and was always pleased to watch them all, and they all honoured and loved him. And I think the traveller must be yourself, dear Grandfather, because this is what you do to us, and what we do to you.

JOHN DOS PASSOS

Vag

The young man waits at the edge of the concrete, with one hand he grips a rubbed suitcase of phony leather, the other hand almost making a fist, thumb up

that moves in ever so slight an arc when a car slithers past, a truck roars clatters; the wind of cars passing ruffles his hair, slaps grit in his face.

Head swims, hunger has twisted the belly tight,

he has skinned a heel through the torn sock, feet ache in the broken shoes, under the threadbare suit carefully brushed off with the hand, the torn drawers have a crummy feel, the feel of having slept in your clothes; in the nostrils lingers the staleness of discouraged carcasses crowded into a transient camp, the carbolic stench of the jail, on the taut cheeks the shamed flush from the boring eyes of cops and deputies, railroadbulls (they eat three squares a day, they are buttoned into wellmade clothes, they have wives to sleep with, kids to play with after supper, they work for the big men who buy their way, they stick their chests out with the sureness of power behind their backs). Git the hell out, scram. Know what's good for you, you'll make yourself scarce. Gittin' tough, eh? Think you kin take it, eh?

The punch in the jaw, the slam on the head with the nightstick, the wrist grabbed and twisted behind the back, the big knee brought up sharp into the crotch,

the walk out of town with sore feet to stand and wait at the edge of the hissing speeding string of cars where the reek of ether and lead and gas melts into the silent grassy smell of the earth.

Eyes black with want seek out the eyes of the drivers, a hitch, a hundred miles down the road.

Overhead in the blue a plane drones. Eyes follow the silver Douglas that flashes once in the sun and bores its smooth way out of sight into the blue.

(The transcontinental passengers sit pretty, big men with bank accounts, highly paid jobs, who are saluted by doormen; telephone-girls say goodmorning to them. Last night after a fine dinner, drinks with friends, they left Newark. Roar of climbing motors slanting up into the inky haze. Lights drop away. An hour staring along a silvery wing at a big lonesome moon hurrying west through curdling scum. Beacons flash in a line across Ohio.

At Cleveland the plane drops banking in a smooth spiral, the string of lights along the lake swings in a circle. Climbing roar of the motors again; slumped in the soft seat drowsing through the flat moonlight night.

Chi. A glimpse of the dipper. Another spiral swoop from cool into hot air thick with dust and the reek of burnt prairies.

Beyond the Mississippi dawn creeps up behind through the murk over the great plains. Puddles of mist go white in the Iowa hills, farms, fences, silos, steel glint from a river. The blinking eyes of the beacons reddening into day. Watercourses vein the eroded hills.

Omaha. Great cumulus clouds, from coppery churning to creamy to silvery white, trail brown skirts of rain over the hot plains. Red and yellow badlands, tiny horned shapes of cattle.

Cheyenne. The cool high air smells of sweetgrass.

The tightbaled clouds to westward burst and scatter in tatters over the strawcolored hills. Indigo mountains jut rimrock. The plane breasts a huge crumbling cloudbank and toboggans over bumpy air across green and crimson slopes into the sunny dazzle of Salt Lake.

The transcontinental passenger thinks contracts, profits, vacation-trips, mighty continent between Atlantic and Pacific, power, wires humming dollars, cities jammed, hills empty, the indiantrail leading into the wagonroad, the macadamed pike, the concrete skyway; trains, planes: history the billiondollar speedup,

and in the bumpy air over the desert ranges towards Las Vegas

sickens and vomits into the carton container the steak and mushrooms he ate in New York. No matter, silver in the pocket, greenbacks in the wallet, drafts, certified checks, plenty restaurants in L.A.)

The young man waits on the side of the road; the plane has gone; thumb moves in a small arc when a car tears hissing past. Eyes seek the driver's eyes. A hundred miles down the road. Head swims, belly tightens, wants crawl over his skin like ants:

went to school, books said opportunity, ads promised speed, own your home, shine bigger than your neighbor, the radiocrooner whispered girls, ghosts of platinum girls coaxed from the screen, millions in winnings were chalked up on the boards in the offices, pay-checks were for hands willing to work, the cleared desk of an executive with three telephones on it;

waits with swimming head, needs knot the belly; idle hands numb, beside the speeding traffic.

A hundred miles down the road.

Fyodor Dostoevsky

The Heavenly Christmas Tree

I am a novelist, and I suppose I have made up this story. I write "I suppose," though I know for a fact that I have made it up, but yet I keep fancying that it must have happened on Christmas Eve in some great town in a time of terrible frost.

I have a vision of a boy, a little boy, six years old or even younger. This boy woke up that morning in a cold damp cellar. He was dressed in a sort of little dressing-gown and was shivering with cold. There was a cloud of white steam from his breath, and sitting on a box in the corner, he blew the steam out of his mouth and amused himself in his dullness watching it float away. But he was terribly hungry. Several times that morning he went up to the plank bed where his sick mother was lying on a mattress as thin as a pancake, with some sort of bundle under her head for a pillow. How had she come here? She must have come with her boy from some other town and suddenly fallen ill. The landlady who let the "corners" had been taken two days before to the police station, the lodgers were out and about as the holiday was so near, and the only one left had been lying for the last twenty-four hours dead drunk, not having waited for Christmas. In another corner of the room a wretched old woman of eighty, who had once been a children's nurse but was now left to die friendless, was moaning and groaning with rheumatism, scolding and grumbling at the boy so that he was afraid to go near her corner. He had got a drink of water in the outer room, but could not find a crust anywhere, and had been on the point of waking his mother a dozen times. He felt frightened at last in the darkness: it had long been dusk, but no light was kindled. Touching his mother's face, he was surprised that she did not move at all, and that she was as cold as the wall. "It is very cold here," he thought. He stood a little, unconsciously letting his hands rest on the dead woman's shoulders, then he breathed on his fingers to warm them, and then quietly fumbling for his cap on the bed, he went out of the cellar. He would have gone earlier, but was afraid of the big dog which had been howling all day at the neighbour's door at the top of the stairs. But the dog was not there now, and he went out into the street.

Mercy on us, what a town! He had never seen anything like it before. In the town from which he had come, it was always such black darkness at night. There was one lamp for the whole street, the little, low-pitched, wooden houses were closed up with shutters, there was no one to be seen in the street after dusk, all the people shut themselves up in their houses, and there was nothing but the howling of packs of dogs, hundreds and thousands of them barking and howling all night. But there it was so warm and he was given food, while here—oh, dear, if he only had something to eat! And what a noise and rattle here, what light and what people, horses and carriages, and what a frost! The frozen steam hung in clouds over the horses, over their warmly breathing mouths; their hoofs clanged against the stones through the powdery snow, and everyone pushed so, and—oh, dear, how he longed for some morsel to eat, and how wretched he suddenly felt. A policeman walked by and turned away to avoid seeing the boy.

There was another street—oh, what a wide one, here he would be run over for certain; how everyone was shouting, racing and driving along, and the light, the light! And what was this? A huge glass window, and through the window a tree reaching up to the ceiling; it was a fir tree, and on it were ever so many lights, gold papers and apples and little dolls and horses; and there were children clean and dressed in their best running about the room, laughing and playing and eating and drinking something. And then a little girl began dancing with one of the boys, what a pretty little girl! And he could hear the music through the window. The boy looked and wondered and laughed, though his toes were aching with the cold and his fingers were red and stiff so that it hurt him to move them. And all at once the boy remembered how his toes and fingers hurt him, and began crying, and ran on; and again through another window-pane he saw another Christmas tree, and on a table cakes of all sorts—almond cakes, red cakes and yellow cakes, and three grand young ladies were sitting there, and they gave the cakes to any one who went up to them, and the door kept opening, lots of gentlemen and ladies went in from the street. The boy crept up, suddenly opened the door and went in. Oh, how they shouted at him and waved him back! One lady went up to him hurriedly and slipped a kopeck into his hand, and with her own hands opened the door into the street for him! How frightened he was. And the kopeck rolled away and clinked upon the steps; he could not bend his red fingers to hold it right. The boy ran away and went on, where he did not know. He was ready to cry again but he was afraid, and ran on and on and blew his fingers. And he was miserable because he felt suddenly so lonely and terrified, and all at once, mercy on us! What was this again? People were standing in a crowd admiring. Behind a glass window there were three little dolls, dressed in red and green dresses, and exactly, exactly as though they were alive. One was a little old man sitting and playing a big violin, the two others were standing close by and playing little violins, and nodding in time, and looking at one another, and their lips moved, they were speaking, actually speaking, only one couldn't hear through the glass. And at first the boy thought they were alive, and when he grasped that they were dolls he laughed. He had never seen such dolls before, and had no idea there were such dolls! And he wanted to cry, but he felt amused, amused by the dolls. All at once he fancied that some one caught at his smock behind: a wicked big boy was standing beside him and suddenly hit him on the head, snatched off his cap and tripped him up. The boy fell down on the ground, at once there was a shout, he was numb with fright, he jumped up and ran away. He ran, and not knowing where he was going, ran in at the gate of some one's courtyard, and sat down behind a stack of wood: "They won't find me here, besides it's dark!"

He sat huddled up and was breathless from fright, and all at once, quite suddenly, he felt so happy: his hands and feet suddenly left off aching and grew so warm, as warm as though he were on a stove; then he shivered all over, then he gave a start, why, he must have been asleep. How nice to have a sleep here! "I'll sit here a little and go and look at the dolls again," said the boy, and smiled thinking of them. "Just as though they were alive! . . ." And suddenly he heard his mother singing over him. "Mammy, I am asleep; how nice it is to sleep here!"

"Come to my Christmas tree, little one," a soft voice suddenly whispered over his head.

He thought that this was still his mother, but no, it was not she. Who it was calling him, he could not see, but someone bent over and embraced him in the darkness; and he stretched out his hands to him, and . . . and all at once—oh, what a bright light! Oh, what a Christmas tree! And yet it was not a fir tree, he had never seen a tree like that! Where was he now? Everything was bright and shining, and all round him were dolls; but no, they were not dolls, they were little boys and girls, only so bright and shining. They all came flying round him, they all kissed him, took him and carried him along with them, and he was flying himself, and he saw that his mother was looking at him and laughing joyfully. "Mammy, Mammy; oh, how nice it is here, Mammy!" And again he kissed the children and wanted to tell them at once of those dolls in the shop window.

"Who are you, boys? Who are you, girls?" he asked, laughing and admiring them.

"This is Christ's Christmas tree," they answered. "Christ always has a Christmas tree on this day, for the little children who have no tree of their own . . ." And he found out that all these little boys and girls were children just like himself; that some had been frozen in the baskets in which they had as babies been laid on the doorsteps of well-to-do Petersburg people, others had been boarded out with Finnish women by the Foundling and had been suffocated, others had died at their starved mother's breasts (in the Samara famine), others had died in third-class railway carriages from the foul air; and yet they were all here, they were all like angels about Christ, and He was in the midst of them and held out His hands to them and blessed them and their sinful mothers. . . . And the mothers of these children stood on one side weeping; each one knew her boy or girl, and the children flew up to them and kissed them and wiped away their tears with their little hands, and begged them not to weep because they were so happy.

And down below in the morning the porter found the little dead body of the frozen child on the woodstack; they sought out his mother too. . . . She had died before him. They met before the Lord God in heaven.

Why have I made up such a story, so out of keeping with an ordinary diary, and a writer's above all? And I promised two stories dealing with real events! But that is just it, I keep fancying that all this may have happened really—that is, what took place in the cellar and on the woodstack; but as for Christ's Christmas tree, I cannot tell you whether that could have happened or not.

CAROLYN FORCHÉ

The Colonel

What you have heard is true. I was in his house. His wife carried a tray of coffee and sugar. His daughter filed her nails, his son went out for the night. There were daily papers, pet dogs, a pistol on the cushion beside him. The moon swung bare on its black cord over the house. On the television was a cop show. It was in English. Broken bottles were embedded in the walls around the house to scoop the kneecaps from a man's legs or cut his hands to lace. On the windows there were gratings like those in liquor stores. We had dinner, rack of lamb, good wine, a gold bell was on the table for calling the maid. The maid brought green mangoes, salt, a type of bread. I was asked how I enjoyed the country. There was a brief commercial in Spanish. His wife took everything away. There was some talk then of how difficult it had become to govern. The parrot said hello on the terrace. The colonel told it to shut up, and pushed himself from the table. My friend said to me with his eyes: say nothing. The colonel returned with a sack used to bring groceries home. He spilled many human ears on the table. They were like dried peach halves. There is no other way to say this. He took one of them in his hands, shook it in our faces, dropped it into a water glass. It came alive there. I am tired of fooling around he said. As for the rights of anyone, tell your people they can go fuck themselves. He swept the ears to the floor with his arm and held the last of his wine in the air. Something for your poetry, no? he said. Some of the ears on the floor caught this scrap of his voice. Some of the ears on the floor were pressed to the ground.

E.M. Forster

The Other Side of the Hedge

My pedometer told me that I was twenty-five; and, though it is a shocking thing to stop walking, I was so tired that I sat down on a milestone to rest. People outstripped me, jeering as they did so, but I was too apathetic to feel resentful, and even when Miss Eliza Dimbleby, the great educationist, swept past, exhorting me to persevere, I only smiled and raised my hat.

At first I thought I was going to be like my brother, whom I had had to leave by the roadside a year or two round the corner. He had wasted his breath on singing, and his strength on helping others. But I had travelled more wisely, and now it was only the monotony of the highway that oppressed me—dust under foot and brown crackling hedges on either side, ever since I could remember.

And I had already dropped several things—indeed, the road behind was strewn with the things we all had dropped; and the white dust was settling down on them, so that already they looked no better than stones. My muscles were so weary that I could not even bear the weight of those things I still carried. I slid off the milestone into the road, and lay there prostrate, with my face to the great parched hedge, praying that I might give up.

A little puff of air revived me. It seemed to come from the hedge; and, when I opened my eyes, there was a glint of light through the tangle of boughs and dead leaves. The hedge could not be as thick as usual. In my weak, morbid state, I longed to force my way in, and see what was on the other side. No one was in sight, or I should not have dared to try. For we of the road do not admit in conversation that there is another side at all.

I yielded to the temptation, saying to myself that I would come back in a minute. The thorns scratched my face, and I had to use my arms as a shield, depending on my feet alone to push me forward. Halfway through I would have gone back, for in the passage all the things I was carrying were scraped off me, and my clothes were torn. But I was so wedged that return was impossible, and I had to wiggle blindly forward, expecting every moment that my strength would fail me, and that I should perish in the undergrowth.

Suddenly cold water closed round my head, and I seemed sinking down for ever. I had fallen out of the hedge into a deep pool. I rose to the surface at last, crying for help, and I heard someone on the opposite bank laugh and say: "Another!" And then I was twitched out and laid panting on the dry ground.

Even when the water was out of my eyes, I was still dazed, for I had never been in so large a space, nor seen such grass and sunshine. The blue sky was no longer a strip, and beneath it the earth had risen grandly into hills—clean, bare buttresses, with beech trees in their folds, and meadows and clear pools at their feet. But the hills were not high, and there was in the landscape a sense of human occupation—so that one might have called it a park, or garden, if the words did not imply a certain triviality and constraint.

As soon as I got my breath, I turned to my rescuer and said:

"Where does this place lead to?"

"Nowhere, thank the Lord!" said he, and laughed. He was a man of fifty or sixty—just the kind of age we mistrust on the road—but there was no anxiety in his manner, and his voice was that of a boy of eighteen.

"But it must lead somewhere!" I cried, too much surprised at his answer to thank him for saving my life.

"He wants to know where it leads!" he shouted to some men on the hillside, and they laughed back, and waved their caps.

I noticed then that the pool into which I had fallen was really a moat which bent round to the left and to the right, and that the hedge followed it continually. The hedge was green on this side—its roots showed through the clear water, and fish swam about in them—and it was wreathed over with dog-roses and Traveller's Joy. But it was a barrier, and in a moment I lost all pleasure in the grass, the sky, the trees, the happy men and women, and realized that the place was but a prison, for all its beauty and extent.

We moved away from the boundary, and then followed a path almost parallel to it, across the meadows. I found it difficult walking, for I was always trying to out-distance my companion, and there was no advantage in doing this if the place led nowhere. I had never kept step with anyone since I left my brother.

I amused him by stopping suddenly and saying disconsolately, "This is perfectly terrible. One cannot advance: one cannot progress. Now we of the road—"

"Yes. I know."

"I was going to say, we advance continually."

"I know."

"We are always learning, expanding, developing. Why, even in my short life I have seen a great deal of advance—the Transvaal War, the Fiscal Question, Christian Science, Radium. Here for example—"

I took out my pedometer, but it still marked twenty-five, not a degree more.

"Oh, it's stopped! I meant to show you. It should have registered all the time I was walking with you. But it makes me only twenty-five."

"Many things don't work in here," he said. "One day a man brought in a Lee-Metford, and that wouldn't work."

"The laws of science are universal in their application. It must be the water in the moat that has injured the machinery. In normal conditions everything works. Science and the spirit of emulation—those are the forces that have made us what we are."

I had to break off and acknowledge the pleasant greetings of people whom we passed. Some of them were singing, some talking, some engaged in gardening, hay-making, or other rudimentary industries. They all seemed happy; and I might have been happy too, if I could have forgotten that the place led nowhere.

I was startled by a young man who came sprinting across our path, took a little fence in fine style, and went tearing over a ploughed field till he plunged into a lake, across which he began to swim. Here was true energy, and I exclaimed: "A cross-country race! Where are the others?"

"There are no others," my companion replied; and, later on, when we passed some long grass from which came the voice of a girl singing exquisitely to herself, he said again: "There are no others." I was bewildered at the waste in production, and murmured to myself, "What does it all mean?"

He said: "It means nothing but itself"—and he repeated the words slowly, as if I were a child.

"I understand," I said quietly, "but I do not agree. Every achievement is worthless unless it is a link in the chain of development. And I must not trespass on your kindness any longer. I must get back somehow to the road and have my pedometer mended."

"First, you must see the gates," he replied, "for we have gates, though we never use them."

I yielded politely, and before long we reached the moat again, at a point where it was spanned by a bridge. Over the bridge was a big gate, as white as ivory, which was fitted into a gap in the boundary hedge. The gate opened outwards, and I exclaimed in amazement, for from it ran a road—just such a road as I had left—dusty under foot, with brown crackling hedges on either side as far as the eye could reach.

"That's my road!" I cried.

He shut the gate and said: "But not your part of the road. It is through this gate that humanity went out countless ages ago, when it was first seized with the desire to walk."

I denied this, observing that the part of the road I myself had left was not more than two miles off. But with the obstinacy of his years he repeated:

"It is the same road. This is the beginning, and though it seems to run straight away from us, it doubles so often, that it is never far from our boundary and sometimes touches it." He stooped down by the moat, and traced on its moist margin an absurd figure like a maze. As we walked back through the meadows, I tried to convince him of his mistake.

"The road sometimes doubles to be sure, but that is part of our discipline. Who can doubt that its general tendency is onward? To what goal we know not—it may be to some mountain where we shall touch the sky, it may be over precipices into the sea. But that it goes forward—who can doubt that? It is the thought of that that makes us strive to excel, each in his own way, and gives us an impetus which is lacking with you. Now that man who passed us—it's true that he ran well, and jumped well, and swam well; but we have men who can run better, and men who can jump better, and who can swim better. Specialization has produced results which would surprise you. Similarly, that girl—"

Here I interrupted myself to exclaim: "Good gracious me! I could have sworn it was Miss Eliza Dimbleby over there, with her feet in the fountain!"

He believed that it was.

"Impossible! I left her on the road, and she is due to lecture this evening at Tunbridge Wells. Why, her train leaves Cannon Street in—of course my watch has stopped like everything else. She is the last person to be here."

"People always are astonished at meeting each other. All kinds come through the hedge, and come at all times—when they are drawing ahead in the race, when they are lagging behind, when they are left for dead. I often stand near the boundary listening to the sounds of the road—you know what they are—and wonder if anyone will turn aside. It is my great happiness to help someone out of the moat, as I helped you. For our country fills up slowly, though it was meant for all mankind."

"Mankind have other aims," I said gently, for I thought him well-meaning; "and I must join them." I bade him good evening, for the sun was declining, and I wished to be on the road by nightfall. To my alarm, he caught hold of me, crying: "You are not to go yet!" I tried to shake him off, for we had no interests in common, and his civility was becoming irksome to me. But for all my struggles the tiresome old man would not let go; and, as wrestling is not my specialty, I was obliged to follow him.

It was true that I could have never found alone the place where I came in, and I hoped that, when I had seen the other sights about which he was worrying, he would take me back to it. But I was determined not to sleep in the country, for I mistrusted it, and the people too, for all their friendliness. Hungry though I was, I would not join them in their evening meals of milk and fruit, and, when they gave me flowers, I flung them away as soon as I could do so unobserved. Already they were lying down for the night like cattle—some out on the bare hillside, others in groups under the beeches. In the light of an orange sunset I hurried on with my unwelcome guide, dead tired, faint from want of food, but murmuring indomitably: "Give me life, with its struggles and victories, with its failures and hatreds, with its deep moral meaning and its unknown goal!"

At last we came to a place where the encircling moat was spanned by another bridge, and where another gate interrupted the line of the boundary hedge. It was different from the first gate; for it was half transparent like horn, and opened inwards. But through it, in the waning light, I saw again just such a road as I had left—monotonous, dusty, with brown crackling hedges on either side, as far as the eye could reach.

I was strangely disquieted at the sight, which seemed to deprive me of all self-control. A man was passing us, returning for the night to the hills, with a scythe over his shoulder and a can of some liquid in his hand. I forgot the destiny of our race. I forgot the road that lay before my eyes, and I sprang at him, wrenched the can out of his hand, and began to drink.

It was nothing stronger than beer, but in my exhausted state it overcame me in a moment. As in a dream, I saw the old man shut the gate, and heard him say: "This is where your road ends, and through this gate humanity—all that is left of it—will come in to us."

Though my senses were sinking into oblivion, they seemed to expand ere they reached it. They perceived the magic song of nightingales, and the odour of invisible hay, and stars piercing the fading sky. The man whose beer I had stolen lowered me down gently to sleep off its effects, and, as he did so, I saw that he was my brother.

Janet Frame

The Press Gang

Many years ago now the Press Gang used to follow me whenever I set foot in the street after the sun had gone down. I do not know why the going down of the sun should have been a signal for the Gang to appear. They carried ropes to bind me, gags to thrust in my mouth to prevent me from screaming, and a sheet of canvas like a shroud to wind about me and carry me along the dark streets until we arrived at the wharf where the ship was waiting. I was to serve aboard this ship for seven years, and another seven years after that, and so on, until my time was up. I had understood that little girls did not serve aboard ship, but I was informed by the Leader of the Press Gang himself that any human being or animal was subject to demand and was searched for each night when the sun had gone down in all the streets of the towns or the countries of the world.

You can be sure they never caught me. Sometimes when I heard muffled screams in the distance and the hurrying feet on the path outside our gate I would go to the front room and lift aside the blind and watch the shadowy figures passing. Seven years at sea! It was in my sleep one night that I met the Leader of the Press Gang himself. He told me about his work and purpose and stressed the fact that being a little girl made no difference to the need for compulsory service.

In the daytime I worried about the Press Gang. They were said to come upon you so suddenly. You never escaped once you had been seized.

The world was an unaccountable place. Why did a strange transformation occur at night when the tar-sealed roads disappeared, the modern buildings toppled, grass grew in the streets, and people walked from door to door crying Bring out your Dead, Bring out your Dead! Black rats crouched in the doorways, bearded wild-eyed men were hanged in the main street of the realm—why did I live in a realm?—for stealing a loaf of bread or an apple. Did the officials know that I stole apples every morning from the cut-glass dish on the counter of the little shop by the bridge? That I picked holes in the new bread on the way home from school? That I bought a pound of best biscuits, putting them down on the bill and saving half to eat by myself, in secret?

I trembled to think what the officials might know.

Also at night the body-snatchers were about, wearing long cloaks and visiting the opera disguised as phantoms. And the graves in the grassy cemetery over the hill opened to yield their dead who looked surprised, swathed and damp, like papier-mâché.

And always the ships put out to sea, past the breakwater and the lighthouse, moving swiftly clear of the coast toward the dark horizon. And the cargo of doomed little boys and girls was never seen again.

I grew up; that is not unusual; they say it is destined.

Shadowy night you have not altered in dream or substance. Even now as I tremble with terror and stare at my pale face in the glass, I know the Press Gang waits for me, that I must serve another seven years, and another seven, until the three score and ten are concluded, and the ship and the sun go down together, and Death at last subdues the piratical activities indulged in by Life.

BRUCE JAY FRIEDMAN

The Subversive

My friend Ed Stamm was the most all-American person I've ever met. It came out when he brushed his teeth and shaved. He did both at the same time, using enormous quantities of toothpaste and shaving cream. When you approached him in the morning, he looked like a white, foaming symbol of Free World cleanliness.

I knew him in the Air Force when he was waiting to get into jet fighter training, and I was waiting to get into something small and inconspicuous where my general lack of military know-how would do the least amount of damage. He looked like a recruiting poster, with clear blue eyes and perfect profile and a sweet countryness about his mouth. Audie Murphy is the Hollywood star he most resembled, although next to him, Murphy would have seemed swarthy. He had wonderful manners and said to me at the base swimming pool when we met, "I'd certainly enjoy your compny this evening." I've known people who wouldn't have minded hanging around with me for a few hours, but the idea of anyone wanting my "compny" was something else again. It was a phony kind of line, but he said it with such all-American sweetness it actually became disarming. I worked it into my repertoire and even *I* was able to get away with it, although I used "company" instead of "compny." He also fell right on top of little children, getting right down on the ground when one came along, his face scrubbed and beaming, and then saying, "Hello, little boy (or girl)," which came out more like "Heddo, lidder booey." He wasn't trying to impress anyone. He did it when people were around or when rooms were empty. He just felt like hugging and kissing little children. I do that one too, now. I felt kind of pretentious the first few times, but then I swung into it and now I get right down there with children just as naturally as I'd check my watch for the time.

I understand that Hollywood puts its new screenwriters into categories such as "adventure," "comedy," "suspense," "war," a typecasting, incidentally, from which I'm told they never escape. Ed's background might have been concocted by one of the lesser lights in "homespun." He came from a small town in the Midwest, lived with his family in a two-story frame house (mortgage just about paid up), had a kid sister with freckles, earned enough working part-time at a gas station to get through the local college, won four letters in sports. His dad: football and track coach at the high school. His Girl Back Home: the bank president's daughter, cheerleader at the college, voted "Prettiest" in her senior class. Tennis wasn't one of his sports, although when we played at the air base, he picked it up quickly, performing with the instinctive grace he would have brought to anything from jai alai to hammer throwing. I was better than him, though. I'd been playing for years and I beat him, not overwhelmingly, but consistently.

One day I wrapped him up pretty solidly and teased him about it and he said, "Do you want to play for money? Forty bucks." He picked just the right amount of money to get me nervous. In all our playing he'd never won a single set. Yet he looked at me in a funny way and made me back down. I said, "You can't play for money without a referee. Anyway, I'm not taking your money." I knew that in some crazy way, even though he never had before, he'd outlast me, or outgut me, or outheart me, or do whatever special thing it is that all-Americans do, and beat me no matter how much better a player I was.

I automatically gave up in all competitions with him. Where girls were concerned, we'd run neck and neck for a few minutes, but then I'd begin to peter out self-consciously and Ed would say, "We certainly would enjoy your compny in my car," whereupon I would stand by while he hooked arms with the cuter of the two and I fell in behind with the bomb. Even when a rare, offtrail girl made it perfectly plain she preferred my swarthiness to his clean-cut wholesomeness, I would begin to do a lot of staring down at the ground until she disgustedly marched off to join Ed's "compny," leaving me to guard her heavily acned friend. Once, with Ed along, I completely mastered a girl. It was at a bar in Illinois, and the girl was serving drinks to the tables. I'd come in after a Bogart movie at the base, spit something out at her through clenched teeth, and she had loved it. Through sheer accident, I'd evidently found myself a pretty little masochist. "Did I do anything wrong?" she asked, and, catching on, I spit out another line, twice as hard. "Could I call you somewhere?" she asked me, and this time, giddy in the role, I said the liquor was rotgut and knocked the shotglass off the table. "What did I do?" she asked Ed, who looked on in fascination. "For Christ's sakes, she's yours," he said to me. "Do you know what I'd do if she was giving me invitations like that?" I stared off into the distance, not really sure of what to do next, and said, "I don't go for that." She kept coming up to me, beseechingly, practically purring with hurt, and then finally I said, "All right. You can call me at Base Operations, extension 976. Any night except Wednesdays when I'm on duty."

"I see," she said, the fire dying in her eyes. Later, I saw her dancing with Ed.

This is not one of those stories in which one guy is better than his friend in a million things, and then at the end there's this one thing the friend is able to win out in, proving it's really better to be a terrible fellow with just one talent. As a matter of fact, there were quite a few things at which I was able to top him. Tennis is one I mentioned and then there is singing (he had no voice at all), general smartness (he had read very few books), and jokes. There was one girl I was sure I'd have the edge with because of the jokes and general routines I did, a new singer at the base club. As the welcoming committee that week, we were to meet her at the club and be her escorts for the evening. We sat with her awhile, Ed assuring her it was swell to be in her compny. I thought I'd work my routines in naturally, rather than announce, "Now I'll do some routines." But before I knew it, Ed was doing them, all of the best ones: Joe Louis commenting on the Ezzard Charles–Marciano fight, a Durante thing I do with a few variations of my own, and a short take from an old Fred Allen script in which two potatoes are the only characters in an avant-garde play. His Joe Louis was too Midwestern, his Durante came out Jimmy Stewart, and he blew the punchline on the Allen skit. His timing was awful, too, but the girl was giggling away just the same. After a while he said, "Now you do one, Tony," forcing me to serve up an Edward Everett Horton imitation I'd far from perfected. The singer listened patiently and in a short while was, inevitably, walking to the jukebox with Ed, nibbling at his ear.

The other all-American things I remember about him are sort of scattered and don't really sound *that* all-American when you set them down. He got the snuggest fit out of his jockey underwear of anyone I've ever known. He drove a new Nash, and instead of making out payment checks to the bank, he was paying off someone named "Old Man Bagley" in a combination of money and chores he was to do during his furloughs. In driving the Nash, long before he came to stops, his brake foot would begin to fidget on the pedal, caressing it, pumping it a little, testing it, until, if you were a passenger, you had ridiculous amounts of confidence that he would be able to pull off the stop. He called everyone "old buddy" and it was a thrilling and special thing to have him pat you on the back and say, "Old buddy, what'll we do tonight?"

One night, a short colonel with a twisted body and a reputation for being touchy about his youth and the quick promotions he'd received, announced he was going off to the flight line to shoot landings in jets. Ed heard him and said, "I'd certainly consider it a great privilege to go along with you, sir." It meant he was willing to squat on the floor of the plane while the colonel took off and landed and took off and landed long hours into the night. It really wasn't necessary for him to do all this and he'd be getting plenty of it in pilot training. But it was something like sweeping floors in grocery stores and doing lowly things in banks and walking several miles to school each morning, and if you're an all-American worth your salt, you don't miss chances to do these things. The colonel explained that it was going to be a pretty miserable kind of evening, but Ed said if the colonel didn't mind his company, he'd like to go up with him. The colonel, a sour man, melted before Ed's sweetness and said okay.

I'm not entirely sure how this last thing fits into the all-American picture. It has something to do with it. In any case, I did discover that for all his pretenses of all-Americanism, the freckled sister, the gas station job, the chores for Old Man Bagley, my friend Ed Stamm was a subversive.

I found this out during a weekend in which Ed invited me and a mutual "old buddy" of ours named Rig to his home in Iowa for the weekend. We made a perfect movie combat trio with Ed, the hero; Rig, the slow-talker from Texas; and me, the Brooklyn boy, telling jokes about my mother's potato pancakes. We drove in shifts, with Ed, by silent agreement, taking over my turn, since my driving was uneven and I was obviously unable to do those confidence-inspiring pumps with my brake foot. Our first stop in Ed's town was at his girl's house; she came running out the way they do in Andy Hardy movies, predictably and agonizingly pretty, filling the car with a minty Seventeen freshness, kissing Ed's head like a puppy, and then flouncing herself around and teasing with Ed's "Old buddies" while Ed drove to the—you guessed it—tree-lined street on which he lived. Ed's father and sister were on the lawn waiting for us, his dad a slender, slightly taller and gray-haired Ed, his sister freckled, and surprisingly (rather disappointingly, since she was to be my date) broad-shouldered. Mr. Stamm took to Rig immediately, regarding me with a hint of suspicion. He had heard that Rig was in charge of painting at the air base and said to us all, "Now don't forget, boys. You're going to work for your meals. I've got a fence back there could use a good coat of paint."

Not much more that night. We all ate dinner together, with Mr. Stamm, after donning apron and cook's hat, fixing and serving the meal. Later, when Ed's girl had gone home, Mr. Stamm turned down our beds and said good night to us. The following day, Ed went off early to do one of those chores for Mr. Bagley. Rig and I ate breakfast with Mr. Stamm and then we really did paint the fence. I thought the idea was wholesome and everything, but I could have done without it. In the afternoon, we all went to a roadside place and danced, Rig and Ed taking turns with Ed's girl. I danced with Ed's sister. A female version of Ed should have been wonderful, and she certainly was healthy looking, but when you analyzed her, she turned out to be all back and no bosom. It was that night at dinner that Ed was unmasked as a subversive.

We had all decided to wear our dress uniforms at the dance that night, and were sitting around the table with Ed's sister, as though we were at a festive NATO conference. Mr. Stamm, in apron and cook's hat, once again was serving platters of food. Ed had just done a George Sanders takeoff of mine, poorly, and then, as though to sell me to his father, said, "That one was made up by my old buddy here, Tony."

"That Rig can certainly paint a fence," said Mr. Stamm. "I could use a boy like that around here. I'd keep him jumping." Rig said, "Yes, I believe you would, too," drawling out the line, and Mr. Stamm slapped him on the back and said, "Oh that Rig, he's a corker."

Ed said, "I know how to pick my old buddies," and then a wheelchair came into the room carrying a shriveled woman in a bathrobe with deep crevasses in her face and beautiful blue eyes. Her bathrobe went flat below her waist, concealing either withered legs or none at all.

Ed stood up at the table, his eyes shut and his fists clenched, screaming in a monotone, "SON OF A BITCH. SON OF A BITCH. GET IT OUT OF HERE. DIRTY. DIRTY. SON OF A BITCH. OH, DIRTY, DIRTY BITCH."

The woman said, sweetly, "Now Ed. Now Ed," and he screamed, "YAAH, YAAH, YAAH."

Mr. Stamm came over quickly and said, "Now Ed," spinning the wheelchair around and taking it out the door, with the woman saying, "Now Ed, now Ed," patiently and sweetly, and giving off an odor of camphor.

When Mr. Stamm got back, we continued the meal, the chatter starting up again, with Mr. Stamm teasing Rig about getting a bargain on some Air Force paint, Ed telling Mr. Stamm about the books I'd read, and Mr. Stamm finally succumbing and saying to me, "We had a Brooklyn boy at school here once. Got along just fine." Later, we went to the dance on schedule and I got in several dances with Ed's girl, her sharp, pointed bosoms a fine relief from my date's vague ones. We started back for the base around noon the following day, after shoveling a little coal for Mr. Stamm, who'd jokingly suggested we do it to work off our meals.

Weeks later, Ed and I drifted apart, or possibly got wrenched apart. My assignment came through before he got into jet pilot training. In the first weeks of getting oriented in my new job in base information, I didn't call him at all, and once, when I did see him, I failed to introduce him to my new friends. They were flip and waspish and, for one brief second, I was a little ashamed of Ed. He must have sensed it. In any case, I violated some crazy all-American code of his for friendship. When I saw him later, there was a flatness between us, and we were never to be close again. This was much to my regret, because many times I longed for his company and for his arm around my shoulder and for him saying, "What are we doing tonight, old buddy?"

In any case, I think of him as the most all-American person I ever knew (or perhaps I should drop the all-American part—because that's sarcastic and I don't mean to be—and just say "American"), his looks, his manners, his sweetness, the bit with the little boys and girls. Or at least I *would* think of him that way if I could forget that one subversive thing he pulled at dinner that night. It proved to me that you probably can't trust a goddamned soul in this country.

EDUARDO GALEANO

The Story of the Lizard Who Had a Habit of Dining on His Wives

Translated from the Spanish by Mark Fried

At the edge of the river, hidden by the tall grass, a woman is reading.

Once upon a time, the book tells, there lived a man of very great substance. Everything belonged to him: the town of Lucanamarca, everything around it, the dry and the wet, the tamed and the wild, all that had memory, all that had oblivion.

But that lord of all things had no heir. Every day his wife offered a thousand prayers, begging for the blessing of a son, and every night she lit a thousand candles.

God was fed up with the demands of that persistent woman, who asked for what He had not wished to grant. Finally, either to avoid having to hear her voice any longer or from divine mercy, He performed the miracle. And joy descended on that household.

The child had a human face and the body of a lizard.

With time, he spoke, but he slithered along on his belly. The finest teachers from Ayacucho taught him to read, but his claws prevented him from writing.

At the age of eighteen, he asked for a wife.

His well-heeled father found him one, and the wedding was celebrated with great pomp in the priest's house.

The first night, the lizard threw himself on his wife and devoured her. When the sun rose, in the marriage bed there was only the widower asleep, surrounded by small bones.

The lizard then demanded another wife, and there was another wedding and another devouring, and the glutton asked for yet another, and so on.

Fiancées were never lacking. In the households of the poor, there was always some spare girl.

His scaly belly lapped by river water, Dulcidio is taking his siesta.

Opening one eye, he sees her. She is reading. Never before in his life has he seen a woman wearing glasses.

Dulcidio pokes forward his long snout:

—*What are you reading?*

She lowers her book, looks at him calmly, and replies:

—*Legends.*

—*Legends?*

—*Ancient voices.*

—*What for?*

She shrugs her shoulders:

—*Company.*

This woman does not seem to be from the mountains, nor the jungle, nor the coast.

—*I know how to read too,* says Dulcidio.

She closes her book and turns her face away.

Before the woman disappears, Dulcidio managers to ask:

—*Where are you from?*

The following Sunday, when Dulcidio wakes from his siesta, she is there. Bookless, but wearing glasses.

Sitting on the sand, her feet hidden under many bright-colored skirts, she is very much there, rooted there. She casts her eye on the intruder.

Dulcidio plays all his cards. He raises a horny claw and waves it toward the blue mountains on the horizon.

—*Everything you see and don't see, it's all mine.*

She does not even glance at the vast expanse, and remains silent. A very silent silence.

The heir presses on. Many lambs, many Indians, all his to command. He is lord of all that expanse of earth and water and air, and also of the small strip of sand she sits on.

—*But you have my permission,* he assures her.

Tossing her long black tresses, she bows:

—*Thank you.*

Then the lizard adds that he is rich but humble, studious, a worker and above all a gentleman who wishes to make a home but has been doomed to widowerhood by the cruelties of fate.

She looks away. Lowering her head, she reflects on the situation.

Dulcidio hovers.

He whispers:

—*May I ask a favor of you?*

And he turns his side to her, offering his back.

—*Would you scratch my shoulder? I can't reach.*
She puts out her hand to touch the metallic scales, and exclaims:
—*It's like silk.*
Dulcidio stretches, closes his eyes, opens his mouth, stiffens his tail, and feels as he has never felt.
But when he turns his head, she is no longer there.
He looks for her, rushing full tilt across the field of tall grass, back and forth, on all sides. No trace of her. The woman has evaporated, as before.

The following Sunday, she does not come to the riverbank. Nor the next Sunday. Nor the following one.
Since he first saw her, he sees only her and nothing but her.
The famous sleeper no longer sleeps, the glutton no longer eats.
Dulcidio's bedroom is no longer the pleasant sanctuary he took his rest in, watched over by his dead wives. Their photographs are all there, covering the walls from top to bottom, in heart-shaped frames garlanded with orange blossom; but Dulcidio, now condemned to solitude, lies slumped into his cushions and into despair. Doctors and medicine men come from all over, but can do nothing for the course of his fever and the collapse of everything else.
With his small battery radio, bought from a passing Turk, Dulcidio spends his nights and days sighing and listening to melodies long out of fashion. His parents, despairing, watch him pine away. He no longer asks for a wife, declaring *I'm hungry.* Now he pleads, *I am made a poor beggar for love,* and in a broken voice, and showing an alarming tendency to rhyme, he

pays painful homage to that certain She
who stole his soul and his serenity.

The whole populace sets out to find her. Searchers scour heaven and earth, but they do not even know the name of the vanished one, and no one has seen a woman wearing glasses in the neighborhood or beyond.

One Sunday afternoon, Dulcidio has a premonition. He gets up, in pain, and sets out painfully for the riverbank.
She is there.
In floods of tears, Dulcidio announces his love for the elusive and indifferent dream-girl. He confesses that he *has died of thirst for the honeys of your mouth,* allows that *I don't deserve your disregard, my beautiful dove,* and showers her with compliments and caresses.

The wedding day arrives. Everyone is delighted, for the people have gone a long time without a fiesta, and Dulcidio is the only one there of the marrying kind. The priest gives him a good price, as a special client.

Guitar music engulfs the sweethearts, the harp and the violins sound in all their glory. A toast of everlasting love is raised to the happy pair, and rivers of punch flow under the great bouquets of flowers.

Dulcidio is sporting a new skin, pink on his shoulders and greenish blue on his prodigious tail.

When at last the two are alone and the hour of truth arrives, he declares to her: —*I give you my heart, for you to tread on.*

She blows out the candle in a single breath, lets fall her wedding dress, spongy with lace, slowly removes her glasses, and tells him, *Don't be an asshole, knock off the bullshit.* With one tug, she unsheathes him like a sword, flings his skin on the floor, embraces his naked body, and sets him on fire.

Afterward Dulcidio sleeps deeply, curled up against this woman, and dreams for the first time in his life.

She eats him while he is still sleeping. She goes on consuming him in small bites, from head to tail, making little sound and chewing as gently as possible, taking care not to wake him, so that he will not carry away a bad impression.

GABRIEL GARCÍA MÁRQUEZ

A Very Old Man with Enormous Wings

Translated by Gregory Rabassa

On the third day of rain they had killed so many crabs inside the house that Pelayo had to cross his drenched courtyard and throw them into the sea, because the newborn child had a temperature all night and they thought it was due to the stench. The world had been sad since Tuesday. Sea and sky were a single ash-gray thing and the sands of the beach, which on March nights glimmered like powdered light, had become a stew of mud and rotten shellfish. The light was so weak at noon that when Pelayo was coming back to the house after throwing away the crabs, it was hard for him to see what it was that was moving and groaning in the rear of the courtyard. He had to go very close to see that it was an old man, a very old man, lying face down in the mud, who, in spite of his tremendous efforts, couldn't get up, impeded by his enormous wings.

Frightened by that nightmare, Pelayo ran to get Elisenda, his wife, who was putting compresses on the sick child, and he took her to the rear of the courtyard. They both looked at the fallen body with mute stupor. He was dressed like a ragpicker. There were only a few faded hairs left on his bald skull and very few teeth in his mouth, and his pitiful condition of a drenched great-grandfather had taken away any sense of grandeur he might have had. His huge buzzard wings, dirty and half-plucked, were forever entangled in the mud. They looked at him so long and so closely that Pelayo and Elisenda very soon overcame their surprise and in the end found him familiar. Then they dared speak to him, and he answered in an incomprehensible dialect with a strong sailor's voice. That was how they skipped over the inconvenience of the wings and quite intelligently concluded that he was a lonely castaway from some foreign ship wrecked by the storm. And yet, they called in a neighbor woman who knew everything about life and death to see him, and all she needed was one look to show them their mistake.

"He's an angel," she told them. "He must have been coming for the child, but the poor fellow is so old that the rain knocked him down."

On the following day everyone knew that a flesh-and-blood angel was held captive in Pelayo's house. Against the judgment of the wise neighbor woman, for whom angels in those times were the fugitive survivors of a celestial conspiracy, they did not have the heart to club him to death. Pelayo watched over him all afternoon from the kitchen, armed with his bailiff's club, and before going to bed he dragged him out of the mud and locked him up with the hens in the wire chicken coop. In the middle of the night, when the rain stopped, Pelayo and Elisenda were still killing crabs. A short time afterward the child woke up without a fever and with a desire to eat. Then they felt magnanimous and decided to put the angel on a raft with fresh water and provisions for three days and leave him to his fate on the high seas. But when they went out into the courtyard with the first light of dawn, they found the whole neighborhood in front of the chicken coop having fun with the angel, without the slightest reverence, tossing him things to eat through the openings in the wire as if he weren't a supernatural creature but a circus animal.

Father Gonzaga arrived before seven o'clock, alarmed at the strange news. By that time onlookers less frivolous than those at dawn had already arrived and they were making all kinds of conjectures concerning the captive's future. The simplest among them thought that he should be named mayor of the world. Others of sterner mind felt that he should be promoted to the rank of five-star general in order to win all wars. Some visionaries hoped that he could be put to stud in order to implant on earth a race of winged wise men who could take charge of the universe. But Father Gonzaga, before becoming a priest, had been a robust woodcutter. Standing by the wire, he reviewed his catechism in an instant and asked them to open the door so that he could take a close look at that pitiful man who looked more like a huge decrepit hen among the fascinated chickens. He was lying in a corner drying his open wings in the sunlight among the fruit peels and breakfast leftovers that the early risers had thrown him. Alien to the impertinences of the world, he only lifted his antiquarian eyes and murmured something in his dialect when Father Gonzaga went into the chicken coop and said good morning to him in Latin. The parish priest had his first suspicion of an impostor when he saw that he did not understand the language of God or know how to greet His ministers. Then he noticed that seen close up he was much too human: he had an unbearable smell of the outdoors, the back side of his wings was strewn with parasites and his main feathers had been mistreated by terrestrial winds, and nothing about him measured up to the proud dignity of angels. Then he came out of the chicken coop and in a brief sermon warned the curious against the risks of being ingenuous. He reminded them that the devil had the bad habit of making use of carnival tricks in order to confuse the unwary. He argued that if wings were not the essential element in determining the difference between a hawk and an airplane, they were even less so in the recognition of angels. Nevertheless, he promised to write a letter to his bishop so that the latter would write to his primate so that the latter would write to the Supreme Pontiff in order to get the final verdict from the highest courts.

His prudence fell on sterile hearts. The news of the captive angel spread with such rapidity that after a few hours the courtyard had the bustle of a marketplace and they had to call in troops with fixed bayonets to disperse the mob that was about to knock the house down. Elisenda, her spine all twisted from sweeping up so much marketplace trash, then got the idea of fencing in the yard and charging five cents admission to see the angel.

The curious came from far away. A traveling carnival arrived with a flying acrobat who buzzed over the crowd several times, but no one paid any attention to him because his wings were not those of an angel but, rather, those of a sidereal bat. The most unfortunate invalids on earth came in search of health: a poor woman who since childhood had been counting her heartbeats and had run out of numbers; a Portuguese man who couldn't sleep because the noise of the stars disturbed him; a sleep-walker who got up at night to undo the things he had done while awake; and many others with less serious ailments. In the midst of that shipwreck disorder that made the earth tremble, Pelayo and Elisenda were happy with fatigue, for in less than a week they had crammed their rooms with money and the line of pilgrims waiting their turn to enter still reached beyond the horizon.

The angel was the only one who took no part in his own act. He spent his time trying to get comfortable in his borrowed nest, befuddled by the hellish heat of the oil lamps and sacramental candles that had been placed along the wire. At first they tried to make him eat some mothballs, which, according to the wisdom of the wise neighbor woman, were the food prescribed for angels. But he turned them down, just as he turned down the papal lunches that the penitents brought him, and they never found out whether it was because he was an angel or because he was an old man that in the end he ate nothing but eggplant mush. His only supernatural virtue seemed to be patience. Especially during the first days, when the hens pecked at him, searching for the stellar parasites that proliferated in his wings, and the cripples pulled out feathers to touch their defective parts with, and even the most merciful threw stones at him, trying to get him to rise so they could see him standing. The only time they succeeded in arousing him was when they burned his side with an iron for branding steers, for he had been motionless for so many hours that they thought he was dead. He awoke with a start, ranting in his hermetic language and with tears in his eyes, and he flapped his wings a couple of times, which brought on a whirlwind of chicken dung and lunar dust and a gale of panic that did not seem to be of this world. Although many thought that his reaction had been one not of rage but of pain, from then on they were careful not to annoy him, because the majority understood that his passivity was not that of a hero taking his ease but that of a cataclysm in repose.

Father Gonzaga held back the crowd's frivolity with formulas of maid servant inspiration while awaiting the arrival of a final judgment on the nature of the captive. But the mail from Rome showed no sense of urgency. They spent their time finding out if the prisoner had a navel, if his dialect had any connection with Aramaic, how many times he could fit on the head of a pin, or whether he wasn't just a Norwegian with wings. Those meager letters might have come and gone until the end of time if a providential event had not put an end to the priest's tribulations.

It so happened that during those days, among so many other carnival attractions, there arrived in town the traveling show of the woman who had been changed into a spider for having disobeyed her parents. The admission to see her was not only less than the admission to see the angel, but people were permitted to ask her all manner of questions about her absurd state and to examine her up and down so that no one would ever doubt the truth of her horror. She was a frightful tarantula the size of a ram and with the head of a sad maiden. What was most heart-rending, however, was not her outlandish shape but the sincere affliction with which she recounted the details of her misfortune. While still practically a child she had sneaked out of her parents' house to go to a dance, and while she was coming back through the woods after having danced all night without permission, a fearful thunderclap rent the sky in two and through the crack came the lightning bolt of brimstone that changed her into a spider. Her only nourishment came from the meatballs that charitable souls chose to toss into her mouth. A spectacle like that, full of so much human truth and with such a fearful lesson, was bound to defeat without even trying that of a haughty angel who scarcely deigned to look at mortals. Besides, the few miracles attributed to the angel showed a certain mental disorder, like the blind man who didn't recover his sight but grew three new teeth, or the paralytic who didn't get to walk but almost won the lottery, and the leper whose sores sprouted sunflowers. Those consolation miracles, which were more like mocking fun, had already ruined the angel's reputation when the woman who had been changed into a spider finally crushed him completely. That was how Father Gonzaga was cured forever of his insomnia and Pelayo's courtyard went back to being as empty as during the time it had rained for three days and crabs walked through the bedrooms.

The owners of the house had no reason to lament. With the money they saved they built a two-story mansion with balconies and gardens and high netting so that crabs wouldn't get in during the winter, and with iron bars on the windows so that angels wouldn't get in. Pelayo also set up a rabbit warren close to town and gave up his job as bailiff for good, and Elisenda bought some satin pumps with high heels and many dresses of iridescent silk, the kind worn on Sunday by the most desirable women in those times. The chicken coop was the only thing that didn't receive any attention. If they washed it down with creolin and burned tears of myrrh inside it every so often, it was not in homage to the angel but to drive away the dungheap stench that still hung everywhere like a ghost and was turning the new house into an old one. At first, when the child learned to walk, they were careful that he not get too close to the chicken coop. But then they began to lose their fears and got used to the smell, and before the child got his second teeth he'd gone inside the chicken coop to play, where the wires were falling apart. The angel was no less standoffish with him than with other mortals, but he tolerated the most ingenious infamies with the patience of a dog who had no illusions. They both came down with chicken pox at the same time. The doctor who took care of the child couldn't resist the temptation to listen to the angel's heart, and he found so much whistling in the heart and so many sounds in his kidneys that it seemed impossible for him to be alive. What surprised him most, however, was the logic of his wings. They seemed so natural on that completely human organism that he couldn't understand why other men didn't have them too.

When the child began school it had been some time since the sun and rain had caused the collapse of the chicken coop. The angel went dragging himself about here and there like a stray dying man. They would drive him out of the bedroom with a broom and a moment later find him in the kitchen. He seemed to be in so many places at the same time that they grew to think that he'd been duplicated, that he was reproducing himself all through the house, and the exasperated and unhinged Elisenda shouted that it was awful living in that hell full of angels. He could scarcely eat and his antiquarian eyes had also become so foggy that he went about bumping into posts. All he had left were the bare cannulae of his last feathers. Pelayo threw a blanket over him and extended him the charity of letting him sleep in the shed, and only then did they notice that he had a temperature at night, and was delirious with the tongue twisters of an old Norwegian. That was one of the few times they became alarmed, for they thought he was going to die and not even the wise neighbor woman had been able to tell them what to do with dead angels.

And yet he not only survived his worst winter, but seemed improved with the first sunny days. He remained motionless for several days in the farthest corner of the courtyard, where no one would see him, and at the beginning of December some large, stiff feathers began to grow on his wings, the feathers of a scarecrow, which looked more like another misfortune of decrepitude. But he must have known the reason for those changes, for he was quite careful that no one should notice them, that no one should hear the sea chanteys that he sometimes sang under the stars. One morning Elisenda was cutting some bunches of onions for lunch when a wind that seemed to come from the high seas blew into the kitchen. Then she went to the window and caught the angel in his first attempts at flight. They were so clumsy that his fingernails opened a furrow in the vegetable patch and he was on the point of knocking the shed down with the ungainly flapping that slipped on the light and couldn't get a grip on the air. But he did manage to gain altitude. Elisenda let out a sigh of relief, for herself and for him, when she saw him pass over the last houses, holding himself up in some way with the risky flapping of a senile vulture. She kept watching him even when she was through cutting the onions and she kept on watching until it was no longer possible for her to see him, because then he was no longer an annoyance in her life but an imaginary dot on the horizon of the sea.

Nadine Gordimer

Is There Nowhere Else Where We Can Meet?

It was a cool grey morning and the air was like smoke. In that reversal of the elements that sometimes takes place, the grey, soft, muffled sky moved like the sea on a silent day.

The coat collar pressed rough against her neck and her cheeks were softly cold as if they had been washed in ice-water. She breathed gently with the air; on the left a strip of veld fire curled silently, flameless. Overhead a dove purred. She went on over the flat straw grass, following the trees, now on, now off the path. Away ahead, over the scribble of twigs, the sloping lines of black and platinum grass—all merging, tones but no colour, like an etching—was the horizon, the shore at which cloud lapped.

Damp burnt grass puffed black, faint dust from beneath her feet. She could hear herself swallow.

A long way off she saw a figure with something red on its head, and she drew from it the sense of balance she had felt at the particular placing of the dot of a figure in a picture. She was here; someone was over there . . . Then the red dot was gone, lost in the curve of the trees. She changed her bag and parcel from one arm to the other and felt the morning, palpable, deeply cold and clinging against her eyes.

She came to the end of a direct stretch of path and turned with it round a dark-fringed pine and a shrub, now delicately boned, that she remembered hung with bunches of white flowers like crystals in the summer. There was a native in a red woollen cap standing at the next clump of trees, where the path crossed a ditch and was bordered by white-splashed stones. She had pulled a little sheath of pine needles, three in a twist of thin brown tissue, and as she walked she ran them against her thumb. Down; smooth and stiff.

Up; catching in gentle resistance as the minute serrations snagged at the skin. He was standing with his back towards her, looking along the way he had come; she pricked the ball of her thumb with the needle-ends. His one trouser leg was torn off above the knee, and the back of the naked leg and half-turned heel showed the peculiarly dead, powdery black of cold. She was nearer to him now, but she knew he did not hear her coming over the damp dust of the path. She was level with him, passing him; and he turned slowly and looked beyond her, without a flicker of interest as a cow sees you go.

The eyes were red, as if he had not slept for a long time, and the strong smell of old sweat burned at her nostrils. Once past, she wanted to cough, but a pang of guilt at the red weary eyes stopped her. And he had only a filthy rag—part of an old shirt?—without sleeves and frayed away into a great gap from underarm to waist. It lifted in the currents of cold as she passed. She had dropped the neat trio of pine needles somewhere, she did not know at what moment, so now, remembering something from childhood, she lifted her hand to her face and sniffed: yes, it was as she remembered, not as chemists pretend it in the bath salts, but a dusty green scent, vegetable rather than flower. It was clean, unhuman. Slightly sticky too; tacky on her fingers. She must wash them as soon as she got there. Unless her hands were quite clean, she could not lose consciousness of them, they obtruded upon her.

She felt a thudding through the ground like the sound of a hare running in fear and she was going to turn around and then he was there in front of her, so startling, so utterly unexpected, panting right into her face. He stood dead still and she stood dead still. Every vestige of control, of sense, of thought, went out of her as a room plunges into dark at the failure of power and she found herself whimpering like an idiot or a child. Animal sounds came out of her throat. She gibbered. For a moment it was Fear itself that had her by the arms, the legs, the throat; not fear of the man, of any single menace he might present, but Fear, absolute, abstract. If the earth had opened up in fire at her feet, if a wild beast had opened its terrible mouth to receive her, she could not have been reduced to less than she was now.

There was a chest heaving through the tear in front of her; a face panting; beneath the red hairy woollen cap the yellowish-red eyes holding her in distrust. One foot, cracked from exposure until it looked like broken wood, moved, only to restore balance in the dizziness that follows running, but any move seemed towards her and she tried to scream and the awfulness of dreams came true and nothing would come out. She wanted to throw the handbag and the parcel at him, and as she fumbled crazily for them she heard him draw a deep, hoarse breath and he grabbed out at her and—ah! It came. His hand clutched her shoulder.

Now she fought with him and she trembled with strength as they struggled. The dust puffed round her shoes and his scuffling toes. The smell of him choked her—It was an old pyjama jacket, not a shirt—His face was sullen and there was a pink place where the skin had been grazed off. He sniffed desperately, out of breath. Her teeth chattered, wildly she battered him with her head, broke away, but he snatched at the skirt of her coat and jerked her back. Her face swung up and she saw the waves of a grey sky and a crane breasting them, beautiful as the figurehead of a ship. She staggered for balance and the handbag and parcel fell. At once he was upon them, and she wheeled about; but as she was about to fall on her knees to get there first, a sudden relief, like a rush of tears, came to her and, instead, she ran. She ran and ran, stumbling wildly off through the stalks of dead grass, turning over her heels against hard winter tussocks, blundering through trees and bushes. The young mimosas closed in, lowering a thicket of twigs right to the ground, but she tore herself through, feeling the dust in her eyes and the scaly twigs hooking at her hair. There was a ditch, knee-high in blackjacks; like pins responding to a magnet they fastened along her legs, but on the other side there was a fence and then the road . . . She clawed at the fence—her hands were capable of nothing—and tried to drag herself between the wires, but her coat got caught on a barb, and she was imprisoned there, bent in half, while waves of terror swept over her in heat and trembling. At last the wire tore through its hold on the cloth; wobbling, frantic, she climbed over the fence.

And she was out. She was out on the road. A little way on there were houses, with gardens, postboxes, a child's swing. A small dog sat at a gate. She could hear a faint hum, as of life, of talk somewhere, or perhaps telephone wires.

She was trembling so that she could not stand. She had to keep on walking, quickly, down the road. It was quiet and grey, like the morning. And cool. Now she could feel the cold air round her mouth and between her brows, where the skin stood out in sweat. And in the cold wetness that soaked down beneath her armpits and between her buttocks. Her heart thumped slowly and stiffly. Yes, the wind was cold; she was suddenly cold, damp-cold, all through. She raised her hand, still fluttering uncontrollably, and smoothed her hair; it was wet at the hairline. She guided her hand into her pocket and found a handkerchief to blow her nose.

There was the gate of the first house, before her.

She thought of the woman coming to the door, of the explanations, of the woman's face, and the police. Why did I fight, she thought suddenly. What did I fight for? Why didn't I give him the money and let him go? His red eyes, and the smell and those cracks in his feet, fissures, erosion. She shuddered. The cold of the morning flowed into her.

She turned away from the gate and went down the road slowly, like an invalid, beginning to pick the blackjacks from her stockings.

GRAHAM GREENE

The Innocent

It was a mistake to take Lola there. I knew it the moment we alighted from the train at the small country station. On an autumn evening one remembers more of childhood than at any other time of year, and her bright veneered face, the small bag which hardly pretended to contain our things for the night, simply didn't go with the old grain warehouses across the small canal, the few lights up the hill, the posters of an ancient film. But she said, 'Let's go into the country,' and Bishop's Hendron was, of course, the first name which came into my head. Nobody would know me there now, and it hadn't occurred to me that it would be I who remembered.

Even the old porter touched a chord. I said, 'There'll be a four-wheeler at the entrance,' and there was, though at first I didn't notice it, seeing the two taxis and thinking, 'The old place is coming on.' It was very dark, and the thin autumn mist, the smell of wet leaves and canal water were deeply familiar.

Lola said, 'But why did you choose this place? It's grim.' It was no use explaining to her why it wasn't grim to me, that that sand heap by the canal had always been there (when I was three I remember thinking it was what other people meant by the seaside). I took the bag (I've said it was light; it was simply a forged passport of respectability) and said we'd walk. We came up over the little humpbacked bridge and passed the alms-houses. When I was five I saw a middle-aged man run into one to commit suicide; he carried a knife and all the neighbours pursued him up the stairs. She said, 'I never thought the country was like *this*.' They were ugly alms-houses, little grey stone boxes, but I knew them as I knew nothing else. It was like listening to music, all that walk.

But I had to say something to Lola. It wasn't her fault that she didn't belong here. We passed the school, the church, and came round into the old wide High Street and the sense of the first twelve years of life. If I hadn't come, I shouldn't have known that sense would be so strong, because those years hadn't been particularly happy or particularly miserable; they had been ordinary years, but now with the smell of wood fires, of the cold striking up from the dark damp paving stones, I thought I knew what it was that held me. It was the smell of innocence.

I said to Lola, 'It's a good inn, and there'll be nothing here, you'll see, to keep us up. We'll have dinner and drinks and go to bed.' But the worst of it was that I couldn't help wishing that I were alone. I hadn't been back all these years; I hadn't realized how well I remembered the place. Things I'd quite forgotten, like that sand heap, were coming back with an effect of pathos and nostalgia. I could have been very happy that night in a melancholy autumnal way, wandering about the little town, picking up clues to that time of life when, however miserable we are, we have expectations. It wouldn't be the same if I came back again, for then there would be the memories of Lola, and Lola meant just nothing at all. We had happened to pick each other up at a bar the day before and liked each other. Lola was all right, there was no one I would rather spend the night with, but she didn't fit in with *these* memories. We ought to have gone to Maidenhead. That's country too.

The inn was not quite where I remembered it. There was the Town Hall, but they had built a new cinema with a Moorish dome and a café, and there was a garage which hadn't existed in my time. I had forgotten too the turning to the left up a steep villaed hill.

'I don't believe that road was there in my day,' I said.

'Your day?' Lola asked.

'Didn't I tell you? I was born here.'

'You must get a kick out of bringing me here,' Lola said. 'I suppose you used to think of nights like this when you were a boy.'

'Yes,' I said, because it wasn't her fault. She was all right. I liked her scent. She used a good shade of lipstick. It was costing me a lot, a fiver for Lola and then all the bills and fares and drinks, but I'd have thought it money well spent anywhere else in the world.

I lingered at the bottom of that road. Something was stirring in the mind, but I don't think I should have remembered what, if a crowd of children hadn't come down the hill at that moment into the frosty lamplight, their voices sharp and shrill, their breath fuming as they passed under the lamps. They all carried linen bags, and some of the bags were embroidered with initials. They were in their best clothes and a little self-conscious. The small girls kept to themselves in a kind of compact beleaguered group, and one thought of hair ribbons and shining shoes and the sedate tinkle of a piano. It all came back to me: they had been to a dancing lesson, just as I used to go, to a small square house with a drive of rhododendrons half-way up the hill. More than ever I wished that Lola were not with me, less than ever did she fit, as I thought 'something's missing from the picture', and a sense of pain glowed dully at the bottom of my brain.

We had several drinks at the bar, but there was half an hour before they would agree to serve dinner. I said to Lola, 'You don't want to drag round this town. If you don't mind, I'll just slip out for ten minutes and look at a place I used to know.' She didn't mind. There was a local man, perhaps a schoolmaster, at the bar simply longing to stand her a drink. I could see how he envied me, coming down with her like this from town just for a night.

I walked up the hill. The first houses were all new. I resented them. They hid such things as fields and gates I might have remembered. It was like a map which had got wet in the pocket and pieces had stuck together; when you opened it there were whole patches hidden. But half-way up, there the house really was, the drive; perhaps the same old lady was giving lessons. Children exaggerate age. She may not in those days have been more than thirty-five. I could hear the piano. She was following the same routine. Children under eight, 6–7 p.m. Children eight to thirteen, 7–8. I opened the gate and went in a little way. I was trying to remember.

I don't know what brought it back. I think it was simply the autumn, the cold, the wet frosting leaves, rather than the piano, which had played different tunes in those days. I remembered the small girl as well as one remembers anyone without a photograph to refer to. She was a year older than I was: she must have been just on the point of eight. I loved her with an intensity I have never felt since, I believe, for anyone. At least I have never made the mistake of laughing at children's love. It has a terrible inevitability of separation because there *can* be no satisfaction. Of course one invents tales of houses on fire, of war and forlorn charges which prove one's courage in her eyes, but never of marriage. One knows without being told that that can't happen, but the knowledge doesn't mean that one suffers less. I remembered all the games of blind-man's buff at birthday parties when I vainly hoped to catch her, so that I might have the excuse to touch and hold her, but I never caught her; she always kept out of my way.

But once a week for two winters I had my chance: I danced with her. That made it worse (it was cutting off our only contact) when she told me during one of the last lessons of the winter that next year she would join the older class. She liked me too, I knew it, but we had no way of expressing it. I used to go to her birthday parties and she would come to mine, but we never even ran home together after the dancing class. It would have seemed odd; I don't think it occurred to us. I had to join my own boisterous teasing male companions, and she the besieged, the hustled, the shrilly indignant sex on the way down the hill.

I shivered there in the mist and turned my coat collar up. The piano was playing a dance from an old C. B. Cochran revue. It seemed a long journey to have taken to find only Lola at the end of it. There *is* something about innocence one is never quite resigned to lose. Now when I am unhappy about a girl, I can simply go and buy another one. Then the best I could think of was to write some passionate message and slip it into a hole (it was extraordinary how I began to remember everything) in the woodwork of the gate. I had once told her about the hole, and sooner or later I was sure she would put in her fingers and find the message. I wondered what the message could have been. One wasn't able to express much, I thought, in those days; but because the expression was inadequate, it didn't mean that the pain was shallower than what one sometimes suffered now. I remembered how for days I had felt in the hole and always found the message there. Then the dancing lessons stopped. Probably by the next winter I had forgotten.

As I went out of the gate I looked to see if the hole existed. It was there. I put in my finger, and, in its safe shelter from the seasons and the years, the scrap of paper rested yet. I pulled it out and opened it. Then I struck a match, a tiny glow of heat in the mist and dark. It was a shock to see by its diminutive flame a picture of crude obscenity. There could be no mistake; there were my initials below the childish inaccurate sketch of a man and woman. But it woke fewer memories than the fume of breath, the linen bags, a damp leaf, or the pile of sand. I didn't recognize it; it might have been drawn by a dirty-minded stranger on a lavatory wall. All I could remember was the purity, the intensity, the pain of that passion.

I felt at first as if I had been betrayed. 'After all,' I told myself, 'Lola's not so much out of place here.' But later that night, when Lola turned away from me and fell asleep, I began to realize the deep innocence of that drawing. I had believed I was drawing something with a meaning and beautiful; it was only now after thirty years of life that the picture seemed obscene.

Nathaniel Hawthorne

The Hollow of the Three Hills

In those strange old times, when fantastic dreams and madmen's rever-
ies were realized among the actual circumstances of life, two persons met
together at an appointed hour and place. One was a lady, graceful in form
and fair of feature, though pale and troubled, and smitten with an untimely
blight in what should have been the fullest bloom of her years; the other was
an ancient and meanly dressed woman, of ill-favored aspect, and so withered, shrunken and decrepit; that even the space since she began to decay
must have exceeded the ordinary term of human existence. In the spot where
they encountered, no mortal could observe them. Three little hills stood near
each other, and down in the midst of them sunk a hollow basin, almost
mathematically circular, two or three hundred feet in breadth, and of such
depth that a stately cedar might but just be visible above the sides. Dwarf
pines were numerous upon the hills, and partly fringed the outer verge of
the intermediate hollow; within which there was nothing but the brown
grass of October, and here and there a tree-trunk, that had fallen long ago,
and lay mouldering with no green successor from its roots. One of these
masses of decaying wood, formerly a majestic oak, rested close beside a pool
of green and sluggish water at the bottom of the basin. Such scenes as this (so
gray tradition tells) were once the resort of a Power of Evil and his plighted
subjects; and here, at midnight or on the dim verge of evening, they were
said to stand round the mantling pool, disturbing its putrid waters in the
performance of an impious baptismal rite. The chill beauty of an autumnal
sunset was now gilding the three hill-tops, whence a paler tint stole down
their sides into the hollow.

"Here is our pleasant meeting come to pass," said the aged crone, "according as thou hast desired. Say quickly what thou wouldst have of me, for there is but a short hour that we may tarry here."

As the old withered woman spoke, a smile glimmered on her countenance, like lamplight on the wall of a sepulchre. The lady trembled, and cast her eyes upward to the verge of the basin, as if meditating to return with her purpose unaccomplished. But it was not so ordained.

"I am stranger in this land, as you know," said she at length. "Whence I come it matters not;—but I have left those behind me with whom my fate was intimately bound, and from whom I am cut off forever. There is a weight in my bosom that I cannot away with, and I have come hither to inquire of their welfare."

"And who is there by this green pool, that can bring thee news from the ends of the Earth?" cried the old woman, peering into the lady's face. "Not from my lips mayst thou hear these tidings; yet, be thou bold, and the daylight shall not pass away from yonder hill-top, before thy wish be granted."

"I will do your bidding though I die," replied the lady desperately.

The old woman seated herself on the trunk of the fallen tree, threw aside the hood that shrouded her gray locks, and beckoned her companion to draw near.

"Kneel down," she said, "and lay your forehead on my knees."

She hesitated a moment, but the anxiety, that had long been kindling, burned fiercely up within her. As she knelt down, the border of her garment was dipped into the pool; she laid her forehead on the old woman's knees, and the latter drew a cloak about the lady's face, so that she was in darkness. Then she heard the muttered words of a prayer, in the midst of which she started, and would have arisen.

"Let me flee,—let me flee and hide myself, that they may not look upon me!" she cried. But, with returning recollection, she hushed herself, and was still as death.

For it seemed as if other voices—familiar in infancy, and unforgotten through many wanderings, and in all the vicissitudes of her heart and fortune—were mingling with the accents of the prayer. At first the words were faint and indistinct, not rendered so by distance, but rather resembling the dim pages of a book, which we strive to read by an imperfect and gradually brightening light. In such a manner, as the prayer proceeded, did those voices strengthen upon the ear; till at length the petition ended, and the conversation of an aged man, and of a woman broken and decayed like himself, became distinctly audible to the lady as she knelt. But those strangers appeared not to stand in the hollow depth between the three hills. Their voices were encompassed and re-echoed by the walls of a chamber, the windows of which were rattling in the breeze; the regular vibration of a clock, the crackling of a fire, and the tinkling of the embers as they fell among the ashes, rendered the scene almost as vivid as if painted to the eye. By a melancholy hearth sat these two old people, the man calmly despondent, the woman querulous and tearful, and their words were all of sorrow. They spoke of a daughter, a wanderer they knew not where, bearing dishonor along with her, and leaving shame and affliction to bring their gray heads to the grave. They alluded also to other and more recent woe, but in the midst of their talk, their voices seemed to melt into the sound of the wind sweeping mournfully among the autumn leaves; and when the lady lifted her eyes, there was she kneeling in the hollow between three hills.

"A weary and lonesome time yonder old couple have of it," remarked the old woman, smiling in the lady's face.

"And did you also hear them!" exclaimed she, a sense of intolerable humiliation triumphing over her agony and fear.

"Yea; and we have yet more to hear," replied the old woman. "Wherefore, cover thy face quickly."

Again the withered hag poured forth the monotonous words of a prayer that was not meant to be acceptable in Heaven; and soon, in the pauses of her breath, strange murmurings began to thicken, gradually increasing so as to drown and overpower the charm by which they grew. Shrieks pierced through the obscurity of sound, and were succeeded by the singing of sweet female voices, which in their turn gave way to a wild roar of laughter, broken suddenly by groanings and sobs, forming altogether a ghastly confusion of terror and mourning and mirth. Chains were rattling, fierce and stern voices uttered threats, and the scourge resounded at their command. All these noises deepened and became substantial to the listener's ear, till she could distinguish every soft and dreamy accent of the love songs, that died causelessly into funeral hymns. She shuddered at the unprovoked wrath which blazed up like the spontaneous kindling of flame, and she grew faint at the fearful merriment, raging miserably around her. In the midst of this wild scene, where unbound passions jostled each other in a drunken career, there was one solemn voice of a man, and a manly and melodious voice it might once have been. He went to-and-fro continually, and his feet sounded upon the floor. In each member of that frenzied company, whose own burning thoughts had become their exclusive world, he sought an auditor for the story of his individual wrong, and interpreted their laughter and tears as his reward of scorn or pity. He spoke of woman's perfidy, of a wife who had broken her holiest vows, of a home and heart made desolate. Even as he went on, the shout, the laugh, the shriek, the sob, rose up in unison, till they changed into the hollow, fitful, and uneven sound of the wind, as it fought among the pine-trees on those three lonely hills. The lady looked up, and there was the withered woman smiling in her face.

"Couldst thou have thought there were such merry times in a Mad House?" inquired the latter.

"True, true," said the lady to herself; "there is mirth within its walls, but misery, misery without."

"Wouldst thou hear more?" demanded the old woman.

"There is one other voice I would fain listen to again," replied the lady faintly.

"Then lay down thy head speedily upon my knees, that thou may'st get thee hence before the hour be past."

The golden skirts of day were yet lingering upon the hills, but deep shades obscured the hollow and the pool, as if sombre night were rising thence to overspread the world. Again that evil woman began to weave her spell. Long did it proceed unanswered, till the knolling of a bell stole in among the intervals of her words, like a clang that had travelled far over valley and rising ground, and was just ready to die in the air. The lady shook upon her companion's knees, as she heard that boding sound. Stronger it grew and sadder, and deepened into the tone of a death-bell, knolling dolefully from some ivy-mantled tower, and bearing tidings of mortality and woe to the cottage, to the hall, and to the solitary wayfarer, that all might weep for the doom appointed in turn to them. Then came a measured tread, passing slowly, slowly on, as of mourners with a coffin, their garments trailing on the ground, so that the ear could measure the length of their melancholy array. Before them went the priest, reading the burial-service, while the leaves of his book were rustling in the breeze. And though no voice but his was heard to speak aloud, still there were revilings and anathemas, whispered but distinct, from women and from men, breathed against the daughter who had wrung the aged hearts of her parents,—the wife who had betrayed the trusting fondness of her husband,—the mother who had sinned against natural affection, and left her child to die. The sweeping sound of the funeral train faded away like a thin vapour, and the wind, that just before had seemed to shake the coffin-pall, moaned sadly round the verge of the Hollow between three Hills. But when the old woman stirred the kneeling lady, she lifted not her head.

"Here has been a sweet hour's sport!" said the withered crone, chuckling to herself.

ERNEST HEMINGWAY

A Very Short Story

One hot evening in Padua they carried him up onto the roof and he could look out over the top of the town. There were chimney swifts in the sky. After a while it got dark and the searchlights came out. The others went down and took the bottles with them. He and Luz could hear them below on the balcony. Luz sat on the bed. She was cool and fresh in the hot night.

Luz stayed on night duty for three months. They were glad to let her. When they operated on him she prepared him for the operating table; and they had a joke about friend or enema. He went under the anæsthetic holding tight on to himself so he would not blab about anything during the silly, talky time. After he got on crutches he used to take the temperatures so Luz would not have to get up from the bed. There were only a few patients, and they all knew about it. They all liked Luz. As he walked back along the halls he thought of Luz in his bed.

Before he went back to the front they went into the Duomo and prayed. It was dim and quiet, and there were other people praying. They wanted to get married, but there was not enough time for the banns, and neither of them had birth certificates. They felt as though they were married, but they wanted every one to know about it, and to make it so they could not lose it.

Luz wrote him many letters that he never got until after the armistice. Fifteen came in a bunch to the front and he sorted them by the dates and read them all straight through. They were all about the hospital, and how much she loved him and how it was impossible to get along without him and how terrible it was missing him at night.

After the armistice they agreed he should go home to get a job so they might be married. Luz would not come home until he had a good job and could come to New York to meet her. It was understood he would not drink, and he did not want to see his friends or any one in the States. Only to get a job and be married. On the train from Padua to Milan they quarrelled about her not being willing to come home at once. When they had to say good-bye, in the station at Milan, they kissed good-bye, but were not finished with the quarrel. He felt sick about saying good-bye like that.

He went to America on a boat from Genoa. Luz went back to Pordonone to open a hospital. It was lonely and rainy there, and there was a battalion of arditi quartered in the town. Living in the muddy, rainy town in the winter, the major of the battalion made love to Luz, and she had never known Italians before, and finally wrote to the States that theirs had been only a boy and girl affair. She was sorry, and she knew he would probably not be able to understand, but might some day forgive her, and be grateful to her, and she expected, absolutely unexpectedly, to be married in the spring. She loved him as always, but she realized now it was only a boy and girl love. She hoped he would have a great career, and believed in him absolutely. She knew it was for the best.

The major did not marry her in the spring, or any other time. Luz never got an answer to the letter to Chicago about it. A short time after he contracted gonorrhea from a sales girl in a loop department store while riding in a taxicab through Lincoln Park.

AMY HEMPLE

Weekend

The game was called on account of dogs—Hunter in the infield, Tucker in the infield, Bosco and Boone at first base. First-grader Donald sat down on second base, and Kirsten grabbed her brother's arm and wouldn't let him leave third to make his first run.

"Unfair!" her brother screamed, and the dogs, roving umpires, ran to third.

"Good power!" their uncle yelled, when Joy, in a leg cast, swung the bat and missed. "Now put some wood to it."

And when she did, Joy's designated runner, Cousin Zeke, ran to first, the ice cubes in his gin and tonic clacking like dog tags in the glass.

And when Kelly broke free from Kirsten and this time came in to make the run, members of the Kelly team made Tucker in the infield dance on his hind legs.

"It's not who wins—" their coach began, and was shouted down by one of the boys, "There's *first* and there's *forget it.*"

Then Hunter retrieved a foul ball and carried it off in the direction of the river.

The other dogs followed—barking, mutinous.

Dinner was a simple picnic on the porch, paper plates in laps, the only conversation a debate as to which was the better grip for throwing shoes.

After dinner, the horseshoes were handed out, the post pounded in, the rules reviewed with a new rule added due to falling-down shorts. The new rule: Have attire.

The women smoked on the porch, the smoke repelling mosquitoes, and the men and children played on even after dusk when it got so dark that a candle was rigged to balance on top of the post, and was knocked off and blown out by every single almost-ringer.

Then the children went to bed, or at least went upstairs, and the men joined the women for a cigarette on the porch, absently picking ticks engorged like grapes off the sleeping dogs. And when the men kissed the women good night, and their weekend whiskers scratched the women's cheeks, the women did not think *shave*, they thought: *stay*.

O. Henry

The Gift of the Magi

One dollar and eighty-seven cents. That was all. And sixty cents of it was in pennies. Pennies saved one and two at a time by bulldozing the grocer and the vegetable man and the butcher until one's cheeks burned with the silent imputation of parsimony that such close dealing implied. Three times Della counted it. One dollar and eighty-seven cents. And the next day would be Christmas.

There was clearly nothing to do but flop down on the shabby little couch and howl. So Della did it. Which instigates the moral reflection that life is made up of sobs, sniffles, and smiles, with sniffles predominating.

While the mistress of the home is gradually subsiding from the first stage to the second, take a look at the home. A furnished flat at $8 per week. It did not exactly beggar description, but it certainly had that word on the lookout for the mendicancy squad.

In the vestibule below was a letter-box into which no letter would go, and an electric button from which no mortal finger could coax a ring. Also appertaining thereunto was a card bearing the name "Mr. James Dillingham Young."

The "Dillingham" had been flung to the breeze during a former period of prosperity when its possessor was being paid $30 per week. Now, when the income was shrunk to $20, the letters of "Dillingham" looked blurred, as though they were thinking seriously of contracting to a modest and unassuming D. But whenever Mr. James Dillingham Young came home and reached his flat above he was called "Jim" and greatly hugged by Mrs. James Dillingham Young, already introduced to you as Della. Which is all very good.

Della finished her cry and attended to her cheeks with the powder rag. She stood by the window and looked out dully at a gray cat walking a gray fence in a gray backyard. Tomorrow would be Christmas Day and she had only $1.87 with which to buy Jim a present. She had been saving every penny she could for months, with this result. Twenty dollars a week doesn't go far. Expenses had been greater than she had calculated. They always are. Only $1.87 to buy a present for Jim. Her Jim. Many a happy hour she had spent planning for something nice for him. Something fine and rare and sterling—something just a little bit near to being worthy of the honor of being owned by Jim.

There was a pier-glass between the windows of the room. Perhaps you have seen a pier-glass in an $8 flat. A very thin and very agile person may, by observing his reflection in a rapid sequence of longitudinal strips, obtain a fairly accurate conception of his looks. Della, being slender, had mastered the art.

Suddenly she whirled from the window and stood before the glass. Her eyes were shining brilliantly, but her face had lost its color within twenty seconds. Rapidly she pulled down her hair and let it fall to its full length.

Now, there were two possessions of the James Dillingham Youngs in which they both took a mighty pride. One was Jim's gold watch that had been his father's and his grandfather's. The other was Della's hair. Had the Queen of Sheba lived in the flat across the airshaft, Della would have let her hair hang out the window some day to dry just to depreciate Her Majesty's jewels and gifts. Had King Solomon been the janitor, with all his treasures piled up in the basement, Jim would have pulled out his watch every time he passed, just to see him pluck at his beard from envy.

So now Della's beautiful hair fell about her rippling and shining like a cascade of brown waters. It reached below her knee and made itself almost a garment for her. And then she did it up again nervously and quickly. Once she faltered for a minute and stood still while a tear or two splashed on the worn red carpet.

On went her old brown jacket; on went her old brown hat. With a whirl of skirts and with the brilliant sparkle still in her eyes, she fluttered out the door and down the stairs to the street.

Where she stopped the sign read: "Mme. Sofronie. Hair Goods of All Kinds." One flight up Della ran, and collected herself, panting. Madame, large, too white, chilly, hardly looked the "Sofronie."

"Will you buy my hair?" asked Della.

"I buy hair," said Madame. "Take yer hat off and let's have a sight at the looks of it."

Down rippled the brown cascade.

"Twenty dollars," said Madame, lifting the mass with a practised hand.

"Give it to me quick," said Della.

Oh, and the next two hours tripped by on rosy wings. Forget the hashed metaphor. She was ransacking the stores for Jim's present.

She found it at last. It surely had been made for Jim and no one else. There was no other like it in any of the stores, and she had turned all of them inside out. It was a platinum fob chain simple and chaste in design, properly proclaiming its value by substance alone and not by meretricious ornamentation—as all good things should do. It was even worthy of The Watch. As soon as she saw it she knew that it must be Jim's. It was like him. Quietness and value—the description applied to both. Twenty-one dollars they took from her for it, and she hurried home with the 87 cents. With that chain on his watch Jim might be properly anxious about the time in any company. Grand as the watch was, he sometimes looked at it on the sly on account of the old leather strap that he used in place of a chain.

When Della reached home her intoxication gave way a little to prudence and reason. She got out her curling irons and lighted the gas and went to work repairing the ravages made by generosity added to love. Which is always a tremendous task, dear friends—a mammoth task.

Within forty minutes her head was covered with tiny, close-lying curls that made her look wonderfully like a truant schoolboy. She looked at her reflection in the mirror long, carefully, and critically.

"If Jim doesn't kill me," she said to herself, "before he takes a second look at me, he'll say I look like a Coney Island chorus girl. But what could I do—oh! what could I do with a dollar and eighty-seven cents?"

At 7 o'clock the coffee was made and the frying-pan was on the back of the stove hot and ready to cook the chops.

Jim was never late. Della doubled the fob chain in her hand and sat on the corner of the table near the door that he always entered. Then she heard his step on the stair away down on the first flight, and she turned white for just a moment. She had a habit of saying little silent prayers about the simplest everyday things, and now she whispered: "Please God, make him think I am still pretty."

The door opened and Jim stepped in and closed it. He looked thin and very serious. Poor fellow, he was only twenty-two—and to be burdened with a family! He needed a new overcoat and he was without gloves.

Jim stepped inside the door, as immovable as a setter at the scent of quail. His eyes were fixed upon Della, and there was an expression in them that she could not read, and it terrified her. It was not anger, nor surprise, nor disapproval, nor horror, nor any of the sentiments that she had been prepared for. He simply stared at her fixedly with that peculiar expression on his face.

Della wriggled off the table and went for him.

"Jim, darling," she cried, "don't look at me that way. I had my hair cut off and sold it because I couldn't have lived through Christmas without giving you a present. It'll grow out again—you won't mind, will you? I just had to do it. My hair grows awfully fast. Say 'Merry Christmas!' Jim, and let's be happy. You don't know what a nice—what a beautiful, nice gift I've got for you."

"You've cut off your hair?" asked Jim, laboriously, as if he had not arrived at that patent fact yet even after the hardest mental labor.

"Cut it off and sold it," said Della. "Don't you like me just as well, anyhow? I'm me without my hair, ain't I?"

Jim looked about the room curiously.

"You say your hair is gone?" he said, with an air almost of idiocy.

"You needn't look for it," said Della. "It's sold, I tell you—sold and gone, too. It's Christmas Eve, boy. Be good to me, for it went for you. Maybe the hairs on my head were numbered," she went on with a sudden serious sweetness, "but nobody could ever count my love for you. Shall I put the chops on, Jim?"

Out of his trance Jim seemed quickly to wake. He enfolded his Della. For ten seconds let us regard with discreet scrutiny some inconsequential object in the other direction. Eight dollars a week or a million a year—what is the difference? A mathematician or a wit would give you the wrong answer. The magi brought valuable gifts, but that was not among them. This dark assertion will be illuminated later on.

Jim drew a package from his overcoat pocket and threw it upon the table.

"Don't make any mistake, Dell," he said, "about me. I don't think there's anything in the way of a haircut or a shave or a shampoo that could make me like my girl any less. But if you'll unwrap that package you may see why you had me going a while at first."

White fingers and nimble tore at the string and paper. And then an ecstatic scream of joy; and then, alas! a quick feminine change to hysterical tears and wails, necessitating the immediate employment of all the comforting powers of the lord of the flat.

For there lay The Combs—the set of combs, side and back, that Della had worshipped for long in a Broadway window. Beautiful combs, pure tortoise shell, with jewelled rims—just the shade to wear in the beautiful vanished hair. They were expensive combs, she knew, and her heart had simply craved and yearned over them without the least hope of possession. And now, they were hers, but the tresses that should have adorned the coveted adornments were gone.

But she hugged them to her bosom, and at length she was able to look up with dim eyes and a smile and say: "My hair grows so fast, Jim!"

And then Della leaped up like a little singed cat and cried, "Oh, oh!"

Jim had not yet seen his beautiful present. She held it out to him eagerly upon her open palm. The dull precious metal seemed to flash with a reflection of her bright and ardent spirit.

"Isn't it a dandy, Jim? I hunted all over town to find it. You'll have to look at the time a hundred times a day now. Give me your watch. I want to see how it looks on it."

Instead of obeying, Jim tumbled down on the couch and put his hands under the back of his head and smiled.

"Dell," said he, "let's put our Christmas presents away and keep 'em a while. They're too nice to use just at present. I sold the watch to get the money to buy your combs. And now suppose you put the chops on."

The magi, as you know, were wise men—wonderfully wise men—who brought gifts to the Babe in the manger. They invented the art of giving Christmas presents. Being wise, their gifts were no doubt wise ones, possibly bearing the privilege of exchange in case of duplication. And here I have lamely related to you the uneventful chronicle of two foolish children in a flat who most unwisely sacrificed for each other the greatest treasures of their house. But in a last word to the wise of these days let it be said that of all who give gifts these two were the wisest. Of all who give and receive gifts, such as they are wisest. Everywhere they are wisest. They are the magi.

CHESTER HIMES

A Penny for Your Thoughts

His name was Frank Hacket but people in Red River, Texas, where he lived, called him Cap Coty. He stood six feet-two, weighed two hundred, and at seventy years was still straight as a ram-rod and agile as a marine. He wore a big black hat and a cowhide vest and his trousers outside his boot tops; and when he spoke, which was seldom, it was always in a slow, courteous drawl.

In Texas, where the babies teeth on gun butts, his marksmanship and speed on the draw were legendary. And what is more, he had a skyrocketing temper and a steady hand. During his twenty-seven years as a Ranger it is said he killed some sixty-odd badmen with his favorite gun, a pearl-handled, brass-lined. 44, which he called 'Becky'.

He quit the Rangers in December of 1932 when a woman was elected governor of Texas for the second time, and for twelve years he stayed in retirement, raising a few hundred white-faced Herefords on his rocky ranch. But in April of 1944, when a mob formed to lynch a Negro soldier accused of rape, he came out of retirement violently and abruptly.

It was in the morning he first got word. It was a warm Spring morning, and he'd been up since dawn shooting a few early rattlers out on the range when he saw the mail man and cantered over to the box to pass the time of day.

'Caught a nigger,' the mail man said, idling down his hot Model-A and spitting in the dust.

'What for?' Cap Coty asked.

'Same thing,' the mail man said, smacking his lips juicily, and spat again.

Cap Coty pulled his stallion out his sidewise drift and turned to face the mail man from another angle. 'Drifter?' he asked.

'Soldier boy this time,' the mail man said.

Cap Coty's expression did not change, but his eyes got reflective, 'Say he done it?'

The mail man spat this time before he replied. Then he said, 'Now, Cap, you know ain't no nigger gonna confess to raping no white woman. But he's the right nigger all right; got a scar on the right side o' his face jes like she say.'

He waited a while for Cap Coty to make some further remark, and when Cap Coty didn't, he pulled into first and rattled along. For all of five minutes Cap Coty sat motionless on his stallion, drifting in the dust, then he turned and cantered back to his ranch house and called the sheriff.

'If any trouble starts, Tim, better call me,' he said.

'Ain't gonna be no trouble,' the sheriff said. He sounded peeved. 'I got everything under hand. Town's quiet as a graveyard.'

But already a mob was forming. Battered dusty cars began pulling in before noon, lining the one main street from end to end; and weatherbeaten men gathered in tight hard knots, going in and out the three saloons with steady intermittence, getting up their gage. They talked loud, their harsh voices lacerating their own taut nerves; and walked tough; and their buck-wild gazes never steadied. For a black man to walk that street was a way into eternity.

They were going to lynch a nigger. But they weren't ready yet. Indecision held them like a live mine; the weight of a foot would set them off.

Bobbie Barker rode into town in a dusty, low slung, Cadillac touring, and did it. She came down the grade from the Amarillo road, doing a hundred and twelve by the needle, dust pluming out behind like smoke from a mountain manifest, and dragged to a stop in the center of the triangle of the three saloons.

When the dust died down she jumped up on the seat, a cigar in her mouth and a pistol in her hand. 'Ah thought sho ah'd be late,' she said, licking her dusty lips.

She was a thin, sun-burned, long-boned woman with slick red hair and slitted gray eyes; but her breasty body in sweater and slacks was raw with sex—she looked like a broad who could line them up. Two months before she had beat a murder rap in Dallas, and they didn't know until they had let her out that she was wanted, along with two ex-convicts, by the Ft Worth sheriff for a filling station robbery.

But she was known best for her lightning trigger finger and a heart bearing the name 'Dan' tattoed on her right thigh. Dannie Lambright was the name of her husband serving a double murder buck in Houston. Any kind of thrill could make her respond.

The cowboys stood and gaped at her. No one asked where she came from or why she was there; the one didn't matter, and the other they knew.

A big, white-haired, solid looking rancher in a fifty dollar Stetson and hand-tooled boots, who had been leaning in the doorway of the grocery store, sauntered across the street.

'I can guess who you are, sister,' he said. 'But there ain't gonna be no lynching in Red River today.' He had the level-voiced authority of a man well respected.

'Why, you nigger-lovin' bastard, what's Texas comin' to when a white woman . . .' She drew back and slapped him across the mouth with the barrel of her gun.

He reached for her leg. She kicked him in the face with the heel of her boot. Then four furtive-faced cowboys who'd been waiting for the chance, ganged him. He'd fired them the week before for rustling his steers for the black market, although he'd been unable to prove it and they'd been laying in town for him ever since.

One drew a rusty length of pipe and slugged him across the head. He reeled back from the blow, his hat falling off, but turned and came back in again. But they were on him like white on rice. Two grabbed his arms and the third his feet, and the pipe wielder slugged him across the head until blood matted red in his white hair.

This turn had been unexpected; gaged for a nigger-lynching the cowboys had stood and watched, thought-blank and unmoving; now they came in to take the rancher's part. But the woman wouldn't be cheated by a free-for-all. She leaned over and knocked the pipe-wielder unconscious with the butt of her gun, snarling at the other three, 'Let the nigger-lover be—we got other business.'

A tall, angle-faced man with crazy red eyes and a blue stubble of two days beard, stepped forward and twirled a rope. He had a pistol tucked in the front of his jeans, and just stood there, wide-legged, twirling the rope.

She jumped down and joined him, waving for the others to follow. For a moment there was silence. The thought ate into them, gutting them with a raw excitement. To one side a youth sneezed, and his legs began shaking visibly.

Then a harsh voice said, 'Let's cut out his . . .' and the woman gave a short blast of laughter.

And suddenly they were ready; it went over them like a wave, going from one to the other without sound. Ready to lynch a goddamned nigger's raping soul. It was in their buck-wild eyes, a savage gleam like cannibal fires in the jungle; in their snarling, twisted faces, white skin taut over bone-angles like dried sheepskin on death' heads; in their hearts, pumping hatred through their souls like gut-corroding poison eating up their tissues.

The thin red-headed woman took a tentative step and the blue-bearded man fell in beside . . . Another step; slow, waiting . . . The rest surged in behind. Down the dusty street toward the Red River jail, to lynch a nigger, to dip their immortal souls in the river of hate, to canker their hearts with a violence eternity couldn't cleanse; walking ever faster, talking ever louder.

'Less roast the nigger in gasoline . . .'

'Less cut the bastard into steak—nigger steak . . .'

One took out his gun and fired into the air; others followed suit. Behind them the afternoon sun reddened, throwing long grotesque shadows out before them like images of hell . . .

At a quarter past five Cap Coty got a call from a craven deputy that the mob was breaking down the doors. They were using a railroad tie as a battering ram and the door couldn't hold out much longer.

By car it was fifteen minutes from the ranch house into town. Motion had come into Cap Coty's feet before he dropped the receiver. Passing, he grabbed his holstered 'Becky' from the hook, bucked it about him in one deft motion on the go; grabbed for his .503 over the back door as he went out, missed it and didn't stop. He went across the back yard in a crab-like dog-trot, fast but not showy, and was inside his Plymouth coupe without ever having stopped. He backed a curve on the starter; the motor didn't catch until he took the dip down to the road. When he came into the main highway he got caught behind the five-thirty Greyhound and rode it piggy-back until he found an opening. He rode that little joppy like a hill-country cowboy on a Spring roundup, and it was five-twenty-four when he pulled up back of the jail.

The deputy was waiting to let him through the small, steel, bulletproof rear door. He went past without speaking, down the corridor by the cells, did not take one glance at the frightened Negro soldier huddled on his cot.

As if timed by Omnipotence, as he came into the jail vestibule from one side, the door crashed down and the mob surged in from the other, led by the red-headed woman and the blue-bearded man. Neither hurrying nor hesitating, with his bare hands hanging at his sides and his lips a light bloodless seam in his clay-baked face, eyes a tricky gleam beneath the low-pulled brim of his big black hat, he kept on walking, and when he had reached the man and woman in front, drew back in the same hard, unhurried motion and slapped the man his length on the concrete floor. He caught the woman by both shoulders with his two hands and holding her at arm's distance, shook her until her gun rattled on the floor and her face was as red as her loose flying hair. Then he spun her about and pushed her face first into the mob.

The blue bearded man rolled over and lunged for the gun he had dropped, got his hand on it and started to his feet, his eyes white with dead fury.

There was no visible motion of Cap Coty's hand. One moment it was empty and the next the gun was in it. He tied three shots together in one long continuous sound, and three black holes like period marks, dotted the man's white forehead just above the blue-black arch of his eyebrows. He was already dead when the sound had ceased.

In the raw silence following the echo, Cap Coty in his slow, courteous drawl said: 'Y' all understand, I don't give a damn 'bout the nigger; it's the uniform I revere. Now goddamit y'all go on home.'

He stood there, a big straight man in a big black hat until they had all gone from his sight, thinking.

PAM HOUSTON

Symphony

Sometimes life is ridiculously simple. I lost fifteen pounds and the men want me again. I can see it in the way they follow my movements, not just with their eyes but with their whole bodies, the way they lean into me until they almost topple over, the way they always seem to have itches on the back of their necks. And I'll admit this: I am collecting them like gold-plated sugar spoons, one from every state.

This is a difficult story to tell because what's right about what I have to say is only as wide as a tightrope, and what's wrong about it yawns wide, beckoning, on either side. I have always said I have no narcotic, smiling sadly at stories of ruined lives, safely remote from the twelve-step program and little red leather booklets that say "One Day at a Time." But there is something so sweet about the first kiss, the first surrender that, like the words "I want you," can never mean precisely the same thing again. It is delicious and addicting. It is, I'm guessing, the most delicious thing of all.

There are a few men who matter, and by writing them down in this story I can make them seem like they have an order, or a sequence, or a priority, because those are the kinds of choices that language forces upon us, but language can't touch the joyful and slightly disconcerting feeling of being very much in love, but not knowing exactly with whom.

First I will tell you about Phillip, who is vast and dangerous, his desires uncontainable and huge. He is far too talented, a grown-up tragedy of a gifted child, massively in demand. He dances, he weaves, he writes a letter that could wring light from a black hole. He has mined gold in the Yukon, bonefished in Belize. He has crossed Iceland on a dogsled, he is the smartest man that all his friends know. His apartment smells like wheat bread, cooling. His body smells like spice. Sensitive and scared scared scared of never becoming a father, he lives in New York City and is very careful about his space. It is easy to confuse what he has learned to do in bed for love or passion or art, but he is simply a master craftsman, and very proud of his good work.

Christopher is innocent. Very young and wide-open. He's had good mothering and no father to make him afraid to talk about his heart. In Nevada he holds hands with middle-aged women while the underground tests explode beneath them. He studies marine biology, acting, and poetry, and is not yet quite aware of his classic good looks. Soon someone will tell him, but it won't be me. A few years ago he said in a few more years he'd be old enough for me, and in a few more years, it will be true. For now we are friends and I tell him my system, how I have learned to get what I want from many sources, and none. He says this: You are a complicated woman. Even when you say you don't want anything, you want more than that.

I have a dream in which a man becomes a wolf. He is sleeping, cocooned, and when he stretches and breaks the parchment there are tufts of hair across his back and shoulders, and on the backs of his hands. It is Christopher, I suspect, though I can't see his face. When I wake up I am in Phillip's bed. My back is to his side and yet we are touching at all the pressure points. In the predawn I can see the line of electricity we make, a glow like neon, the curve of a wooden instrument. As I wake, "Symphony" is the first word that forms in my head.

Jonathan came here from the Okavango Delta in Botswana; he's tall and hairy and clever and strong. In my living room I watch him reach inside his shirt and scratch his shoulder. It is a savage movement, rangy and impatient, lazy too, and without a bit of self-consciousness. He is not altogether human. He has spent the last three years in the bush. I cook him T-bone steaks because he says he won't eat complicated food. He is skeptical of the hibachi, of the barely glowing coals. Where he comes from, they cook everything with fire. He says things against my ear, the names of places: Makgadikgadi Pans, Nxamaseri, Mpandamatenga, Gabarone. Say these words out loud and see what happens to you. Mosi-oa-Toenja, "The Smoke That Thunders." Look at the pictures: a rank of impalas slaking their thirst, giraffes, their necks entwined, a young bull elephant rising from the Chobe River. When I am with Jonathan I have this thought which delights and frightens me: It has been the animals that have attracted me all along. Not the cowboys, but the horses that carried them. Not the hunters, but the caribou and the bighorn. Not Jonathan, in his infinite loveliness, but the hippos, the kudu, and the big African cats. You fall in love with a man's animal spirit, Jonathan tells me, and then when he speaks like a human being, you don't know who he is.

There's one man I won't talk about, not because he is married, but because he is sacred. When he writes love letters to me he addresses them "my dear" and signs them with the first letter of his first name and one long black line. We have only made love one time. I will tell you only the one thing that must be told: After the only part of him I will ever hold collapsed inside me he said, "You are so incredibly gentle." It was the closest I have ever come to touching true love.

Another dream: I am in the house of my childhood, and I see myself, at age five, at the breakfast table; pancakes and sausage, my father in his tennis whites. The me that is dreaming, the older me, kneels down and holds out her arms waiting for the younger me to come and be embraced. Jonathan's arms twitch around me and I am suddenly awake inside a body, inside a world where it has become impossible to kneel down and hold out my arms. Still sleeping, Jonathan pulls my hand across his shoulder, and presses it hard against his face.

I'm afraid of what you might be thinking. That I am a certain kind of person, and that you are the kind of person who knows more about my story than me. But you should know this: I could love any one of them, in an instant and with every piece of my heart, but none of them nor the world will allow it, and so I move between them, on snowy highways and crowded airplanes. I was in New York this morning. I woke up in Phillip's bed. Come here, he's in my hair. You can smell him.

Langston Hughes

Jazz, Jive, and Jam

"It Being Negro History Week," said Simple, "Joyce took me to a pay lecture to hear some Negro hysterian——"

"Historian," I corrected.

"—hysterian speak," continued Simple, "and he laid our Negro race low. He said we was misbred, misread, and misled, also losing our time good-timing. Instead of time-taking and money-making, we are jazz-shaking. Oh, he enjoyed his self at the expense of the colored race—and him black as me. He really delivered a lecture—in which, no doubt, there is some truth."

"Constructive criticism, I gather—a sort of tearing down in order to build up."

"He tore us down good," said Simple. "Joyce come out saying to me, her husband, that he had really got my number. I said, 'Baby, he did not miss you, neither.' But Joyce did not consider herself included in the bad things he said.

"She come telling me on the way home by subway, 'Jess Semple, I have been pursuing culture since my childhood. But you, when I first met you, all you did was drape yourself over some beer bar and argue with the barflies. The higher things of life do not come out of a licker trough.'

"I replied, 'But, Joyce, how come culture has got to be so dry?'

"She answers me back, 'How come your gullet has got to be so wet? You are sitting in this subway right now looking like you would like to have a beer.'

" 'Solid!' I said. 'I would. How did you guess it?'

" 'Married to you for three years, I can read your mind,' said Joyce. 'We'll buy a couple of cans to take home. I might even drink one myself.'

" 'Joyce, baby,' I said, 'in that case, let's buy three cans.'

"Joyce says, 'Remember the budget, Jess.'

"I says, 'Honey, you done busted the budget going to that lecture program which cost One Dollar a head, also we put some small change in the collection to help Negroes get ahead.'

" 'Small change?' says Joyce, 'I put a dollar.'

" 'Then our budget is busted real good,' I said, 'so we might as well dent it some more. Let's get six cans of beer.'

" 'All right,' says Joyce, 'go ahead, drink yourself to the dogs—instead of saving for that house we want to buy!'

" 'Six cans of beer would not pay for even the bottom front step,' I said. 'But they would lift my spirits this evening. That Negro high-speaking doctor done tore my spirits down. I did not know before that the colored race was so misled, misread, and misbred. According to him there is hardly a pure black man left. But I was setting in the back, so I guess he did not see me.'

" 'Had you not had to go to sleep in the big chair after dinner,' says Joyce, 'we would have been there on time and had seats up front.'

" 'I were near enough to that joker,' I said. 'Loud as he could holler, we did not need to set no closer. And he certainly were nothing to look at!'

" 'Very few educated men look like Harry Belafonte,' said Joyce.

" 'I am glad I am handsome instead of wise,' I said. But Joyce did not crack a smile. She had that lecture on her mind.

" 'Dr. Conboy is smart,' says Joyce. 'Did you hear him quoting Aristotle?'

" 'Who were Harry Stottle?' I asked.

" 'Some people are not even misread,' said Joyce. 'Aristotle was a Greek philosopher like Socrates, a great man of ancient times.'

" 'He must of been before Booker T. Washington then,' I said, 'because, to tell the truth, I has not heard of him at all. But tonight being *Negro* History Week, how come Dr. Conboy has to quote some Greek?'

" 'There were black Greeks,' said Joyce. 'Did you not hear him say that Negroes have played a part in all history, throughout all time, from Eden to now?'

" 'Do you reckon Eve was brownskin?' I requested.

" 'I do not know about Eve,' said Joyce, 'but Cleopatra was of the colored race, and the Bible says Sheba, beloved of Solomon, was black but comely.'

" 'I wonder would she come to me?' I says.

" 'Solomon also found Cleopatra comely. He was a king,' says Joyce.

" 'And I am Jesse B. Semple,' I said.

"But by that time the subway had got to our stop. At the store Joyce broke the budget again, opened up her pocket purse, and bought us six cans of beer. So it were a good evening. It ended well—except that I ain't for going to any more meetings—especially interracial meetings."

"Come now! Don't you want to improve race relations?"

"Sure," said Simple, "but in my opinion, jazz, jive, and jam would be better for race relations than all this high-flown gab, gaff, and gas the orators put out. All this talking that white folks do at meetings, and big Negroes, too, about how to get along together—just a little jam session would have everybody getting along fine without having to listen to so many speeches. Why, last month Joyce took me to a Race Relations Seminar which her club and twenty other clubs gave, and man, it lasted three days! It started on a Friday night and it were not over until Sunday afternoon. They had sessions' mammy! Joyce is a fiend for culture."

"And you sat through all that?"

"I did not set," said Simple. "I stood. I walked in and walked out. I smoked on the corner and snuck two drinks at the bar. But I had to wait for Joyce, and I thought them speeches would never get over! My wife were a delegate from her club, so she had to stay, although I think Joyce got tired her own self. But she would not admit it. Joyce said, 'Dr. Hillary Thingabod was certainly brilliant, were he not?'

"I said, 'He were not.'

"Joyce said, 'What did you want the man to say?'

"I said, 'I wish he had sung, instead of *said*. That program needed some music to keep folks awake.'

"Joyce said, 'Our forum was not intended for a musical. It was intended to see how we can work out integration.'

"I said, 'With a jazz band, they could work out integration in ten minutes. Everybody would have been dancing together like they all did at the Savoy—colored and white—or down on the East Side at them Casinos on a Friday night where jam holds forth—and we would have been integrated.'

"Joyce said, 'This was a serious seminar, aiming at facts, not fun.'

" 'Baby,' I said, 'what is more facts than acts? Jazz makes people get into action, move! Didn't nobody move in that hall where you were—except to jerk their head up when they went to sleep, to keep anybody from seeing that they was nodding. Why, that chairman, Mrs. Maxwell-Reeves, almost lost her glasses off her nose, she jerked her head up so quick one time when that man you say was so brilliant were speaking!'

" 'Jess Semple, that is not so!' yelled Joyce. 'Mrs. Maxwell-Reeves were just lost in thought. And if you think you saw *me* sleeping—'

" 'You was too busy trying to look around and see where I was,' I said. 'Thank God, I did not have to set up there like you with the delegation. I would not be a delegate to no such gabfest for nothing on earth.'

" 'I thought you was so interested in saving the race!' said Joyce. 'Next time I will not ask you to accompany me to no cultural events, Jesse B., because I can see you do not appreciate them. That were a discussion of ways and means. And you are talking about jazz bands!'

" 'There's more ways than one to skin a cat,' I said. 'A jazz band like Duke's or Hamp's or Basie's sure would of helped that meeting. At least on Saturday afternoon, they could have used a little music to put some pep into the proceedings. Now, just say for instant, baby, they was to open with jazz and close with jam—and do the talking in between. Start out, for example, with "The St. Louis Blues," which is a kind of colored national anthem. That would put every human in a good humor. Then play "Why Don't You Do Right?" which could be addressed to white folks. They could pat their feet to that. Then for a third number before introducing the speaker, let some guest star like Pearl Bailey sing "There'll Be Some Changes Made"—which, as I understand it, were the theme of the meeting, anyhow—and all the Negroes could say *Amen!*

" 'Joyce, I wish you would let me plan them interracial seminaries next time. After the music, let the speechmaking roll for a while—with maybe a calypso between speeches. Then, along about five o'clock, bring on the jam session, extra-special. Start serving tea to "Tea For Two," played real cool. Whilst drinking tea and dancing, the race relationers could relate, the integraters could integrate, and the desegregators desegregate. Joyce, you would not have to beg for a crowd to come out and support your efforts then. Jam—and the hall would be jammed! Even I would stick around, and not be outside sneaking a smoke, or trying to figure how I can get to the bar before the resolutions are voted on. *Resolved*: that we solve the race problem! Strike up the band! Hit it, men! Aw, play that thing! "How High the Moon!" How high! Wheee-ee-e!' "

"What did Joyce say to that?" I demanded.

"Joyce just thought I was high," said Simple.

SHIRLEY JACKSON

Janice

First, to me on the phone, in a half-amused melancholy: "Guess I'm not going back to school . . ."

"Why not, Jan?"

"Oh, my *mother*. She says we can't afford it." How can I reproduce the uncaring inflections of Janice's voice, saying conversationally that what she wanted she could not have? "So I guess I'm not going back."

"I'm so sorry, Jan."

But then, struck by another thought: "Y'know *what?*"

"What?"

"Darn near killed myself this afternoon."

"Jan! How?"

Almost whimsical, indifferent: "Locked myself in the garage and turned on the car motor."

"But why?"

"I dunno. 'Cause I couldn't go back, I suppose."

"What happened?"

"Oh, the fellow that was cutting our lawn heard the motor and came and got me. I was pretty near out."

"But that's terrible, Jan. What ever possessed—"

"Oh, well. Say—" changing again, "—going to Sally's tonight?" . . .

And, later, that night at Sally's where Janice was not the center of the group, but sat talking to me and to Bob: "Nearly killed myself this afternoon, Bob."

"What!"

Lightly: "Nearly killed myself. Locked myself in the garage with the car motor running."

"But why, Jan?"

"I guess because they wouldn't let me go back to school."

"Oh, I'm sorry about that, Jan. But what about this afternoon? What did you do?"

"Man cutting the grass got me out."

Sally coming over: "What's this, Jan?"

"Oh, I'm not going back to school."

Myself, cutting in: "How did it feel to be dying, Jan?"

Laughing "Gee, funny. All black." Then, to Sally's incredulous stare: "Nearly killed myself this afternoon, Sally . . ."

First Person: Shirley Jackson, "Notes for a Young Writer"

These are some notes, not necessarily complete, on the writing of short stories; they were originally written as a stimulus to my daughter Sally, who wants to be a writer.

In the country of the story the writer is king. He makes all the rules, with only the reservation that he must not ask more than a reader can reasonably grant. Remember, the reader is a very tough customer indeed, stubborn, dragging his feet, easily irritated. He will willingly agree to suspend disbelief for a time: he will go along with you if it is necessary for your story that you both assume temporarily that there really is a Land of Oz, but he will not suspend reason, he will not agree, for any story ever written, that he can see the Land of Oz from his window. As a matter of fact, you would do well to picture your typical reader as someone lying in a hammock on a soft summer day, with children playing loudly near by, a television set and a radio both going at once, a sound truck blaring past in the street, birds singing and dogs barking; this fellow has a cool drink and a pillow for his head, and all you have to do with your story is catch his attention and hold it. Remember, your story is an uneasy bargain with your reader. Your end of the bargain is to play fair, and keep him interested, his end of the bargain is to keep reading. It is just terribly terribly easy to put a story down half-read and go off and do something else. Nevertheless, for as long as the story does go on you are the boss. You have the right to assume that the reader will accept the story on your own terms. You have the right to assume that the reader, however lazy, will exert some small intelligence while he is reading. Suppose you are writing a story about a castle. You do not need to describe every tower, every man at arms, every stone; your reader must bring his own complement of men at arms and towers; you need only describe one gardener to imply that the castle is well stocked with servants. In your stories, then, set your own landscape with its own horizons, put your characters in where you think they belong, and move them as you please.

Your story must have a surface tension, which can be considerably stretched but not shattered; you cannot break your story into pieces with jagged odds and ends that do not belong. You cannot begin a story in one time and place, say, and then intrude a major flashback or a little sermon or a shift in emphasis to another scene or another character, without seriously marring the story, and turning the reader dizzy with trying to keep up. Consider simple movement from one place to another; if some movement is necessary and inevitable—as of course it is in most stories—then let the reader come along with you; do not jolt him abruptly from one place to another; in other words, let your story move as naturally and easily as possible, without side trips into unnecessary spots of beauty. Suppose you are writing a story about a boy and a girl meeting on a corner; your reader wants to go to that very corner and listen in; if, instead, you start your boy and girl toward the corner and then go off into a long description of the streetcar tracks and a little discussion of the background of these two characters and perhaps a paragraph or so about the town improvement which is going to remove the streetcar tracks they are crossing, and the girl's father's long-time aversion to any form of wheeled traffic—you will lose your reader and your story will fall apart. Always, always, make the duller parts of your story work *for* you; the necessary passage of time, the necessary movement must not stop the story dead, but must push it forward.

Avoid small graceless movements. As much as possible free yourself from useless and clumsy statements about action. "They got in the car and drove home" is surely too much ground to cover in one short simple sentence; assuming that your characters did get into the car and did have to drive home, you have just the same wasted a point where your action might work for your story; let the process of their getting home be an unobtrusive factor in another, more important action: "On their way home in the car they saw that the boy and the girl were still standing talking earnestly on the corner." Let each such potentially awkward spot contribute to your total action. In almost every story you will face some unwanted element, something your characters *have* to do to keep the story going at all; people have to get from one place to another, or get dressed, or eat their dinners, before the story can continue; try always to make these actions positive. For instance: "She dealt the cards; her fingers clung to each card as though unwilling to let go of anything they had once touched," or, "During all of dinner the singing went on upstairs, and no one said a word." (I would like to see someone write that story.) Or, "It was only one block to walk, so she counted her footsteps anxiously." Does your unfortunate heroine have to do the dishes before she can go out and meet her hero in the rose garden? "She washed and dried the dishes with extreme care, wondering all the time if she dared to smash a cup against the wall."

All of this has applied to necessary but essentially uninteresting action. The same thing is true of description and some conversation; certainly in every story there comes a time when you have to give in and let your reader know what something looks like, or that your hero and heroine said good-morning-how-are-you-today-isn't-the-weather-lovely-how's-your-mother before they got on to the most important business of the story, or to the rose garden. Try to remember with description that you must never just let it lie there; nothing in your story should ever be static unless you have a very good reason indeed for keeping your reader still; the essence of the story is motion. Do not let your chair be "a straight chair, with no arms and a hard wooden seat." Let your heroine go over and take a firm hold of the back of a straight wooden chair, because at the moment it is stronger than she. Naturally it is assumed that you are not going to try to describe anything you don't need to describe. If it is a sunny day let the sun make a pattern through the fence rail; if you don't care what the weather is don't bother your reader with it. Inanimate objects are best described in use or motion: "Because his cigarette lighter was platinum he had taken to smoking far too much." "The battered chimney seemed eager to hurl down bricks on anyone passing." Also, if your heroine's hair is golden, call it yellow.

Conversation is clearly one of the most difficult parts of the story. It is not enough to let your characters talk as people usually talk because the way people usually talk is extremely dull. Your characters are not going to stammer, or fumble for words, or forget what they are saying, or stop to clear their throats, at least not unless you want them to. Your problem is to make your characters sound as though they were real people talking (or, more accurately, that this is "real" conversation being read by a reader; look at some written conversation that seems perfectly smooth and plausible and natural on the page, and then try reading it aloud; what looks right on the page frequently sounds very literary indeed when read aloud; remember that you are writing to be read silently). Now the sounds and cadences of spoken speech are perfectly familiar to you; you have been talking and listening all your life. You know, for instance that most people speak in short sentences, tending to overuse certain words. You know that whenever anyone gets the floor and a chance to tell a story or describe an incident he will almost always speak in a series of short sentences joined by "and"; this is of course a device to insure that his audience will have no chance to break in before he has finished his story. You know that in a conversation people do say the same things over and over; there is very little economy in spoken speech. There is a great deal of economy in written speech. Your characters will use short sentences, and will tell long stories only under exceptional circumstances, and even then only in the most carefully stylized and rhythmic language; nothing can dissolve a short story quite so effectively as some bore who takes up the middle of it with a long account of something that amuses him and no one else. A bore is a bore, on the page or off it.

Listen always to people talking. Listen to patterns of talking. Listen to patterns of thinking displayed in talking. Think about this: if a husband comes home at night and says to his wife, "What do you think happened to me? When I got onto the bus tonight I sat down next to a girl and when the conductor came along he had a live penguin riding on his head, a live penguin, can you imagine? And when I looked at it, it turned out it was a talking penguin and it said 'Tickets, please,' and there was this guy across the aisle and you really won't believe this but it turned out *he* had a parrot in his pocket and the parrot put out his head and he and the penguin got to talking and I never heard anything like it in my life," don't you know that after the husband has said all this his wife is going to say, "What did the girl look like?" Your characters will make their remarks only once unless there is a good reason for repeating them; people hear better in stories than in real life. Your characters will start all their conversations in the middle unless you have a very good reason for their telling each other good morning and how are you. Remember the importance of the pattern, as important on paper as in real life; a character who says habitually, with one of those silly little laughs, "Well, that's the story of my life," is not ever going to turn around and say, with a silly little laugh, "Well, that's my life story."

Now look at this device: "'I hate fresh asparagus,' she said to her kitchen clock, and found herself saying it again ten minutes later to Mrs. Butler in the grocery; 'I hate fresh asparagus,' she said, 'it always takes so long to cook.'" You are, at this moment, well into a conversation with Mrs. Butler; your reader, being a common-sense type, no doubt assumes that before the remark about asparagus your heroine and Mrs. Butler said good morning my aren't you out early and isn't that a charming hat. Your reader may also assume, if he is perceptive, that your heroine in some fashion turned away from her kitchen clock, got her hat and coat on, picked up her pocketbook, forgot her shopping list, and in some fashion either walked or drove or bicycled to the store. She is there, she is in the middle of a conversation with Mrs. Butler; not ten words ago she was at home talking to the clock. The transition has been relatively painless; your reader has been required to read only one sentence and get around one semicolon, and the asparagus remark has been repeated simply to tie together the two halves of the sentence.

Your characters in the story, surely, are going to be separate and widely differing people, even though they are not necessarily described to the reader. You yourself have some idea of what they are like and how they differ; there is, for instance, in almost everyone's mind, an essential difference between the hero and the heroine. They don't look alike, even if you are the only one who knows it; your reader will assume it; after all, he has seen people before. They don't dress alike, they don't sound alike. They have small individualities of speech, arising naturally out of their actions and their personalities and their work in the story. Suppose you are using three little girls talking together; you *could* distinguish them by saying that one wore a blue dress, the second had curly hair, and the third was on roller skates, but wouldn't it be simply better writing to identify them by their positions in the group of three; that is, making their actions and their conversations more meaningful because the girls are related to one another at once? They form a hierarchy: first there is a leader who does most of the talking, makes the plans, and provokes the action. The second must be subordinate, but not too much so; she does not initiate, but by following the leader encourages the leader into further action; she will disagree and perhaps even rebel up to a point. The third is of course the tagalong, the one left out when three is a crowd, and her actions and conversation are echoing and imitative of the other two, particularly the leader. The third character will throw her support to whichever of the other two seems stronger at the moment, and can thus, although a very minor character indeed, bring force to bear and influence action. Once three such characters are determined, the entire course of their conversation, no matter how trivial it might be in the story, is predetermined and strong. Once again: people in stories tend to talk in patterns. If your heroine is prepared to be so violent about fresh asparagus it would be reasonable to suppose that her conversation and opinions would generally be a little more emphatic than another character's. She would "adore that silly hat," for instance, or "die if that noise doesn't stop." She will carry out this positive manner in her actions; she will put out a cigarette, for instance, with forceful little poundings, she will set the table carelessly and noisily, but quickly, there will be no nonsense about her likes and dislikes. You might oppose to her a character who is uncertain, who lets cigarettes burn out in the ash tray, who rarely finishes a sentence or who will substitute a phrase like *"you* know" for a finished thought: "I usually carry an umbrella but sometimes . . . *you* know." "I guess it's time I left. I guess you're pretty busy?" Your character, remember, must not talk one way and act another, and can only outrage this consistency for a reason; a character who breaks out of a pattern is shocking and generally insane.

Use all your seasoning sparingly. Do not worry about making your characters shout, intone, exclaim, remark, shriek, reason, holler, or any such thing, unless they are doing it for a reason. All remarks can be *said*. Every time you use a fancy word your reader is going to turn his head to look at it going by and sometimes he may not turn his head back again. My own name for this kind of overexcited talking is the-other-responded. As in this example: " 'Then I'm for a swim,' " cried Jack, a gallant flush mantling his cheek. " 'And I am with you!' the other responded."

Your coloring words, particularly adjectives and adverbs, must be used where they will do the most good. Not every action needs a qualifying adverb, not every object needs a qualifying adjective. Your reader probably has a perfectly serviceable mental picture of a lion; when a lion comes into your story you need not burden him with adjectives unless it is necessary, for instance, to point out that he is a green lion, something of which your reader might not have a very vivid mental picture.

Use all the tools at your disposal. The language is infinitely flexible, and your use of it should be completely deliberate. Never forget the grotesque effect of the absolutely wrong words: "He swept her into his arms; 'I will always love you,' he giggled." "Top the finished cake with a smear of whipped cream." "'I am not afraid of anything in the world,' he said thinly."

Remember, too, that words on a page have several dimensions: they are seen, they are partially heard, particularly if they seem to suggest a sound, and they have a kind of tangible quality—think of the depressing sight of a whole great paragraph ahead of you, solidly black with huge heavy-sounding words. Moreover, some words seem soft and some hard, some liquid, some warm, some cold; your reader will respond to "soft laughter" but not to "striped laughter"; he will respond more readily to "soft laughter" than to "sweet laughter," because he can hear it more easily. There are also words like "itchy" and "greasy" and "smelly" and "scratchy" that evoke an almost physical response in the reader; use these only if you need them. Exclamation points, italics, capitals, and, most particularly, dialect, should all be used with extreme caution. Consider them as like garlic, and use them accordingly.

Do not try to puzzle your reader unnecessarily; a puzzled reader is an antagonistic reader. Do not expect him to guess why a character does something or how it happens that some remark is made; it may be that you want him to stop and wonder for a minute; if so, make it perfectly clear that everything is going to be all right later on. If you want the reader to be troubled by a nagging question, and go through a part of your story with a kind of expectancy, let one of your characters do something outrageous—turn, perhaps, and throw an apple core through an open window. But then be sure that before your story is finished you explain in some manner that inside the open window lives the character's great-uncle, who keeps a monkey who devours apple cores and catches them on the fly as they come through the window. The reader brings with him a great body of knowledge which you may assume, but he must rely on you for all information necessary to the understanding of this story which, after all, you have written.

Someone—I forget who—once referred to the easier sections of his work as "benches for the reader to sit down upon," meaning, of course, that the poor reader who had struggled through the complex maze of ideas for several pages could rest gratefully at last on a simple clear paragraph. Provide *your* reader with such assistance. If you would like him to rest for a minute so you can sneak up behind him and sandbag him, let him have a little peaceful description, or perhaps a little something funny to smile over, or a little moment of superiority. If you want him to stop dead and think, do something that will make him stop dead; use a wholly inappropriate word, or a startling phrase—"pretty as a skunk"—or an odd juxtaposition: "Her hair was curly and red and she had great big feet," or something that will make him think back: "Fresh asparagus is most significant symbolically." Give him something to worry about: "Although the bank had stood on that corner for fifty years it had never been robbed." Or something to figure out: "If John had not had all that tooth trouble there would never have been any question about the rabbits." In all this, though, don't let the reader stop for more than a second or he might get away. Catch him fast with your next sentence and send him reeling along.

And if you want your reader to go faster and faster make your writing go faster and faster. "The room was dark. The windows were shaded, the furniture invisible. The door was shut and yet from somewhere, some small hidden precious casket of light buried deep in the darkness of the room, a spark came, moving in mad colored circles up and down, around and in and out and over and under and lighting everything it saw." (Those adjectives are unspeakable in every sense of the word, and wholly unnecessary; this is an example, not a model.) If you want your reader to go slower and slower make your writing go slower and slower: "After a wild rush of water and noise the fountain was at last turned off and the water was gone. Only one drop hung poised and then fell, and fell with a small musical touch. Now, it rang. Now."

Now I want to say something about words artificially weighted; you can, and frequently must, make a word carry several meanings or messages in your story if you use the word right. This is a kind of shorthand. I once had occasion to send a heroine on a long journey during which she expressed her loneliness and lack of a home by imagining dream lives in various places she passed; this daydream is climaxed when at lunch she hears a little girl at a nearby table ask for her milk in a cup of stars; the lonely girl thinks that what she too is asking for is a cup of stars, and when she finally finds her home she will drink from a cup of stars. Later, when other characters are talking of their own comfort and security the lonely girl announces proudly that *she* has a cup of stars; this is by then not only recognizable as an outright lie, but a pathetic attempt to pretend that she is neither lonely nor defenseless. "Cup of stars" has become a shorthand phrase for all her daydreams. Notice, however, that once such a word or phrase has been given a weighting you cannot afford to use the word or phrase *without* the weighting; my lonely girl cannot refer idly to cups of stars anywhere else, because those words are carrying an extra meaning which must not be dissipated.

If you announce early in your story that your lady with the aversion to asparagus is wearing a diamond-and-ruby wrist watch your reader will be intrigued: here is a detail apparently not essential to the story and yet you thought it worthwhile to put it in; the reader will be watching to see what you are going to do with it. If you then turn up another character who is wearing a solid-gold wrist watch your reader will begin to wonder whether you are just queer for watches or whether this is going to amount to something in the story. You must satisfy his curiosity. If you then remark that the diamond-and-ruby wrist watch was a gift from an old boy friend of the lady's, the watch is then carrying something extra, and when at the end of the story she throws the watch at her husband's head she is throwing her old boy friend too. The reader is also going to have to know who gave the other fellow the solid-gold wrist watch and whose head *that* one is going to hit; nothing can be left suspended in mid-air, abandoned. If you start your story on a small boy going home to pick up his football so he can get into the game in the corner lot, and then let him fall into one adventure after another until the end of the story, your reader is going to come out of that story fighting mad unless he is told whether or not the boy got his football and whether he ever got back to the game.

Now about this business of the beginning implying the ending, something which all the textbooks insist upon. You will actually find that if you keep your story tight, with no swerving from the proper path, it will curl up quite naturally at the end, provided you stop when you have finished what you have to say. One device, of course, is beginning and ending on what is essentially the same image, so that a story beginning, say, "It was a beautiful sunny day," might end, "The sun continued to beat down on the empty street." This is not a bad policy, although it can be limiting. There is no question but that the taut stretched quality of the good short story is pulled even tighter by such a construction. You can tie your story together, however, with similar devices—how about a story which opens on a lady feeding her cat, and ends on a family sitting down to dinner? Or a story which opens on your heroine crying and closes on her laughing? The beginning and ending should of course belong together; the ending must be implicit in the beginning, although there have been stories which were defeated because the author thought of a wonderful last line and then tried to write a story to go with it; this is not wrong, just almost impossible. I am not going to try to tell you how to set up a plot. Just remember that primarily, in the story and out of it, you are living in a world of people. A story must have characters in it; work with concrete rather than abstract nouns, and always dress your ideas immediately. Suppose you want to write a story about what you might vaguely think of as "magic." You will be hopelessly lost, wandering around formlessly in notions of magic and incantations; you will never make any forward progress at all until you turn your idea, "magic," into a person, someone who wants to do or make or change or act in some way. Once you have your first character you will of course need another to put into opposition, a person in some sense "anti-magic"; when both are working at their separate intentions, dragging in other characters as needed, you are well into your story. All you have to do then is write it, paying attention, please, to grammar and punctuation.

James Joyce

Araby

North Richmond Street, being blind, was a quiet street except at the hour when the Christian Brothers' School set the boys free. An uninhabited house of two storeys stood at the blind end, detached from its neighbours in a square ground. The other houses of the street, conscious of decent lives within them, gazed at one another with brown imperturbable faces.

The former tenant of our house, a priest, had died in the back drawing-room. Air, musty from having been long enclosed, hung in all the rooms, and the waste room behind the kitchen was littered with old useless papers. Among these I found a few paper-covered books, the pages of which were curled and damp: *The Abbot*, by Walter Scott, *The Devout Communicant* and *The Memoirs of Vidocq*. I liked the last best because its leaves were yellow. The wild garden behind the house contained a central apple-tree and a few straggling bushes under one of which I found the late tenant's rusty bicycle-pump. He had been a very charitable priest; in his will he had left all his money to institutions and the furniture of his house to his sister.

When the short days of winter came dusk fell before we had well eaten our dinners. When we met in the street the houses had grown sombre. The space of sky above us was the colour of ever-changing violet and towards it the lamps of the street lifted their feeble lanterns. The cold air stung us and we played till our bodies glowed. Our shouts echoed in the silent street. The career of our play brought us through the dark muddy lanes behind the houses where we ran the gauntlet of the rough tribes from the cottages, to the back doors of the dark dripping gardens where odours arose from the ashpits, to the dark odorous stables where a coachman smoothed and combed the horse or shook music from the buckled harness. When we returned to the street light from the kitchen windows had filled the areas. If my uncle was seen turning the corner we hid in the shadow until we had seen him safely housed. Or if Mangan's sister came out on the doorstep to call her brother in to his tea we watched her from our shadow peer up and down the street. We waited to see whether she would remain or go in and, if she remained, we left our shadow and walked up to Mangan's steps resignedly. She was waiting for us, her figure defined by the light from the half-opened door. Her brother always teased her before he obeyed and I stood by the railings looking at her. Her dress swung as she moved her body and the soft rope of her hair tossed from side to side.

Every morning I lay on the floor in the front parlour watching her door. The blind was pulled down to within an inch of the sash so that I could not be seen. When she came out on the doorstep my heart leaped. I ran to the hall, seized my books and followed her. I kept her brown figure always in my eye and, when we came near the point at which our ways diverged, I quickened my pace and passed her. This happened morning after morning. I had never spoken to her, except for a few casual words, and yet her name was like a summons to all my foolish blood.

Her image accompanied me even in places the most hostile to romance. On Saturday evenings when my aunt went marketing I had to go to carry some of the parcels. We walked through the flaring streets, jostled by drunken men and bargaining women, amid the curses of labourers, the shrill litanies of shop-boys who stood on guard by the barrels of pigs' cheeks, the nasal chanting of street-singers, who sang a *come-all-you* about O'Donovan Rossa, or a ballad about the troubles in our native land. These noises converged in a single sensation of life for me: I imagined that I bore my chalice safely through a throng of foes. Her name sprang to my lips at moments in strange prayers and praises which I myself did not understand. My eyes were often full of tears (I could not tell why) and at times a flood from my heart seemed to pour itself out into my bosom. I thought little of the future. I did not know whether I would ever speak to her or not or, if I spoke to her, how I could tell her of my confused adoration. But my body was like a harp and her words and gestures were like fingers running upon the wires.

One evening I went into the back drawing-room in which the priest had died. It was a dark rainy evening and there was no sound in the house. Through one of the broken panes I heard the rain impinge upon the earth, the fine incessant needles of water playing in the sodden beds. Some distant lamp or lighted window gleamed below me. I was thankful that I could see so little. All my senses seemed to desire to veil themselves and, feeling that I was about to slip from them, I pressed the palms of my hands together until they trembled, murmuring: "*O love! O love!*" many times.

At last she spoke to me. When she addressed the first words to me I was so confused that I did not know what to answer. She asked me was I going to *Araby*. I forgot whether I answered yes or no. It would be a splendid bazaar, she said she would love to go.

"And why can't you ?" I asked.

While she spoke she turned a silver bracelet round and round her wrist. She could not go, she said, because there would be a retreat that week in her convent. Her brother and two other boys were fighting for their caps and I was alone at the railings. She held one of the spikes, bowing her head towards me. The light from the lamp opposite our door caught the white curve of her neck, lit up her hair that rested there and, falling, lit up the hand upon the railing. It fell over one side of her dress and caught the white border of a petticoat, just visible as she stood at ease.

"It's well for you," she said.

"If I go," I said, "I will bring you something."

What innumerable follies laid waste my waking and sleeping thoughts after that evening! I wished to annihilate the tedious intervening days. I chafed against the work of school. At night in my bedroom and by day in the classroom her image came between me and the page I strove to read. The syllables of the word *Araby* were called to me through the silence in which my soul luxuriated and cast an Eastern enchantment over me. I asked for leave to go to the bazaar on Saturday night. My aunt was surprised and hoped it was not some Freemason affair. I answered few questions in class. I watched my master's face pass from amiability to sternness; he hoped I was not beginning to idle. I could not call my wandering thoughts together. I had hardly any patience with the serious work of life which, now that it stood between me and my desire, seemed to me child's play, ugly monotonous child's play.

On Saturday morning I reminded my uncle that I wished to go to the bazaar in the evening. He was fussing at the hallstand, looking for the hatbrush, and answered me curtly:

"Yes, boy, I know."

As he was in the hall I could not go into the front parlour and lie at the window. I left the house in bad humour and walked slowly towards the school. The air was pitilessly raw and already my heart misgave me.

When I came home to dinner my uncle had not yet been home. Still it was early. I sat staring at the clock for some time and, when its ticking began to irritate me, I left the room. I mounted the staircase and gained the upper part of the house. The high cold empty gloomy rooms liberated me and I went from room to room singing. From the front window I saw my companions playing below in the street. Their cries reached me weakened and indistinct and, leaning my forehead against the cool glass, I looked over at the dark house where she lived. I may have stood there for an hour, seeing nothing but the brown-clad figure cast by my imagination, touched discreetly by the lamplight at the curved neck, at the hand upon the railings and at the border below the dress.

When I came downstairs again I found Mrs. Mercer sitting at the fire. She was an old garrulous woman, a pawnbroker's widow, who collected used stamps for some pious purpose. I had to endure the gossip of the tea-table. The meal was prolonged beyond an hour and still my uncle did not come. Mrs. Mercer stood up to go: she was sorry she couldn't wait any longer, but it was after eight o'clock and she did not like to be out late, as the night air was bad for her. When she had gone I began to walk up and down the room, clenching my fists. My aunt said:

"I'm afraid you may put off your bazaar for this night of Our Lord."

At nine o'clock I heard my uncle's latchkey in the halldoor. I heard him talking to himself and heard the hallstand rocking when it had received the weight of his overcoat. I could interpret these signs. When he was midway through his dinner I asked him to give me the money to go to the bazaar. He had forgotten.

"The people are in bed and after their first sleep now," he said.

I did not smile. My aunt said to him energetically:

"Can't you give him the money and let him go? You've kept him late enough as it is."

My uncle said he was very sorry he had forgotten. He said he believed in the old saying: "All work and no play makes Jack a dull boy." He asked me where I was going and, when I had told him a second time he asked me did I know *The Arab's Farewell to his Steed*. When I left the kitchen he was about to recite the opening lines of the piece to my aunt.

I held a florin tightly in my hand as I strode down Buckingham Street towards the station. The sight of the streets thronged with buyers and glaring with gas recalled to me the purpose of my journey. I took my seat in a third-class carriage of a deserted train. After an intolerable delay the train moved out of the station slowly. It crept onward among ruinous houses and over the twinkling river. At Westland Row Station a crowd of people pressed to the carriage doors; but the porters moved them back, saying that it was a special train for the bazaar. I remained alone in the bare carriage. In a few minutes the train drew up beside an improvised wooden platform. I passed out on to the road and saw by the lighted dial of a clock that it was ten minutes to ten. In front of me was a large building which displayed the magical name.

I could not find any sixpenny entrance and, fearing that the bazaar would be closed, I passed in quickly through a turnstile, handing a shilling to a weary-looking man. I found myself in a big hall girdled at half its height by a gallery. Nearly all the stalls were closed and the greater part of the hall was in darkness. I recognised a silence like that which pervades a church after a service. I walked into the centre of the bazaar timidly. A few people were gathered about the stalls which were still open. Before a curtain, over which the words *Café Chantant* were written in coloured lamps, two men were counting money on a salver. I listened to the fall of the coins.

Remembering with difficulty why I had come I went over to one of the stalls and examined porcelain vases and flowered tea-sets. At the door of the stall a young lady was talking and laughing with two young gentlemen. I remarked their English accents and listened vaguely to their conversation.

"O, I never said such a thing!"

"O, but you did!"

"O, but I didn't!"

"Didn't she say that?"

"Yes, I heard her."

"O, there's a . . . fib!"

Observing me the young lady came over and asked me did I wish to buy anything. The tone of her voice was not encouraging; she seemed to have spoken to me out of a sense of duty. I looked humbly at the great jars that stood like eastern guards at either side of the dark entrance to the stall and murmured:

"No, thank you."

The young lady changed the position of one of the vases and went back to the two young men. They began to talk of the same subject. Once or twice the young lady glanced at me over her shoulder.

I lingered before her stall, though I knew my stay was useless, to make my interest in her wares seem the more real. Then I turned away slowly and walked down the middle of the bazaar. I allowed the two pennies to fall against the sixpence in my pocket. I heard a voice call from one end of the gallery that the light was out. The upper part of the hall was now completely dark.

Gazing up into the darkness I saw myself as a creature driven and derided by vanity; and my eyes burned with anguish and anger.

Commentary: Jerome Mandel, "Medieval Romance and the Structure of 'Araby'"

In "Araby" the medieval and romance imagery of chalice, chapel, church, and the Virgin Mary has long been noted, but only recently has John Freimarck in "'Araby': A Quest for Meaning" suggested that the story "raises echoes of the Grail Quest story-pattern" because "several actions and images . . . [are] common to basic versions of the Quest." Professor Freimarck is more concerned with these echoes and images than he is with structure. It is my belief that "Araby" is constructed with rigorous precision upon a paradigm of medieval romance, that the unnamed boy reflects in detail and in general the action and behavior of smitten courtly lovers, and that the story as a whole shows Joyce working with the well-defined structure of a traditional genre, the medieval romance. Such a paradigm would include the following: 1) the *enfance* (which defines the hero's youth before his coming to manhood or knighthood), 2) the introduction of the lady, 3) the commitment to a quest, 4) the quest.

The first three paragraphs of "Araby" define the hero's *enfance*, a matter of location as well as upbringing. It has long been noted that the details of these three introductory paragraphs—the blind and quiet street, being set free from the Christian Brothers School, the waste room, books, useless papers, wild garden, central apple tree, rusty bicycle pump, charitable priest, and so on—with greater or less symbolic value and irony establish the terms in which we understand the youth of the boy as hero by defining the world in which he lives. The youthful games are the practice wars of knighthood in which one runs the "gantlet" and fights against the "rough tribes from the cottages" in "darky muddy lanes" or kitchen-lit streets, where the adversaries are an uncle and an older sister and perhaps a coachman.

The *enfance* ends with the introduction of the heroine. As a romance heroine she must be above the knight in station, and she must be taboo. Mangan's sister is both older and the sister of a friend. Publicly she is an "enemy" (they hide from her); but as the object of the boy's private adoration, she is also an "enemy" in the courtly love sense: one who makes the lover's life unquiet. His position is that of Lancelot and Tristan who must maintain public distance from the one they most adore. To be sure, the boy's attitude reflects the conventions of pubescent boys in dealing with girls, but that same attitude also reflects the conventions of medieval romance.

The boy's response is precisely that of the courtly lover whose characteristic action is to look, to adore from a distance. Since he honors her above all women, he cannot take her name in jest: "Her brother always teased her before he obeyed and I stood by the railings looking at her." What some have called his voyeurism, his peeping beneath the blinds, reflects both the lover's desire to protect his beloved and the emotional imperative which insists the courtly knight long always for sight of his lady. In the mornings he watches for and follows her, at once protective and prepared to do her bidding. The regularity of his performance ("This happened morning after morning") affirms his absolute devotion which must remain thankless and publicly unrecognized. In medieval romance the lover almost never addresses his lady ("I had never spoken to her except for a few casual words") but he indicates his total commitment to her by his acts of devotion and by growing weak or blanching or flushing in her presence. For the boy in "Araby" "her name was like a summons to all my foolish blood" and "when she came out on the doorstep my heart leaped." The reduction of noble knight to tonguetied, blushing courtly lover is epitomized elsewhere by the boy in the phrase "my confused adoration."

The next two paragraphs—beginning "Her image accompanied me even in places the most hostile to romance" and ending with his "murmuring: *O love! O love!* many times" —have long been examined for images from romance and need not be recapitulated here. As the boy continues to perform his public duties in the world (to win worship: "I had . . . to carry some of the parcels") he retains the attitude and response of the courtly lover. As a lover totally possessed by love, he moves out of time, and all worldly, public, and temporal considerations pass from him: "I thought little of the future." He is swept by strange emotions—"My eyes were often full of tears (I could not tell why)"—and rendered inarticulate. When all his "senses seem to desire to veil themselves" and he trembles in adoration, he exhibits the proper response of a courtly lover committed to love.

In the passage that establishes and defines the quest (and which ends with the lover's commitment: "I will bring you something"—), the lady speaks first in her double role as the object of the lover's adoration and the lady for whose sake the adventure is to be undertaken. "At last she spoke to me"—the lady at last recognizes the miserable, worshipful knight who has adored her from a distance without hope of success but with unrelenting devotion. He responds as do all courtly lovers when they first come to the attention of the beloved: he is "so confused that I did not know what to answer." When she asks if he is going to *Araby*, "I forget whether I answered yes or no." Her wish, "she would love to go," is his command: he must take upon himself the fulfillment of an adventure to which he has been called by love—one she herself is prevented from accomplishing.

Medieval knights generally complete the quest successfully. Only the quest for the Grail produces widespread failure, shows the knights their own limitations and lack of purity, leads to general disaffection, and destroys a brilliant civilization. In "Araby" Joyce conflates these two traditions, that of the successful and that of the unsuccessful quest. It is important to "Araby," to *Dubliners*, and to Joyce that the quest dissolve in a double failure: 1) a failure in the world: what had been "a splendid bazaar" and "Eastern enchantment" in the imagination is tawdry in this world—a hollow hall, dark and silent except for the fall of coin on a salver and the flirtatious (pre-sexual?) play of "a young lady" and her "two young gentlemen" at the door of a stall; and 2) a failure of will: the boy's paralysis shows him caught in a sequence of events in which he is unable to fill his part.

But only in a special sense has the quest been unsuccessful: he expected to buy a trinket for a girl and he failed. In quite another sense—and one more important to Joyce—the quest is successful since it leads to vision and epiphany: coming to some understanding of oneself "as a creature driven and derided by vanity." In slightly different terms, this is the understanding of himself Gawain achieves at the end of *Sir Gawain and the Green Knight*: he realizes that he thought himself better than he was. In Malory, Lancelot comes to a similar understanding when he discovers that precisely what made him the greatest knight in the world—his strength and his brilliant love for Guenivere—renders him imperfect and impure, unable to achieve the Grail. But something of value derives from failure, some painful human truth. We discover, like Gawain, that we are not so good as we thought ourselves to be; or, like Lancelot, that we are not so perfect and pure. We are not so brave or just or wise or compassionate. To be alive, to be human, is to be less than what we think we are. It is not that the Arabys for which we search are tawdry but that we ourselves are less than the Arabys we imagine. The boy discovers not that *Araby* is worldly and impure but that he is. His vision is not about the world but about himself—and us. The boy's anguish at the end derives from his realization about mankind; his anger is with himself that he should be only human after all, that he should allow himself to be the victim of his own vanity.

I have spoken throughout as though the structure of "Araby" were created by Joyce. But if we understand the narrator to be the boy grown older, telling a story about himself from a position of maturity and distance which allows him to treat his youthful infatuation with wit, then the relation between the events of the story and the structure of medieval romance takes on slightly different meaning. The romance structure becomes the means by which the narrator laughs at himself. The older narrator teases himself by ordering events according to a paradigm of medieval romance he as a boy may not have been clearly aware of. But the act of imposing form on experience necessarily establishes distance between narrator (as the one who imposes form) and event. The romance structure becomes part of the narrator's ironic dramatization of himself as a figure out of stories about knights and ladies. Or, if the narrator is the boy himself, then his adolescent self-dramatization is in terms of the material of medieval romance and equally amusing. Either way—whether the narrator is mature or adolescent—the vanity of which he finds himself a victim derives from presenting himself as a character in medieval romance.

Commentary: James Sonoski, "Analyzing 'Araby' as Story and Discourse"

Narrative Voice:

> When we speak of "expression," we pass . . . to the province of narrative voice, the medium through which perception, conception, and everything else are communicated. Thus point of view is *in* in the story . . ., but voice is always outside, in the discourse. From *A Portrait of the Artist as a Young Man*: "A few moments [later] he found himself on the stage amid the garish gas and the dim scenery." The perceptual point of view is Stephen's, but the voice is the narrator's. Character's perceptions need not be articulated—Stephen is not saying to himself the *words* "garish gas and dim scenery"; the words are the narrator's. This is a narrator's report.

We can make the same analysis of many of the sentences in "Araby." For example, of the sentence: ". . . her name was like a summons to all my foolish blood" or the sentence, "Gazing up into the darkness I saw myself as a creature driven and derided by vanity; and my eyes burned with anguish and anger." We can say that "the perceptual point of view is [the boy's], but the voice is the narrator's." The boy is not saying to himself the *words*: "foolish blood" and "driven and derided"; the words are the narrator's. The narrator's voice is often quite audible in "Araby." We hear him in phrases like: "conscious of decent lives within them" (3), "most hostile to romance" (30), "like fingers running upon the wires," (38), and many others.

Point of view: If we can say that in "Araby" the perceptual point of view is the boy's though the voice is the narrator's, then we also have to say that the perceptual point of view is limited to the boy since the narrator is looking back at his own earlier perceptions. According to Chatman, "looking back" is a conception, no longer a perception. Our analysis reveals that "Araby" is structured, in part, by the continuous contrast in the narration between the narrator's retrospective conceptual point of view and the boy's perceptual point of view usually presupposed. Procedurally, we identified the boy's perceptual point of view only in statements that presuppose the boy perceived or could have perceived an actual physical situation in the world of the fiction. Once the narrator's voice and perspective were identified, we experienced little difficulty in assigning "perceptions" to the boy. Though in some statements the boy's perception is almost completely expressed in the narrator's diction, it remains clear that it is the boy's perception which is reported. For example, it is without doubt that the boy did see Mangan's sister at the railing, even though the words used to describe her are those of the older narrator. In other statements the boy's conceptual point of view seems to be presupposed. These were often difficult to analyze. In a sentence such as, "Her name was like a summons to all my foolish blood" (29), we are given a conceptualization of the boy's experience from the narrator's point of view. Since the sentence at issue does not imply a perception on the part of the boy, should we presuppose that (*a*) the boy understood and conceived of his experience as a "summons" even if he might have chosen a different expression to signify it, and/or (*b*) he also conceived of his experience as "foolish"? In general we assumed a "common sense" attitude in identifying the boy's conceptual point of view. This is an important consideration, however. In many sentences, it seemed to us that the boy would not have conceived of his experience in the terms the narrator selects. Accordingly, we construed these statements as retrospective conceptual points of view that do *not* reflect what the boy was "thinking" at the time. The most important sentence in the category, "the boy's conceptual point of view," is the last sentence of the text. It seemed to us that the boy's conceptual point of view which the sentence presupposes must modify any irony we might hear in the narrator's voice. If the narrator, despite his diction, is reporting an event in the boy's life, then, despite the ironic tone of the phrase he uses, its semantic range forces us to presuppose that the boy understood himself ("saw himself") ironically. It is therefore important to distinguish this sentence from others which seem to presuppose some understanding on the part of the boy. In the last sentence of the text, the narrator directly attributes understanding to the boy at a specific point of time in the story. In sentences like "Her name was like a summons to all my foolish blood" (29) there is no such direct attribution. In this instance we are not constrained to presuppose that the boy has any understanding of his experience at the point of time in the story to which the sentence refers. But in the final sentence the narrator attributes understanding to the boy; according to Chatman, therefore, we are not free to presuppose otherwise. Whatever we presuppose the boy understood must necessarily come within the semantic range of the phrase, "a creature driven and derided by vanity." It is not enough to presuppose only that the boy understood that he had been vain. Rather we have to presuppose that he understood not simply that he had been vain, but also that he couldn't help being unreflectively naive, and therefore, that he couldn't help being mocked by another side of himself. The conceptual force of *"derided by* vanity" presupposes self-reflection, whereas *"driven by* vanity" presupposes its absence. Hence, the combined phrases imply that the boy "saw himself" from two perspectives, one of which is an ironic comment on the other. Notice that in the phrase, "driven by vanity," the word "vanity" retains its usual lexical meaning; whereas in the phrase, "derided by vanity," it is personified and thus becomes a synecdoche for the boy.

It has always been difficult to analyze ironic patterns in Joyce's texts. Why do we, for example, tend to keep ourselves as readers simultaneously at an ironic distance from Stephen and in sympathy with him in *A Portrait*? In "Araby" readers similarly situate themselves. Why is this such a common experience in Joyce's texts? Our analysis of narrative expression may shed some light on this difficult question.

Narrative expression: It is obvious to any reader that "Araby" is "overtly narrated." The first person pronoun dominates the narration. What a sentence by sentence analysis of the text yields, however, is a picture of the varying degrees to which the reader senses the presence of the adult narrator, the way in which the reader is manipulated by the narration.

The most common "narrative expressions" in the text are statements which contain first person pronouns, temporal summaries, and set descriptions, all overt narrative features of a discourse. If we designate this typical narrative expression the "NORM," then we can identify those statements that are "DEVIANT." Following this procedure, we can easily identify two kinds of deviations from the norm: (*a*) statements that do not contain overt narrative features and therefore diminish a reader's awareness of the narrator, and (*b*) statements that contain other overt narrative features, especially "philosophic generalizations" or "commentary," and therefore heighten a reader's awareness of the narrator. As we move from statement to statement, noting when the narrator's presence is either diminished or heightened, an interesting pattern emerges. "Araby" begins with the narrator's presence very much in the forefront of our awareness. However, when we first hear of the boy's uncle and Mangan's sister, the narration "drops down" to "the normal expression," lessening the reader's awareness of the narrator. In sequences 5, 6, 7, and the first part of 8, where we are given an account of the girl's impact on the boy from the narrator's point of view, the presence of the narrator is heightened significantly. Suddenly, the narration "drops down" all the way to "non-narrative" features, surely diminishing our sense of the narrator's presence and giving the reader the impression of an "unmediated" report of events. Since sequence 8 is the account of the conversation with the girl, we can see that the reader experiences a subtle contrast between the sense of being told by an older man what impact Mangan's sister had upon him as a boy and the sense of receiving a report of an actual conversation between the boy and Mangan's sister. The rest of the story is narrated in a relatively "normal" mode with three outstanding exceptions. Both of the boy's encounters with his uncle and his encounter with the "young lady" are "reported." Since the narrator has at his command three different ways of recounting conversations, it is interesting to notice which conversations he chooses to "non-narrate." For example, the narrator sometimes "summarizes" a conversation (see 64–67), the most overt form of "telling." At other times, conversations are narrated as such (see 87), a more "covert" narrative technique. At specific times the narrator chooses to report the "dialogue," a "non-narrative" mode, one in which the presence of the narrator is diminished. One might infer from the pattern of narrative expressions that, on the one hand, the reader is being given a set of events narrated emphatically from the narrator's point of view, and, on the other, a set of events, reported without any "interference" from the narrator, which the reader "interprets" independently. If so, the reader is given a "neutral" point of view, an "unbiased" vantage point from which he or she can judge, interpret, evaluate the boy's role in the events. From such a neutral vantage point, the narrator's judgments, interpretations, and evaluations seem somewhat too harsh. Hence, the reader, manipulated by the narration, learns to modify the narrator's point of view. If these inferences are warranted, they would then support our analyses of the structure of points of view and of the merging of the boy's character traits with those of the narrator.

Commentary: Steven Doloff, "Aspects of Milton's *Paradise Lost* in 'Araby'"

It has been argued that James Joyce drew heavily on John Milton's *Paradise Lost* in his structuring of *Ulysses* and that he also incorporated extensive references to this epic into *Finnegans Wake*. It may well be that Joyce used several other reflections of Milton's story of the Fall in an earlier work as well, "Araby," the *Dubliners* tale of a boy's disappointing excursion to a bazaar.

While it is the name of an actual traveling bazaar visited in 1894 by the young Joyce, "Araby" also appears in Book 4 of *Paradise Lost* and is associated with the Garden of Eden; Milton compares the sensual impact upon Satan of the newly created paradise on earth with the effect upon sailors of the scented breezes from the "spicie shoar/Of Arabie." Joyce's story similarly suggests a link between Araby and Eden. The boy's imagination focuses on exotic associations with the bazaar's name—"[t]he syllables of the word *Araby* were called to me through the silence in which my soul luxuriated and cast an Eastern enchantment over me"—and symbolic imagery in the story collaterally implies an Edenic motif to his romantically colored state of innocent egotism—"[t]he wild garden behind the house contained a central apple-tree."

Another *Paradise Lost* association may help to answer questions raised by some scholars concerning Joyce's word choice in the story's final sentence: "Gazing up into the darkness I saw myself as a creature driven and derided by vanity; and my eyes burned with anguish and anger." Harry Stone, for instance, notes: "'Driven and derided,' 'anguish and anger'—these reactions [by the boy] seem far too strong." Bernard Benstock writes, "[The boy's] self-accusation of vanity is something of an enigma." Some of these same descriptive terms chosen by Joyce for this sentence are used by the fallen angel Belial in *Paradise Lost*. In counseling Satan and the rest of the fallen host to accept defeat prudently, he depicts how they all must appear to the eye of God:

> for what can force or guile
> With him, or who deceive his mind, whose eye
> Views all things at one view? he from heav'ns highth
> All these our motions vain, sees and derides. (2.188–91)

Joyce's phrasing, "a creature driven and derided by vanity," taken as a possible echo of Belial's description of the fallen angels (humiliated creatures as well), might thus appear quite fitting.

Other parallels may additionally link the end of "Araby" to the defeated angels in *Paradise Lost*. The "big hall" of the bazaar, the upper part of which becomes "completely dark" accompanying the boy's crushing disillusionment, can be seen as corresponding to "the spacious Hall" of Satan's council (1.762) in the "darkness" (2.377) where Belial and the others convene. The darkness in the last sentence in which the boy "sees" himself so painfully may also recall the "darkness visible" of Milton's Hell, which "[s]erv'd only to discover sights of woe" (1.63–64).

Finally, Belial's speech to the fallen angels, if indeed glancingly alluded to in "Araby," may even hold some thematic significance for the stories that follow in *Dubliners* as well. For Belial proposes the following:

This horror will grow mild, this darkness light,
Besides what hope the never-ending flight
Of future dayes may bring, what chance, what change
Worth waiting, since our present lot appeers
For happy though but ill, for ill not worst,
If we procure not to our selves more woe.
    Thus Belial with words cloath'd in reason's garb
Counsel'd ignoble ease, and peaceful sloath. (2.220–27)

Such self-deceptive acceptance of defeat may aptly suggest the kind of complicity that Joyce seems to suggest concerning many of his fallen Dubliners and their own various psychological and spiritual failures.

Franz Kafka

First Sorrow

Translated by Willa and Edwin Muir

A trapeze artist—this art, practiced high in the vaulted domes of the great variety theaters, is admittedly one of the most difficult humanity can achieve—had so arranged his life that, as long as he kept working in the same building, he never came down from his trapeze by night or day, at first only from a desire to perfect his skill, but later because custom was too strong for him. All his needs, very modest needs at that, were supplied by relays of attendants who watched from below and sent up and hauled down again in specially constructed containers whatever he required. This way of living caused no particular inconvenience to the theatrical people, except that, when other turns were on the stage, his being still up aloft, which could not be dissembled, proved somewhat distracting, as also the fact that, although at such times he mostly kept very still, he drew a stray glance here and there from the public. Yet the management overlooked this, because he was an extraordinary and unique artist. And of course they recognized that this mode of life was no mere prank, and that only in this way could he really keep himself in constant practice and his art at the pitch of its perfection.

Besides, it was quite healthful up there, and when in the warmer seasons of the year the side windows all around the dome of the theater were thrown open and sun and fresh air came pouring irresistibly into the dusky vault, it was even beautiful. True, his social life was somewhat limited, only sometimes a fellow acrobat swarmed up the ladder to him, and then they both sat on the trapeze, leaning left and right against the supporting ropes, and chatted, or builders' workmen repairing the roof exchanged a few words with him through an open window, or the fireman, inspecting the emergency lighting in the top gallery, called over to him something that sounded respectful but could hardly be made out. Otherwise nothing disturbed his seclusion, occasionally, perhaps, some theater hand straying through the empty theater of an afternoon gazed thoughtfully up into the great height of the roof, almost beyond eyeshot, where the trapeze artist, unaware that he was being observed, practiced his art or rested.

The trapeze artist could have gone on living peacefully like that, had it not been for the inevitable journeys from place to place, which he found extremely trying. Of course his manager saw to it that his sufferings were not prolonged one moment more than necessary; for town travel, racing automobiles were used, which whirled him, by night if possible or in the earliest hours of the morning, through the empty streets at breakneck speed, too slow all the same for the trapeze artist's impatience; for railway journeys, a whole compartment was reserved, in which the trapeze artist, as a possible though wretched alternative to his usual way of living, could pass the time up on the luggage rack; in the next town on their circuit, long before he arrived, the trapeze was already slung up in the theater and all the doors leading to the stage were flung wide open, all corridors kept free—yet the manager never knew a happy moment until the trapeze artist set his foot on the rope ladder and in a twinkling, at long last, hung aloft on his trapeze.

Despite so many journeys having been successfully arranged by the manager, each new one embarrassed him again, for the journeys, apart from everything else, got on the nerves of the artist a great deal.

Once when they were again traveling together, the trapeze artist lying on the luggage rack dreaming, the manager leaning back in the opposite window seat reading a book, the trapeze artist addressed his companion in a low voice. The manager was immediately all attention. The trapeze artist, biting his lips, said that he must always in future have two trapezes for his performance instead of only one, two trapezes opposite each other. The manager at once agreed. But the trapeze artist, as if to show that the manager's consent counted for as little as his refusal, said that never again would he perform on only one trapeze, in no circumstances whatever. The very idea that it might happen at all seemed to make him shudder. The manager, watchfully feeling his way, once more emphasized his entire agreement, two trapezes were better than one, besides it would be an advantage to have a second bar, more variety could be introduced into the performance. At that the trapeze artist suddenly burst into tears. Deeply distressed, the manager sprang to his feet and asked what was the matter, then getting no answer climbed up on the seat and caressed him, cheek to cheek, so that his own face was bedabbled by the trapeze artist's tears. Yet it took much questioning and soothing endearment until the trapeze artist sobbed: "Only the one bar in my hands—how can I go on living!" That made it somewhat easier for the manager to comfort him; he promised to wire from the very next station for a second trapeze to be installed in the first town on their circuit; reproached himself for having let the artist work so long on only one trapeze; and thanked and praised him warmly for having at last brought the mistake to his notice. And so he succeeded in reassuring the trapeze artist, little by little, and was able to go back to his corner. But he himself was far from reassured, with deep uneasiness he kept glancing secretly at the trapeze artist over the top of his book. Once such ideas began to torment him, would they ever quite leave him alone? Would they not rather increase in urgency? Would they not threaten his very existence? And indeed the manager believed he could see, during the apparently peaceful sleep which had succeeded the fit of tears, the first furrows of care engraving themselves upon the trapeze artist's smooth, childlike forehead.

Yasunari Kawabata

The Grasshopper and the Bell Cricket

Translated by Lane Dunlop

Walking along the tile-roofed wall of the university, I turned aside and approached the upper school. Behind the white board fence of the school playground, from a dusky clump of bushes under the black cherry trees, an insect's voice could be heard. Walking more slowly and listening to that voice, and furthermore reluctant to part with it, I turned right so as not to leave the playground behind. When I turned to the left, the fence gave way to an embankment planted with orange trees. At the corner, I exclaimed with surprise. My eyes gleaming at what they saw up ahead, I hurried forward with short steps.

At the base of the embankment was a bobbing cluster of beautiful vari-colored lanterns, such as one might see at a festival in a remote country village. Without going any farther, I knew that it was a group of children on an insect chase among the bushes of the embankment. There were about twenty lanterns. Not only were there crimson, pink, indigo, green, purple, and yellow lanterns, but one lantern glowed with five colors at once. There were even some little red store-bought lanterns. But most of the lanterns were beautiful square ones which the children had made themselves with love and care. The bobbing lanterns, the coming together of children on this lonely slope—surely it was a scene from a fairy tale?

One of the neighborhood children had heard an insect sing on this slope one night. Buying a red lantern, he had come back the next night to find the insect. The night after that, there was another child. This new child could not buy a lantern. Cutting out the back and front of a small carton and papering it, he placed a candle on the bottom and fastened a string to the top. The number of children grew to five, and then to seven. They learned how to color the paper that they stretched over the windows of the cutout cartons, and to draw pictures on it. Then these wise child-artists, cutting out round, three-cornered, and lozenge leaf shapes in the cartons, coloring each little window a different color, with circles and diamonds, red and green, made a single and whole decorative pattern. The child with the red lantern discarded it as a tasteless object that could be bought at a store. The child who had made his own lantern threw it away because the design was too simple. The pattern of light that one had had in hand the night before was unsatisfying the morning after. Each day, with cardboard, paper, brush, scissors, penknife, and glue, the children made new lanterns out of their hearts and minds. Look at my lantern! Be the most unusually beautiful! And each night, they had gone out on their insect hunts. These were the twenty children and their beautiful lanterns that I now saw before me.

Wide-eyed, I loitered near them. Not only did the square lanterns have old fashioned patterns and flower shapes, but the names of the children who had made them were cut out in squared letters of the syllabary. Different from the painted-over red lanterns, others (made of thick cutout cardboard) had their designs drawn onto the paper windows, so that the candle's light seemed to emanate from the form and color of the design itself. The lanterns brought out the shadows of the bushes like dark light. The children crouched eagerly on the slope wherever they heard an insect's voice.

"Does anyone want a grasshopper?" A boy, who had been peering into a bush about thirty feet away from the other children, suddenly straightened up and shouted.

"Yes! Give it to me!" Six or seven children came running up. Crowding behind the boy who had found the grasshopper, they peered into the bush. Brushing away their outstretched hands and spreading out his arms, the boy stood as if guarding the bush where the insect was. Waving the lantern in his right hand, he called again to the other children.

"Does anyone want a grasshopper? A grasshopper!"

"I do! I do!" Four or five more children came running up. It seemed you could not catch a more precious insect than a grasshopper. The boy called out a third time.

"Doesn't anyone want a grasshopper?"

Two or three more children came over.

"Yes. I want it."

It was a girl, who just now had come up behind the boy who'd discovered the insect. Lightly turning his body, the boy gracefully bent forward. Shifting the lantern to his left hand, he reached his right hand into the bush.

"It's a grasshopper."

"Yes. I'd like to have it."

The boy quickly stood up. As if to say "Here!" he thrust out his fist that held the insect at the girl. She, slipping her left wrist under the string of her lantern enclosed the boy's fist with both hands. The boy quietly opened his fist. The insect was transferred to between the girl's thumb and index finger.

"Oh! It's not a grasshopper. It's a bell cricket." The girl's eyes shone as she looked at the small brown insect.

"It's a bell cricket! It's a bell cricket!" The children echoed in an envious chorus.

"It's a bell cricket. It's a bell cricket."

Glancing with her bright intelligent eyes at the boy who had given her the cricket, the girl opened the little insect cage hanging at her side and released the cricket in it.

"It's a bell cricket."

"Oh, it's a bell cricket," the boy who'd captured it muttered. Holding up the insect cage close to his eyes, he looked inside it. By the light of his beautiful many-colored lantern, also held up at eye level, he glanced at the girl's face.

Oh, I thought. I felt slightly jealous of the boy, and sheepish. How silly of me not to have understood his actions until now! Then I caught my breath in surprise. Look! It was something on the girl's breast which neither the boy who had given her the cricket, nor she who had accepted it, nor the children who were looking at them noticed.

In the faint greenish light that fell on the girl's breast, wasn't the name "Fujio" clearly discernible? The boy's lantern, which he held up alongside the girl's insect cage, inscribed his name, cut out in the green papered aperture, onto her white cotton kimono. The girl's lantern, which dangled loosely from her wrist, did not project its pattern so clearly, but still one could make out, in a trembling patch of red on the boy's waist, the name "Kiyoko." This chance interplay of red and green—if it was chance or play—neither Fujio nor Kiyoko knew about.

Even if they remembered forever that Fujio had given her the cricket and that Kiyoko had accepted it, not even in dreams would Fujio ever know that his name had been written in green on Kiyoko's breast or that Kiyoko's name had been inscribed in red on his waist, nor would Kiyoko ever know that Fujio's name had been inscribed in green on her breast or that her own name had been written in red on Fujio's waist.

Fujio! Even when you have become a young man, laugh with pleasure at a girl's delight when, told that it's a grasshopper, she is given a bell cricket; laugh with affection at a girl's chagrin when, told that it's a bell cricket, she is given a grasshopper.

Even if you have the wit to look by yourself in a bush away from the other children, there are not many bell crickets in the world. Probably you will find a girl like a grasshopper whom you think is a bell cricket.

And finally, to your clouded, wounded heart, even a true bell cricket will seem like a grasshopper. Should that day come, when it seems to you that the world is only full of grasshopper, I will think it a pity that you have no way to remember tonight's play of light, when your name was written in green by your beautiful lantern on a girl's breast.

Jamaica Kincaid

Girl

Wash the white clothes on Monday and put them on the stone heap; wash the color clothes on Tuesday and put them on the clothesline to dry; don't walk barehead in the hot sun; cook pumpkin fritters in very hot sweet oil; soak your little cloths right after you take them off; when buying cotton to make yourself a nice blouse, be sure that it doesn't have gum on it, because that way it won't hold up well after a wash; soak salt fish overnight before you cook it; is it true that you sing benna[1] in Sunday school?; always eat your food in such a way that it won't turn someone else's stomach; on Sundays try to walk like a lady and not like the slut you are so bent on becoming; don't sing benna in Sunday school; you mustn't speak to wharf-rat boys, not even to give directions; don't eat fruits on the street—flies will follow you; *but I don't sing benna on Sundays at all and never in Sunday school*; this is how to sew on a button; this is how to make a button-hole for the button you have just sewed on; this is how to hem a dress when you see the hem coming down and so to prevent yourself from looking like the slut I know you are so bent on becoming; this is how you iron your father's khaki shirt so that it doesn't have a crease; this is how you iron your father's khaki pants so that they don't have a crease; this is how you grow okra—far from the house, because okra tree harbors red ants; when you are growing dasheen, make sure it gets plenty of water or else it makes your throat itch when you are eating it; this is how you sweep a corner; this is how you sweep a whole house; this is how you sweep a yard; this is how you smile to someone you don't like too much; this is how you smile to someone you don't like at all;

---

[1] Benna: Calypso music.

this is how you smile to someone you like completely; this is how you set a table for tea; this is how you set a table for dinner; this is how you set a table for dinner with an important guest; this is how you set a table for lunch; this is how you set a table for breakfast; this is how to behave in the presence of men who don't know you very well, and this way they won't recognize immediately the slut I have warned you against becoming; be sure to wash every day, even if it is with your own spit; don't squat down to play marbles—you are not a boy, you know; don't pick people's flowers—you might catch something; don't throw stones at blackbirds, because it might not be a blackbird at all; this is how to make a bread pudding; this is how to make doukona;[2] this is how to make pepper pot; this is how to make a good medicine for a cold; this is how to make a good medicine to throw away a child before it even becomes a child; this is how to catch a fish; this is how to throw back a fish you don't like, and that way something bad won't fall on you; this is how to bully a man; this is how a man bullies you; this is how to love a man, and if this doesn't work there are other ways, and if they don't work don't feel too bad about giving up; this is how to spit up in the air if you feel like it, and this is how to move quick so that it doesn't fall on you; this is how to make ends meet; always squeeze bread to make sure it's fresh; *but what if the baker won't let me feel the bread?*; you mean to say that after all you are really going to be the kind of woman who the baker won't let near the bread?

---

[2] Doukona: A spicy plantain pudding.

Ursula K. Le Guin

The Ones Who Walk Away from Omelas

With a clamor of bells that set the swallows soaring, the Festival of Summer came to the city. Omelas, bright-towered by the sea. The rigging of the boats in harbor sparkled with flags. In the streets between houses with red roofs and painted walls, between old moss-grown gardens and under avenues of trees, past great parks and public buildings, processions moved. Some were decorous: old people in long stiff robes of mauve and grey, grave master workmen, quiet, merry women carrying their babies and chatting as they walked. In other streets the music beat faster, a shimmering of gong and tambourine, and the people went dancing, the procession was a dance. Children dodged in and out, their high calls rising like the swallows' crossing flights over the music and the singing. All the processions wound towards the north side of the city, where on the great water-meadow called the Green Fields boys and girls, naked in the bright air, with mud-stained feet and ankles and long, lithe arms, exercised their restive horses before the race. The horses wore no gear at all but a halter without bit. Their manes were braided with streamers of silver, gold, and green. They flared their nostrils and pranced and boasted to one another; they were vastly excited, the horse being the only animal who has adopted our ceremonies as his own. Far off to the north and west the mountains stood up half encircling Omelas on her bay. The air of morning was so clear that the snow still crowning the Eighteen Peaks burned with white-gold fire across the miles of sunlit air, under the dark blue of the sky. There was just enough wind to make the banners that marked the racecourse snap and flutter now and then. In the silence of the broad green meadows one could hear the music winding through the city streets, farther and nearer and ever approaching, a cheerful faint sweetness of the air that from time to time trembled and gathered together and broke out into the great joyous clanging of the bells.

Joyous! How is one to tell about joy? How describe the citizens of Omelas?

They were not simple folk, you see, though they were happy. But we do not say the words of cheer much any more. All smiles have become archaic. Given a description such as this one tends to make certain assumptions. Given a description such as this one tends to look next for the King, mounted on a splendid stallion and surrounded by his noble knights, or perhaps in a golden litter borne by great-muscled slaves. But there was no king. They did not use swords, or keep slaves. They were not barbarians. I do not know the rules and laws of their society, but I suspect that they were singularly few. As they did without monarchy and slavery, so they also got on without the stock exchange, the advertisement, the secret police, and the bomb. Yet I repeat that these were not simple folk, not dulcet shepherds, noble savages, bland utopians. They were not less complex than us. The trouble is that we have a bad habit, encouraged by pedants and sophisticates, of considering happiness as something rather stupid. Only pain is intellectual, only evil interesting. This is the treason of the artist: a refusal to admit the banality of evil and the terrible boredom of pain. If you can't lick 'em, join 'em. If it hurts, repeat it. But to praise despair is to condemn delight, to embrace violence is to lose hold of everything else. We have almost lost hold; we can no longer describe a happy man, nor make any celebration of joy. How can I tell you about the people of Omelas? They were not naïve and happy children—though their children were, in fact, happy. They were mature, intelligent, passionate adults whose lives were not wretched. O miracle! but I wish I could describe it better. I wish I could convince you. Omelas sounds in my words like a city in a fairy tale, long ago and far away, once upon a time. Perhaps it would be best if you imagined it as your own fancy bids, assuming it will rise to the occasion, for certainly I cannot suit you all. For instance, how about technology? I think that there would be no cars or helicopters in and above the streets; this follows from the fact that the people of Omelas are happy people. Happiness is based on a just discrimination of what is necessary, what is neither necessary nor destructive, and what is destructive. In the middle category, however—that of the unnecessary but undestructive, that of comfort, luxury, exuberance, etc.—they could perfectly well have central heating, subway trains, washing machines, and all kinds of marvelous devices not yet invented here, floating light-sources, fuelless power, a cure for the common cold. Or they could have none of that: it doesn't matter. As you like it. I incline to think that people from towns up and down the coast have been coming in to Omelas during the last days before the Festival on very fast little trains and double-decked trams and that the train station of Omelas is actually the handsomest building in town, though plainer than the magnificent Farmers' Market. But even granted trains, I fear that Omelas so far strikes some of you as goody-goody. Smiles, bells, parades, horses, bleh.

If so, please add an orgy. If an orgy would help, don't hesitate. Let us not, however, have temples from which issue beautiful nude priests and priest-esses already half in ecstasy and ready to copulate with any man or woman, lover or stranger, who desires union with the deep godhead of the blood, al-though that was my first idea. But really it would be better not to have any temples in Omelas—at least, not manned temples. Religion yes, clergy no. Surely the beautiful nudes can just wander about, offering themselves like divine soufflés to the hunger of the needy and the rapture of the flesh. Let them join the processions. Let tambourines be struck above the copulations, and the glory of desire be proclaimed upon the gongs, and (a not unimpor-tant point) let the offspring of these delightful rituals be beloved and looked after by all. One thing I know there is none of in Omelas is guilt. But what else should there be? I thought at first there were no drugs, but that is puri-tanical. For those who like it, the faint insistent sweetness of *drooz* may per-fume the ways of the city, *drooz* which first brings a great lightness and brilliance to the mind and limbs, and then after some hours a dreamy lan-guor, and wonderful visions at last of the very arcana and inmost secrets of the Universe, as well as exciting the pleasure of sex beyond all belief; and it is not habit-forming. For more modest tastes I think there ought to be beer. What else, what else belongs in the joyous city? The sense of victory, surely, the celebration of courage. But as we did without clergy, let us do without soldiers. The joy built upon successful slaughter is not the right kind of joy; it will not do; it is fearful and it is trivial. A boundless and generous content-ment, a magnanimous triumph felt not against some outer enemy but in communion with the finest and fairest in the souls of all men everywhere and the splendor of the world's summer: this is what swells the hearts of the people of Omelas, and the victory they celebrate is that of life. I really don't think many of them need to take *drooz*.

Most of the processions have reached the Green Fields by now. A mar-velous smell of cooking goes forth from the red and blue tents of the provi-sioners. The faces of small children are amiably sticky; in the benign grey beard of a man a couple of crumbs of rich pastry are entangled. The youths and girls have mounted their horses and are beginning to group around the starting line of the course. An old woman, small, fat, and laughing, is pass-ing out flowers from a basket, and tall young men wear her flowers in their shining hair. A child of nine or ten sits at the edge of the crowd, alone, play-ing on a wooden flute. People pause to listen, and they smile, but they do not speak to him, for he never ceases playing and never sees them, his dark eyes wholly rapt in the sweet, thin magic of the tune.

He finishes, and slowly lowers his hands holding the wooden flute.

As if that little private silence were the signal, all at once a trumpet sounds from the pavillion near the starting line: imperious, melancholy, piercing. The horses rear on their slender legs, and some of them neigh in answer. Sober-faced, the young riders stroke the horses' necks and soothe them, whispering, "Quiet, quiet, there my beauty, my hope. . . ." They begin to form in rank along the starting line. The crowds along the racecourse are like a field of grass and flowers in the wind. The Festival of Summer has begun.

Do you believe? Do you accept the festival, the city, the joy? No? Then let me describe one more thing.

In a basement under one of the beautiful public buildings of Omelas, or perhaps in the cellar of one of its spacious private homes, there is a room. It has one locked door, and no window. A little light seeps in dustily between cracks in the boards, secondhand from a cobwebbed window somewhere across the cellar. In one corner of the little room a couple of mops, with stiff, clotted, foul-smelling heads, stand near a rusty bucket. The floor is dirt, a little damp to the touch, as cellar dirt usually is. The room is about three paces long and two wide: a mere broom closet or disused tool room. In the room a child is sitting. It could be a boy or a girl. It looks about six, but actually is nearly ten. It is feeble-minded. Perhaps it was born defective, or perhaps it has become imbecile through fear, malnutrition, and neglect. It picks its nose and occasionally fumbles vaguely with its toes or genitals, as it sits hunched in the corner farthest from the bucket and the two mops. It is afraid of the mops. It finds them horrible. It shuts its eyes, but it knows the mops are still standing there; and the door is locked; and nobody will come. The door is always locked; and nobody ever comes, except that sometimes—the child has no understanding of time or interval—sometimes the door rattles terribly and opens, and a person, or several people, are there. One of them may come in and kick the child to make it stand up. The others never come close, but peer in at it with frightened, disgusted eyes. The food bowl and the water jug are hastily filled, the door is locked, the eyes disappear. The people at the door never say anything, but the child, who has not always lived in the tool room, and can remember sunlight and its mother's voice, sometimes speaks. "I will be good," it says. "Please let me out. I will be good!" They never answer. The child used to scream for help at night, and cry a good deal, but now it only makes a kind of whining, "eh-haa, eh-haa," and it speaks less and less often. It is so thin there are no calves to its legs; its belly protrudes; it lives on a half-bowl of corn meal and grease a day. It is naked. Its buttocks and thighs are a mass of festered sores, as it sits in its own excrement continually.

They all know it is there, all the people of Omelas. Some of them have come to see it, others are content merely to know it is there. They all know that it has to be there. Some of them understand why, and some do not, but they all understand that their happiness, the beauty of their city, the tenderness of their friendships, the health of their children, the wisdom of their scholars, the skill of their makers, even the abundance of their harvest and the kindly weathers of their skies, depend wholly on this child's abominable misery.

This is usually explained to children when they are between eight and twelve, whenever they seem capable of understanding; and most of those who come to see the child are young people, though often enough an adult comes, or comes back, to see the child. No matter how well the matter has been explained to them, these young spectators are always shocked and sickened at the sight. They feel disgust, which they had thought themselves superior to. They feel anger, outrage, impotence, despite all the explanations. They would like to do something for the child. But there is nothing they can do. If the child were brought up into the sunlight out of that vile place, if it were cleaned and fed and comforted, that would be a good thing, indeed; but if it were done, in that day and hour all the prosperity and beauty and delight of Omelas would wither and be destroyed. Those are the terms. To exchange all the goodness and grace of every life in Omelas for that single, small improvement: to throw away the happiness of thousands for the chance of the happiness of one: that would be to let guilt within the walls indeed.

The terms are strict and absolute; there may not even be a kind word spoken to the child.

Often the young people go home in tears, or in a tearless rage, when they have seen the child and faced this terrible paradox. They may brood over it for weeks or years. But as time goes on they begin to realize that even if the child could be released, it would not get much good of its freedom: a little vague pleasure of warmth and food, no doubt, but little more. It is too degraded and imbecile to know any real joy. It has been afraid too long ever to be free of fear. Its habits are too uncouth for it to respond to humane treatment. Indeed, after so long it would probably be wretched without walls about it to protect it, and darkness for its eyes, and its own excrement to sit in. Their tears at the bitter injustice dry when they begin to perceive the terrible justice of reality and to accept it. Yet it is their tears and anger, the trying of their generosity and the acceptance of their helplessness, which are perhaps the true source of the splendor of their lives. Theirs is no vapid, irresponsible happiness. They know that they, like the child, are not free. They know compassion. It is the existence of the child, and their knowledge of its existence, that makes possible the nobility of their architecture, the poignancy of their music, the profundity of their science. It is because of the child that they are so gentle with children. They know that if the wretched one were not there snivelling in the dark, the other one, the flute-player, could make no joyful music as the young riders line up in their beauty for the race in the sunlight of the first morning of summer.

Now do you believe in them? Are they not more credible? But there is one more thing to tell, and this is quite incredible.

At times one of the adolescent girls or boys who go to see the child does not go home to weep or rage, does not, in fact, go home at all. Sometimes also a man or woman much older falls silent for a day or two, and then leaves home. These people go out into the street, and walk down the street alone. They keep walking, and walk straight out of the city of Omelas, through the beautiful gates. They keep walking across the farmlands of Omelas. Each one goes alone, youth or girl, man or woman. Night falls; the traveler must pass down village streets, between the houses with yellow-lit windows, and on out into the darkness of the fields. Each alone, they go west or north, towards the mountains. They go on. They leave Omelas, they walk ahead into the darkness, and they do not come back. The place they go towards is a place even less imaginable to most of us than the city of happiness. I cannot describe it at all. It is possible that it does not exist. But they seem to know where they are going, the ones who walk away from Omelas.

First Person: Ursula K. Le Guin, "The Sound of Your Writing," "Sentence Length and Complete Syntax," and "Point of View"

THE SOUND OF YOUR WRITING

The sound of the language is where it all begins and what it all comes back to. The basic elements of language are physical: the noise words make and the rhythm of their relationships. This is just as true of written prose as it is of poetry, though the sound-effects of prose are usually subtle and always irregular.

Most children enjoy the sound of language for its own sake. They wallow in repetitions and luscious word-sounds and the crunch and slither of onomatopoeia; they fall in love with musical or impressive words and use them in all the wrong places. Some writers keep this childish love for the sounds of language. For them language is not a way to deliver a message, but, as McLuhan said, *is* the message. Others "outgrow" their oral/aural sense of language as they learn to read in silence. That's a loss. I think an awareness of what your own writing sounds like is an essential skill for a writer. Fortunately it's one quite easy to cultivate, to relearn, reawaken.

A good reader has a mind's ear. Though we read most of our narratives in silence, a keen inner ear does hear them. Dull, choppy, droning, jerky, feeble: these are all faults in the sound of prose, though we may not know we hear them as we read. Lively, well-paced, flowing, strong, beautiful: these are all qualities of the sound of prose, and we rejoice in them as we read. And so good writers train their mind's ear to listen to their own prose—to hear as they write.

Now the chief duty of a narrative sentence is to lead to the next sentence—to keep the story going. . . . But pace and movement depend above all on rhythm, and you have to hear your writing to feel its rhythm.

SENTENCE LENGTH AND COMPLEX SYNTAX

As I said before, when we were being gorgeous: The chief duty of a narrative sentence is to lead to the next sentence. Beyond this basic, invisible job, the narrative sentence can do an infinite number of beautiful, surprising, powerful, audible, visible things (see *all* the examples). But the basic function of the narrative sentence is to keep the story going and keep the reader going with it.

Its rhythm is part of the rhythm of the whole piece; all its qualities are part of the quality and tone of the whole piece. As a narrative sentence, it isn't serving the story well if its rhythm is so unexpected, or its beauty so striking, or its similes or metaphors so dazzling, that it stops the reader, even to say Ooh, Ah! Poetry can do that. Poetry can be visibly, immediately dazzling. In poetry a line, a few words, can make the reader's breath catch and her eyes fill with tears. But for the most part, prose sets its proper beauty and power deeper, hiding it in the work as a whole. In a story it's the *scene*— the setting/characters/action/interaction/dialogue/feelings—that makes us hold our breath, and cry . . . and turn the page to find out what happens next. And so, until the scene ends, each sentence should lead to the next sentence.

Rhythm is what keeps the song going, the horse galloping, the story moving. Sentence length has a lot to do with the rhythm of prose. So an important aspect of the narrative sentence is—prosaically—its length.

Teachers trying to get school kids to write clearly, and journalists with their weird rules of writing, have filled a lot of heads with the notion that the only good sentence is a short sentence.

This is true for convicted criminals.

Very short sentences, isolated or in a series, are terrifically effective in the right place. Prose consisting entirely of short, syntactically simple sentences is monotonous, choppy, a blunt instrument. If short-sentence prose goes on very long, whatever its content, the thump-thump beat gives it a false simplicity that soon just sounds dumb. See Spot. See Jane. See Spot bite Jane.

Narrative prose consisting largely of long, complex sentences, full of embedded clauses and all the rest of the syntactical armature, is fairly rare these days. Some people have never read any and so are anxious about reading it, let alone writing it. Very long sentences have to be carefully and knowledgeably managed, solidly constructed; their connections must be clear, so that they flow, carrying the reader along easily.

It's a myth that short-sentence prose is "more like the way we speak." A writer can build a sentence in a more deliberate way than a speaker can, because a writer can revise. But a lot of people who are nervous about constructing a long sentence in writing actually speak in long, well-articulated sentences. People following a complex thought aloud often do so by using a wealth of clauses and qualifiers. Dictation, indeed, is notoriously wordy. When Henry James began dictating his novels to a secretary, his tendency to qualify and parenthesize and embed clause within clause got out of hand, clogging the narrative flow and making his prose totter on the edge of self-parody. Listening with a careful ear to one's prose isn't the same thing as falling in love with the sound of one's voice.

To avoid long sentences and the marvelously supple connections of a complex syntax is to deprive your prose of an essential quality. Connectedness is what keeps a narrative going.

As Strunk and White say, variety in sentence length is what's needed. All short will sound stupid. All long will sound stuffy.

In revision you can consciously check for variety, and if you've fallen into a thumping of all short sentences or a wambling of all long ones, change them to achieve a varied rhythm and pace.

What the sentence says and does is essential in determining its length: "Kate fires the gun." —A short sentence.

"Kate perceives that her husband's not paying any real attention to what she's saying to him, but also observes that she doesn't much care if he's paying attention or not, and that this lack of feeling may be a sinister symptom of something she doesn't want to think about just now."—This kind of subject may well require a complicated sentence that can work itself out at some length.

POINT OF VIEW

Point of view, POV for short and when scribbled in margins of manuscripts, is the technical term for describing *who is telling the story and what their relation to the story is.*

This person, if a character in the story, is called the *viewpoint character.* (The only other person it can be is the author.)

Voice is a word critics often use in discussing narrative. It's always metaphorical, since what's written is voiceless. Often it signifies the authenticity of the writing (writing in your own voice; catching the true voice of a kind of person; and so on). I'm using it naively and pragmatically to mean *the voice or voices that tell the story,* the narrating voice. For our purposes in this book, at this point, I'll treat voice and point of view as so intimately involved and interdependent as to be the same thing.

The Principal Points of View

What follows is my attempt to define and describe the five principal narrative points of view. Each description is followed by an example: a paragraph told in that POV, from a nonexistent story called "Princess Sefrid." It's the same scene each time, the same people, the same events. Only the viewpoint changes.

A Note on the "Reliable Narrator"   In autobiography and memoir, in nonfiction narrative of any kind, the "I" (whether the writer uses it or not) is the author. In these forms, the reader has a right, I think, to expect the author/narrator to be reliable—to try to tell us as honestly as possible what happened. Reading nonfiction, we assume that the author is not inventing, but relating, and won't change facts to make the story neater—at least, not blatantly.

In fiction, the "I" narrator (or the third-person narrator) is *not* the author. Most first- and third-person narrators in serious fiction used to be trustworthy, just like memoirists. But "unreliable narrators" are now fairly common in fiction, narrators who—deliberately or innocently—misrepresent the facts.

Fictional narrators who suppress facts, or who make mistakes in relating or interpreting the events, are almost always telling us something about themselves (and perhaps about us.) The author lets us see or guess what "really" happened, and using this as a touchstone, we readers are led to understand how other people see the world, and why they (and we?) see it that way.

A familiar example of a semireliable narrator is Huck Finn. Huck misinterprets a good deal of what he sees. For instance, he never understands that Jim is the only adult in his world who treats him with love and honor; he never really understands that he loves and honors Jim. The fact that he *can't* understand it tells us an appalling truth about the world he and Jim—and we—live in.

Princess Sefrid, as you will see by comparing her relation with those of other viewpoint characters, is entirely reliable.

First Person.   In first-person narration, the viewpoint character is "I." "I" tells the story and is centrally involved in it. Only what "I" knows, feels, perceives, thinks, guesses, hopes, remembers, etc., can be told. The reader can infer what other people feel and who they are only from what "I" sees, hears, and says of them.

Princess Sefrid: First Person Narration

I felt so strange and lonesome entering the room crowded with strangers that I wanted to turn around and run, but Rassa was right behind me, and I had to go ahead. People spoke to me, asked Rassa my name. In my confusion I couldn't tell one face from another or understand what people were saying to me, and answered them almost at random. Only for a moment I caught the glance of a person in the crowd, a woman looking directly at me, and there was a kindness in her eyes that made me long to go to her. She looked like somebody I could talk to.

Limited Third Person.   The viewpoint character is "he" or "she." "He" or "she" tells the story and is centrally involved in it. Only what the viewpoint character knows, feels, perceives, thinks, guesses, hopes, remembers, etc., can be told. The reader can infer what other people feel and are only from what the viewpoint character observes of their behavior. This limitation to the perceptions of one person may be consistent throughout a whole book, or the narrative may shift from one viewpoint character to another. Such shifts are usually signalled in some way, and usually don't happen at very short intervals.

Tactically, limited third is identical to first person. It has exactly the same essential limitation: that nothing can be seen, known, or told except what the narrator sees, knows, and tells. That limitation concentrates the voice and gives apparent authenticity.

It seems that you could change the narration from first to limited third person by merely instructing the computer to switch the pronoun, then correct verb endings throughout, and *voilá*. But it isn't that simple. First person is a different voice from limited third. The reader's relationship to that voice is different—because the author's relationship to it is different. Being "I" is not the same as being "he" or "she." In the long run, it takes a quite different imaginative energy, both for the writer and for the reader.

There is no guarantee, by the way, that the limited third person narrator is reliable.

"Stream-of-consciousness" is a particularly inward form of limited third person.

Princess Sefrid: Limited Third Person

Sefrid felt isolated, conspicuous, as she entered the room crowded with strangers. She would have turned around and run back to her room, but Rassa was right behind her, and she had to go ahead. People spoke to her. They asked Rassa her name. In her confusion she could not tell one face from another or understand what people said to her. She answered them at random. Only once, for a moment, a woman looked directly at her through the crowd, a keen, kind gaze that made Sefrid long to cross the room and talk to her.

Involved Author ("Omniscient Author").   The story is not told from within any single character. There may be numerous viewpoint characters, and the narrative voice may change at any time from one to another character within the story, or to a view, perception, analysis, or prediction that only the author could make. (For example: the description of what a person who is quite alone looks like; or the description of a landscape or a room at a moment when there's nobody there to see it.) The writer may tell us what anyone is thinking and feeling, interpret behavior for us, and even make judgments on characters.

This is the familiar voice of the storyteller, who knows what's going on in all the different places the characters are at the same time, and what's going on inside the characters, and what has happened, and what has to happen.

All myths and legends and folktales, all young children's stories, almost all fiction until about 1915, and a vast amount of fiction since then, use this voice.

I don't like the common term "omniscient author," because I hear a judgmental sneer in it. I think "authorial narration" is the most neutral term, and "involved author" the most exact.

Limited third person is the predominant modern fictional voice—partly in reaction to the Victorian fondness for involved-author narration, and the many possible abuses of it.

Involved author is the most openly, obviously manipulative of the points of view. But the voice of the narrator who knows the whole story, tells it because it is important, and is profoundly involved with *all* the characters, cannot be dismissed as old-fashioned or uncool. It's not only the oldest and the most widely used storytelling voice, it's also the most versatile, flexible, and complex of the points of view—and probably, at this point, the most difficult for the writer.

Princess Sefrid: Involved Author ("Omniscient Author")

The Tufarian girl entered the room hesitantly, her arms close to her sides, her shoulders hunched; she looked both frightened and indifferent, like a captured wild animal. The big Hemmian ushered her in with a proprietary air and introduced her complacently as "Princess Sefrid," or "the Princess of Tufar." People pressed close to meet her or simply to stare at her. She endured them, seldom raising her head, replying to their inanities briefly, in a barely audible voice. Even in the pressing, chattering crowd she created a space around herself, a place to be lonely in. No one touched her. They were not aware that they avoided her, but she was. Out of that solitude she looked up to meet a gaze that was not curious, but open, intense, compassionate—a face that said to her, through the sea of strangeness, "I am your friend."

Detached Author ("Fly on the Wall," "Camera Eye," "Objective Narrator"). There is no viewpoint character. The narrator is not one of the characters, and can say of the characters only what a neutral observer (an intelligent fly on the wall) might infer of them from behavior and speech. The author never enters a character's mind. People and places may be exactly described, but values and judgments can be implied only indirectly. A popular voice around 1900 and in "minimalist" and "brand-name" fiction, it is the most covertly manipulative of the points of view.

It's excellent practice for writers who expect codependent readers. When we're new at writing we may expect our readers to respond just as we respond to what we're writing about—to cry because we're crying. But this is a childish, not a writerly, relation to the reader. If you can move a reader while using this cool voice, you've got something really moving going on.

Princess Sefrid: Detached Author ("Fly on the Wall," "Camera Eye," "Objective Narrator")

The princess from Tufar entered the room followed closely by the big man from Hemm. She walked with long steps, her arms close to her sides and her shoulders hunched. Her hair was thick and frizzy. She stood still while the Hemmian introduced her, calling her Princess Sefrid of Tufar. Her eyes did not meet the eyes of any of the people who crowded around her, staring at her and asking her questions. None of them tried to touch her. She replied briefly to everything said to her. She and an older woman near the tables of food exchanged a brief glance.

Observer-Narrator, Using the First Person. The narrator is one of the characters, but not the principal character—present, but not a major actor in the events. The difference from first-person narration is that the story is not about the narrator. It's a story the narrator witnessed and wants to tell us. Both fiction and nonfiction use this voice.

Princess Sefrid: Observer-Narrator in First Person

She wore Tufarian clothing, the heavy red robes I had not seen for so long; her hair stood out like a storm cloud around the dark, narrow face. Crowded forward by her owner, the Hemmian slavemaster called Rassa, she looked small, hunched, defensive, but she preserved around herself a space that was all her own. She was a captive, an exile, yet I saw in her young face the pride and kindness I had loved in her people, and I longed to speak with her.

Observer-Narrator, Using the Third Person. This point of view is limited to fiction. The tactic is much the same as the last one. The viewpoint character is a limited third-person narrator who witnesses the events.

As unreliability is a complex and subtle way of showing the *narrator's* character, and the observer-narrator isn't the protagonist, the reader is usually safe in assuming this viewpoint character is reliable, or at least perfectly transparent, both in first and third person.

Princess Sefrid: Observer-Narrator in Third Person

She wore Tufarian clothing, the heavy red robes Anna had not seen for fifteen years. Crowded forward by her owner, the Hemmian slavemaster called Rassa, the princess looked small, hunched, defensive, but she preserved around herself a space that was all her own. She was a captive, an exile, yet Anna saw in her young face the pride and kindness she had loved in the Tufarians, and longed to speak with her.

FURTHER READING. Look at a bunch of stories in an anthology or pull down a bunch of novels from your shelf (from as wide a span of time as possible) and identify the viewpoint character(s) and the point(s) of view of the narration. Notice if they change, and if so, how often.

Considerations on Changing Point of View

I'm going into all this detail because the narrative problem I meet most often in workshop stories (and often in published work) is in handling POV: inconsistency and frequent changes of POV.

It's a problem even in nonfiction, when the author starts telling the reader what Aunt Jane was thinking and why Uncle Fred swallowed the grommet. A memoirist doesn't have the right to do this without clearly indicating that Aunt Jane's thoughts and Uncle Fred's motives aren't known facts, but the author's guesswork, opinion, or interpretation. Memoirists can't be omniscient, even for a moment.

In fiction, inconsistent POV is a very frequent problem. Unless handled with awareness and skill, frequent POV shifts jerk the reader around, bouncing in and out of incompatible identifications, confusing emotion, garbling the story.

Any shift from one of the five POVs outlined above to another is a dangerous one. It's a major change of voice to go from first to third person, or from involved author to observer-narrator. The shift will affect the whole tone and structure of your narrative.

Shifts within limited third person—from one character's mind to another's—call for equal awareness and care. A writer must be aware of, have a reason for, and be in control of all shifts of viewpoint character.

I feel like writing the last two paragraphs all over again, but that would be rude. Could I ask you to read them over again?

The POV exercises are intended to make you temporarily super-conscious, and forever conscious, of what POV you're using and when and how you shift it.

Limited third is, at present, the person most fiction writers are most used to using. First person is, of course, the voice memoirists mostly use. I think it's a good idea for all of us to try all the other possibilities.

CLARICE LISPECTOR

Soulstorm

Ah, had I but known, I wouldn't have come into this world, ah, had I but known, I wouldn't have come into this world. Madness is neighbor to the cruelest prudence. I swallow madness because it calmly leads me to hallucinations. Jack and Jill went up the hill to fetch a pail of water, Jack fell down, Jill kissed his crown, and they lived happy-unhappy ever after. The chair is an object to me. It is useless while I look at it. Tell me, please, what time it is, so I'll know I'm alive at that time. Creativity is unleashed by a germ and I don't have that germ today, but I do have an incipient madness which in itself is a valid creation. I have nothing more to do with the validity of things. I am free or lost. I'm going to tell you a secret: life is lethal. We maintain the secret in utter silence, each of us, as we face ourselves, because to do so is convenient and doing otherwise would make each moment lethal. The object chair has always interested me. I look at this one, which is old, bought at an antique shop, an Empire chair; one couldn't imagine a greater simplicity of line contrasting with the seat of red felt. I love objects in proportion to how little they love me. But if I don't understand what I am writing, the fault isn't mine. I have to speak, for speaking saves me. But I don't have a single word to say. I am gagged by words already spoken. What does one person say to another? How about "how's it going?" If the madness of honesty worked, what would people say to one another? The worst of it is what a person would say to himself, yet that would be his salvation, even if honesty is determined on a conscious level while the terror of honesty comes from the part it plays in the vast unconscious that links me to the world and to the creative unconscious of the world. Today is a day for a starry sky, at least so promises this sad afternoon that a human word could save.

I open my eyes wide, but it does no good: I merely see. But the secret, that I neither see nor feel. The record player is broken, and to live without music is to betray the human condition, which is surrounded by music. Besides, music is an abstraction of thought, I'm speaking of Bach, Vivaldi, Handel. I can only write if I am free, uncensored, otherwise I succumb. I look at the Empire chair, and this time it is as if it too had looked and seen me. The future is mine as long as I live. In the future there will be more time to live and, higgledy-piggledy, to write. In the future one will say: had I but known, I wouldn't have come into this world. Marli de Oliveira, I don't write to you because I only know how to be intimate. In fact, all I can do, whatever the circumstances, is be intimate: that's why I'm even more silent. Everything that never got done, will it one day get done? The future of technology threatens to destroy all that is human in man, but technology does not touch madness; and it is there that the human in man takes refuge. I see the flowers in the vase: they are wildflowers, born without having been planted, they are beautiful and yellow. But my cook says: what ugly flowers. Just because it is difficult to understand and love what is spontaneous and Franciscan. To understand the difficult is no advantage, but to love what is easy to love is a great step upward on the human ladder. How many lies I am forced to tell. But with myself I don't want to be forced to lie. Otherwise what remains to me? Truth is the final residue of all things, and in my unconscious is the same truth as that of the world. The Moon, as Paul Eluard would say, is *éclatante de silence*. I don't know if the Moon will show at all today, since it is already late and I don't see it anywhere in the sky. Once I looked up at the night sky, circumscribing it with my head tilted back, and I became dizzy from the many stars that appear in the country, for the country sky is clear. There is no logic, if one were to think a bit about it, in the perfectly balanced illogicity of nature. Nor in that of human nature either. What would the world be like, the cosmos, if man did not exist? If I could always write as I am writing now, I would be in the midst of a *tempestade de cérebro*, a "brainstorm." Who might have invented the chair? Someone who loved himself. He therefore invented a greater comfort for his body. Then centuries passed and no one really paid attention anymore to a chair, for using it is simply automatic. You have to have courage to stir up a brainstorm: you never know what may come to frighten us. The sacred monster died: in its place a solitary girl was born. I understand, of course, that I will have to stop, not for lack of words, but because such things, and above all those things I've only thought and not written down, usually don't make it into print.

LUKE

The Prodigal Son

A certain man had two sons: and the younger of them said to his father, "Father, give me the portion of goods that falleth to me." And he divided unto them his living. And not many days after, the younger son gathered all together, and took his journey into a far country, and there wasted his substance with riotous living. And when he had spent all, there arose a mighty famine in that land, and he began to be in want. And he went and joined himself to a citizen of that country, and he sent him into his fields to feed swine. And he would fain have filled his belly with the husks that the swine did eat: and no man gave unto him. And when he came to himself, he said, "How many hired servants of my father's have bread enough and to spare, and I perish with hunger? I will arise and go to my father, and will say unto him, 'Father, I have sinned against heaven, and before thee. And am no more worthy to be called thy son: make me as one of thy hired servants.' " And he arose, and came to his father. But when he was yet a great way off, his father saw him, and had compassion, and ran, and fell on his neck, and kissed him. And the son said unto him, "Father, I have sinned against heaven, and in thy sight, and am no more worthy to be called thy son." But the father said to his servants, "Bring forth the best robe, and put it on him, and put a ring on his hand, and shoes on his feet. And bring hither the fatted calf, and kill it, and let us eat, and be merry. For this my son was dead, and is alive again; he was lost, and is found." And they began to be merry. Now his elder son was in the field, and as he came and drew nigh to the house, he heard music and dancing. And he called one of the servants, and asked what these things meant. And he said unto him, "Thy brother is come, and thy father hath killed the fatted calf, because he hath received him safe and sound." And he was angry, and would not go in: therefore came his father out, and entreated him. And he answering said to his father, "Lo, these many years do I serve thee, neither transgressed I at any time thy commandment, and yet thou never gavest me a kid, that I might make merry with my friends: but as soon as this thy son was come, which hath devoured thy living with harlots, thou hast killed for him the fatted calf." And he said unto him, "Son, thou art ever with me, and all that I have is thine. It was meet that we should make merry, and be glad: for this thy brother was dead, and is alive again: and was lost, and is found."

Naguib Mafouz

Half a Day

Translated by Denys Johnson-Davies

I proceeded alongside my father, clutching his right hand, running to keep up with the long strides he was taking. All my clothes were new: the black shoes, the green school uniform, and the red tarboosh. My delight in my new clothes, however, was not altogether unmarred, for this was no feast day but the day on which I was to be cast into school for the first time.

My mother stood at the window watching our progress, and I would turn toward her from time to time, as though appealing for help. We walked along a street lined with gardens; on both sides were extensive fields planted with crops, prickly pears, henna trees, and a few date palms.

"Why school?" I challenged my father openly. "I shall never do anything to annoy you."

"I'm not punishing you," he said, laughing. "School's not a punishment. It's the factory that makes useful men out of boys. Don't you want to be like your father and brothers?"

I was not convinced. I did not believe there was really any good to be had in tearing me away from the intimacy of my home and throwing me into this building that stood at the end of the road like some huge, high-walled fortress, exceedingly stern and grim.

When we arrived at the gate we could see the courtyard, vast and crammed full of boys and girls. "Go in by yourself," said my father, "and join them. Put a smile on your face and be a good example to others."

I hesitated and clung to his hand, but he gently pushed me from him. "Be a man," he said. "Today you truly begin life. You will find me waiting for you when it's time to leave."

I took a few steps, then stopped and looked but saw nothing. Then the faces of boys and girls came into view. I did not know a single one of them, and none of them knew me. I felt I was a stranger who had lost his way. But glances of curiosity were directed toward me, and one boy approached and asked, "Who brought you?"

"My father," I whispered.

"My father's dead," he said quite simply.

I did not know what to say. The gate was closed, letting out a pitiable screech. Some of the children burst into tears. The bell rang. A lady came along, followed by a group of men. The men began sorting us into ranks. We were formed into an intricate pattern in the great courtyard surrounded on three sides by high buildings of several floors; from each floor we were overlooked by a long balcony roofed in wood.

"This is your new home," said the woman. "Here too there are mothers and fathers. Here there is everything that is enjoyable and beneficial to knowledge and religion. Dry your tears and face life joyfully."

We submitted to the facts, and this submission brought a sort of contentment. Living beings were drawn to other living beings, and from the first moments my heart made friends with such boys as were to be my friends and fell in love with such girls as I was to be in love with, so that it seemed my misgivings had had no basis. I had never imagined school would have this rich variety. We played all sorts of different games: swings, the vaulting horse, ball games. In the music room we chanted our first songs. We also had our first introduction to language. We saw a globe of the Earth, which revolved and showed the various continents and countries. We started learning the numbers. The story of the Creator of the universe was read to us, we were told of His present world and of His Hereafter, and we heard examples of what He said. We ate delicious food, took a little nap, and woke up to go on with friendship and love, play and learning.

As our path revealed itself to us, however, we did not find it as totally sweet and unclouded as we had presumed. Dust-laden winds and unexpected accidents came about suddenly, so we had to be watchful, at the ready, and very patient. It was not all a matter of playing and fooling around. Rivalries could bring about pain and hatred or give rise to fighting. And while the lady would sometimes smile, she would often scowl and scold. Even more frequently she would resort to physical punishment.

In addition, the time for changing one's mind was over and gone and there was no question of ever returning to the paradise of home. Nothing lay ahead of us but exertion, struggle, and perseverance. Those who were able took advantage of the opportunities for success and happiness that presented themselves amid the worries.

The bell rang announcing the passing of the day and the end of work. The throngs of children rushed toward the gate, which was opened again. I bade farewell to friends and sweethearts and passed through the gate. I peered around but found no trace of my father, who had promised to be there. I stepped aside to wait. When I had waited for a long time without avail, I decided to return home on my own. After I had taken a few steps, a middle-aged man passed by, and I realized at once that I knew him. He came toward me, smiling, and shook me by the hand, saying, "It's a long time since we last met—how are you?"

With a nod of my head, I agreed with him and in turn asked, "And you, how are you?"

"As you can see, not all that good, the Almighty be praised!"

Again he shook me by the hand and went off. I proceeded a few steps, then came to a startled halt. Good Lord! Where was the street lined with gardens? Where had it disappeared to? When did all these vehicles invade it? And when did all these hordes of humanity come to rest upon its surface? How did these hills of refuse come to cover its sides? And where were the fields that bordered it? High buildings had taken over, the street surged with children, and disturbing noises shook the air. At various points stood conjurers showing off their tricks and making snakes appear from baskets. Then there was a band announcing the opening of a circus, with clowns and weight lifters walking in front. A line of trucks carrying central security troops crawled majestically by. The siren of a fire engine shrieked, and it was not clear how the vehicle would cleave its way to reach the blazing fire. A battle raged between a taxi driver and his passenger, while the passenger's wife called out for help and no one answered. Good God! I was in a daze. My head spun. I almost went crazy. How could all this have happened in half a day, between early morning and sunset? I would find the answer at home with my father. But where was my home? I could see only tall buildings and hordes of people. I hastened on to the crossroads between the gardens and Abu Khoda. I had to cross Abu Khoda to reach my house, but the stream of cars would not let up. The fire engine's siren was shrieking at full pitch as it moved at a snail's pace, and I said to myself, "Let the fire take its pleasure in what it consumes." Extremely irritated, I wondered when I would be able to cross. I stood there a long time, until the young lad employed at the ironing shop on the corner came up to me. He stretched out his arm and said gallantly, "Grandpa, let me take you across."

BERNARD MALAMUD

A Lost Grave

Hecht was a born late bloomer.

One night he woke hearing rain on his windows and thought of his young wife in her wet grave. This was something new, because he hadn't thought of her in too many years to be comfortable about. He saw her in her uncovered grave, rivulets of water streaming in every direction, and Celia, whom he had married when they were of unequal ages, lying alone in the deepening wet. Not so much as a flower grew on her grave, though he could have sworn he had arranged perpetual care.

He stepped into his thoughts perhaps to cover her with a plastic sheet, and though he searched in the cemetery under dripping trees and among many wet plots, he was unable to locate her. The dream he was into offered no tombstone name, row, or plot number, and though he searched for hours, he had nothing to show for it but his wet self. The grave had taken off. How can you cover a woman who isn't where she is supposed to be? That's Celia.

The next morning, Hecht eventually got himself out of bed and into a subway train to Jamaica to see where she was buried. He hadn't been to the cemetery in many years, no particular surprise to anybody considering past circumstances. Life with Celia wasn't exactly predictable. Yet things change in a lifetime, or seem to. Hecht had lately been remembering his life more vividly, for whatever reason. After you hit sixty-five, some things that have two distinguishable sides seem to pick up another that complicates the picture as you look or count. Hecht counted.

Now, though Hecht had been more or less in business all his life, he kept few personal papers, and though he had riffled through a small pile of them that morning, he had found nothing to help him establish Celia's present whereabouts; and after a random looking at gravestones for an hour he felt the need to call it off and spent another hour with a young secretary in the main office, who fruitlessly tapped his name and Celia's into a computer and came up with a scramble of interment dates, grave plots and counter plots, that exasperated him.

"Look, my dear," Hecht said to the flustered young secretary, "if that's how far you can go on this machine, we have to find another way to go further, or I will run out of patience. This grave is lost territory as far as I am concerned, and we have to do something practical to find it."

"What do you think I'm doing, if I might ask?"

"Whatever you are doing doesn't seem to be much help. This computer is supposed to have a good mechanical memory, but it's either out of order or rusty in its parts. I admit I didn't bring any papers with me but so far the only thing your computer has informed us is that it has nothing much to inform us."

"It has informed us it is having trouble locating the information you want."

"Which adds up to zero minus zero," Hecht said. "I wish to remind you that a lost grave isn't a missing wedding ring we are talking about. It is a lost cemetery plot of the lady who was once my wife that I wish to recover."

The pretty young woman he was dealing with had a tight-lipped conversation with an unknown person, then the buzzer on her desk sounded, and Hecht was given permission to go into the director's office.

"Mr. Goodman will now see you."

He resisted "Good for Mr. Goodman." Hecht nodded only and followed the young woman to an inner office. She knocked once and disappeared, as a friendly voice talked through the door.

"Come in, come in."

"Why should I worry if it's not my fault?" Hecht told himself.

Mr. Goodman pointed to a chair in front of his desk and Hecht was soon seated, watching him pour orange juice from a quart container into a small green glass.

"Will you join me in a sweet mouthful?" he asked, nodding at the container. "I usually take refreshment this time of the morning. It keeps me balanced."

"Thanks," said Hecht, meaning he had more serious problems. "Why I am here is that I am looking for my wife's grave, so far with no success." He cleared his throat, surprised at the emotion that had gathered there.

Mr. Goodman observed Hecht with interest.

"Your outside secretary couldn't find it," Hecht went on, regretting he hadn't found the necessary documents that would identify the grave site. "Your young lady tried her computer in every combination but couldn't produce anything. What was lost is still lost, in other words, a woman's grave."

"*Lost* is premature," Goodman offered. "*Displaced* might be better. In my twenty-eight years in my present capacity, I don't believe we have lost a single grave."

The director tapped lightly on the keys of his desk computer, studied the screen with a squint, and shrugged. "I am afraid that we now draw a blank. The letter *H* volume of our ledgers that we used before we were computerized seems to be missing. I assure you this can't be more than a temporary condition."

"That's what your young lady already informed me."

"She's not my young lady, she's my secretarial assistant."

"I stand corrected," Hecht said. "This meant no offense."

"Likewise," said Goodman. "But we will go on looking. Could you kindly tell me, if you don't mind, what was the status of your relationship to your wife at the time of her death?" He peered over half-moon glasses to check the computer reading.

"There was no status. We were separated. What has that got to do with her burial plot?"

"The reason I inquire is, I thought it might refresh your memory. For example, is this the correct cemetery, the one you are looking in—Mount Jereboam? Some people confuse us with Mount Hebron."

"I guarantee you it was Mount Jereboam."

Hecht, after a hesitant moment, gave these facts: "My wife wasn't the most stable woman. She left me twice and disappeared for months. Although I took her back twice, we weren't together at the time of her death. Once she threatened to take her life, though eventually she didn't. In the end she died of a normal sickness, not cancer. This was years later, when we weren't living together anymore, but I carried out her burial, to the best of my knowledge, in this exact cemetery. I also heard she had lived for a short time with some guy she met somewhere, but when she died, I was the one who buried her. Now I am sixty-five, and lately I have had this urge to visit the grave of someone who lived with me when I was a young man. This is a grave that everybody now tells me they can't locate."

Goodman rose at his desk, a short man, five feet tall. "I will institute a careful research."

"The quicker, the better," Hecht replied. "I am still curious what happened to her grave."

Goodman almost guffawed, but caught himself and thrust out his hand. "I will keep you well informed, don't worry."

Hecht left irritated. On the train back to the city he thought of Celia and her various unhappinesses. He wished he had told Goodman she had spoiled his life.

That night it rained. To his surprise he found a wet spot on his pillow.

The next day Hecht again went to the graveyard. "What did I forget that I ought to remember?" he asked himself. Obviously the grave plot, row, and number. Though he sought it diligently he could not find it. Who can remember something he has once and for all put out of his mind? It's like trying to grow beans out of a bag of birdseed.

"But I must be patient and I will find out. As time goes by I am bound to recall. When my memory says yes, I won't argue no."

But weeks passed and Hecht still could not remember what he was trying to. "Maybe I have reached a dead end?"

Another month went by and at last the cemetery called him. It was Mr. Goodman clearing his throat. Hecht pictured him at his desk sipping orange juice.

"Mr. Hecht?"

"The same."

"This is Mr. Goodman. A happy Rosh-ha-shonah."

"A happy Rosh-ha-shonah to you."

"Mr. Hecht, I wish to report progress. Are you prepared for an insight?"

"You name it," Hecht said.

"So let me use a better word. We have tracked your wife, and it turns out she isn't in the grave there where the computer couldn't find her. To be frank, we found her in a grave with another gentleman."

"What kind of gentleman? Who in God's name is he? I am her legal husband."

"This one, if you will pardon me, is the man who lived with your wife after she left you. They lived together on and off, so don't blame yourself too much. After she died he got a court order, and they removed her to a different grave, where we also laid him after his death. The judge gave him the court order because he convinced him that he had loved her for many years."

Hecht was embarrassed. "What are you talking about? How could he transfer her grave anywhere if it wasn't his legal property? Her grave belonged to me. I paid cash for it."

"That grave is still there," Goodman explained, "but the names were mixed up. His name was Kaplan but the workmen buried her under Caplan. Your grave is still in the cemetery, though we had it under Kaplan and not Hecht. I apologize to you for this inconvenience but I think we now have got the mystery cleared up."

"So thanks," said Hecht. He felt he had lost a wife but was no longer a widower.

"Also," Goodman reminded him, "don't forget you gained an empty grave for future use. Nobody is there and you own the plot."

Hecht said that was obviously true.

The story had astounded him. Yet whenever he felt like telling it to someone he knew, or had just met, he wasn't sure he wanted to.

Thomas Mann

A Vision

As I mechanically roll another cigarette and the speckles of brown dust tumble onto the yellow-white blotting paper of my writing folder, I find it hard to believe that I am still awake. And as the warm damp evening air, flowing in through the open window beside me, shapes the clouds of smoke so strangely, wafting them out of the light of the green-shaded lamp into matte black darkness, I am convinced I am dreaming.

How wild it is! My notion is snapping its reins on fantasy's back. Behind me the chair-back creaks, secretly nattering, sending a sudden shudder through all my nerve ends. It annoys me and disturbs my deep study of the bizarre shapes of smoke drifting around me, through which I had already resolved to draw a connecting thread.

Now the silence has gone to the dogs. Jangling movement flows through all my senses. Feverish, nervous, crazed. Every sound a stab! And tangled up in all this, forgotten things rise up. Things long ago imprinted on my sense of sight now strangely renew themselves, along with their old forgotten feelings.

With interest I notice that my awareness expands hungrily, embracing that area in the darkness in which the bright forms of smoke stand out with increasing clarity. I notice how my glance engulfs these things, only imaginings, yet full of bliss. And my sight takes in more and more, it lets itself go more and more, creates more and more, conjures more and more, more . . . and . . . more.

Now the creation, the artwork of chance, emerges, clear, just like in the past, looming from things forgotten, re-created, formed, painted by fantasy, that magically talented artist.

Not large: small. And not really a whole, but perfect, as it had been back then. And yet infinitely blurring into darkness in all directions. A world. A universe. In it light trembles, and a powerful mood, but no sound. Nothing of the laughing noises around it can penetrate: the laughing noises not of now, but of then.

Right at the base, dazzling damask. Across it, woven flowers zigzag and curve and wind. Translucently pressed upon it and rising up slender a crystalline goblet, half-filled with pallid gold. Before it, dreaming, a hand stretches out, the fingers draped loosely around the goblet's base. Clinging to one finger is a matte silver ring upon which a ruby bleeds.

Where the vision strives to form an arm above the delicate wrist, in a crescendo of shapes, it blurs into the whole. A sweet enigma. The girl's hand lies dreamy and still. Only where a light-blue vein snakes its way over its pearly whiteness does life pulse and passion pound, slowly and violently. And as it feels my glance it becomes swifter and swifter, wilder and wilder, till it turns into a pleading flutter: stop, don't . . .

But my glance is heavy and cruelly sensual, as it was then. It weighs upon the quaking hand in which, in the fight with love, love's victory pulsates . . . like then . . . like then.

Slowly, from the bottom of the goblet, a pearl detaches itself and floats upward. As it moves into the ruby's orbit of light it flames up blood red, and then on the surface is suddenly quenched. The disturbance threatens to dissipate everything, and my eyes struggle to rekindle the vision's soft contours.

Now it is gone, faded into darkness. I breathe, breathe deeply, for I notice that I had forgotten now, as I had back then . . .

I lean back, fatigued, and pain flares up. But I know now as surely as I did then: You *did* love me . . . Which is why I can cry now.

Katherine Mansfield

Miss Brill

Although it was so brilliantly fine—the blue sky powdered with gold and great spots of light like white wine splashed over the Jardins Publiques—Miss Brill was glad that she had decided on her fur. The air was motionless, but when you opened your mouth there was just a faint chill, like a chill from a glass of iced water before you sip, and now and again a leaf came drifting—from nowhere, from the sky. Miss Brill put up her hand and touched her fur. Dear little thing! It was nice to feel it again. She had taken it out of its box that afternoon, shaken out the moth-powder, given it a good brush, and rubbed the life back into the dim little eyes. "What has been happening to me?" said the sad little eyes. Oh, how sweet it was to see them snap at her again from the red eiderdown! . . . But the nose, which was of some black composition, wasn't at all firm. It must have had a knock, some-how. Never mind—a little dab of black sealing-wax when the time came—when it was absolutely necessary. . . . Little rogue! Yes, she really felt like that about it. Little rogue biting its tail just by her left ear. She could have taken it off and laid it on her lap and stroked it. She felt a tingling in her hands and arms, but that came from walking, she supposed. And when she breathed, something light and sad—no, not sad, exactly—something gentle seemed to move in her bosom.

There were a number of people out this afternoon, far more than last Sunday. And the band sounded louder and gayer. That was because the Sea-son had begun. For although the band played all the year round on Sundays, out of season it was never the same. It was like some one playing with only the family to listen; it didn't care how it played if there weren't any strangers present. Wasn't the conductor wearing a new coat, too? She was sure it was new. He scraped with his foot and flapped his arms like a rooster about to crow, and the bandsmen sitting in the green rotunda blew out their cheeks and glared at the music. Now there came a little "flutey" bit—very pretty!—a little chain of bright drops. She was sure it would be repeated. It was; she lifted her head and smiled.

Only two people shared her "special" seat: a fine old man in a velvet coat, his hands clasped over a huge carved walking-stick, and a big old woman, sitting upright, with a roll of knitting on her embroidered apron. They did not speak. This was disappointing, for Miss Brill always looked forward to the conversation. She had become really quite expert, she thought, at listening as though she didn't listen, at sitting in other people's lives just for a minute while they talked round her.

She glanced, sideways, at the old couple. Perhaps they would go soon. Last Sunday, too, hadn't been as interesting as usual. An Englishman and his wife, he wearing a dreadful Panama hat and she button boots. And she'd gone on the whole time about how she ought to wear spectacles; she knew she needed them; but that it was no good getting any; they'd be sure to break and they'd never keep on. And he'd been so patient. He'd suggested every-thing—gold rims, the kind that curved round your ears, little pads inside the bridge. No, nothing would please her. "They'll always be sliding down my nose!" Miss Brill had wanted to shake her.

The old people sat on the bench, still as statues. Never mind, there was always the crowd to watch. To and fro, in front of the flower-beds and the band rotunda, the couples and groups paraded, stopped to talk, to greet, to buy a handful of flowers from the old beggar who had his tray fixed to the railings. Little children ran among them, swooping and laughing; little boys with big white silk bows under their chins, little girls, little French dolls, dressed up in velvet and lace. And sometimes a tiny staggerer came suddenly rocking into the open from under the trees, stopped, stared, as suddenly sat down "flop," until its small high-stepping mother, like a young hen, rushed scolding to its rescue. Other people sat on the benches and green chairs, but they were nearly always the same, Sunday after Sunday, and—Miss Brill had often noticed—there was something funny about nearly all of them. They were odd, silent, nearly all old, and from the way they stared they looked as though they'd just come from dark little rooms or even—even cupboards!

Behind the rotunda the slender trees with yellow leaves down droop-ing, and through them just a line of sea, and beyond the blue sky with gold-veined clouds.

Tum-tum-tum tiddle-um! tiddle-um! tum tiddley-um tum ta! blew the band.

Two young girls in red came by and two young soldiers in blue met them, and they laughed and paired and went off arm-in-arm. Two peasant women with funny straw hats passed, gravely, leading beautiful smoke-coloured donkeys. A cold, pale nun hurried by. A beautiful woman came along and dropped her bunch of violets, and a little boy ran after to hand them to her, and she took them and threw them away as if they'd been poisoned. Dear me! Miss Brill didn't know whether to admire that or not! And now an ermine toque and a gentleman in grey met just in front of her. He was tall, stiff, dignified, and she was wearing the ermine toque she'd bought when her hair was yellow. Now everything, her hair, her face, even her eyes, was the same colour as the shabby ermine, and her hand, in its cleaned glove, lifted to dab her lips, was a tiny yellowish paw. Oh, she was so pleased to see him—delighted! She rather thought they were going to meet that afternoon. She described where she'd been—everywhere, here, there, along by the sea. The day was so charming—didn't he agree? And wouldn't he, perhaps? . . . But he shook his head, lighted a cigarette, slowly breathed a great deep puff into her face, and, even while she was still talking and laughing, flicked the match away and walked on. The ermine toque was alone; she smiled more brightly than ever. But even the band seemed to know what she was feeling and played more softly, played tenderly, and the drum beat, "The Brute! The Brute!" over and over. What would she do? What was going to happen now? But as Miss Brill wondered, the ermine toque turned, raised her hand as though she'd seen some one else, much nicer, just over there, and pattered away. And the band changed again and played more quickly, more gaily than ever, and the old couple on Miss Brill's seat got up and marched away, and such a funny old man with long whiskers hobbled along in time to the music and was nearly knocked over by four girls walking abreast.

Oh, how fascinating it was! How she enjoyed it! How she loved sitting here, watching it all! It was like a play. It was exactly like a play. Who could believe the sky at the back wasn't painted? But it wasn't till a little brown dog trotted on solemn and then slowly trotted off, like a little "theatre" dog, a little dog that had been drugged, that Miss Brill discovered what it was that made it so exciting. They were all on the stage. They weren't only the audience, not only looking on; they were acting. Even she had a part and came every Sunday. No doubt somebody would have noticed if she hadn't been there; she was part of the performance after all. How strange she'd never thought of it like that before! And yet it explained why she made such a point of starting from home at just the same time each week—so as not to be late for the performance—and it also explained why she had quite a queer, shy feeling at telling her English pupils how she spent her Sunday afternoons. No wonder! Miss Brill nearly laughed out loud. She was on the stage. She thought of the old invalid gentleman to whom she read the newspaper four afternoons a week while he slept in the garden. She had got quite used to the frail head on the cotton pillow, the hollowed eyes, the open mouth and the high pinched nose. If he'd been dead she mightn't have noticed for weeks; she wouldn't have minded. But suddenly he knew he was having the paper read to him by an actress! "An actress!" The old head lifted; two points of light quivered in the old eyes. "An actress—are ye?" And Miss Brill smoothed the newspaper as though it were the manuscript of her part and said gently: "Yes, I have been an actress for a long time."

The band had been having a rest. Now they started again. And what they played was warm, sunny, yet there was just a faint chill—a something, what was it?—not sadness—no, not sadness—a something that made you want to sing. The tune lifted, lifted, the light shone; and it seemed to Miss Brill that in another moment all of them, all the whole company, would begin singing. The young ones, the laughing ones who were moving together, they would begin, and the men's voices, very resolute and brave, would join them. And then she too, she too, and the others on the benches—they would come in with a kind of accompaniment—something low, that scarcely rose or fell, something so beautiful—moving. . . . And Miss Brill's eyes filled with tears and she looked smiling at all the other members of the company. Yes, we understand, we understand, she thought—though what they understood she didn't know.

Just at that moment a boy and a girl came and sat down where the old couple had been. They were beautifully dressed; they were in love. The hero and heroine, of course, just arrived from his father's yacht. And still soundlessly singing, still with that trembling smile, Miss Brill prepared to listen.

"No, not now," said the girl. "Not here, I can't."

"But why? Because of that stupid old thing at the end there?" asked the boy. "Why does she come here at all—who wants her? Why doesn't she keep her silly old mug at home?"

"It's her fu-fur which is so funny," giggled the girl. "It's exactly like a fried whiting."

"Ah, be off with you!" said the boy in an angry whisper. Then: "Tell me, ma??? petite chére—"

"No, not here," said the girl. "Not *yet*."

On her way home she usually bought a slice of honey-cake at the baker's. It was her Sunday treat. Sometimes there was an almond in her slice, sometimes not. It made a great difference. If there was an almond it was like carrying home a tiny present—a surprise—something that might very well not have been there. She hurried on the almond Sundays and struck the match for the kettle in quite a dashing way.

But to-day she passed the baker's by, climbed the stairs, went into the little dark room—her room like a cupboard—and sat down on the red eiderdown. She sat there for a long time. The box that the fur came out of was on the bed. She unclasped the necklet quickly; quickly, without looking, laid it inside. But when she put the lid on she thought she heard something crying.

First Person: Katherine Mansfield on "Crafting Miss Brill"

TO RICHARD MURRY, 17 JANUARY 1921

It's a very queer thing how *craft* comes into writing. I mean down to details. Par exemple. In "Miss Brill" I choose not only the length of every sentence, but even the sound of every sentence. I choose the rise and fall of every paragraph to fit her, and to fit her on that day at that very moment. After I'd written it I read it aloud—numbers of times—just as one would *play over* a musical composition—trying to get it nearer and nearer to the expression of Miss Brill—until it fitted her.

Don't think I'm vain about the little sketch. It's only the method I wanted to explain. I often wonder whether other writers do the same—If a thing has really come off it seems to me there mustn't be one single word out of place or one word that could be taken out. That's how I AIM at writing. It will take some time to get anywhere near there.

But you know, Richard, I was only thinking last night people have hardly begun to write yet. Put poetry out of it for a moment and leave out Shakespeare—now I mean prose. Take the very best of it. Aren't they still cutting up sections rather than tackling the whole of a mind? I had a moment of absolute terror in the night. I suddenly thought of *a living mind*—a whole mind—with absolutely nothing left out. With *all* that one knows how much does one not know? I used to fancy one knew all but some kind of mysterious core (or one could). But now I believe just the opposite. The unknown is far, far greater than the known. The known is only a mere shadow. This is a fearful thing and terribly hard to face. But it must be faced.

SADAT HASAN MANTO

The Return

The special train left Amritsar at two in the afternoon, arriving at Mughalpura, Lahore, eight hours later. Many had been killed on the way, a lot more injured and countless lost.

It was at 10 o'clock the next morning that Sirajuddin regained consciousness. He was lying on bare ground, surrounded by screaming men, women and children. It did not make sense.

He lay very still, gazing at the dusty sky. He appeared not to notice the confusion or the noise. To a stranger, he might have looked like an old man in deep thought, though this was not the case. He was in shock, suspended, as it were, over a bottomless pit.

Then his eyes moved and, suddenly, caught the sun. The shock brought him back to the world of living men and women. A succession of images raced through his mind. Attack . . . fire . . . escape . . . railway station . . . night . . . Sakina. He rose abruptly and began searching through the milling crowd in the refugee camp.

He spent hours looking, all the time shouting his daughter's name . . . Sakina, Sakina . . . but she was nowhere to be found.

Total confusion prevailed, with people looking for lost sons, daughters, mothers, wives. In the end Sirajuddin gave up. He sat down, away from the crowd, and tried to think clearly. Where did he part from Sakina and her mother? Then it came to him in a flash—the dead body of his wife, her stomach ripped open. It was an image that wouldn't go away.

Sakina's mother was dead. That much was certain. She had died in front of his eyes. He could hear her voice: 'Leave me where I am. Take the girl away.'

The two of them had begun to run. Sakina's *dupatta* had slipped to the ground and he had stopped to pick it up and she had said: 'Father, leave it.'

He could feel a bulge in his pocket. It was a length of cloth. Yes, he recognized it. It was Sakina's *dupatta*, but where was she?

Other details were missing. Had he brought her as far as the railway station? Had she got into the carriage with him? When the rioters had stopped the train, had they taken her with them?

All questions. There were no answers. He wished he could weep, but tears would not come. He knew then that he needed help.

A few days later, he had a break. There were eight of them, young men armed with guns. They also had a truck. They said they brought back women and children left behind on the other side.

He gave them a description of his daughter. 'She is fair, very pretty. No, she doesn't look like me, but her mother. About seventeen. Big eyes, black hair, a mole on the left cheek. Find my daughter. May God bless you.'

The young men had said to Sirajuddin: 'If your daughter is alive, we will find her.'

And they had tried. At the risk of their lives, they had driven to Amritsar, recovered many women and children and brought them back to the camp, but they had not found Sakina.

On their next trip out, they had found a girl on the roadside. They seemed to have scared her and she had started running. They had stopped the truck, jumped out and run after her. Finally, they had caught up with her in a field. She was very pretty and she had a mole on her left cheek. One of the men had said to her: 'Don't be frightened. Is your name Sakina?' Her face had gone pale, but when they had told her who they were, she had confessed that she was Sakina, daughter of Sirajuddin.

The young men were very kind to her. They had fed her, given her milk to drink and put her in their truck. One of them had given her his jacket so that she could cover herself. It was obvious that she was ill-at-ease without her *dupatta*, trying nervously to cover her breasts with her arms.

Many days had gone by and Sirajuddin had still not had any news of his daughter. All his time was spent running from camp to camp, looking for her. At night, he would pray for the success of the young men who were looking for his daughter. Their words would ring in his ears: 'If your daughter is alive, we will find her.'

Then one day he saw them in the camp. They were about to drive away. 'Son,' he shouted after one of them, 'have you found Sakina, my daughter?'

'We will, we will,' they replied all together.

The old man again prayed for them. It made him feel better.

That evening there was sudden activity in the camp. He saw four men carrying the body of a young girl found unconscious near the railway tracks. They were taking her to the camp hospital. He began to follow them.

He stood outside the hospital for some time, then went in. In one of the rooms, he found a stretcher with someone lying on it.

A light was switched on. It was a young woman with a mole on her left cheek. 'Sakina,' Sirajuddin screamed.

The doctor, who had switched on the light, stared at Sirajuddin.

'I am her father,' he stammered.

The doctor looked at the prostrate body and felt for the pulse. Then he said to the old man: 'Open the window.'

The young woman on the stretcher moved slightly. Her hands groped for the cord which kept her *shalwar* tied round her waist. With painful slowness, she unfastened it, pulled the garment down and opened her thighs.

'She is alive. My daughter is alive,' Sirajuddin shouted with joy.

The doctor broke into a cold sweat.

W. Somerset Maugham

The Ant and the Grasshopper

When I was a very small boy I was made to learn by heart certain of the fables of La Fontaine, and the moral of each was carefully explained to me. Among those learned was *The Ant and the Grasshopper*, which is devised to bring home to the young the useful lesson that in an imperfect world industry is rewarded and giddiness punished. In this admirable fable (I apologise for telling something which everyone is politely, but inexactly, supposed to know) the ant spends a laborious summer gathering its winter store, while the grasshopper sits on a blade of grass singing to the sun. Winter comes and the ant is comfortably provided for, but the grasshopper has an empty larder: he goes to the ant and begs for a little food. Then the ant gives him her classic answer:

"What were you doing in the summer time?"

"Saving your presence, I sang. I sang all day, all night."

"You sang. Why, then go and dance."

I do not ascribe it to perversity on my part, but rather to the inconsequence of childhood, which is deficient in moral sense, that I could never quite reconcile myself to the lesson. My sympathies were with the grasshopper and for some time I never saw an ant without putting my foot on it. In this summary (and as I have discovered since, entirely human) fashion I sought to express my disapproval of prudence and common-sense.

I could not help thinking of this fable when the other day I saw George Ramsay lunching by himself in a restaurant. I never saw anyone wear an expression of such deep gloom. He was staring into space. He looked as though the burden of the whole world sat upon his shoulders. I was sorry for him: I suspected at once that his unfortunate brother had been causing trouble again. I went up to him and held out my hand.

"How are you?" I asked.

"I'm not in hilarious spirits," he answered.

"Is it Tom again?"

He sighed.

"Yes, it's Tom again."

"Why don't you chuck him? You've done everything in the world for him. You must know by now that he's quite hopeless."

I suppose every family has a black sheep. Tom had been a sore trial to his for twenty years. He had begun life decently enough: he went into business, married and had two children. The Ramsays were perfectly respectable people and there was every reason to suppose that Tom Ramsay would have a useful and honourable career. But one day, without warning, he announced that he didn't like work and that he wasn't suited for marriage. He wanted to enjoy himself. He would listen to no expostulations. He left his wife and his office. He had a little money and he spent two happy years in various capitals of Europe. Rumours of his doings reached his relations from time to time and they were profoundly shocked. He certainly had a very good time. They shook their heads and asked what would happen when his money was spent. They soon found out: he borrowed. He was charming and unscrupulous. I have never met anyone to whom it was more difficult to refuse a loan. He made a steady income from his friends and he made friends easily. But he always said that the money you spent on necessities was boring; the money that was amusing to spend was the money you spent on luxuries. For this he depended on his brother George. He did not waste his charm on him. George was respectable. Once or twice he fell to Tom's promises of amendment and gave him considerable sums in order that he might make a fresh start. On these Tom bought a motorcar and some very nice jewellery. But when circumstances forced George to realise that his brother would never settle down and he washed his hands of him, Tom, without a qualm, began to blackmail him. It was not very nice for a respectable lawyer to find his brother shaking cocktails behind the bar of his favourite restaurant or to see him waiting on the box-seat of a taxi outside his club. Tom said that to serve in a bar or to drive a taxi was a perfectly decent occupation, but if George could oblige him with a couple of hundred pounds he didn't mind for the honour of the family giving it up. George paid.

Once Tom nearly went to prison. George was terribly upset. He went into the whole discreditable affair. Really Tom had gone too far. He had been wild, thoughtless and selfish, but he had never before done anything dishonest, by which George meant illegal; and if he were prosecuted he would assuredly be convicted. But you cannot allow your only brother to go to gaol. The man Tom had cheated, a man called Cronshaw, was vindictive. He was determined to take the matter into court; he said Tom was a scoundrel and should be punished. It cost George an infinite deal of trouble and five hundred pounds to settle the affair. I have never seen him in such a rage as when he heard that Tom and Cronshaw had gone off together to Monte Carlo the moment they cashed the cheque. They spent a happy month there.

For twenty years Tom raced and gambled, philandered with the prettiest girls, danced, ate in the most expensive restaurants, and dressed beautifully. He always looked as if he had just stepped out of a bandbox. Though he was forty-six you would never have taken him for more than thirty-five. He was a most amusing companion and though you knew he was perfectly worthless you could not but enjoy his society. He had high spirits, an unfailing gaiety and incredible charm. I never grudged the contributions he regularly levied on me for the necessities of his existence. I never lent him fifty pounds without feeling that I was in his debt. Tom Ramsay knew everyone and everyone knew Tom Ramsay. You could not approve of him, but you could not help liking him.

Poor George, only a year older than his scapegrace brother, looked sixty. He had never taken more than a fortnight's holiday in the year for a quarter of a century. He was in his office every morning at nine-thirty and never left it till six. He was honest, industrious and worthy. He had a good wife, to whom he had never been unfaithful even in thought, and four daughters to whom he was the best of fathers. He made a point of saving a third of his income and his plan was to retire at fifty-five to a little house in the country where he proposed to cultivate his garden and play golf. His life was blameless. He was glad that he was growing old because Tom was growing old too. He rubbed his hands and said:

"It was all very well when Tom was young and good-looking, but he's only a year younger than I am. In four years he'll be fifty. He won't find life too easy then. I shall have thirty thousand pounds by the time I'm fifty. For twenty-five years I've said that Tom would end in the gutter. And we shall see how he likes that. We shall see if it really pays best to work or be idle."

Poor George! I sympathised with him. I wondered now as I sat down beside him what infamous thing Tom had done. George was evidently very much upset.

"Do you know what's happened now?" he asked me.

I was prepared for the worst. I wondered if Tom had got into the hands of the police at last. George could hardly bring himself to speak.

"You're not going to deny that all my life I've been hard working, decent, respectable and straightforward. After a life of industry and thrift I can look forward to retiring on a small income in gilt-edged securities. I've always done my duty in that state of life in which it has pleased Providence to place me."

"True."

"And you can't deny that Tom has been an idle, worthless dissolute and dishonourable rogue. If there were any justice he'd be in the workhouse."

"True."

George grew red in the face.

"A few weeks ago he became engaged to a woman old enough to be his mother. And now she's died and left him everything she had. Half a million pounds, a yacht, a house in London and a house in the country."

George Ramsay beat his clenched fist on the table.

"It's not fair, I tell you, it's not fair. Damn it, it's not fair."

I could not help it. I burst into a shout of laughter as I looked at George's wrathful face. I rolled in my chair, I very nearly fell on the floor. George never forgave me. But Tom often asks me to excellent dinners in his charming house in Mayfair, and if he occasionally borrows a trifle from me, that is merely from force of habit. It is never more than a sovereign.

GUY DE MAUPASSANT

A Piece of String

Along all the roads around Goderville the peasants and their wives were coming toward the burgh because it was market day. The men were proceeding with slow steps, the whole body bent forward at each movement of their long twisted legs, deformed by their hard work, by the weight on the plow which, at the same time, raised the left shoulder and swerved the figure, by the reaping of the wheat which made the knees spread to make a firm "purchase," by all the slow and painful labors of the country. Their blouses, blue, "stiff-starched," shining as if varnished, ornamented with a little design in white at the neck and wrists, puffed about their bony bodies, seemed like balloons ready to carry them off. From each of them a head, two arms, and two feet protruded.

Some led a cow or a calf by a cord, and their wives, walking behind the animal, whipped its haunches with a leafy branch to hasten its progress. They carried large baskets on their arms from which, in some cases, chickens and, in others, ducks thrust out their heads. And they walked with a quicker, livelier step than their husbands. Their spare straight figures were wrapped in a scanty little shawl, pinned over their flat bosoms, and their heads were enveloped in a white cloth glued to the hair and surmounted by a cap.

Then a wagon passed at the jerky trot of a nag, shaking strangely, two men seated side by side and a woman in the bottom of the vehicle, the latter holding on to the sides to lessen the hard jolts.

In the public square of Goderville there was a crowd, a throng of human beings and animals mixed together. The horns of the cattle, the tall hats with long nap of the rich peasant, and the headgear of the peasant women rose above the surface of the assembly. And the clamorous, shrill, screaming voices made a continuous and savage din which sometimes was dominated by the robust lungs of some countryman's laugh, or the long lowing of a cow tied to the wall of a house.

All that smacked of the stable, the dairy and the dirt heap, hay and sweat, giving forth that unpleasant odor, human and animal, peculiar to the people of the field.

Maître Hauchecome, of Breaute, had just arrived at Goderville, and he was directing his steps toward the public square, when he perceived upon the ground a little piece of string. Maître Hauchecome, economical like a true Norman, thought that everything useful ought to be picked up, and he bent painfully, for he suffered from rheumatism. He took the bit of thin cord from the ground and began to roll it carefully when he noticed Maître Malandain, the harness-maker, on the threshold of his door, looking at him. They had heretofore had business together on the subject of a halter, and they were on bad terms, being both good haters. Maître Hauchecome was seized with a sort of shame to be seen thus by his enemy, picking a bit of string out of the dirt. He concealed his "find" quickly under his blouse, then in his trousers' pocket; then he pretended to be still looking on the ground for something which he did not find, and he went toward the market, his head forward, bent double by his pains.

He was soon lost in the noisy and slowly moving crowd, which was busy with interminable bargainings. The peasants milked, went and came, perplexed, always in fear of being cheated, not daring to decide, watching the vender's eye, ever trying to find the trick in the man and the flaw in the beast.

The women, having placed their great baskets at their feet, had taken out the poultry which lay upon the ground, tied together by the feet, with terrified eyes and scarlet crests.

They heard offers, stated their prices with a dry air and impassive face, or perhaps, suddenly deciding on some proposed reduction, shouted to the customer who was slowly going away: "All right, Maître Authirne, I'll give it to you for that."

Then little by little the square was deserted, and the Angelus ringing at noon, those who had stayed too long, scattered to their shops. ·

At Jourdain's the great room was full of people eating, as the big court was full of vehicles of all kinds, carts, gigs, wagons, dump carts, yellow with dirt, mended and patched, raising their shafts to the sky like two arms, or perhaps with their shafts in the ground and their backs in the air.

Just opposite the diners seated at the table, the immense fireplace, filled with bright flames, cast a lively heat on the backs of the row on the right. Three spits were turning on which were chickens, pigeons, and legs of mutton; and an appetizing odor of roast beef and gravy dripping over the nicely browned skin rose from the hearth, increased the jovialness, and made everybody's mouth water.

All the aristocracy of the plow ate there, at Maître Jourdain's, tavern keeper and horse dealer, a rascal who had money.

The dishes were passed and emptied, as were the jugs of yellow cider. Everyone told his affairs, his purchases, and sales. They discussed the crops. The weather was favorable for the green things but not for the wheat.

Suddenly the drum beat in the court, before the house. Everybody rose except a few indifferent persons, and ran to the door, or to the windows, their mouths still full and napkins in their hands.

After the public crier had ceased his drum-beating, he called out in a jerky voice, speaking his phrases irregularly:

"It is hereby made known to the inhabitants of Goderville, and in general to all persons present at the market, that there was lost this morning, on the road to Benzeville, between nine and ten o'clock, a black leather pocketbook containing five hundred francs and some business papers. The finder is requested to return same with all haste to the mayor's office or to Maître Fortune Houlbreque of Manneville; there will be twenty francs reward."

Then the man went away. The heavy roll of the drum and the crier's voice were again heard at a distance.

Then they began to talk of this event discussing the chances that Maître Houlbreque had of finding or not finding his pocketbook.

And the meal concluded. They were finishing their coffee when a chief of the gendarmes appeared upon the threshold.

He inquired:

"Is Maître Hauchecome, of Breaute, here?"

Maître Hauchecome, seated at the other end of the table, replied:

"Here I am."

And the officer resumed:

"Maître Hauchecome, will you have the goodness to accompany me to the mayor's office? The mayor would like to talk to you."

The peasant, surprised and disturbed, swallowed at a draught his tiny glass of brandy, rose, and, even more bent than in the morning, for the first steps after each rest were specially difficult, set out, repeating: "Here I am, here I am."

The mayor was awaiting him, seated on an armchair. He was the notary of the vicinity, a stout, serious man, with pompous phrases.

"Maître Hauchecome," said he, "you were seen this morning to pick up, on the road to Benzeville, the pocketbook lost by Maître Houlbreque of Manneville."

The countryman, astounded, looked at the mayor, already terrified, by this suspicion resting on him without his knowing why.

"Me? Me? Me pick up the pocketbook?"

"Yes, you, yourself."

"Word of honor, I never heard of it."

"But you were seen."

"I was seen, me? Who says he saw me?"

"Monsieur Malandain, the harness-maker."

The old man remembered, understood, and flushed with anger.

"Ah, he saw me, the clodhopper, he saw me pick up this string, here, M'sieu the Mayor." And rummaging in his pocket he drew out the little piece of string.

But the mayor, incredulous, shook his head.

"You will not make me believe, Maître Hauchecome, that Monsieur Malandain, who is a man worthy of credence, mistook this cord for a pocketbook."

The peasant, furious, lifted his hand, spat at one side to attest his honor, repeating:

"It is nevertheless the truth of the good God, the sacred truth, M'sieu' the Mayor. I repeat it on my soul and my salvation."

The mayor resumed:

"After picking up the object, you stood like a stilt, looking a long while in the mud to see if any piece of money had fallen out."

The good, old man choked with indignation and fear.

"How anyone can tell—how anyone can tell—such lies to take away an honest man's reputation! How can anyone—"

There was no use in his protesting, nobody believed him. He was confronted with Monsieur Malandain, who repeated and maintained his affirmation. They abused each other for an hour. At his own request, Maître Hauchecome was searched, nothing was found on him.

Finally the mayor, very much perplexed, discharged him with the warning that he would consult the public prosecutor and ask for further orders.

The news had spread. As he left the mayor's office, the old man was surrounded and questioned with a serious or bantering curiosity, in which there was no indignation. He began to tell the story of the string. No one believed him. They laughed at him.

He went along, stopping his friends, beginning endlessly his statement and his protestations, showing his pockets turned inside out, to prove that he had nothing.

They said:

"Old rascal, get out!"

And he grew angry, becoming exasperated, hot, and distressed at not being believed, not knowing what to do and always repeating himself.

Night came. He must depart. He started on his way with three neighbors to whom he pointed out the place where he had picked up the bit of string; and all along the road he spoke of his adventure.

In the evening he took a turn in the village of Breaute, in order to tell it to everybody. He only met with incredulity.

It made him ill at night.

The next day about one o'clock in the afternoon, Marius Paumelle, a hired man in the employ of Maître Breton, husbandman at Ymanville, returned the pocketbook and its contents to Maître Houlbreque of Manneville.

This man claimed to have found the object in the road; but not knowing how to read, he had carried it to the house and given it to his employer.

The news spread through the neighborhood. Maître Hauchecome was informed of it. He immediately went the circuit and began to recount his story completed by the happy climax. He was in triumph.

"What grieved me so much was not the thing itself, as the lying. There is nothing so shameful as to be placed under a cloud on account of a lie."

He talked of his adventure all day long, he told it on the highway to people who were passing by, in the wine-shop to people who were drinking there, and to persons coming out of church the following Sunday. He stopped strangers to tell them about it. He was calm now, and yet something disturbed him without his knowing exactly what it was. People had the air of joking while they listened. They did not seem convinced. He seemed to feel that remarks were being made behind his back.

On Tuesday of the next week he went to the market at Goderville, urged solely by the necessity he felt of discussing the case.

Malandain, standing at his door, began to laugh on seeing him pass. Why?

He approached a farmer from Crequetot, who did not let him finish, and giving him a thump in the stomach said to his face:

"You big rascal."

Then he turned his back on him.

Maître Hauchecome was confused, why was he called a big rascal?

When he was seated at the table in Jourdain's tavern he commenced to explain "the affair."

A horse dealer from Monvilliers called to him:

"Come, come, old sharper, that's an old trick; I know all about your piece of string!"

Hauchecome stammered:

"But since the pocketbook was found."

But the other man replied:

"Shut up, papa, there is one that finds, and there is one that reports. At any rate you are mixed with it."

The peasant stood choking. He understood. They accused him of having had the pocketbook returned by a confederate, by an accomplice.

He tried to protest. All the table began to laugh.

He could not finish his dinner and went away, in the midst of jeers.

He went home ashamed and indignant, choking with anger and confusion, the more dejected that he was capable with his Norman cunning of doing what they had accused him of, and even boasting of it as of a good turn. His innocence to him, in a confused way, was impossible to prove, as his sharpness was known. And he was stricken to the heart by the injustice of the suspicion.

Then he began to recount the adventures again, prolonging his history every day, adding each time, new reasons, more energetic protestations, more solemn oaths which he imagined and prepared in his hours of solitude, his whole mind given up to the story of the string. He was believed so much the less as his defense was more complicated and his arguing more subtle.

"Those are lying excuses," they said behind his back.

He felt it, consumed his heart over it, and wore himself out with useless efforts. He wasted away before their very eyes.

The wags now made him tell about the string to amuse them, as they make a soldier who has been on a campaign tell about his battles. His mind, touched to the depth, began to weaken.

Toward the end of December he took to his bed.

He died in the first days of January, and in the delirium of his death struggles he kept claiming his innocence, reiterating:

"A piece of string, a piece of string,—look—here it is, M'sieu' the Mayor."

HERMAN MELVILLE

Daniel Orme

A profound portrait-painter like Titian or our famous country-man Stewart, what such an observer sees in any face he may earnestly study, that essentially is the man. To disentangle his true history from contemporary report is superfluous. Not so with us who are scarce Titians and Stewarts. Occasionally we are struck by some exceptional aspect instantly awakening our interest. But it is an interest that in its ignorance is full of commonplace curiosity. We try to ascertain from somebody the career and experience of the man, or may seek to obtain the information from himself. But what we hear from others may prove but unreliable gossip, and he himself, if approached, prove uncommunicative. In short, in most instances he turns out to be like a meteoric stone in a field. There it lies. The neighbours have their say about it, and an odd enough say it may prove. But what is it? Whence did it come? In what unimaginable sphere did it get that strange, igneous, metallic look, the kine now cropping the dewy grass about it?

Any attempt to depict such a character as is here suggested must be an imperfect one. Nevertheless, it is a man of this description who is the subject of the present essay at a sketch.

A sailor's name as it appears on a crew-list is not always his real name, nor in every instance does it indicate his country. This premised, be it said that by the name at the head of this writing long went an old man-of-war's man of whose earlier history it may verily be said that nobody knew any-thing but himself; and it was idle to seek it in that quarter. Conscientious, constantly so, in discharging his duties, the respect of his officers naturally followed. And for his fellow-sailors, if none had reason to like one so un-like themselves, none dared to take the slightest liberties with him. Any approach to it, and his eye was a tutoring and deterring one. Getting in years at last, he was retired as captain of a top, and assigned to a lower grade and post, namely, at the foot of the mainmast, his business there being simply to stand by, to let go, and make fast. But even this, with the night-watches, ere long exacted too much from a sailor, a septuagenarian. In brief, he belays his last halyard, and slips into obscure moorings ashore. What-ever his disposition may originally have been, there, in his latter cruise at least, had he been specially noted for his unsociability. Not that he was gruff like some marine veterans with the lumbago, nor stealthily taciturn like an Indian; but moody, frequently muttering to himself. And from such mut-tered soliloquy he would sometimes start, and with a look or gesture so uncheerfully peculiar that the Calvinistic imagination of a certain frigate's chaplain construed it into remorseful condemnation of some dark deed in the past.

His features were large, strong, cast as in iron; but the effect of a car-tridge explosion had peppered all below the eyes with dense dottings of black-blue. When according to custom he as mainmast man used to doff his hat in less laconic speech with the officer-of-the-deck, his tanned brow showed like October's tawny moon revealed in crescent above an ominous cloud. Along with his moody ways, was it this uncanny physical aspect, the result of a mere chance, was it this, and this alone, that had suggested the germ of the rumour among certain afterguardsmen that in earlier life he had been a bucanier of the Keys and the Gulf, one of Lafitte's murderous crew? Certain it is, he had once served on a letter-of-marque.

In stature, though bowed somewhat in the shoulders, akin to the cham-pion of Gath. Hands heavy and hard; short nails like withered horn. A pow-erful head, and shaggy. An iron-gray beard broad as a commodore's pennant, and about the mouth indelibly streaked with the moodily dribbled tobacco juice of all his cruises. In his day watch-below silently couched by himself on the gun-deck in a bay between black cannon, he might have sug-gested an image of the Great Grizzly of the California Sierras, his coat the worse for wear, grim in his last den awaiting the last hour.

In his shore moorings—hard by the waters, not very far from the docks—what with his all-night-in and easier lot in every particular, with choice of associates when he desired them, which was not always, happily he lost most of his gruffness as the old mastiff of the mainmast exposed to all weathers and with salt-horse for his diet. A stranger accosting him sunning himself upon some old spar on the strand, and kindly saluting him there, would receive no surly response, and if more than mere salutation was ex-changed, would probably go away with the impression that he had been talking with an interesting oddity, a salt philosopher, not lacking in a sort of grim common-sense.

After being ashore for a period, a singularity in his habits was re-marked. At times, but only when he might think himself quite alone, he would roll aside the bosom of his darned Guernsey frock and steadfastly contemplate something on his body. If by chance discovered in this, he would quickly conceal all and growl his resentment.

This peculiarity awakening the curiosity of certain idle observers, lodgers under the same roof with him, and none caring to be so bold as to question him as to the reason of it, or to ask what it was on his body, a drug was enlisted as a means of finding out the secret. In prudent quantities it was slyly slipped into his huge bowl of tea at supper. Next morning a certain old-clothes-man whispered to his gossips the result of his sorry intrusion overnight.

Drawing them into a corner, and looking around furtively, "Listen," said he, and told them an eerie story, following it up with shuddering conjectures, vague enough, but dear to the superstitious and ignorant mind. What he had really discovered was this: a crucifix in indigo and vermilion tattooed on the chest and on the side of the heart. Slanting across the crucifix and paling the pigment there ran a whitish scar, long and thin, such as might ensue from the slash of a cutlass imperfectly parried or dodged. The cross of the Passion is often tattooed upon the sailor, upon the forearm generally, sometimes, though but rarely, on the trunk. As for the scar, the old mastman had in legitimate naval service known what it was to repel boarders and not without receiving a sabre mark from them. It may be. The gossips of the lodging, however, took another view of the discovery, and at last reported to the landlady that the old sailor was a sort of *man forbid*, a man branded by the Evil Spirit, and it would be well to get rid of him, lest the charm in the horse-shoe nailed over the house-door should be fatally counteracted and be naught. The good woman, however, was a sensible lady with no belief in the horse-shoe, though she tolerated it, and as the old mastman was regular in his weekly dues, and never made noise or gave trouble, she turned a deaf ear to all solicitations against him.

Since in his presence it was ever prudently concealed, the old mariner was not then aware of underhand proceedings. At sea it had never come to his ears that some of his shipmates thought him a bucanier, for there was a quiet leonine droop about the angles of his mouth that said—*hands off*. So now he was ignorant of the circumstances that the same rumour had followed him ashore. Had his habits been social, he would have socially felt the effect of this and cast about in vain for the cause; whether having basis or not, some ill-report is in certain instances like what sailors call a *dry tempest*, during which there is neither rain nor lightning, though none the less the viewless and intangible winds make a shipwreck and then ask—who did it?

So Orme pursued his solitary way with not much from without to disturb him. But Time's moments still keep descending upon the quietest hour, and though it were adamant they would wear it. In his retirement the superannuated giant begins to mellow down into a sort of animal decay. In hard, rude natures, especially such as have passed their lives among the elements, farmers or sailors, this animal decay mostly affects the memory by casting a haze over it; not seldom, it softens the heart as well, besides more or less, perhaps, drowsing the conscience, innocent or otherwise.

But, let us come to the close of a sketch necessarily imperfect. One fine Easter Day, following a spell of rheumatic weather, Orme was discovered alone and dead on a height overlooking the seaward sweep of the great haven to whose shore, in his retirement from sea, he had moored. It was an evened terrace, destined for use in war, but in peace neglected and offering a sanctuary for anybody. Mounted on it was an obsolete battery of rusty guns. Against one of these he was found leaning, his legs stretched out before him; his clay pipe broken in twain, the vacant bowl and no spillings from it, attesting that his pipe had been smoked out to the last of its contents. He faced the outlet to the ocean. The eyes were open, still continuing in death the vital glance fixed on the hazy waters and the dim-seen sails coming and going or at anchor near by. What had been his last thoughts? If aught of reality lurked in the rumours concerning him, had remorse, had penitence any place in those thoughts? Or was there just nothing of either? After all, were his moodiness and mutterings, his strange freaks, starts, eccentric shrugs and grimaces, were these but the grotesque additions like the wens and knobs and distortions of the trunk of an old chance apple-tree in an inclement upland, not only beaten by many storms, but also obstructed in its natural development by the chance of its having first sprouted among hard-packed rock? In short, that fatality, no more encrusting him, made him what he came to be? Even admitting that there was something dark that he chose to keep to himself, what then? Such reticence may sometimes be more for the sake of others than one's self. No, let us believe that the animal decay before mentioned still befriended him to the close, and that he fell asleep recalling through the haze of memory many a far-off scene of the wide world's beauty dreamily suggested by the hazy waters before him.

He lies buried among other sailors, for whom also strangers performed one last rite in a lonely plot overgrown with wild eglantine uncared for by man.

W. S. MERWIN

Sand

An ant was born in an hourglass. Before it hatched out there was nothing to notice—and who would have looked, who would have suspected that one instant in each measure of time was an egg? And after the ant had emerged, it was too late to ask whether the birth was a mistake. Anyway, there was no one to ask, except those nameless hosts, his brothers, at once much older and much younger than he was, who nudged and ground past him, rustling toward the neck of the glass, and fell, and lay blind, deaf, and dreamless in the mountain made of each other, and would never hatch, though the mountain itself turned over again and again and sent them smoking down from its tip like souls into time. Besides, it never occurred to him that there was a question to ask. He did not know that things ever had been or ever could be any different, and whatever capacity for speech he may have been born with slept on inside him like a grain of sand.

There was nothing to eat. But he had never been told about hunger, and ants, particularly those of his species, can subsist for long periods, sometimes for generations, without consuming other life of any kind. The same was true of thirst, dry though that place surely was, made of nothing but those rocks his family. Whatever discomfort he may have become aware of, arising from either hunger or thirst, seemed to him to be like something that we would no doubt call a memory, returning inexplicably to trouble him in a new life, and certain to fade. It stirred in him like some ghost from his days as a grain of sand, but he could not remember what use it had been to him then. And he would hold it to him and save it for a while, as though there was a danger of losing it. He would hold it, trying to understand it, not knowing that it was pain. Something of the kind was true also of breathing.

He was breathing. But he knew nothing of breath. What, after all, reached him through the glass? The light. The darkness. Sounds. Gravity. The desire to climb. What reached the grains of sand? Light. Darkness. Vibrations. Gravity. No one knows what else.

His brothers tried to crush him. He tried to count them. He could see that they were not infinite. But he could never start at the beginning. He would count them as they edged past him faster and faster. He had no names for numbers, but he tried to count the brothers even so, as he was borne along with them, as he climbed on their shoulders, as he swam on their heads, falling with them. He tried to count them as they fell on him and rolled after him to the foot of the next mountain, to the glass. He would start to the top again at once, trying to count them as they slipped under his feet. He would climb, counting, till the mountain turned over, and then he would begin again. Each time the mountain flowed out from under him he delayed the falling for an instant, and a measure of time paused while he clung to the neck of the glass, climbing on sand. Then everything went on just the same.

No one had told him about time. He did not know why he was trying to count. He did not know what a number, a final sum, would tell him, what use it would be to him, what he would call it, where he would put it. He did not know that they were not his real brothers. He thought he was a grain of sand.

He did not know that he was alone.

MARK MILLS

Under the Heavens

I saw the vision there.

A transcendental error led to my Harlem team playing in Long Island's premier 16-and-under tournament, rather than the nationals.

Sitting on the aluminum courtside bleachers with her crew of 16-year-old proteges, she looked 16. She clearly gave the girls beaming up at her Venus envy.

I stomped up the bleachers, stopped right in front of her, and said, "Those sneakers are *on!*"

She giggled, as if to say, I know what you really like. She was wrong.

She told me about the sneakers for 10 or 15 minutes, concluding with a coy smile, "They rock!" I looked up at the pristine sky and then back into those bluest of eyes. My strongest muscle thumped, my mouth dried. I shook my head, not believing my luck.

I introduced myself and said, "This club is way too small. They really need to expand it."

She giggled again because the place is the size of Puerto Rico.

"Come on," she said, "I'll give you the tour of our little place." We walked and talked before she watched me lose a close match to their No. 1 singles player.

In the snack bar, we sat at a round white enamel table, shaded by a blue and white umbrella. In between bites of rocky road, she told me about what she described as her "bor-ing" life of coaching, clam bakes, sun-bathing and trying to figure out her next move after recently graduating from a small Jesuit college in Connecticut, where she had majored in zoology before losing interest in med school and everything but tennis, which she'd played since she could walk. And she didn't want to stop the only positive constant, because then her whole world would crumble, but she didn't tell me that yet. You could tell she'd been playing since birth, because one honey-colored forearm was slightly larger than the other.

As we talked, we fell into a debate about "What is a pure truth?"

"The only pure truth is applied mathematics," she said. Like many Aries, she can be very strong, confident, direct, and a little bumptious. "It's the only universal language and it *can* be proven."

"Typical pre-med," I said, remembering my best friend Steve's sister, a former Howard U. zoology major now at Hopkins med. "Do you think Shakespeare, or any of the romantic poets, like Shelley or Keats, would add love?"

She paused for a long while before saying, in a dubious tone, ". . . Maybe."

Looking at her oval face, with its soft slopes, I realized that sometimes when you first meet someone, the knowledge that it isn't the first time transcends logic and reality. And the unexpected has already been felt. I wondered, as she looked at me intensely with her sapphire gems, could she see my anger, my fear, my strength?

"Do you," I asked, "think a person predatory animal instincts can be trained to trust completely?"

Julie, unlike my friend Steve's sister, said, "No!"

We continued talking at length about diverse topics: Islam and women, Mormons and marriage, the beautiful handling of fast cars, existentialism—the nature of freedom, responsibility, and the unexplainable in a Godless universe. As we talked, we unconsciously moved closer, drinking in each other's words, and faces, kissing mid-sentence. Our lips didn't want to part, but did so, out of propriety, with a slow sweet stickiness that reminded me of strawberry cotton candy. Her eyes shimmered, incandescent.

"*Wow,*" she said, almost out of breath and fell back dizzily into her seat. "I feel like I'm going to faint." She pushed her hands through hair golden as wine. After she caught her breath, she jolted forward and slapped my hand—"Hey, stop making me swoon!" Smiling, she fell back against her seat just as suddenly, laughing, as if I was a humorous impostor: "Are you *sure* you're 16?"

I returned her warm smile. I had fallen marching up the bleachers.

"Hey, you're the one making *me* swoon," I said. I got the sense she didn't like to lose control. But that was my whole game. I like to see what's at the core. I believe in strokes of genius. The power of art over everything. Like the strength of water over stone. A slow constant pressure.

We continued talking, cracking each other up, getting into arguments, simultaneously concluding each other's sentences. Three hours passed like seconds.

"God," she said, "you know it's funny, but I really feel like I can talk to you."

"I guess we fit together—"

"Because we're opposites . . ." she paused, thinking about everything that had been said, ". . . or because we're?—"

"Not," we said. We looked at each other for a moment, sensing something strange yet comfortable. . . .

I noticed her very delicate hands; uncoated nails; hands like Georgia O'Keefe's; I noticed scars on the inside of her wrists that resembled horizontal coke lines.

"The doctors said I killed all the nerves there."

I respectfully declined the invitation to pry. "I'd love to kiss them," I said, trying to read her mind.

She let out a nervous little laugh.

We discussed our love of tiger-boxer dogs, why animals were often more valuable than humans, how little dogs were a sign of fidelity and given as wedding presents—like the one given to the Arnolfino's at their wedding —why humans had waged conflicts in all but 14 years since our existence on the planet, and why landscapes were better than portraits of people like the Arnolfinos.

"Let me finish showing you around." She pointed out areas of interest on the 18-acre club—the fastest Deco II hard courts; the brick-red clays that ruined your socks; a breathtaking, open-air weight room, with gleaming silver free-weights, an Olympic-size pool, whirl pools, and Jacuzzis, all overlooking the murky green Atlantic, which rolled toward us on small curls of foam.

"I love the smell of the Atlantic!" she said, inhaling deeply.

"But not the Pacific," I said.

She looked at me as if she had received a small electrical shock. Her mouth opened slightly, for a second.

"Huh," she said finally, like OK.

She continued the tour, opened a door marked "READING ROOM," revealing overstuffed leather arm chairs; dimpled, burgundy, leather "Chesterfield" couches; ceiling-to-floor bookcases; and oil paintings of fox-hunting scenes on forest-green walls. It looked like an English study, very *Masterpiece Theater*. On the leather-topped desk sat a small, graceful bronze of a partially nude woman stomping a partially nude, bearded man: "Virtue Triumphing Over Vice" it read at the base. Both the male and the female were wearing togas that had become loose in the fight. One was wearing a wreath, the woman. Julie spun the large antique globe, showed me the gigantic dictionary, and pointed out the palatial white marble fireplace, with its green veins, containing black and white birch logs. . . . the fireplace was taller and wider than both of our bodies combined . . .

I picked up the phone and dialed: "Hi, Dad . . . I'm going to spend the night at Steve's. . . . Love you too, bye."

Leaning nude against the desk now, both of us bewildered and too tired to flip back over the couch, stayed put, hugging, motionless. Her arms draped around my neck, her head rested on my shoulder then moved slightly, glancing at my numerous red wrappers on the worn Oriental rugs; we tossed our heads back and laughed carefree.

"*God!*" she said.

"*God damn*" I said.

Her hair smelled like lavender and vanilla. I inhaled deeply as my fingers caressed the nape of her neck. We were enjoying the warmth of the fire, basking in its glow, the mellow radiance of our bodies, and the way we fit perfectly with each other; to use her words, she slid into all my "nooks and crannies." The smell of ocean salt whispered into the room through the windows, mixing with the aroma of the burning birch. Her head nestled against my shoulder.

She whispered in my ear, "You won't want to see me again."

I chuckled, because that's what I do when I'm afraid.

She squeezed me very tightly, as if she were scared, and buried her head into my neck. I could barely hear the words: "I'm going pro." I felt a trickle of dampness on the side of my neck.

I looked past the French doors framed by green velvet drapes, out to an Atlantic now glossy from the early evening sun. The sky with red and pink and orange, all brilliantly illuminated from behind by an invisible sun that did not want to bow.

I tried to understand, put myself in her shoes. I lost all cares and sense of responsibility. I hugged her with all my strength.

Time passed silently. The dramatic pastel sky faded to a chalky moon. She explained how her father's father had always begun by rubbing the back of her dad's neck when he was a 6-year-old boy, then he would jokingly run his hands through the boy's large golden "David Copperfield curls," and then he would proceed to crawl his fingers up the 6-year-old's thigh while singing, " 'The itsy bitsy spider . . .' "

No relative spoke of what they feared or confirmed. The boy, soon diagnosed as a mild epileptic, had looked angelic with his chubby cheeks and mop of sunshine curls streaming down. And this same boy became a father and sang the same song to her, not knowing why, but unable to stop, destroying the love she had wanted most.

Ostensibly, tennis-playing Barbie was still perfect for all who cared to look.

Her father could not acknowledge his shame. And he could not love what he could not comprehend. He mastered bourbon, squash, capital markets. But not her, not the defiant ram.

Parent-teacher conferences, graduations, concealed humiliation, invisible hypocrisy. Girls envious of her gifts. Unvoiced shame. Boys she would not let come close. The pistil removed from the flower. The flower that would not. Petals of blood.

"He still thinks he's better than his father because he didn't do it to his son!" Her fist coiled. The bronze sailed through the air, slamming down on the Oriental rug. This was the fighter with the killer instinct that I had known.

Living in "*that* house," she couldn't take it; she tried a variety of exit visas immediately after her reversal of fortune. Numerous Neoflaxin, embracing a tree with a Porsche, "his Wilkinson double-edged razors."

So now Juliet's wanting to become a prostitute would be what? So many unspeakable things: a way to disgrace the standard-bearer of a wealthy community, proof that love doesn't exist, something to do to fight ennui. I took her left arm from around my neck, kissed the little speed bumps on the inside of her wrist . . . heard the whisper of a moan.

Yukio Mishima

Swaddling Clothes

Translated by Ivan Morris

He was always busy, Toshiko's husband. Even tonight he had to dash off to an appointment, leaving her to go home alone by taxi. But what else could a woman expect when she married an actor—an attractive one? No doubt she had been foolish to hope that he would spend the evening with her. And yet he must have known how she dreaded going back to their house, unhomely with its Western-style furniture and with the bloodstains still showing on the floor.

Toshiko had been oversensitive since girlhood: that was her nature. As the result of constant worrying she never put on weight, and now, an adult woman, she looked more like a transparent picture than a creature of flesh and blood. Her delicacy of spirit was evident to her most casual acquaintance.

Earlier that evening, when she had joined her husband at a night club, she had been shocked to find him entertaining friends with an account of "the incident." Sitting there in his American-style suit, puffing at a cigarette, he had seemed to her almost a stranger.

"It's a fantastic story," he was saying, gesturing flamboyantly as if in an attempt to outweigh the attractions of the dance band. "Here this new nurse for our baby arrives from the employment agency, and the very first thing I notice about her is her stomach. It's enormous—as if she had a pillow stuck under her kimono! No wonder, I thought, for I soon saw that she could eat more than the rest of us put together. She polished off the contents of our rice bin like that. . . ." He snapped his fingers. "'Gastric dilation'—that's how she explained her girth and her appetite. Well, the day before yesterday we heard groans and moans coming from the nursery. We rushed in and found her squatting on the floor, holding her stomach in her two hands, and moan-ing like a cow. Next to her our baby lay in his cot, scared out of his wits and crying at the top of his lungs. A pretty scene, I can tell you!"

"So the cat was out of the bag?" suggested one of their friends, a film actor like Toshiko's husband.

"Indeed it was! And it gave me the shock of my life. You see, I'd com-pletely swallowed that story about 'gastric dilation.' Well, I didn't waste any time. I rescued our good rug from the floor and spread a blanket for her to lie on. The whole time the girl was yelling like a stuck pig. By the time the doc-tor from the maternity clinic arrived, the baby had already been born. But our sitting room was a pretty shambles!"

"Oh, that I'm sure of!" said another of their friends, and the whole company burst into laughter.

Toshiko was dumbfounded to hear her husband discussing the horrify-ing happening as though it were no more than an amusing incident which they chanced to have witnessed. She shut her eyes for a moment and all at once she saw the newborn baby lying before her: on the parquet floor the in-fant lay, and his frail body was wrapped in bloodstained newspapers.

Toshiko was sure that the doctor had done the whole thing out of spite. As if to emphasize his scorn for this mother who had given birth to a bastard under such sordid conditions, he had told his assistant to wrap the baby in some loose newspapers, rather than proper swaddling. This callous treat-ment of the newborn child had offended Toshiko. Overcoming her disgust at the entire scene, she had fetched a brand-new piece of flannel from her cupboard and, having swaddled the baby in it, had laid him carefully in an armchair.

This all had taken place in the evening after her husband had left the house. Toshiko had told him nothing of it, fearing that he would think her oversoft, oversentimental; yet the scene had engraved itself deeply in her mind. Tonight she sat silently thinking back on it, while the jazz orchestra brayed and her husband chatted cheerfully with his friends. She knew that she would never forget the sight of the baby, wrapped in stained newspapers and lying on the floor—it was a scene fit for a butchershop. Toshiko, whose own life had been spent in solid comfort, poignantly felt the wretchedness of the illegitimate baby.

I am the only person to have witnessed its shame, the thought occurred to her. The mother never saw her child lying there in its newspaper wrap-pings, and the baby itself of course didn't know. I alone shall have to pre-serve that terrible scene in my memory. When the baby grows up and wants to find out about his birth, there will be no one to tell him, so long as I pre-serve silence. How strange that I should have this feeling of guilt! After all, it was I who took him up from the floor, swathed him properly in flannel, and laid him down to sleep in the armchair.

They left the night club and Toshiko stepped into the taxi that her hus-band had called for her. "Take this lady to Ushigomé," he told the driver and shut the door from the outside. Toshiko gazed through the window at her husband's smiling face and noticed his strong, white teeth. Then she leaned back in the seat, oppressed by the knowledge that their life together was in some way too easy, too painless. It would have been difficult for her to put her thoughts into words. Through the rear window of the taxi she took a last look at her husband. He was striding along the street toward his Nash car, and soon the back of his rather garish tweed coat had blended with the figures of the passers-by.

The taxi drove off, passed down a street dotted with bars and then by a theatre, in front of which the throngs of people jostled each other on the pavement. Although the performance had only just ended, the lights had already been turned out and in the half dark outside it was depressingly obvious that the cherry blossoms decorating the front of the theatre were merely scraps of white paper.

Even if that baby should grow up in ignorance of the secret of his birth, he can never become a respectable citizen, reflected Toshiko, pursuing the same train of thoughts. Those soiled newspaper swaddling clothes will be the symbol of his entire life. But why should I keep worrying about him so much? Is it because I feel uneasy about the future of my own child? Say twenty years from now, when our boy will have grown up into a fine, carefully educated young man, one day by a quirk of fate he meets that other boy, who then will also have turned twenty. And say that the other boy, who has been sinned against, savagely stabs him with a knife. . . .

It was a warm, overcast April night, but thoughts of the future made Toshiko feel cold and miserable. She shivered on the back seat of the car.

No, when the time comes I shall take my son's place, she told herself suddenly. Twenty years from now I shall be forty-three. I shall go to that young man and tell him straight out about everything—about his newspaper swaddling clothes, and about how I went and wrapped him in flannel.

The taxi ran along the dark wide road that was bordered by the park and by the Imperial Palace moat. In the distance Toshiko noticed the pinpricks of light which came from the blocks of tall office buildings.

Twenty years from now that wretched child will be in utter misery. He will be living a desolate, hopeless, poverty-stricken existence—a lonely rat. What else could happen to a baby who has had such a birth? He'll be wandering through the streets by himself, cursing his father, loathing his mother.

No doubt Toshiko derived a certain satisfaction from her somber thoughts: she tortured herself with them without cease. The taxi approached Hanzomon and drove past the compound of the British Embassy. At that point the famous rows of cherry trees were spread out before Toshiko in all their purity. On the spur of the moment she decided to go and view the blossoms by herself in the dark night. It was a strange decision for a timid and unadventurous young woman, but then she was in a strange state of mind and she dreaded the return home. That evening all sorts of unsettling fancies had burst open in her mind.

She crossed the wide street—a slim, solitary figure in the darkness. As a rule when she walked in the traffic Toshiko used to cling fearfully to her companion, but tonight she darted alone between the cars and a moment later had reached the long narrow park that borders the Palace moat. Chidorigafuchi, it is called—the Abyss of the Thousand Birds.

Tonight the whole park had become a grove of blossoming cherry trees. Under the calm cloudy sky the blossoms formed a mass of solid whiteness. The paper lanterns that hung from wires between the trees had been put out; in their place electric light bulbs, red, yellow, and green, shone dully beneath the blossoms. It was well past ten o'clock and most of the flower-viewers had gone home. As the occasional passers-by strolled through the park, they would automatically kick aside the empty bottles or crush the waste paper beneath their feet.

Newspapers, thought Toshiko, her mind going back once again to those happenings. Bloodstained newspapers. If a man were ever to hear of that piteous birth and know that it was he who had lain there, it would ruin his entire life. To think that I, a perfect stranger, should from now on have to keep such a secret—the secret of a man's whole existence. . . .

Lost in these thoughts, Toshiko walked on through the park. Most of the people still remaining there were quiet couples; no one paid her any attention. She noticed two people sitting on a stone bench beside the moat, not looking at the blossoms, but gazing silently at the water. Pitch black it was, and swathed in heavy shadows. Beyond the moat the somber forest of the Imperial Palace blocked her view. The trees reached up, to form a solid dark mass against the night sky. Toshiko walked slowly along the path beneath the blossoms hanging heavily overhead.

On a stone bench, slightly apart from the others, she noticed a pale object—not, as she had at first imagined, a pile of cherry blossoms, nor a garment forgotten by one of the visitors to the park. Only when she came closer did she see that it was a human form lying on the bench. Was it, she wondered, one of those miserable drunks often to be seen sleeping in public places? Obviously not, for the body had been systematically covered with newspapers, and it was the whiteness of those papers that had attracted Toshiko's attention. Standing by the bench, she gazed down at the sleeping figure.

It was a man in a brown jersey who lay there, curled up on layers of newspapers, other newspapers covering him. No doubt this had become his normal night residence now that spring had arrived. Toshiko gazed down at the man's dirty, unkempt hair, which in places had become hopelessly matted. As she observed the sleeping figure wrapped in its newspapers, she was inevitably reminded of the baby who had lain on the floor in its wretched swaddling clothes. The shoulder of the man's jersey rose and fell in the darkness in time with his heavy breathing.

It seemed to Toshiko that all her fears and premonitions had suddenly taken concrete form. In the darkness the man's pale forehead stood out, and it was a young forehead, though carved with the wrinkles of long poverty and hardship. His khaki trousers had been slightly pulled up; on his sockless feet he wore a pair of battered gym shoes. She could not see his face and suddenly had an overmastering desire to get one glimpse of it.

She walked to the head of the bench and looked down. The man's head was half buried in his arms, but Toshiko could see that he was surprisingly young. She noticed the thick eyebrows and the fine bridge of his nose. His slightly open mouth was alive with youth.

But Toshiko had approached too close. In the silent night the newspaper bedding rustled, and abruptly the man opened his eyes. Seeing the young woman standing directly beside him, he raised himself with a jerk, and his eyes lit up. A second later a powerful hand reached out and seized Toshiko by her slender wrist.

She did not feel in the least afraid and made no effort to free herself. In a flash the thought had struck her, Ah, so the twenty years have already gone by! The forest of the Imperial Palace was pitch dark and utterly silent.

LORRIE MOORE

The Kid's Guide to Divorce

Put extra salt on the popcorn because your mom'll say that she needs it because the part where Inger Berman almost dies and the camera does tricks to elongate her torso sure gets her every time.

Think: Geeze, here she goes again with the Kleenexes.

She will say thanks honey when you come slowly, slowly around the corner in your slippers and robe, into the living room with Grandma's old used-to-be-salad-bowl piled high. I made it myself, remind her, and accidentally drop a few pieces on the floor. Mittens will bat them around with his paws.

Mmmmm, good to replenish those salts, she'll munch and smile soggily.

Tell her the school nurse said after a puberty movie once that salt is bad for people's hearts.

Phooey, she'll say. It just makes it thump, that's all. Thump, thump, thump—oh look! She will talk with her mouth full of popcorn. Cary Grant is getting her out of there. Did you unplug the popper?

Pretend you don't hear her. Watch Inger Berman look elongated; wonder what it means.

You'd better check, she'll say.

Groan. Make a little *tsk* noise with your tongue on the roof of your mouth. Run as fast as you can because the next commercial's going to be the end. Unplug the popper. Bring Mittens back in with you because he is mewing by the refrigerator. He'll leave hair on your bathrobe. Dump him in your mom's lap.

Hey baby, she'll coo at the cat, scratching his ears. Cuddle close to your mom and she'll reach around and scratch one of your ears too, kissing your cheek. Then she'll suddenly lean forward, reaching toward the bowl on the coffee table, carefully so as not to disturb the cat. I always think he's going to realize faster than he does, your mom will say between munches, hand to hand to mouth. Men can be so dense and frustrating. She will wink at you.

Eye the tube suspiciously. All the bad guys will let Cary Grant take Inger Berman away in the black car. There will be a lot of old-fashioned music. Stand and pull your bathrobe up on the sides. Hang your tongue out and pretend to dance like a retarded person at a ball. Roll your eyes. Waltz across the living room with exaggerated side-to-side motions, banging into furniture. Your mother will pretend not to pay attention to you. She will finally say in a flat voice: How wonderful, gee, you really send me.

When the music is over, she will ask you what you want to watch now. She'll hand you the *TV Guide*. Look at it. Say: The Late, Late Chiller. She'll screw up one of her eyebrows at you, but say *please, please* in a soft voice and put your hands together like a prayer. She will smile back and sigh, okay.

Switch the channel and return to the sofa. Climb under the blue afghan with your mother. Tell her you like this beginning cartoon part best where the mummy comes out of the coffin and roars, *CHILLER!!* Get up on one of the arms of the sofa and do an imitation, your hands like claws, your elbows stiff, your head slumped to one side. Your mother will tell you to sit back down. Snuggle back under the blanket with her.

When she says, Which do you like better, the mummy or the werewolf, tell her the werewolf is scary because he goes out at night and does things that no one suspects because in the day he works in a bank and has no hair.

What about the mummy? she'll ask, petting Mittens.

Shrug your shoulders. Fold in your lips. Say: The mummy's just the mummy.

With the point of your tongue, loosen one of the chewed, pulpy kernels in your molars. Try to swallow it, but get it caught in your throat and begin to gasp and make horrible retching noises. It will scare the cat away.

Good god, be careful, your mother will say, thwacking you on the back. Here, drink this water.

Try groaning root beer, root beer, like a dying cowboy you saw on a commercial once, but drink the water anyway. When you are no longer choking, you face is less red, and you can breathe again, ask for a Coke. Your mom will say: I don't think so; Dr. Atwood said your teeth were atrocious.

Tell her Dr. Atwood is for the birds.

What do you mean by that? she will exclaim.

Look straight ahead. Say: I dunno.

The mummy will be knocking down telephone poles, lifting them up, and hurling them around like Lincoln Logs.

Wow, all wrapped up and no place to go, your mother will say.

Cuddle close to her and let out a long, low, admiring *Neato*.

The police will be in the cemetery looking for a monster. They won't know whether it's the mummy or the werewolf, but someone will have been hanging out there leaving little smoking piles of bones and flesh that even the police dogs get upset and whine at.

Say something like gross-out, and close your eyes.

Are you sure you want to watch this?

Insist that you are not scared.

There's a rock concert on Channel 7, you know.

Think about it. Decide to try Channel 7, just for your mom's sake. Somebody with greasy hair who looks like Uncle Jack will be saying something boring.

Your mother will agree that he does look like Uncle Jack. A little.

A band with black eyeshadow on will begin playing their guitars. Stand and bounce up and down like you saw Julie Steinman do once.

God, why do they always play them down at their crotches? your mom will ask.

Don't answer, simply imitate them, throwing your hair back and fiddling bizarrely with the crotch of your pajama bottoms. Your mother will slap you and tell you you're being fresh.

Act hurt. Affect a slump. Pick up a magazine and pretend you're reading it. The cat will rejoin you. Look at the pictures of the food.

Your mom will try to pep you up. She'll say: Look! Pat Benatar! Let's dance.

Tell her you think Pat Benatar is stupid and cheap. Say nothing for five whole minutes.

When the B-52's come on, tell her you think *they're* okay.

Smile sheepishly. Then the two of you will get up and dance like wild maniacs around the coffee table until you are sweating, whooping to the oo-ah-oo's, jumping like pogo sticks, acting like space robots. Do razz-ma-tazz hands like your mom at either side of your head. During a commercial, ask for an orange soda.

Water or milk, she will say, slightly out of breath, sitting back down.

Say shit, and when she asks what did you say, sigh: Nothing.

Next is Rod Stewart singing on a roof somewhere. Your mom will say: He's sort of cute.

Tell her Julie Steinman saw him in a store once and said he looked really old.

Hmmmm, your mother will say.

Study Rod Stewart carefully. Wonder if you could make your legs go like that. Plan an imitation for Julie Steinman.

When the popcorn is all gone, yawn. Say: I'm going to bed now.

Your mother will look disappointed, but she'll say, okay, honey. She'll turn the TV off. By the way, she'll ask hesitantly like she always does. How did the last three days go?

Leave out the part about the lady and the part about the beer. Tell her they went all right, that he's got a new silver dart-board and that you went out to dinner and this guy named Hudson told a pretty funny story about peeing in the hamper. Ask for a 7-Up.

Alberto Moravia

The Fetish

Immediately after the wedding they had gone to live in a penthouse flat in the Parioli district of Rome which Livio's father-in-law had made over to his daughter as a dowry. The flat was almost empty, except for such pieces of furniture as were indispensable; but the bride declared she was in no hurry: she wished to furnish it in her own way. And so, in a leisurely manner, she started to acquire, here and there, furniture, fittings, ornaments and pictures, all in a very "modern" taste which to Livio, convinced that she was following the fashion rather than a reasoned preference, seemed at the same time both conceited and snobbish. The fetish was discovered by his wife in the back shop of a rather special kind of antique-dealer, an elderly American who had set up a small shop in order to liquidate the stuff he had accumulated, in a villa belonging to him, during twenty years of travel all over the world. It—the fetish—was a cylinder of grey stone of the most ordinary kind, as tall as a man but much broader, terminating in a head shaped like a pointed cone, with strongly stylized features: all that was indicated was the arches of the eyebrows, the septum of the nose, and the chin. At each side of the cylinder, where the junctions of the arms should have been, two round bosses, like two buttons, were carved in the stone. The figure, rough and imprecise though evilly expressive, at once aroused extreme antipathy in Livio. He did not admit it to himself, but the reason for this antipathy lay, in truth, in his wife's infatuation for the fetish—one infatuation amongst many that he disapproved of because he did not understand it.

Livio took to calling the figure "The Martian"; it did in fact somewhat resemble the clumsy puppets by which the illustrators of comic papers usually represent those imaginary celestial creatures. "I'm not going to kiss you good-morning to-day," he would say; "the Martian is watching us." "The Martian seems more than usually ill-humoured to-day; d'you see how sulky he looks?" "Last night I went into the bathroom and what did I see? The Martian brushing his teeth." "Don Giovanni had the statue of the Commendatore, I have the Martian. That's an idea: why don't we invite him to supper?"

This last remark, contrary to what was usual, elicited a response. They were eating in the living-room, right in front of the fetish, which appeared to be watching them intently from its half-dark corner. "I'm almost inclined," she said, "to take you at your word and leave you to finish eating with *him*."

She spoke calmly, pronouncing each syllable distinctly, her head lowered. But with so obvious a hostility that Livio had almost a feeling of fear. Nevertheless, carried away by his own joke, he persisted: "The first thing to do is to see whether he'll accept the invitation."

"In fact," she went on, as though she had not heard him, "I'll leave you anyhow. Enjoy your meal." She put down her napkin on the table, rose and left the room.

Livio remained seated and tried for a little to imagine how the fetish would manage to leave its corner, roll on its circular base up to the table, and then sit down and eat. A few days before he had been to a performance of *Don Giovanni* at the Opera; and the coincidence amused him. But what sort of a voice would the fetish have? In what language would it speak? To what Papuan or Polynesian hell would it drag him down at the end of the supper-party?

These fancies, however, did not suffice to distract him from his wife's gesture. He hoped it was a piece of momentary ill-humour, he expected to see her reappear in the doorway; but nothing happened. Now, after his previous amusement, the idea of the fetish coming to dine with him disgusted him. And the fetish itself, looking at him from its dark corner, filled him with embarrassment. Finally he called out in a loud voice: "Alina!"; but no one answered, the flat seemed empty. The maid had come in with the dishes on a tray. Livio told her to put it down on the table, then rose and went out.

The bedroom was at the far end of the passage; the door was ajar; Livio pushed it and went in. This room, too, contained no furniture apart from the bed and two chairs. There was a suitcase on the bed, open. His wife, standing in front of the wide-open wall-cupboard, was taking a dress off its hanger.

For a moment Livio was dumbfounded, not knowing what to say. Then he realized that his wife was on the point of leaving him, two months after their wedding; and an icy chill ran up his spine. "Why, Alina," he said, "what in the world are you doing?"

At the sound of his voice she at once let go of the coat-hanger and sat down on the bed. Livio also sat down, put his arm round her waist and murmured: "But why, Alina, why? What's come over you?"

He expected a conciliatory reply but, when he looked at her, he saw that he was mistaken. His wife's face, round, massive, of a livid pallor in which her pale blue eyes stood out conspicuously, was darkened by a settled hostility. "What has come over me," she said, "is that you make jokes about everything and that I can't stand your jokes any longer."

"But it's my nature; I like making jokes—and what's the harm in it?"

"There may not be any harm in it, but I can't stand it any longer."

"But why, my love?"

"Don't call me 'my love'. You never talk seriously, you have to be witty about everything, you always have to show that you're superior to everything."

"Come, come, Alina, don't you think you're exaggerating?"

"I'm not exaggerating at all. Every time you make a joke, I feel my heart sink. One would think . . ."

"What would one think?"

"One would think that, since you can't bring yourself up to the level of certain things, you try, by means of sarcasm, to bring them down to *your* level. Besides, it's not only that . . ."

"What is it, then?"

"You even make jokes at moments when no man would make jokes. During our honeymoon you said something that I shall remember all my life."

"What was that?"

"That I shall never tell you."

Silence followed. Livio was still clasping her round the waist, as he sat beside her. Then, as he looked at her, he realized, with the feeling that he was making an important discovery, that it was the first time since they had come to know each other that he had spoken to her seriously, in a sincere, affectionate way, without hiding behind a mask of jokes. He reflected that it had needed nothing less than a threat of abandonment to induce him to change his tone, and suddenly he felt remorseful. "Now, Alina," he said, "let's consider what it is that has really happened. You bought that fetish, which I didn't like, and brought it home. Why did I begin to make jokes about the fetish? Not, certainly, because it's ugly or ridiculous or clumsy; there are already plenty of clumsy, ugly, ridiculous things in this flat. No, it was because you became infatuated with it to such a degree . . ."

His wife sat listening to him with an attentiveness that seemed to emanate from the whole of her compact, heavy body and become concentrated in the small, fleshy ear which peeped out from beneath her black hair. All of a sudden she clapped her hands and turned towards Livio: "You've said it, you've said it, once and for all."

"What d'you mean?"

"You can't endure what you call my infatuations."

"No, of course not; and so . . . ?"

"But don't you realize that what you call my infatuations are my feelings, my affections, myself, in fact?"

"Have you then a feeling, an affection for that stone puppet?"

"I might have—who knows? I have—or rather, I had—a feeling for you, certainly. And you've treated it as an infatuation, you've thrown your icy shower-bath of jokes over it."

"When have I ever done that?"

"I've already told you, during our honeymoon."

"I made jokes about your feeling for me during our honeymoon?"

"Yes, in Venice, to be precise, in the hotel room, the first night. And you didn't make jokes only about my feeling but also about my physical appearance, and just at a moment when no man—and mind, I say this with the utmost seriousness—when no man would have dared to do so."

"I made jokes about your physical appearance?"

"Yes, about one detail of my appearance."

Livio suddenly blushed up to his ears, although he was quite unable to recall having made a joke on that occasion. At last he said: "It may be true, but I don't remember. Anyhow I should like to know what the joke was. It may have been an innocent thing, like the remark I made about your fetish this evening."

"Certainly it was an innocent thing, inasmuch as you weren't conscious of it. However, it had the same effect on me as if you had put a piece of ice down my neck. It was our first night after our wedding and you didn't realize that I hated you."

"You hated me?"

"Yes, with all my soul."

"And do you hate me now?"

"Now—I don't know."

Livio again remained silent, looking intently at her. Then suddenly he had the feeling that he was face to face with a complete stranger, about whom he knew nothing, neither past nor present, neither feelings nor thoughts. This feeling of estrangement had arisen from her remark: "You didn't realize that I hated you." And indeed he had not realized that he was holding in his arms a woman who hated him. About that night he remembered everything, even the wind that from time to time caused the curtain to swell out slightly over the window wide-open on to the Lagoon; but not her hatred. Moreover, if he had not been aware of so important a feeling, how many other things had escaped his notice, how much of her had remained unknown to him? But it was clear by now that his wife did not intend to leave; that the suitcase open on the bed formed part of a kind of ritual of matrimonial dispute; that he himself must now initiate the reconciliation, however strange and unknown she might seem to him. With an effort, he took her hand and said: "You must forgive me. I am what is generally called an impious man."

"What does impious mean?"

"The opposite of pious. A man for whom sacred things do not exist. But from now onwards I shall try and mend my ways, I promise you."

His wife looked at him, she contemplated him, in fact, with her pale blue, rather sullen eyes; as one looks at a singular and incomprehensible object. Finally she said, quite simply: "Well, go on back, I'll be with you in a moment"; and, leaning forward, she gave him a smacking kiss on the cheek.

Livio would have liked to say something but he could not find anything to say. He rose, went back into the living-room and sat down again at the table. He took a cutlet from the tray, put it on his plate and prepared to start eating. Then he dropped his knife and fork and looked in front of him.

The fetish, as before, was right opposite him; its brow low above its eyes like a vizor, it seemed to be staring at him with a menacing, demanding air. As though it wished to say to him: 'This is only the beginning. There will be all too many other things about which you will have to stop making jokes.'

Livio remembered Don Giovanni and reflected that he at least had had the consolation of being punished for mocking at the principles of a recognized and respected religion. But he himself had to pay respect to an unconsecrated world, without hell and without paradise, a world that was mute and absurd, like the stone fetish.

A rustling sound made him start. His wife had come back and was now seated opposite to him again. Livio noticed that, in perspective, his wife's face appeared to be closely coupled with the stupid, ferocious face of the fetish. And he shuddered anxiously.

First Person: Alberto Moravia on "The Short Story and the Novel"

A definition of the short story as a distinct and autonomous literary *genre*, with its own special rules and laws, may well be impossible, for, among other things, the short story has an even wider sweep than the novel. It extends from the French-style *récit*, or long short story, whose characters and situations are almost those of a novel, down to the prose-poem, the sketch and the lyrical fragment. Yet when we attempt to make a rough definition of the short story we cannot help considering it in relation to its big brother, rather than in isolation: the short story is not a novel. When thus contrasted with the novel some constant characteristics do appear, and though they lack the character of laws and cannot be quoted as rules, they explain how the short story does in fact constitute a *genre* in its own right and has nothing to do with the novel or any other narrative composition of similar length.

Meanwhile it is worth noting that short story writers, accustomed as they are to expressing themselves within the limits and in accord with the rules of the *genre* however badly defined these may be, find it very difficult to write really good novels. Consider, for example, the two greatest short story writers of the end of the nineteenth century, Maupassant and Chekhov. These have both left us enormous collections of short stories which give an incomparable picture of the life in France and Russia of their time. Quantitively speaking, Maupassant's world is wider and more varied than the world of Flaubert, his contemporary; Chekhov's more so than Dostoievsky's, his immediate predecessor. Indeed, all things considered, we can say that while Maupassant and Chekhov so to speak exhaust the variety of situations and characters of the society of their time, Flaubert and Dostoievsky are rather like those solitary birds that restlessly and loyally repeat the same significant cry. In the last analysis all they did was to write the same novel over and over again, with the same situations and the same characters.

Some centuries earlier Boccaccio, the greatest short story writer of all time, exhibited a similar variety and richness as compared with Dante. If we only had *The Divine Comedy* with its static Gothic figures carved in *bas relief* round and round the monument of the poem, we should certainly know much less than we do about the life of Florence and Italy and the Middle Ages in general. Whereas Boccaccio's depiction of it is incomparable. Unlike *The Divine Comedy*, the *Decameron* presents everything in function of a complete illustration of this life, with no end in view other than that of extolling its richness and variety.

But when Maupassant and Chekhov tried their hand at novels or even *récits* they were far less gifted and convincing than with the short story. Some of Chekhov's novel-like stories, and Maupassant's *Bel Ami*, make us think less of novels than of blown-up, lengthened and watered-down short stories—rather as some frescoes by modern painters are really no more than easel paintings enlarged out of all proportion. In Chekhov's and Maupassant's novels and long short stories we feel the lack of that something that makes a novel, even a bad novel, a novel. Chekhov dilutes his concentrated lyrical feeling with superfluous plots lacking intrinsic necessity, while Maupassant gives us a series of disjointed pictures, seen through a telescope, and only held together by the presence of the protagonist. Indeed it is noteworthy that the very qualities that made these two great as short story writers become defects as soon as they tackle the novel. Someone may point out that we are dealing with different techniques, and Chekhov and Maupassant failed to master the technique of the novel. But this does not solve the problem, it merely states it differently. Technique is the form taken by the writer's inspiration and personality. Chekhov's and Maupassant's technique is unsuited to the novel because they could only say what they wanted to say in the short story, and not vice versa. So we are back where we started from. What is the outstanding distinction between the novel and the short story?

The principal and fundamental difference lies in the groundplan or structure of the narrative. Of course all sorts of novels are being written, and will go on being written, with a variety of bizarre and experimental structures—which seems to give the lie to the validity of what we have just said. Nevertheless the classical novelists, those whose works have created the genre—men like Flaubert, Dostoievsky, Stendhal, Tolstoy, and later Proust, Joyce and Mann—go to prove that some common characteristics do exist in spite of this. The most important of these is what we could call ideology, that is the skeleton of the theme from which the flesh of the story takes its form.

In other words the novel has a bone structure holding it together from top to toe, whereas the short story is, so to speak, boneless. Naturally the novel's ideology is not precise, preconstituted, or reducible to a thesis, just as the skeleton is not introduced into the human body by force when we are adults but has grown along with the body's other parts. It is this ideology that differentiates a novel from a short story and, conversely, it is the absence of bone structure that makes a short story not a novel. It is the ideology, however imprecise and contradictory it may be, with all the contradictions that are to be found in life itself (the novelist is not a philosopher, but a witness), that begets the things that make a novel a novel.

The first of these is what is usually called plot, or the changing succession of events that constitute the story of the novel. It can sometimes happen that the plot is an end in itself, but this is never the case with good novelists; suffice it to say that this obtains most often in detective stories where mechanical device plays the major part. With good novelists, real novelists, the plot is nothing but the sum total of the ideological themes as they conflict and merge with each other in their various ways. So the plot is made up not only of intuitions of feelings (as in the short story) but primarily of ideas expressed poetically but well defined.

The plot, for example, of *Crime and Punishment* is made up of the crisscross, the contrast, the clash and the conflicting claims of the various ideological themes presented to us by the author from the first page: the theme of Raskolnikoff, the theme of Sonia, the theme of Svidrigailoff, the theme of Marmeladoff, the theme of the judge Porphyry, and so on. All these characters are autonomous and entirely human, but they are also ideas and it is not difficult to extract from them the ideological meanings they carry, a thing it would be quite impossible to do with the characters in a short story by Chekhov or Maupassant. The plot of *Crime and Punishment* is born of these themes embodied in characters, in other words from the grandiose ground-plan of this exemplary novel which enables Dostoievsky to proceed for five hundred pages without ever giving the impression that he is either spinning out or watering down events—the impression that we get in Chekhov's longer stories and in Maupassant's novel. The twists and turns of the plot, its surprises, its contradictions, its *coups de scéne*, even its *deus ex machinas*, are never due to extrinsic interventions by the author or to what we could call the inexhaustible resources of life, but to the dialectical and necessary development of the ideological themes. From one point of view nothing could be more misleading than to say that the novel competes with the civil register. It would be more accurate to say this of the short story which passes in review a large variety of characters who have individual characteristics only. The truth is that many novels compete, not with the civil register, but with a philosophical treatise or a moral essay.

Besides the plot, the quality of the characters, too, stems from the presence or absence of ideology. Andreuccio da Perugia, Boule de Suif, the boy of the steppe, are short story characters; Raskolnikoff, Julien Sorel, Madame

Bovary, Prince Andrey, Bloom, Proust's "Je", and the protagonist of Mann's *Doktor Faust* are novel characters. Those familiar with the short stories and novels in which the above-mentioned characters operate cannot fail to perceive the difference between the first group and the second. The first are caught at a particular moment, within narrow limits of time and space, and act in function of a determined event which forms the object of the short story. Whereas the second have a long, ample and tortuous development that unites biographical with ideological data, and they move in a time and space that are both real and abstract, immanent and transcendent. Characters in short stories are the product of lyrical intuitions, Those in novels are symbols. Obviously a character from a novel could never be compressed within the narrow confines of a short story, just as a character from a short story could never be drawn out to the dimensions of a novel without an alteration in his nature.

So the short story is distinguished from the novel in the following ways: non-ideological characters of whom we get foreshortened and tangential glimpses in accord with the needs of an action limited in time and place; a very simple plot, even non-existent in some short stories—when they become prose poems—and in any case one that gets its complexity from life and not from the orchestration of some kind of ideology; psychology in function of facts, not of ideas; technical procedures intended to provide in synthesis what, in the novel, needs long and extended analysis.

Of course all this has little to do with the principal qualities of the short story—I mean that indefinable and inexpressible charm of narration experienced both by the writer and the reader. An exceedingly complex charm, deriving from a literary art which is unquestionably purer, more essential, more lyrical, more concentrated and more absolute than that of the novel. Whereas, by way of compensation, the novel provides a deeper, more complex, more dialectical, more polyhedric and more metaphysical representation of reality than the short story.

So, while the short story comes near to being a lyric, the novel, as we have said, is more likely to rub shoulders with the essay or the philosophical treatise.

BHARATI MUKHERJEE

Courtly Vision

Jahanara Begum stands behind a marble grille in her palace at Fatehpur-Sikri.

Count Barthelmy, an adventurer from beyond frozen oceans, crouches in a lust-darkened arbor. His chest—a tear-shaped fleck of rust—lifts away from the gray, flat trunk of a mango tree. He is swathed in the coarse, quaint clothes of his cool-weather country. Jacket, pantaloons, shawl, swell and cave in ardent pleats. He holds a peacock's feather to his lips. His face is colored in admonitory pink. The feather is dusty aqua, broken-spined. His white-gloved hand pillows a likeness of the Begum, painted on a grain of rice by Basawan, the prized court artist. Two red-eyed parrots gouge the patina of grass at the adventurer's feet; their buoyant, fluffy breasts caricature the breasts of Moghul virgins. The Count is posed full-front; the self-worshipful body of a man who has tamed thirteen rivers and seven seas. Dainty thighs bulge with wayward expectancy. The head twists savagely upward at an angle unreckoned except in death, anywhere but here. In profile the lone prismatic eye betrays the madman and insomniac.

On the terrace of Jahanara Begum's palace, a slave girl kneels; her forearms, starry with jewels, strain toward the fluted handle of a decanter. Two bored eunuchs squat on their fleshy haunches, awaiting their wine. Her simple subservience hints at malevolent dreams, of snake venom rubbed into wine cups or daggers concealed between young breasts, and the eunuchs are menaced, their faces pendulous with premonition.

In her capacious chamber the Begum waits, perhaps for death from the serving-girl, for ravishing, or merely the curtain of fire from the setting sun. The chamber is open on two sides, the desert breeze stiffens her veil into a gauzy disc. A wild peacock, its fanned-out feathers beaten back by the same breeze, cringes on the bit of marble floor visible behind her head. Around the Begum, retainers conduct their inefficient chores. One, her pursed navel bare, slackens her grip on a *morchal* of plumes; another stumbles, biceps clenched, under the burden of a gold hookah bowl studded with translucent rubies and emeralds; a third stoops, her back an eerie, writhing arc, to straighten a low table littered with cosmetics in jewelled pillboxes. The Begum is a tall, rigid figure as she stands behind a marble grille. From her fists, which she holds in front of her like tiny shields, sprouts a closed, up-right lotus bloom. Her gaze slips upward, past the drunken gamblers on the roof-terraces, to the skyline where fugitive cranes pass behind a blue cloud.

Oh, beauteous and beguiling Begum, has your slave-girl apprised the Count of the consequences of a night of bliss?

Under Jahanara Begum's window, in a courtyard cooled with fountains into whose basin slaves have scattered rose petals, sit Fathers Aquaviva and Henriques, ingenuous Portuguese priests. They have dogged the emperor through inclement scenery. Now they pause in the emperor's famed, new capital, eyes closed, abstemious hands held like ledges over their brows to divert the sullen desert breeze. Their faces seem porous; the late afternoon has slipped through the skin and distended the chins and cheeks. Before their blank, radiant gazes, seven itinerant jugglers heap themselves into a shuddering pyramid. A courtier sits with the priests on a divan covered with brocaded silk. He too is blind to the courage of gymnasts. He is distracted by the wondrous paintings the priests have spread out on the arabesques of the rug at their feet. Mother and Child. Child and Mother. The Moghul courtier—child of Islam, ruler of Hindus—finds the motif repetitive. What comforting failure of the imagination these priests are offering. What precar-ious boundaries set on life's playful fecundity. He hears the Fathers murmur. They are devising stratagems on a minor scale. They want to trick the emperor into kissing Christ, who on each huge somber canvas is a bright, white, healthy baby. The giant figures seem to him simple and innocuous, not complicated and infuriating like the Hindu icons hidden in the hills. In the meantime his eyes draw comfort from the unclad angels who watch over the Madonna to protect her from heathens like him. Soft-fleshed, flying women. He will order the court artists to paint him a harem of winged women on a single poppy seed.

The emperor will not kiss Christ tonight. He is at the head of his army, riding a piebald horse out of his new walled city. He occupies the foreground of that agate-colored paper, a handsome young man in a sun-yellow *jama*. Under the *jama* his shoulders pulsate to the canny violent rhythm of his mount. Behind him in a thick choking diagonal stream follow his soldiers. They scramble and spill on the sandy terrain; spiky desert grass slashes their jaunty uniforms of muslin. Tiny, exhilarated profiles crowd the battlements. In the women's palace, tinier figures flit from patterned window grille, to grille. The citizens have begun to celebrate. Grandfathers leading children by the wrists are singing of the emperor's victories over invisible rebels.

Shopkeepers, coy behind their taut paunches, give away their syrupy sweets. Even the mystics with their haggard, numinous faces have allowed themselves to be distracted by yet another parade.

So the confident emperor departs.

The Moghul evening into which he drags his men with the promise of unimaginable satisfactions is grayish gold with the late afternoon, winter light. It spills down the rims of stylized rocks that clog the high horizon. The light is charged with unusual excitement and it discovers the immense intimacy of darkness, the erotic shadowiness of the cave-deep arbor in which the Count crouches and waits. The foliage of the mango tree yields sudden, bountiful shapes. Excessive, unruly life—monkeys, serpents, herons, thieves naked to the waist—bloom and burgeon on its branches. The thieves, their torsos pushing through clusters of leaves, run rapacious fingers on their dagger blades.

They do not discern the Count. The Count does not overhear the priests. Adventurers all, they guard from each other the common courtesy of their subterfuge. They sniff the desert air and the air seems full of portents. In the remote horizon three guards impale three calm, emaciated men. Behind the low wall of a *namaz* platform, two courtiers quarrel, while a small boy sneaks up and unties their horses. A line of stealthy women prostrate themselves and pray at the doorway of a temple in a patch of browning foliage. Over all these details float three elegant whorls of cloud, whorls in the manner of Chinese painting, imitated diligently by men who long for rain.

The emperor leaves his capital, applauded by flatterers and loyal citizens. Just before riding off the tablet's edge into enemy territory, he twists back on his saddle and shouts a last-minute confidence to his favorite court-painter. He is caught in reflective profile, the quarter-arc of his mustache suggests a man who had permitted his second thoughts to confirm his spontaneous judgments.

Give me total vision, commands the emperor. His voice hisses above the hoarse calls of the camels. *You, Basawan, who can paint my Begum on a grain of rice, see what you can do with the infinite vistas the size of my opened hand. Hide nothing from me, my co-wanderer. Tell me how my new capital will fail, will turn to dust and these marbled terraces be home to jackals and infidels. Tell me who to fear and who to kill but tell it to me in a way that makes me smile. Transport me through dense fort walls and stone grilles and into the hearts of men.*

Alice Munro

Prue

Prue used to live with Gordon. This was after Gordon had left his wife and before he went back to her—a year and four months in all. Some time later, he and his wife were divorced. After that came a period of indecision, of living together off and on; then the wife went away to New Zealand, most likely for good.

Prue did not go back to Vancouver Island, where Gordon had met her when she was working as a dining-room hostess in a resort hotel. She got a job in Toronto, working in a plant shop. She had many friends in Toronto by that time, most of them Gordon's friends and his wife's friends. They liked Prue and were ready to feel sorry for her, but she laughed them out of it. She is very likable. She has what eastern Canadians call an English accent, though she was born in Canada—in Duncan, on Vancouver Island. This accent helps her to say the most cynical things in a winning and lighthearted way. She presents her life in anecdotes, and though it is the point of most of her anecdotes that hopes are dashed, dreams ridiculed, things never turn out as expected, everything is altered in a bizarre way and there is no explanation ever, people always feel cheered up after listening to her; they say of her that it is a relief to meet somebody who doesn't take herself too seriously, who is so unintense, and civilized, and never makes any real demands or complaints.

The only thing she complains about readily is her name. Prue is a schoolgirl, she says, and Prudence is an old virgin; the parents who gave her that name must have been too shortsighted even to take account of puberty. What if she had grown a great bosom, she says, or developed a sultry look? Or was the name itself a guarantee that she wouldn't? In her late forties now, slight and fair, attending to customers with a dutiful vivacity, giving pleasure to dinner guests, she might not be far from what those parents had in mind: bright and thoughtful, a cheerful spectator. It is hard to grant her maturity, maternity, real troubles.

Her grownup children, the products of an early Vancouver Island marriage she calls a cosmic disaster, come to see her, and instead of wanting money, like other people's children, they bring presents, try to do her accounts, arrange to have her house insulated. She is delighted with their presents, listens to their advice, and, like a flighty daughter, neglects to answer their letters.

Her children hope she is not staying on in Toronto because of Gordon. Everybody hopes that. She would laugh at the idea. She gives parties and goes to parties; she goes out sometimes with other men. Her attitude toward sex is very comforting to those of her friends who get into terrible states of passion and jealousy, and feel cut loose from their moorings. She seems to regard sex as a wholesome, slightly silly indulgence, like dancing and nice dinners—something that shouldn't interfere with people's being kind and cheerful to each other.

Now that his wife is gone for good, Gordon comes to see Prue occasionally, and sometimes asks her out for dinner. They may not go to a restaurant; they may go to his house. Gordon is a good cook. When Prue or his wife lived with him he couldn't cook at all, but as soon as he put his mind to it he became—he says truthfully—better than either of them.

Recently he and Prue were having dinner at his house. He had made Chicken Kiev, and crème brûlée for dessert. Like most new, serious cooks, he talked about food.

Gordon is rich, by Prue's—and most people's—standards. He is a neurologist. His house is new, built on a hillside north of the city, where there used to be picturesque, unprofitable farms. Now there are one-of-a-kind, architect-designed, very expensive houses on half-acre lots. Prue, describing Gordon's house, will say, "Do you know there are four bathrooms? So that if four people want to have baths at the same time there's no problem. It seems a bit much, but it's very nice, really, and you'd never have to go through the hall."

Gordon's house has a raised dining area—a sort of platform, surrounded by a conversation pit, a music pit, and a bank of heavy greenery under sloping glass. You can't see the entrance area from the dining area, but there are no intervening walls, so that from one area you can hear something of what is going on in the other.

During dinner the doorbell rang. Gordon excused himself and went down the steps. Prue heard a female voice. The person it belonged to was still outside, so she could not hear the words. She heard Gordon's voice, pitched low, cautioning. The door didn't close—it seemed the person had not been invited in—but the voices went on, muted and angry. Suddenly there was a cry from Gordon, and he appeared halfway up the steps, waving his arms.

"The crème brûlée," he said. "Could you?" He ran back down as Prue got up and went into the kitchen to save the dessert. When she returned he was climbing the stairs more slowly, looking both agitated and tired.

"A friend," he said gloomily. "Was it all right?"

Prue realized he was speaking of the crème brûlée, and she said yes, it was perfect, she had got it just in time. He thanked her but did not cheer up. It seemed it was not the dessert he was troubled over but whatever had happened at the door. To take his mind off it, Prue started asking him professional questions about the plants.

"I don't know a thing about them," he said. "You know that."

"I thought you might have picked it up. Like the cooking."

"She takes care of them."

"Mrs. Carr?" said Prue, naming his housekeeper.

"Who did you think?"

Prue blushed. She hated to be thought suspicious.

"The problem is that I think I would like to marry you," said Gordon, with no noticeable lightening of his spirits. Gordon is a large man, with heavy features. He likes to wear thick clothing, bulky sweaters. His blue eyes are often bloodshot, and their expression indicates that there is a helpless, baffled soul squirming around inside this doughty fortress.

"What a problem," said Prue lightly, though she knew Gordon well enough to know that it was.

The doorbell rang again, rang twice, three times, before Gordon could get to it. This time there was a crash, as of something flung and landing hard. The door slammed and Gordon was immediately back in view. He staggered on the steps and held his hand to his head, meanwhile making a gesture with the other hand to signify that nothing serious had happened, Prue was to sit down.

"Bloody overnight bag," he said. "She threw it at me."

"Did it hit you?"

"Glancing."

"It made a hard sound for an overnight bag. Were there rocks in it?"

"Probably cans. Her deodorant and so forth."

"Oh."

Prue watched him pour himself a drink. "I'd like some coffee, if I might," she said. She went to the kitchen to put the water on, and Gordon followed her.

"I think I'm in love with this person," he said.

"Who is she?"

"You don't know her. She's quite young."

"Oh."

"But I do think I want to marry you, in a few years' time."

"After you get over being in love?"

"Yes."

"Well. I guess nobody knows what can happen in a few years' time."

When Prue tells about this, she says, "I think he was afraid I was going to laugh. He doesn't know why people laugh or throw their overnight bags at him, but he's noticed they do. He's such a proper person, really. The lovely dinner. Then she comes and throws her overnight bag. And it's quite reasonable to think of marrying me in a few years' time, when he gets over being in love. I think he first thought of telling me to sort of put my mind at rest."

She doesn't mention that the next morning she picked up one of Gordon's cufflinks from his dresser. The cufflinks are made of amber and he bought them in Russia, on the holiday he and wife took when they got back together again. They look like squares of candy, golden, translucent, and this one warms quickly in her hand. She drops it into the pocket of her jacket. Taking one is not a real theft. It could be a reminder, an intimate prank, a piece of nonsense.

She is alone in Gordon's house; he has gone off early, as he always does. The housekeeper does not come till nine. Prue doesn't have to be at the shop until ten; she could make herself breakfast, stay and have coffee with the housekeeper, who is her friend from olden times. But once she has the cufflink in her pocket she doesn't linger. The house seems too bleak a place to spend an extra moment in. It was Prue, actually, who helped choose the building lot. But she's not responsible for approving the plans—the wife was back by that time.

When she gets home she puts the cufflink in an old tobacco tin. The children bought this tobacco tin in a junk shop years ago, and gave it to her for a present. She used to smoke, in those days, and the children were worried about her, so they gave her this tin full of toffees, jelly beans, and gumdrops, with a note saying, "Please get fat instead." That was for her birthday. Now the tin has in it several things besides the cufflink—all small things, not of great value but not worthless, either. A little enamelled dish, a sterling-silver spoon for salt, a crystal fish. These are not sentimental keepsakes. She never looks at them, and often forgets what she has there. They are not booty, they don't have ritualistic significance. She does not take something every time she goes to Gordon's house, or every time she stays over, or to mark what she might call memorable visits. She doesn't do it in a daze and she doesn't seem to be under a compulsion. She just takes something, every now and then, and puts it away in the dark of the old tobacco tin, and more or less forgets about it.

HECTOR HUGH MUNRO

Reginald's Choir Treat

"Never," wrote Reginald to his most darling friend, "be a pioneer. It's the Early Christian that gets the fattest lion."

Reginald, in his way, was a pioneer.

None of the rest of his family had anything approaching Titian hair or a sense of humour, and they used primroses as a table decoration.

It follows that they never understood Reginald, who came down late to breakfast, and nibbled toast, and said disrespectful things about the universe. The family ate porridge, and believed in everything, even the weather forecast.

Therefore the family was relieved when the vicar's daughter undertook the reformation of Reginald. Her name was Amabel; it was the vicar's one extravagance. Amabel was accounted a beauty and intellectually gifted: she never played tennis, and was reputed to have read Maeterlinck's *Life of the Bee*. If you abstain from tennis *and* read Maeterlinck in a small country village, you are of necessity intellectual. Also she had been twice to Fécamp to pick up a good French accent from the Americans staying there; consequently she had a knowledge of the world which might be considered useful in dealings with a worldling.

Hence the congratulations in the family when Amabel undertook the reformation of its wayward member.

Amabel commenced operations by asking her unsuspecting pupil to tea in the vicarage garden; she believed in the healthy influence of natural surroundings, never having been in Sicily, where things are different.

And like every woman who has ever preached repentance to unregenerate youth, she dwelt on the sin of an empty life, which always seems so much more scandalous in the country, where people rise early to see if a new strawberry has happened during the night.

Reginald recalled the lilies of the field, "which simply sat and looked beautiful, and defied competition."

"But that is not an example for us to follow," gasped Amabel.

"Unfortunately, we can't afford to. You don't know what a world of trouble I take in trying to rival the lilies in their artistic simplicity."

"You are really indecently vain of your appearance. A good life is infinitely preferable to good looks."

"You agree with me that the two are incompatible. I always say beauty is only sin deep."

Amabel began to realize that the battle is not always to the strong-minded. With the immemorial resource of her sex, she abandoned the frontal attack and laid stress on her unassisted labours in parish work, her mental loneliness, her discouragements—and at the right moment she produced strawberries and cream. Reginald was obviously affected by the latter, and when his preceptress suggested that he might begin the strenuous life by helping her to supervise the annual outing of the bucolic infants who composed the local choir, his eyes shone with the dangerous enthusiasm of a convert.

Reginald entered on the strenuous life alone, as far as Amabel was concerned. The most virtuous women are not proof against damp grass, and Amabel kept her bed with a cold. Reginald called it a dispensation; it had been the dream of his life to stage-manage a choir outing. With strategic insight, he led his shy, bullet-headed charges to the nearest woodland stream and allowed them to bathe; then he seated himself on the discarded garments and discoursed on their immediate future, which, he decreed, was to embrace a Bacchanalian procession through the village. Forethought had provided the occasion with a supply of tin whistles, but the introduction of a he-goat from a neighbouring orchard was a brilliant afterthought. Properly, Reginald explained, there should have been an outfit of panther skins; as it was, those who had spotted handkerchiefs were allowed to wear them, which they did with thankfulness. Reginald recognized the impossibility in the time at his disposal, of teaching his shivering neophytes a chant in honour of Bacchus, so he started them off with a more familiar, if less appropriate, temperance hymn. After all, he said, it is the spirit of the thing that counts. Following the etiquette of dramatic authors on first nights, he remained discreetly in the background while the procession, with extreme diffidence and the goat, wound its way lugubriously towards the village. The singing had died down long before the main street was reached, but the miserable wailing of pipes brought the inhabitants to their doors. Reginald said he had seen something like it in pictures; the villagers had seen nothing like it in their lives, and remarked as much freely.

Reginald's family never forgave him. They had no sense of humour.

HECTOR HUGH MUNRO

The Open Window

'My aunt will be down presently, Mr. Nuttel,' said a very self-possessed young lady of fifteen; 'in the meantime you must try and put up with me.'

Framton Nuttel endeavoured to say the correct something which should duly flatter the niece of the moment without unduly discounting the aunt that was to come. Privately he doubted more than ever whether these formal visits on a succession of total strangers would do much towards helping the nerve cure which he was supposed to be undergoing.

'I know how it will be,' his sister had said when he was preparing to migrate to this rural retreat; 'you will bury yourself down there and not speak to a living soul, and your nerves will be worse than ever from moping. I shall just give you letters of introduction to all the people I know there. Some of them, as far as I can remember, were quite nice.'

Framton wondered whether Mrs. Sappleton, the lady to whom he was presenting one of the letters of introduction, came into the nice division.

'Do you know many of the people round here?' asked the niece, when she judged that they had had sufficient silent communion.

'Hardly a soul,' said Framton. 'My sister was staying here, at the rectory, you know, some four years ago, and she gave me letters of introduction to some of the people here.'

He made the last statement in a tone of distinct regret.

'Then you know practically nothing about my aunt?' pursued the self-possessed young lady.

'Only her name and address,' admitted the caller. He was wondering whether Mrs. Sappleton was in the married or widowed state. An undefinable something about the room seemed to suggest masculine habitation.

'Her great tragedy happened just three years ago,' said the child; 'that would be since your sister's time.'

'Her tragedy?' asked Framton; somehow in this restful country spot tragedies seemed out of place.

'You may wonder why we keep that window wide open on an October afternoon,' said the niece, indicating a large French window that opened on to a lawn.

'It is quite warm for the time of the year,' said Framton; 'but has that window got anything to do with the tragedy?'

'Out through that window, three years ago to a day, her husband and her two young brothers went off for their day's shooting. They never came back. In crossing the moor to their favourite snipe-shooting ground they were all three engulfed in a treacherous piece of bog. It had been that dreadful wet summer, you know, and places that were safe in other years gave way suddenly without warning. Their bodies were never recovered. That was the dreadful part of it.' Here the child's voice lost its self-possessed note and became falteringly human. 'Poor aunt always thinks that they will come back some day, they and the little brown spaniel that was lost with them, and walk in at that window just as they used to do. That is why the window is kept open every evening till it is quite dusk. Poor dear aunt, she has often told me how they went out, her husband with his white waterproof coat over his arm, and Ronnie, her youngest brother, singing, "Bertie, why do you bound?" as he always did to tease her, because she said it got on her nerves. Do you know, sometimes on still, quiet evenings like this, I almost get a creepy feeling that they will all walk in through that window—'

She broke off with a little shudder. It was a relief to Framton when the aunt bustled into the room with a whirl of apologies for being late in making her appearance.

'I hope Vera has been amusing you?' she said.

'She has been very interesting,' said Framton.

'I hope you don't mind the open window,' said Mrs. Sappleton briskly; 'my husband and brothers will be home directly from shooting, and they always come in this way. They've been out for snipe in the marshes today, so they'll make a fine mess over my poor carpets. So like you men-folk, isn't it?'

She rattled on cheerfully about the shooting and the scarcity of birds, and the prospects for duck in the winter. To Framton, it was all purely horrible. He made a desperate but only partially successful effort to turn the talk on to a less ghastly topic; he was conscious that his hostess was giving him only a fragment of her attention, and her eyes were constantly straying past him to the open window and the lawn beyond. It was certainly an unfortunate coincidence that he should have paid his visit on this tragic anniversary.

'The doctors agree in ordering me complete rest, an absence of mental excitement, and avoidance of anything in the nature of violent physical exercise,' announced Framton, who laboured under the tolerably wide-spread delusion that total strangers and chance acquaintances are hungry for the least detail of one's ailments and infirmities, their cause and cure. 'On the matter of diet they are not so much in agreement,' he continued.

'No?' said Mrs. Sappleton, in a voice which only replaced a yawn at the last moment. Then she suddenly brightened into alert attention—but not to what Framton was saying.

'Here they are at last.' she cried. 'Just in time for tea, and don't they look as if they were muddy up to the eyes!'

Framton shivered slightly and turned towards the niece with a look intended to convey sympathetic comprehension. The child was staring out through the open window with dazed horror in her eyes. In a chill shock of nameless fear Framton swung round in his seat and looked in the same direction.

In the deepening twilight three figures were walking across the lawn towards the window; they all carried guns under their arms, and one of them was additionally burdened with a white coat hung over his shoulders. A tired brown spaniel kept close at their heels. Noiselessly they neared the house, and then a hoarse young voice chanted out of the dusk: 'I said, Bertie, why do you bound?'

Framton grabbed wildly at his stick and hat; the hall-door, the gravel-drive, and the front gate were dimly noted stages in his headlong retreat. A cyclist coming along the road had to run into the hedge to avoid imminent collision.

'Here we are, my dear,' said the bearer of the white mackintosh, coming in through the window; 'fairly muddy, but most of it's dry. Who was that who bolted out as we came up?'

'A most extraordinary man, a Mr. Nuttel,' said Mrs. Sappleton; 'could only talk about his illnesses, and dashed off without a word of good-bye or apology when you arrived. One would think he had seen a ghost.'

'I expect it was the spaniel,' said the niece calmly; 'he told me he had a horror of dogs. He was once hunted into a cemetery somewhere on the banks of the Ganges by a pack of pariah dogs, and had to spend the night in a newly dug grave with the creatures snarling and grinning and foaming just above him. Enough to make any one lose their nerve.'

Romance at short notice was her speciality.

Vladimir Nabokov

Signs and Symbols

I

For the fourth time in as many years they were confronted with the problem of what birthday present to bring a young man who was incurably deranged in his mind. He had no desires. Man-made objects were to him either hives of evil, vibrant with a malignant activity that he alone could perceive, or gross comforts for which no use could be found in his abstract world. After eliminating a number of articles that might offend him or frighten him (anything in the gadget line for instance was taboo), his parents chose a dainty and innocent trifle: a basket with ten different fruit jellies in ten little jars.

At the time of his birth they had been married already for a long time; a score of years had elapsed, and now they were quite old. Her drab gray hair was done anyhow. She wore cheap black dresses. Unlike other women of her age (such as Mrs. Sol, their next-door neighbor, whose face was all pink and mauve with paint and whose hat was a cluster of brookside flowers), she presented a naked white countenance to the fault-finding light of spring days. Her husband, who in the old country had been a fairly successful businessman, was now wholly dependent on his brother Isaac, a real American of almost forty years' standing. They seldom saw him and had nicknamed him "the Prince."

That Friday everything went wrong. The underground train lost its life current between two stations, and for a quarter of an hour one could hear nothing but the dutiful beating of one's heart and the rustling of newspapers. The bus they had to take next kept them waiting for ages; and when it did come, it was crammed with garrulous high-school children. It was rain-ing hard as they walked up the brown path leading to the sanitarium. There they waited again; and instead of their boy shuffling into the room as he usu-ally did (his poor face blotched with acne, ill shaven, sullen, and confused), a nurse they knew, and did not care for, appeared at last and brightly ex-plained that he had again attempted to take his life. He was all right, she said, but a visit might disturb him. The place was so miserably understaffed, and things got mislaid or mixed up so easily, that they decided not to leave their present in the office but to bring it to him next time they came.

She waited for her husband to open his umbrella and then took his arm. He kept clearing his throat in a special resonant way he had when he was upset. They reached the bus-stop shelter on the other side of the street and he closed his umbrella. A few feet away, under a swaying and dripping tree, a tiny half-dead unfledged bird was helplessly twitching in a puddle.

During the long ride to the subway station, she and her husband did not exchange a word; and every time she glanced at his old hands (swollen veins, brown-spotted skin), clasped and twitching upon the handle of his umbrella, she felt the mounting pressure of tears. As she looked around try-ing to hook her mind onto something, it gave her a kind of soft shock, a mix-ture of compassion and wonder, to notice that one of the passengers, a girl with dark hair and grubby red toenails, was weeping on the shoulder of an older woman. Whom did that woman resemble? She resembled Rebecca Borisovna, whose daughter had married one of the Soloveichiks—in Minsk, years ago.

The last time he had tried to do it, his method had been, in the doctor's words, a masterpiece of inventiveness; he would have succeeded, had not an envious fellow patient thought he was learning to fly—and stopped him. What he really wanted to do was to tear a hole in his world and escape.

The system of his delusions had been the subject of an elaborate paper in a scientific monthly, but long before that she and her husband had puz-zled it out for themselves. "Referential mania," Herman Brink had called it. In these very rare cases the patient imagines that everything happening around him is a veiled reference to his personality and existence. He ex-cludes real people from the conspiracy—because he considers himself to be so much more intelligent than other men. Phenomenal nature shadows him wherever he goes. Clouds in the staring sky transmit to one another, by means of slow signs, incredibly detailed information regarding him. His inmost thoughts are discussed at nightfall, in manual alphabet, by darkly gesticulating trees. Pebbles or stains or sun flecks form patterns representing in some awful way messages which he must intercept. Everything is a cipher and of everything he is the theme. Some of the spies are detached observers, such are glass surfaces and still pools; others, such as coats in store windows, are prejudiced witnesses, lynchers at heart; others again (running water, storms) are hysterical to the point of insanity, have a distorted opinion of him and grotesquely misinterpret his actions. He must be always on his guard and devote every minute and module of life to the decoding of the undulation of things. The very air he exhales is indexed and filed away. If only the interest he provokes were limited to his immediate surroundings— but alas it is not! With distance the torrents of wild scandal increase in volume and volubility. The silhouettes of his blood corpuscles, magnified a million times, flit over vast plains; and still farther, great mountains of unbearable solidity and height sum up in terms of granite and groaning firs the ultimate truth of his being.

II

When they emerged from the thunder and foul air of the subway, the last dregs of the day were mixed with the street lights. She wanted to buy some fish for supper, so she handed him the basket of jelly jars, telling him to go home. He walked up to the third landing and then remembered he had given her his keys earlier in the day.

In silence he sat down on the steps and in silence rose when some ten minutes later she came, heavily trudging upstairs, wanly smiling, shaking her head in deprecation of her silliness. They entered their two-room flat and he at once went to the mirror. Straining the corners of his mouth apart by means of his thumbs, with a horrible masklike grimace he removed his new hopelessly uncomfortable dental plate and severed the long tusks of saliva connecting him to it. He read his Russian-language newspaper while she laid the table. Still reading, he ate the pale victuals that needed no teeth. She knew his moods and was also silent.

When he had gone to bed, she remained in the living room with her pack of soiled cards and her old albums. Across the narrow yard where the rain tinkled in the dark against some battered ash cans, windows were blandly alight and in one of them a black-trousered man with his bare elbows raised could be seen lying supine on an untidy bed. She pulled the blind down and examined the photographs. As a baby he looked more surprised than most babies. From a fold in the album, a German maid they had had in Leipzig and her fat-faced fiance fell out. Minsk, the Revolution, Leipzig, Berlin, Leipzig, a slanting house front badly out of focus. Four years old, in a park: moodily, shyly, with puckered forehead, looking away from an eager squirrel as he would from any other stranger. Aunt Rosa, a fussy, angular, wild-eyed old lady, who had lived in a tremulous world of bad news, bankruptcies, train accidents, cancerous growths—until the Germans put her to death, together with all the people she had worried about. Age six—that was when he drew wonderful birds with human hands and feet, and suffered from insomnia like a grown-up man. His cousin, now a famous chess player. He again, aged about eight, already difficult to understand, afraid of the wallpaper in the passage, afraid of a certain picture in a book which merely showed an idyllic landscape with rocks on a hillside and an old cart wheel hanging from the branch of a leafless tree. Aged ten: the year they left Europe. The shame, the pity, the humiliating difficulties, the ugly, vicious, backward children he was with in that special school. And then came a time in his life, coinciding with a long convalescence after pneumonia, when those little phobias of his which his parents had stubbornly regarded as the eccentricities of a prodigiously gifted child hardened as it were into a dense tangle of logically interacting illusions, making him totally inaccessible to normal minds.

This, and much more, she accepted—for after all living did mean accepting the loss of one joy after another, not even joys in her case—mere possibilities of improvement. She thought of the endless waves of pain that for some reason or other she and her husband had to endure; of the invisible giants hurting her boy in some unimaginable fashion; of the incalculable amount of tenderness contained in the world; of the fate of this tenderness, which is either crushed, or wasted, or transformed into madness; of neglected children humming to themselves in unswept corners; of beautiful weeds that cannot hide from the farmer and helplessly have to watch the shadow of his simian stoop leave mangled flowers in its wake, as the monstrous darkness approaches.

III

It was past midnight when from the living room she heard her husband moan; and presently he staggered in, wearing over his nightgown the old overcoat with astrakhan collar which he much preferred to the nice blue bathrobe he had.

"I can't sleep," he cried.

"Why," she asked, "why can't you sleep? You were so tired."

"I can't sleep because I am dying," he said and lay down on the couch.

"Is it your stomach? Do you want me to call Dr. Solov?"

"No doctors, no doctors," he moaned. "To the devil with doctors! We must get him out of there quick. Otherwise we'll be responsible. Responsible!" he repeated and hurled himself into a sitting position, both feet on the floor, thumping his forehead with his clenched fist.

"All right," she said quietly, "we shall bring him home tomorrow morning."

"I would like some tea," said her husband and retired to the bathroom.

Bending with difficulty, she retrieved some playing cards and a photograph or two that had slipped from the couch to the floor: knave of hearts, nine of spades, ace of spades, Elsa and her bestial beau.

He returned in high spirits, saying in a loud voice:

"I have it all figured out. We will give him the bedroom. Each of us will spend part of the night near him and the other part on this couch. By turns. We will have the doctor see him at least twice a week. It does not matter what the Prince says. He won't have to say much anyway because it will come out cheaper."

The telephone rang. It was an unusual hour for their telephone to ring. His left slipper had come off and he groped for it with his heel and toe as he stood in the middle of the room, and childishly, toothlessly, gaped at his wife. Having more English than he did, it was she who attended the calls.

"Can I speak to Charlie," said a girl's dull little voice.

"What number you want? No. That is not the right number."

The receiver was gently cradled. Her hand went to her old tired heart. "It frightened me," she said.

He smiled a quick smile and immediately resumed his excited monologue.

They would fetch him as soon as it was day. Knives would have to be kept in a locked drawer. Even at his worst he presented no danger to other people.

The telephone rang a second time. The same toneless anxious young voice asked for Charlie.

"You have the incorrect number. I will tell you what you are doing: you are turning the letter O instead of the zero."

They sat down to their unexpected festive midnight tea. The birthday present stood on the table. He sipped noisily; his face was flushed; every now and then he imparted a circular motion to his raised glass so as to make the sugar dissolve more thoroughly. The vein on the side of his bald head where there was a large birthmark stood out conspicuously and although he had shaved that morning, a silvery bristle showed on his chin. While she poured him another glass of tea, he put on his spectacles and re-examined with pleasure the luminous yellow, green, red little jars. His clumsy moist lips spelled out their eloquent labels: apricot, grape, peach, plum, quince. He had got to crab apple, when the telephone rang again.

Commentary: John V. Hagopian, "Decoding Nabokov's 'Signs and Symbols'"

Displaced persons and madmen are recurrent themes in Nabokov's fiction, and both are central to his early—and best—short story, "Signs and Symbols." The nameless family, probably Russian Jews, have shuttled from "Minsk, the Revolution, Leipzig, Berlin, Leipzig" to America where the father, "who in the old country had been a fairly successful business man, was now wholly dependent on his brother Isaac, a real American of almost forty years standing." The geographic and socio-political displacement, however, is subsumed in a larger, cosmic displacement; these people have no place in life or in the universe. The straightforward, declarative style ("That Friday everything went wrong") barely mutes the sombre tone. Unlike the larger, grander treatments of this theme in *Pnin, Bend Sinister* and *Pale Fire*, there is no wit or levity here to relieve the intense sadness of the human experience. That sombre tone is most appropriate to the mother, of whom—or *for* whom—the narrator says, "all living did mean accepting the loss of one joy after another, not even joys in her case—mere possibilities of improvement."

Tone and point of view are closely related, because the external, objective narrator effaces himself and, though he tells the story in the third person, presents only the thoughts and perceptions in her mind. The only factor that prevents a conversion of the story into an I-narrative simply by changing the third-person pronouns into the first person (i.e., "she waited for her husband . . ." to "I waited for my husband . . .") is that the mother, a poor emigre, cannot realistically have such a magnificent command of the English language. But even though the language is Nabokov's, the mind it manifests is the mother's. Hence, it cannot be as William Carroll maintains, in the only full-length commentary on the story in all of Nabokov criticism, that "Nabokov has ensured, through his rhetorical strategy, that the reader will succumb to the same mania." And that perspective is not at all, as W. W. Rowe maintains, "an almost paranoiac mode of perception." On the contrary, the narrative technique serves as an implicit endorsement of her perspective on things. Indeed, the central thematic question of the story is: Is it necessarily paranoid to feel that nature and the universe are enemies of man? to want to "tear a hole in [the] world and escape"? To put it another way, does the story depict a context for human experience so benign that it is obviously madness to want to escape? What do the "signs and symbols" indicate? Dr. Herman Brink, presumably a Freudian psychiatrist and forerunner of John Ray, Jr., in *Lolita* (a breed that Nabokov detested), had diagnosed the boy's condition as "referential mania," a form of paranoia which the *Psychiatric Dictionary* defines as a delusion in which a patient misinterprets everything around him as having "a personal reference of a derogatory character toward him." Dr. Brink used the boy as a subject of a professional paper in which he gave a vivid description of his symptoms and drew the conclusion that to him "everything is a cipher and of everything he is the theme . . . . [that is] the ultimate truth of his being". But is it a fact that the boy's interpretation is a delusion, an aberration inconsistent with the "real" world depicted in the story?

William Carroll endorses Dr. Brink with the comment, "The boy lives in a closed system of signs all of which point, malevolently, toward him." It may be that anyone who seeks to interpret the meaning of the signs and symbols betrays himself as one of another breed that Nabokov detested. In a reply to W. W. Rowe's book he expressed indignation at "the symbolism racket in schools [that] computerizes minds but destroys plain intelligence as well as poetical sense. . . . The various words planted by an idiotically sly novelist to keep schoolmen busy are not labels, not pointers, and certainly not the garbage cans of a Viennese tenement, but live fragments of specific description, rudiments of metaphor, and echoes of creative emotion." But the story is entitled "Signs and Symbols" and clearly depicts characters who are intensely aware of them. The signs are not, as Carroll maintains, merely a "closed system" of the deranged son; nor is it true that "his parents are dull, sad people who are merely oblivious where he is paranoid." The world presented by the narrator and observed by the parents is fully consistent with the boy's vision of it. The parents have suffered much and their greatest suffering issues from their compassion for their unfortunate son. They make great sacrifices for him, go to a great deal of trouble to visit him regularly in the sanatorium, worry about getting him an appropriate present for his birthday, and have poignant reminiscences about his childhood. Upon learning of his renewed attempt to commit suicide, they determine to bring him home and care for him themselves in their cramped two-room flat. Such concerns gainsay Douglas Fowler's bizarre observation that the parents "are allowed to come before us as without genius, beauty, comic vulgarity, or monstrousness because they are marked for extinction, too." To be sure, they lack comic vulgarity and monstrousness, but they have a genius for survival and a beautiful capacity for family love. If they are "marked for extinction," it is only because they are old and have suffered much, and not because they are to be classed with the losers in Nabokov's world.

With respect to the significance of the signs and symbols of the story, it is important to keep in mind that everything is presented from the point of view of the mother. She is fully aware that, unlike Mrs. Sol "whose face was all pink and mauve with paint and whose hat was a cluster of brookside flowers" (i.e., she cosmeticizes the malevolence of nature), she "presented a naked white countenance to the fault-finding light of spring days." It is a fact and not a paranoid fantasy that the world she lives in is not at all friendly or succoring: "the Underground train lost its life current between two stations," "a tiny half-dead unfledged bird was helplessly twitching in a puddle," another passenger, a girl, was weeping on the shoulder of an older woman, the sanatorium was "miserably understaffed and things got mislaid or mixed up so easily," the husband's "clasped and twitchy hands had swollen veins and brown spotted skin," the son's "poor face was blotched with acne." These are not the insane imaginings of the boy, but a hard-fact reality that undermines Dr. Brink's diagnosis. They depict a world from which the urge to escape is not at all a symptom of madness.

Carroll argues that "Nabokov has insured, through his rhetorical strategy, that the reader will succumb to the same mania that afflicts the boy. The story is studded with apparent signs and symbols that the gullible reader—that is, any reader—will attempt to link together in a meaningful pattern." Carroll is clearly a post-modernist who believes that the story does not have a closed form that crystallizes a specific meaning determined by the author and that a reader who feels a "need to see a completed pattern . . . will have, in effect, participated with Nabokov in killing the boy." But Nabokov once said to Alfred Appel, "the design of my novel is fixed in my imagination and every character follows the course I imagine for him. I am a perfect dictator in that private world." It would seem to follow that a reader is obliged to discover the author's fixed design and follow the course he has imagined for his characters. But Carroll would have it that a reader who sees the design as leading inexorably to the death of the boy is guilty of murder! That raises the most crucial plot question: does the boy in fact die in the end?

The story has three parts. Part I depicts the abortive attempt of the parents to deliver a birthday gift, abortive because the boy had attempted to commit suicide. Part II focuses on the mother's meditations after their return to the flat, and Part III on the post-midnight decision to bring the boy home, followed by the ringing of the telephone. In effect, these are (1) the immediate context of the boy's suicide attempt, already examined above; (2) the family's history of pain and death, obviously modeled on Nabokov's own family history; (3) the successful suicide. The principal signs and symbols of Part II are the photographs and playing cards. Apart from the boy, the figures in the photo album include Aunt Rosa, exterminated by the Germans; a famous chess player cousin (readers familiar with Nabokov's sly practice of using principal characters in some works as background figures in others will recognize Luzhin, another suicide); and some "ugly vicious, backward children he was with in that special school" (like those in the school where Adam Krug's own son was killed in *Bend Sinister*)—all symbols of death and violence. At four, the boy looked away from an eager squirrel (like Pnin, he did not consider nature friendly even then); at six, he drew birds with human hands and feet (later, an envious fellow patient thought he was learning to fly—and stopped him from committing suicide), and as a teen-ager he developed "those little phobias. . .the eccentricities of a prodigiously gifted child hardened as it were into a dense tangle of logically inter-acting illusions, making him totally inaccessible to normal minds" (perfect description of Nabokov's own fiction). These images evoke in the mother thoughts of "endless waves of pain. . .of individual giants hurting her boy. . .of beautiful weeds that cannot hide from the farmer and helplessly have to watch the shadow of his simian stoop leave mangled flowers in its wake as the monstrous darkness approaches." That last image in which human perceptions and emotions are projected upon helpless weeds suggests that the mother, too, suffers from what Herman Brink called "referential mania." But the family's history fully justifies the feeling that they live in a malevolent universe.

All this brooding on pain and death leads to Part III, which occurs in a period of "monstrous darkness." The father who cries, "I can't sleep because I am dying," insists that they bring the boy home. The mother readily agrees, stooping to pick up some photos and cards, including the ace of spades (a symbol of death). It is then that they are frightened by the ring of the telephone, a wrong number. When the telephone rings a second time, the mother (who obviously has acute perceptions and intelligence) patiently explains, "I will tell you what you are doing: you are turning the letter O instead of the zero." Carroll says of this, "while it is a plausible explanation of the wrong number, the fact remains that there is no hieroglyphic difference between the letter and the number." He is so determined to keep the story from having a necessary closure that he cites the irrelevant hieroglyphic similarity of O and zero. But in fact on a telephone dial there is a significant hieroglyphic difference: the letter O is a perfect circle, whereas the number zero is a vertical oval. Even more important is the fact that the O appears in the sixth hole on the dial and the zero appears in the tenth! These significant details and the lapse of time between the second and third rings of the telephone make it highly unlikely that the third call is simply another wrong number. Nabokov said, "I like composing riddles with elegant solutions" (see the ending of "The Vane Sisters"). The signs and symbols of the story inexorably accumulate to make that third ring a portent of death. The fears of the parents come true, and the reader experiences the chilling shock of recognition that the sanatorium is calling to report that the boy has at last torn a hole in his world and escaped.

Carroll is clearly wrong in asserting that

> it is just as plausible to argue, though, that the signs and symbols of death have no logically inherent and inescapable conclusion, that they point to nothing finally, and are as "meaning"-less as a sequence of random numbers. It is this ambiguity that makes the story so profoundly eerie. The "cipher" is constructed so that we have to supply the key, constitutionally unable to admit that there is none.

But no legitimate artist produces randomness. Such a reading assumes that the story does not have implicit lines of force shaping a gestalt and leading to the closure of a specific design. The post-modernists must not be allowed to kidnap Nabokov. He may revel in intricacies and labyrinthine complexities and he may relish topsi-turvical coincidences, but John Shade in *Pale Fire* nicely articulates Nabokov's aesthetic: "Not flimsy nonsense, but a web of sense./Yes! It sufficed that I in life could find/Some kind of link-and-bobolink, some kind/Of correlated pattern in the game." As Hagopian observes, "One might say of Nabokov that the more a particular novel engages his own passions, the more he controls and conceals them by converting them into games, puzzles, and various intricate patterns; clear and obvious plots emerge from his pen only when he contemplates the experience with a cool, dispassionate objectivity." In the final analysis, "Signs and Symbols," despite its pessimistic world-view, emerges as one of Nabokov's most beautifully made and poignant short stories.

Commentary: David Field, "Sacred Dangers: Nabokov's Distorted Reflection"

Vladimir Nabokov began his lectures on literature by claiming that "the real writer, the fellow who sends planets spinning and models a man asleep and eagerly tampers with the sleeper's rib, that kind of author has no given values at his disposal: he must create them himself." Like the God of creation, the artist faces an amorphous world and must impose form on it: "The material of this world may be real enough (as far as reality goes) but does not exist at all as an accepted entirety: it is chaos, and to this chaos the author says 'go!' allowing the world to flicker and to fuse. It is now recombined in its very atoms, not merely in its visible and superficial parts." Nabokov thus seems to acknowledge that artists are supreme egotists who vie with Jehovah's power to create a world.

But that god-like creative act involves a tremendous risk because the artist may merely possess the insane notion that he or she is God. Such delusions of grandeur lead to a false sense of creation, for insane artists lack the power to recombine the world "in its very atoms" and must settle instead for an order that distorts reality, an order that they discern in the "visible and superficial parts" of the world. And that false order inevitably replicates the insane artists' imaginations because the chaos merely reflects elements of their own minds.

There is, nevertheless, a point of tangency between the hubris of the artist and the delusions of the insane, and Nabokov repeatedly acknowledged his sympathy for highly personalized and eccentric imaginations. In a lecture he gave his classes at Cornell, for example, Nabokov lashed out at "commonsense" (one word) and praised those who break from shared reality:

> It is instructive to think that there is not a single person in this room, or for that matter in any room in the world, who, at some nicely chosen point in historical space-time would not be put to death there and then, here and now, by a commonsensical majority in righteous rage. The color of one's creed, neckties, eyes, thoughts, manners, speech, is sure to meet somewhere in time or space with a fatal objection from a mob that hates that particular tone. And the more brilliant, the more unusual the man, the nearer he is to the stake. *Stranger* always rhymes with *danger*. The meek prophet, the enchanter in his cave, the indignant artist, the nonconforming little schoolboy, all share in the same sacred danger. And this being so, let us bless them, let us bless the freak; for in the natural evolution of things, the ape would perhaps never have become man had not a freak appeared in the family.

Because such freakish, insane-appearing minds may reach more sacred insight than those who accept society's shared reality, the only "real" worlds are highly personal imaginative creations: "What I feel to be the real modern world is the world the artist creates, his own mirage, which becomes a new *mir* ('world' in Russian) by the very act of his shedding, as it were, the age he lives in."

Nabokov's short story "Signs and Symbols" illustrates this complex relationship between imagination and insanity. The story concerns an emigré family—an elderly woman, her husband, and their son, who is "incurably deranged in his mind" and confined to a sanitarium. Herman Brink, the psychologist in the story, had analyzed the "system of [the boy's] delusions" in "an elaborate paper in a scientific monthly": the boy suffers from "referential mania," a disease which causes him to see messages to himself in all his surroundings. When the parents take the boy a carefully chosen birthday present, a basket with jars of fruit jellies, they learn that he has attempted suicide again—the doctor called his previous attempt "a masterpiece of inventiveness; he would have succeeded, had not an envious fellow patient thought he was learning to fly—and stopped him. What he really wanted to do was to tear a hole in his world and escape." The parents fear another attempt. When they get home, they decide to bring him there and care for him themselves since the hospital does not sufficiently attend to his needs. Late that evening, as the parents grow more convinced that their decision is sound, the phone rings, and "a girl's dull little voice" asks for "Charlie." The phone rings again, and "the same toneless anxious young voice asked for Charlie." The man explains to the young girl the nature of her dialing error. The story ends with the phone ringing for the third time, but we never learn the nature of the call.

Criticism has focused on the way that the reader's attempt to decipher the story's own signs and symbols—especially the reader's quest to determine whether or not the third phone call reports the boy's suicide—duplicates the very nature of the boy's insanity. William Carroll says that in the story "a Nabokovian character's self-consciousness resembles, though in a distorted manner, our own self-consciousness as readers." He claims that "referential mania," the disease from which the insane boy suffers, "is a critical disease all readers of fiction suffer from." Like Carroll, David H. Richter finds that "Signs and Symbols" engages the sensitive reader in a plight similar to that of the main character. "through Nabokov's device of narrative entrapment, we become collaborators not only in crime but in creation."

Larry R. Andrews carries such reasoning further and, after arguing for a reading in which he deciphers the story's ending to show how signs point to the boy's suicide, he unravels his own and all other interpretations to reduce the story to "a configuration of black marks on the page," an abstract aesthetic pattern, "the higher sphere of the artist's fictive world (in which we are characters too)." And Paul J. Rosenzweig insists that "Nabokov undercuts the traditional distances among the realities of author, reader, and text by forcing the reader to become both a character in and author of the text."

Standing in stark contrast to such reader-response critics is John V. Hagopian, who argues that "no legitimate artist produces randomness." For Hagopian, the signs and symbols in the story all point to the boy's suicide; the story cannot metamorphose with each reader's interpretation, and a careful and scrupulous reading can yield its meaning. An example of the signs that alert us to the impending tragedy occurs in the story when the couple comes home: "The underground train lost its life current between two stations," and then, when they've left the subway to walk the rest of the way home, they see "a tiny half-dead unfledged bird" which is "helplessly twitching in a puddle." Their plan to bring the boy home puts him, in a sense, "between two stations." His childhood drawing of "wonderful birds with human hands and feet" and his effort to fly when attempting suicide both associate him with the helpless bird. Hagopian uses such evidence to infer that the boy does, in fact, commit suicide and that the third phone call conveys the bad news from the hospital.

But even Hagopian must grapple with the issue of meaning that inheres in details, and he must express faith in the order of the world of art. The other critics, in fact, acknowledge the evidence that Hagopian presents but refuse to believe in his conclusions. Nevertheless, all the interpretations move from the question of whether or not the boy commits suicide to a consideration of the very foundation of knowledge: can anyone know anything definitely? Are there any principles for determining reality? Are we not in fact all insane as we try to make order of the world? Or, as Nabokov's former student Thomas Pynchon puts it, "life's single lesson" may be that "there is more accident to it than a man can ever admit to in a lifetime and stay sane."

Is the boy in "Signs and Symbols" merely a misunderstood artist, a combination of all the freaks a commonsensical mob might put to death— prophet, enchanter, schoolboy, artist? His first attempt at suicide is "a masterpiece of inventiveness" and his desire to fly into a transcendent world through somehow connecting himself to nature links him with romantic poets. His active imagination, like all creative fancy, colors what he sees and performs a major transformation when it observes nature. According to Dr. Brink's diagnosis, in "referential mania,"

> the patient imagines that everything happening around him is a veiled reference to his personality and existence.. . . Phenomenal nature shadows him wherever he goes. Clouds in the staring sky transmit to one another, by means of slow signs, incredibly detailed information regarding him.. . . Everything is a cipher and of everything he is the theme. Some of the spies are detached observers, such as glass surfaces and still pools; others, such as coats in store windows, are prejudiced witnesses, lynchers at heart.. . . He must be always on his guard and devote every minute and module of life to the decoding of the undulation of things.

As the reader-response critics have pointed out, the boy's quest resembles critical and poetic inquiry as well as insanity. Carol T. Williams extends the argument and calls Nabokov's technique "self-directed irony" because he is "a writer devoted to the 'decoding of the undulation of things.' " Even Nabokov speaks explicitly about the importance of imaginatively connecting himself to "phenomenal nature." In *Speak, Memory*, after recounting the origin of his first poem, he relates that writing the poem was "a phenomenon of orientation" and explains that all poetry involves the attempt "to express one's position in regard to the universe embraced by consciousness." He goes on to say that "[t]he arms of consciousness reach out and grope, and the longer they are the better. Tentacles, not wings, are Apollo's natural members." Like the boy, Nabokov sends out his imaginative tentacles to the universe, enveloping "reality" with his own consciousness.

Commentary: Carole M. Doe, "Innocent Trifles, or 'Signs and Symbols'"

When the phone rings the third time, who is calling? Most discussions of Vladimir Nabokov's "Signs and Symbols" (1948), whether in literary journals or freshman English classes, center around this question. One line of criticism, best represented by John Hagopian, has been to take up the invitation of the title to puzzle out the significance of the phone call by examining the extraordinary number of images imbedded in the story, most obviously the many references to death: the ace of spades, the "tiny half-dead unfledged bird," the train that "lost its life current between two stations." Another line, established by William Carroll in the first full-length essay on the story, has been to take that procedure one step further and conclude that the identity of the caller is irrelevant; Nabokov's insistence that we rely on our knowledge of literary conventions to solve the puzzle is also the insistence that we recognize the fictionality of the story, and that we recognize our reading strategy as very much like the son's "referential mania," a disease in which "the patient imagines that everything happening around him is a veiled reference to his personality and existence" and so must put all his energy into "decoding" the messages of the phenomenal world.

Regardless of critical position, then, readers seem to have found that they cannot analyze the story without taking careful account of its numerous "signs and symbols." A good deal has been written on these symbols, and one commentator, Larry Andrews, has analyzed their interplay in exhaustive detail. Yet no one has fully accounted for the most insistent apparent symbol in the story, the "ten different fruit jellies in ten little jars" that the elderly couple purchase as a birthday present for their institutionalized son. As Andrews has noted, the conspicuous placement of the jelly jars in the story—in the first paragraph, at the beginning of section two, and in the last three sentences of the final section—argues for their symbolic significance. Yet the reader finds it as difficult to arrive at the meaning of the jelly jars as the characters find it to get the jelly jars to their intended destination (not only are the parents unable to deliver the gift to their son, but the father also finds himself locked out of their apartment when he tries to return with the jellies). The "luminous" little jars seem unreadable rather than illuminating. Might Nabokov, then, have been hinting at their very *lack* of meaningfulness when he introduced the basket of jellies as an "innocent trifle," something that even the referential maniac son wouldn't construe as a threatening cipher? Might he be taunting us for hunting symbols in a way that is suspiciously like the maniac son's?

As soon as we start calling the jellies an innocent symbol, though, we face another problem. The jelly jars may not stand for something else in the way symbols conventionally do, but to cite them as proof that objects are no more than they appear is, after all, to accept them as signs, not mere objects. Indeed, in labelling them "innocent" Nabokov uses the jelly jars as a sign-post pointing to his theme: our impulse to restructure a random world into a meaningful pattern, an impulse most evident in our response to fictional worlds. His other clues to this theme—the description of referential mania (the extreme extension of such an impulse), the story's title, the mysterious final telephone call that insists we put our pattern-finding skills into prac-tice—seem to me sufficient argument that the story is about creating and in-terpreting as well as about a crazed boy and his pitiable parents. But, for the unconvinced, Nabokov has hidden in the final lines of the story still another clue to his theme, a clue available only to the reader painstaking (and manic?) enough to decipher his more extravagant riddles.

Nabokov alerts us to this clue by hinting that we should do as the fa-ther does and look again at that recalcitrant symbol, the jellies: "he put on his spectacles and re-examined with pleasure the luminous yellow, green, red little jars." Having dropped this hint, Nabokov immediately concludes the story with a focus on the jellies so conspicuous that we can hardly resist puz-zling over it:

> His clumsy moist lips spelled out their eloquent labels: apricot,
> grape, beech plum, quince. He had got to crab apple, when the
> telephone rang again.

Puzzle long enough, and at last the jelly jars yield a final clue to what Nabokov is up to. We must join the father in spelling. Nabokov, whose fond-ness for puns and puzzles is well known, has concealed an anagram in the list of "eloquent labels." The last letters of the four jellies in the list (aprico*t*, grap*e*, beec*h* plu*m*, quinc*e*) form the word *theme*.

Are the jellies, then, somehow the theme? Once again, they are a sign-post, directing us to the part of the story in which the theme is most evi-dent: the paragraph describing referential mania. It is there, at the very center of the paragraph, that the word *theme* makes its single appearance in the story. And it is there that the activities of reader, writer, and referential maniac reveal their affinities. And so the jellies, unlike the many symbols in the story that seem to point to a meaning within its fictional world, point outside it, to the realm of fiction making and fiction breaking.

ANAÏS NIN

Mallorca

I was spending the summer in Mallorca, in Deya, near the monastery where George Sand and Chopin stayed. In the early morning we would get on small donkeys and travel the hard, difficult road to the sea, down the mountain. It would take about an hour of slow travail, through the red earth paths, the rocks, the treacherous boulders, through the silver olive trees, down to the fishing villages, made of huts built against the mountain flanks.

Every day I went down to the cove, where the sea came into a small round bay of such transparency that one could swim to the bottom and see the coral reefs and unusual plants.

A strange story was told of the place by the fishermen. The Mallorcan women were very inaccessible, puritanical and religious. When they swam they wore the long skirted bathing suits and black stockings of years ago. Most of them did not believe in swimming at all and left this to the shameless European women who spent the summers there. The fishermen also condemned the modern bathing suits and obscene behavior of Europeans. They thought of Europeans as nudists, who waited for only the slightest opportunity to get completely undressed and lie naked in the sun like pagans. They also looked with disapproval on the midnight bathing parties innovated by Americans.

One evening some years ago, a fisherman's daughter of eighteen was walking along the edge of the sea, leaping from rock to rock, her white dress clinging to her body. Walking thus and dreaming and watching the effects of the moon on the sea, the soft lapping of the waves at her feet, she came to a hidden cove where she noticed that someone was swimming. She could see only the head moving and occasionally an arm. The swimmer was quite far away. Then she heard a light voice calling out to her, "Come in and swim. It's beautiful." It was said in Spanish with a foreign accent. "Hello, Maria," it called, so the voice knew her. It must have been one of the young American women who bathed there during the day.

She answered, "Who are you?"

"I'm Evelyn," said the voice, "come and swim with me!"

It was very tempting. Maria could easily take off her white dress and wear only her short white chemise. She looked everywhere. There was no one around. The sea was calm and speckled with moonlight. For the first time Maria understood the European love of midnight bathing. She took off her dress. She had long black hair, a pale face, slanted green eyes, greener than the sea. She was beautifully formed, with high breasts, long legs, a stylized body. She knew how to swim better than any other woman on the island. She slid into the water and began her long easy strokes towards Evelyn.

Evelyn swam under the water, came up to her and gripped her legs. In the water they teased each other. The semidarkness and the bathing cap made it difficult to see the face clearly. American women had voices like boys.

Evelyn wrestled with Maria, embraced her under the water. They came up for air, laughing, swimming nonchalantly away and back to each other. Maria's chemise floated up around her shoulders and hampered her movements. Finally it came off altogether and she was left naked. Evelyn swam under and touched her playfully, wrestling and diving under and between her legs.

Evelyn would part her legs so that her friend could dive between them and reappear on the other side. She floated and let her friend swim under her arched back.

Maria saw that she was naked too. Then suddenly she felt Evelyn embracing her from behind, covering her whole body with hers. The water was lukewarm, like a luxuriant pillow, so salty that it bore them, helped them to float and swim without effort.

"You're beautiful, Maria," said the deep voice, and Evelyn kept her arms around her. Maria wanted to float away, but she was held by the warmth of the water, the constant touch of her friend's body. She let herself be embraced. She did not feel breasts on her friend, but, then, she knew young American women she had seen did not have breasts. Maria's body was languid, and she wanted to close her eyes.

Suddenly what she felt between her legs was not a hand but something else, something so unexpected, so disturbing that she screamed. This was no Evelyn but a young man, Evelyn's younger brother, and he had slipped his erect penis between her legs. She screamed but no one heard, and her scream was only something she had been trained to expect of herself. In reality his embrace seemed to her as lulling and warming and caressing as the water. The water and the penis and the hands conspired to arouse her body. She tried to swim away. But the boy swam under her body, caressed her, gripped her legs, and then mounted her again from behind.

In the water they wrestled, but each movement affected her only more physically, made her more aware of his body against hers, of his hands upon her. The water swung her breasts back and forth like two heavy water lilies floating. He kissed them. With the constant motion he could not really take her, but his penis touched her over and over again in the most vulnerable tip of her sex, and Maria was losing her strength. She swam towards shore, and he followed. They fell on the sand. The waves still lapped them as they lay there panting, naked. The boy then took the girl, and the sea came and washed over them and washed away the virgin blood.

From that night they met only at this hour. He took her there in the water, swaying, floating. The wavelike movements of their bodies as they enjoyed each other seemed part of the sea. They found a foothold on a rock and stood together, caressed by the waves, and shaking from the orgasm.

When I went down to the beach at night, I often felt as though I could see them, swimming together, making love.

First Person: Anaïs Nin, "Out of the Labyrinth: An Interview"

Interview by Jody Hoy, *East West Journal* (August 1974).

EAST WEST JOURNAL: At what point in your life did you recognize your own commitment as a writer?

ANAÏS NIN: Very early, because of a mistaken diagnosis when I was nine years old that I wouldn't walk. I immediately took to writing, and then after that of course I began the diary at eleven.

EWJ: Did you read a great deal as a child?

AN: Yes, voraciously.

EWJ: In the diaries you frequently mention Marcel Proust. Has his work influenced your writing?

AN: Proust was very important; he was the first one to show me how to break down the chronology (which I never like) and to follow the dictates and intuitions of memory, of feeling memory, so that he only wrote things when he felt them, no matter when it happened. And of course this element became very strong in my work. But there were also other influences. I wanted to write a poetic novel, and for that I chose models like Giraudoux, Pierre-Jean Jouve, and also Djuna Barnes, an American writer and author of *Nightwood*. Later on it was D. H. Lawrence. Lawrence showed me the way to find a language for emotion, for instinct, for ambivalence, for intuition.

EWJ: Do you identify yourself now as an American writer?

AN: I'm really writing for America and in English, but I would like to go beyond that. I can't say I'm an American writer, although I'm identified with the new consciousness. I prefer to think of myself in more universal or inter-national terms, particularly as I partake of two cultures. On the other hand, many foreign-born writers have been incorporated into the mainstream of American literature, yet Americans still say "foreign-born Nabokov," and in my case, "Paris-born Anaïs."

EWJ: Is the cross-cultural background to which you refer a possible source of the inner density and flow in your work?

AN: I always felt the inner quality resulted from the trauma of being uprooted and of losing my father, then of realizing I had to build an inner world which would withstand destruction. The child who is uprooted begins to recognize that what he builds within himself is what will endure, what will withstand shattering experiences.

EWJ: Your works often evoke symphonic form. Do you feel that music has influenced your writing?

AN: Very strongly. I even said as directly as that in the diary that my ideal would be a page of writing which would be like a page of music. There must be a language, a way of expressing things, which bypasses the intellect and goes straight to the emotions. I wanted to evoke the same reaction to writing that I have to music.

EWJ: I'm interested in the creative process itself, how you move from the interior vision to its exteriorization in literature.

AN: My concern was for exterior reality as holding a secret of a metaphor. I would never describe the city or the ragpickers or a person without looking for the inner meaning. When you are concerned with the metaphysical meaning, everything becomes transparent. I never described a city for its own sake but immediately had to find what its spiritual qualities were. Its symbolic value is what makes it seem transparent, people would even say dreamlike, but that wasn't what it was.

EWJ: What place would you assign to the dream in your works, and what significance to the constancy of flow and communication between the conscious and the unconscious?

AN: Unfortunately, we tend to separate everything. We separate the body and soul. We separate the dream from our daily life. What I found in psychology was the interrelationship between them, and I wanted to keep those passageways open, to be able to move from one dimension to the other, not to divide them even, so that they were really one. The next step was carrying it into the novel, always starting the novel with a dream, having that dream be the theme of the novel to be developed, understood, and fulfilled if possible at the end in order to be able to move on to the next experience.

EWJ: How do you explain the almost universal identification of your women readers with the characters in your novels?

AN: I believe that what unites us universally is our emotions, our feelings in the face of experience, and not necessarily the actual experiences themselves. The facts were different, but readers felt the same way towards a father even if the father was different. So I think unwittingly I must have gone so deep inside what Ira Progoff calls the "personal well" that I touched the water at a level where it connected all the wells together.

EWJ: Is part of your uniqueness as a writer due to the fact that you venture into realms which relate specifically to woman's situation and experience?

AN: My own subjective attitude towards reality was all I really knew, what I could see and feel. I read a great deal, but I didn't imitate men writers. I wanted to tell what I saw. So it came out a woman's vision of the universe, a highly personal vision. I wanted to translate man to woman and woman to man. I didn't want to lose contact with the language of man, but I knew that there was a distinction of levels.

EWJ: Among your works is there one which, from your own point of view, is the best written?

AN: I could never rewrite the short stories. I couldn't add one word to the short stories in *Under a Glass Bell*. I couldn't change anything in *Collages*.

EWJ: Do you use a different artistic yardstick or measure for the diaries?

AN: In writing the diary, I tried to overlook, to forget all procedures of writing. I wanted to make no demands on myself as to whether I'd written it well or not well. I wanted to shed all that, and I succeeded because I felt it would never be read.

EWJ: The diaries were originally not intended to be published?

AN: No.

EWJ: How did they come to be published?

AN: Occasionally I would have a desire to share a part of the diary, or I would write something I was proud of. I did let some people read a part here and there; for example, I let Henry Miller read his portrait. So, there was a little bit of sharing. But feeling that I could solve the problems of editing a diary didn't come till much later, when as a practiced novelist I felt I could handle the problem of editing. Also, I had to handle the psychological problem of being open, the fear of exposing myself. I had a terrifying dream that I opened my front door and was struck by mortal radiation. But then the opposite happened. I overcame that, I overcame the editing problems and then, of course, I was open.

EWJ: Do you use the diary as a resource for the novels and short stories?

AN: Yes, it's really a notebook. Sometimes if I keep writing about a person who interests me, after a while I have a cumulative portrait. We don't think of our friends in that way, we see them a little bit here and a little bit there. Suddenly I see a total person, then I write the story.

EWJ: Has your exceptional beauty been an asset or a disadvantage?

AN: Sometimes it was an asset when you could charm a critic, and sometimes it really stood in the way. Even in women the feeling persists that beauty means there isn't anything inside. I never believed in mine, so that made it very simple.

EWJ: In the diaries, you speak with great attachment of your home in Louveciennes. Do you consider environment an extension of personality in the same way that clothing constitutes a symbolic extension of character in your novels?

AN: Yes. I also believe we need to change our environment as we evolve. I know the history of Louveciennes ended at a certain time. Looking back on it, it was the right time. Even though it's painful and you are not necessarily aware when you're finished with a certain experience, you do know, something propels you out. I have been propelled out of several homes. When a certain cycle ends, the house itself becomes dead. I think these are reflections of where we are at the moment.

EWJ: In your writings you express a profound belief in the human capacity to grow beyond neurosis. What is the source of your optimism?

AN: I never thought about the source. I always felt that impulse in myself, the way plants have an impulse to grow. I believe what happens are accidental interferences and blockages. We all have that impulse but then it gets damaged occasionally. It's in children, isn't it? They use their strengths, their skills, and explore everything, all possibilities. I believe that we can take notice of the damage which most of us sustain somewhere along the line and we can overcome the damage. We all have interferences, discouragements, and traumatic experiences. I have met young writers who have stopped at the first rejection notice. So it's a question of how much we are willing to struggle in order to overcome the impediments.

EWJ: Would you say that one of the major themes in your works is the conflict between woman's role as a dependent and loving being and the artist's drive toward transcendence?

AN: Yes, I think that is a very great conflict. The creative will pushes you in one direction while you have guilt about using time and energy which is supposed to be devoted to your personal life. It hasn't been a problem for man because the culture incites him to produce, he wants to be obsessed with his work, he is blessed for it. But woman has really been told that the primary concern is her personal life, she hasn't been encouraged to create; in her case it is accidental phenomena.

EWJ: In terms of the growth impulse or process, do you believe that we evolve out of childhood, that we grow away from childhood and leave it behind, or do we, as we grow, effect a reunion with a primary self before trauma? Is growth a linear process of moving away or a circular process of return to an essential self?

AN: I would agree with you that the search should take us to the point of being able to reassemble all the separate pieces of ourselves. Wallace Fowlie defined the poet as one who was able to keep the fresh vision of the child alive within the mature man. I agree with that except during trauma, when pieces break off—so it's really a work of connectiveness.

EWJ: There is an almost archetypal cycle of return to the self at the inner core of your work.

AN: If our mythological journey is supposed to have been through the labyrinth we would ultimately come out, we would have to come out with all of ourselves, we couldn't leave parts of ourselves behind in the labyrinth.

EWJ: You mention in the diaries that you're a Pisces. Do you attribute any of the quality of flow and movement in your writing to the fact that you are a Pisces?

AN: I am very related to water. I feel very close to the sea, I like the idea of travelling and moving about, the whole journey on water. I think it has an influence on my wanting my writing to be fluid, not static. I felt that I wrote better on a houseboat because I could feel the river flowing underneath. I have been described as a Neptunian, for whom illusion was more important than the world of reality, and where the meshing of the dream and reality takes place.

EWJ: What is the source of your inexhaustible energy?

AN: I haven't thought about that. I guess it's curiosity, the fact that I still feel things as keenly. I suppose that when you feel alive something propels you into new experiences, new friendships, and while you're responding you have this energy. It seems to be a quality of responsiveness, of remaining alive to whatever is happening around you. While you have that feeling, you go on exploring. Then, I'm always curious. I was in an airplane accident once. There was only one wheel, one side of the wing had caught fire, we had six minutes to get to Los Angeles, and all I was doing was thinking of all the places I hadn't seen yet. That was my feeling—that it was a shame not to see everything, to hear everything, be everywhere.

EWJ: What are you presently working on?

AN: I'm editing Volume Six [of *The Diary of Anaïs Nin*]. Editing Volume Seven will bring me to the exchange of letters and diaries with other women. Then I will go back and redo my childhood and adolescence, because readers say I started the diary at the point where my life expanded. They would like to see how it went from the narrow to the expanded part.

EWJ: How does it feel to have achieved recognition as a major literary figure?

AN: Well, I never imagined that. It's a lovely feeling, you lose your sense of isolation. And you can live out your universal life. You're in contact with the whole world, which is probably the wish of every writer. I have a feeling of being in touch with the world.

JOYCE CAROL OATES

Politics

She was a cheerful good-natured girl, not a whiner or complainer; everyone liked her for that. On her purple quilted jacket she wore a sunny yellow Happy Face button: "Hi!"

Her new job was salesgirl at The Gap at Sky Hills Mall. She wore all their clothes except those long tunic sweaters where you really had to be skinny or it showed.

Parked off the highway she studied the surface of the compact mirror in which like something floating teasing in a dream her blurred face showed. Particles of powder made it seem shiny, distorted. The skin around the eyes like bruised fruit, the lid of the left eye swollen like an insect had bitten it and red as if she'd been crying which she had not. Not once that morning.

She hadn't gone to the store that morning, she'd driven to the mall and sat in her car for a while. Then she'd driven back home and called in sick. Maybe they believed her, maybe not.

It made her a little crazy to be in the apartment waiting for the telephone to ring, it was a whole lot better to go out again even to drive with no place in mind then, when you come back, you can see if any calls came in on the answering machine, and how many. One time last spring, Memorial Day weekend she'd been away and when she came back she saw there were seven calls. *Seven.*

She would not call him this time. This time, *no*.

He'd warned her never to call him at work which she'd done once, a stupid thing to do but she'd been desperate. If she called his home number there'd been the answering machine, his taped voice clicking on like a stranger's and she couldn't deal with that.

When she was there sometimes the phone'd ring and the tape would click on and whoever was calling, one time it was another girl, an ex-girlfriend, would have to speak and they'd lain there laughing together. She couldn't deal with that.

She was a Sagittarius. She'd cut out her horoscope for June from *Self*. *Your high ideals and romantic heart make you vulnerable. Don't ignore good advice at the office. Don't be overly possessive! Ask: Am I doing all I can for myself? Expect HIGHS and LOWS with the man in your life. Avoid the temptation to control. Exciting times ahead!*

She held the compact mirror up close to her face. This *was* her face—wasn't it? Her neck was stiff. Shoulders and upper back in a shape like a T all glimmering pain. Swallowing aspirin, with black coffee. She was twenty-eight years old and that scared her but she looked five, six years younger, she really did. Even a time like now.

Was there something in her face that invited hurt. Her eyes that were brown, and warm. Her mouth that smiled almost without her knowing it. That look of sympathy of wanting to hear, maybe the word was "vulnerable," that was the word. Once an older guy she'd met at Friday's told her she had a face like a flower, she felt he had singled her out for it. But she didn't remember his name, probably he hadn't told her his real name anyway.

The man she was with now she loved so her heart could break—talk like that embarrassed him. Nor did he kid around, much. If she was a girl for him to marry and have kids with it had to be serious, even solemn like.

Times of hurt, she found herself thinking of: being cut from the cheer-leading try-outs, the finals, sophomore year of high school. You never forget.

The girls on the varsity squad liked her really well, the captain surely did, and Marcy Myers the girls' gym coach, they were all encouraging then impatient, she was better than just about anybody but so nervous and scared so shaky that gets on other people's nerves so she tried to make herself vomit ahead of time but it didn't work and she fucked up and all those hours of prac-tice in the basement at home all that hope and prayer they cut her from the fi-nals picking four out of twelve and her name not spoken so she ran blind from the gym and in a toilet stall cried and cried and after a while she did vomit.

You never forget.

Let him get it out of his system, was what she'd heard off and on, growing up.

So sweet at first, calling her *Doll Baby*. Fitting her snug in the crook of his arm and in his pull-out bed, the thin lumpy mattress smelling of sweat and aftershave. *Love my Doll Baby, my sweet Doll Baby, you're the only one.* Yes and he'd meant it, too.

When he was feeling down, in one of his moods, it was never her fault and in the beginning, at these times, he'd make love to her more tenderly than ever and how and why it changed she would never know. There were other guys like that going back to high school but she didn't want to think it was a pattern or something. That would be just too depressing.

A while back he'd lost it, squeezing her breasts till she cried, digging his fingers up inside her and she'd gnawed the pillow to keep from screaming thinking *Let him get it out of his system.* And it had seemed to work, that time.

Through May, it seemed she couldn't do or say anything right, he'd actually said he felt sorry for her. But Christ she got on his nerves weepy and apologetic and needing to be told all the time he loved her which for sure he did but, Christ. And don't ever call me at work again. Even the married guys, the guys with kids, hated to be called at work.

That time he'd slapped her and her nose started to bleed and the look on his face when he saw the blood!—it'd been worth it, almost.

Oh Jesus honey what'd I do, hey look I didn't mean it honey, you know I wouldn't hurt you for the world and they were both crying saying after we're married and living together things would be different.

Yes. Oh yes.

Expect HIGHS and LOWS with the man in your life.

And: *Don't be overly possessive.*

Last night, when it'd happened so fast she couldn't exactly remember what had happened, she sort of sensed what set him off. After work he'd gone over to his parents' and something must've happened there or got said, not that he'd say what it was or maybe even know himself, that was why he was so quiet so she should have been more cautious trying to cheer him up. At the store the other girls enjoyed her clowning around like she did sometimes, but that was different, it's always different with your girlfriends. She knew that.

Like she had to respect his privacy, not call him too much. Like she couldn't lapse ever, be too familiar like his sister-in-law with his brother, that disgusted him.

Lucky she'd just bought these new sunglasses. Chic white plastic frames and lenses dark as ski lenses, almost black, the guy at the gas station stared at her but couldn't see her bruised eyes.

Hung around while the tank was filling. Asked how she liked that make of car, did she get it new or secondhand, where did she live, yeah okay, he sort of remembered her, he'd graduated from Central and she'd graduated from Valley and he'd been on the Central varsity basketball team, hadn't she been a cheerleader?

Maybe yes maybe no. That's all she said.

Later, in the Sky Hills lot, parking her car thinking, It's a weird fact of life how guys are drawn to you even if black eyes don't show.

Opening the compact, rubbing at the mirror with her thumb to get it clean, seeing her face with tenderness and forgiveness: "Hi!"

First Person: Joyce Carol Oates on "The Very Short Story," "The Nature of Short Fiction; or, The Nature of My Short Fiction," and "Fictions, Dreams, and Revelations"

First Person: The Very Short Story

Very short fictions are nearly always experimental, exquisitely calibrated, reminiscent of Frost's definition of a poem—a structure of words that consumes itself as it unfolds, like ice melting on a stove. The form is sometimes mythical, sometimes merely anecdotal, but it ends with its final sentence, often with its final word. We who love prose fiction love these miniature tales both to read and to write because they are so finite; so highly compressed and highly charged. The tension is that of—one might say—Hagler's eight minutes against Hearns, an epic writ so small one can hardly bear to watch it.

Of course the form, while being contemporary, is also timeless. As old as the human instinct to combine power and brevity in a structure of words. Consider words as disparate as these:

> These are the seductive voices of the night; the Sirens, too, sang that way. It would be doing them an injustice to think that they wanted to seduce; they knew they had claws and sterile wombs, and they lamented this aloud. They could not help it if their laments sounded so beautiful.

Kafka, "The Sirens"

and

> The competitions of the sky
> Corrodeless ply.

Emily Dickinson

and

> Western Wind, when wilt thou blow,
> That the small rain down may rain?
> Christ, that my love were in my arms
> And I in my bed again!

Anonymous

As these selections suggest, the rhythmic form of the short-short story is often more temperamentally akin to poetry than to conventional prose, which generally opens out to dramatize experience and to evoke emotion; in the smallest, tightest spaces, experience can only be suggested. Voice is everything, the melting of the ice on the stove, consuming itself as we watch.

There are those for whom one of Chopin's brilliant little Preludes is worth an entire symphony by one or another "classic" composer whose method is to build upon repetition and contrast . . .

It may well be, however, that all the short fictions in existence cannot match a single great novel: Hardy's *Tess*, for instance. But, fortunately, works of art are not in competition. And surely should not be judged as if they were.

First Person: The Nature of Short Fiction

As to the nature of short fiction? There is no nature to it, but only natures. Different natures. Just as we all have different personalities, so the dreams of our personalities will be different. There are no rules to help us. There used to be a rule—"Don't be boring!"—but that has been by-passed; today writers like Beckett and Albee and Pinter are deliberately boring (though perhaps they succeed more than they know) and anything goes. Outrageous exaggeration. Outrageous understatement. Very short scenes, very long scenes . . . cinematic flashes and impressions, long introspective passages in the manner of Thomas Mann: anything. There is no particular length, certainly, to the short story or to the novel. I believe that any short story can become a novel, and any novel can be converted back into a short story or into a poem. Reality is fluid and monstrous; let us package it in as many shapes as possible, put names on it, publish it in hard-cover. Let us make films of it. Let us declare that everything is sacred and therefore material for art—or, perhaps, nothing is sacred, nothing can be left alone.

The amateur writer wants to write of great things, serious themes. Perhaps he has a social conscience! But there are no "great" things but only great treatments. All themes are serious, or foolish. There are no rules. We are free. Miracles are in the wings, in the ink of unopened typewriter ribbons, craving release. I tell my students to write of their true subjects. How will they know when they are writing of their true subjects? By the ease with which they write. By their reluctance to stop writing. By the headachy, even guilty, joyous sensation of having done something that must be done, having confessed emotions thought unconfessable, having said what had seemed should remain unsaid. If writing is difficult, stop writing. Begin with another subject. The true subject writes itself, it cannot be silenced. Give shape to your dreams, your day-dreams, cultivate your day-dreams and their secret meanings will come out. If you feel that sitting blankly and staring out the window is sinful, then you will never write, and why write anyway? If you feel that sitting in a daze, staring at the sky or at the river, is somehow a sacred event, that your deepest self is pleased by it, then perhaps you are a writer or a poet and in time you will try to communicate your feelings.

Writers write, eventually; but first they feel.

A marvelous life.

First Person: Fiction, Dreams, Revelations

All art is autobiographical. It is the record of an artist's psychic experience, his attempt to explain something to himself: and in the process of explaining it to himself, he explains it to others. When a work of art pleases us it is often because it recounts for us an experience close to our own, something we can recognize. And so we "like" the artist, because he is so human.

But there are works of art that explain nothing, that dispel order and sanity; works of art that contradict our experience and are therefore deeply offensive to us; works of art that refuse to make sense, that are perhaps dangerous because they are unforgettable. Picasso tells us that "Art is a lie that leads to the truth," and we understand by this paradox that a lie can make us see the truth, a lie can illuminate the truth for us, a lie—especially an extravagant, gorgeous lie—can make us sympathize with a part of the truth that we had always successfully avoided. Instinctively, we want either lies that we can know as lies, or truth that we can know as truth. A newspaper in the mid-South declares bluntly: "We Print Only the Truth—No Fiction." But the two are hopeless mixed together, mysteriously confused. Nothing human is simple.

Every person dreams, and every dreamer is a kind of artist. The formal artist is one who arranges his dreams into a shape that can be experienced by other people. There is no guarantee that art will be understood, not even by the artist; it is not meant to be understood but to be experienced. Emotions flow from one personality to another, altering someone's conception of the world: this is the moment of art, the magical experience of art. It is a revelation. This impact of another personality upon us—our terrible, reluctant, unavoidable acknowledgment of another person, other people, all the consciousness outside ourselves that we cannot control and cannot possess, despite our deepest wishes—all that is humanly sacred is present in this exchange, which is art.

Frank O'Connor

The Bridal Night

It was sunset, and the two great humps of rock made a twilight in the cove where the boats were lying high up the strand. There was one light only in a little whitewashed cottage. Around the headland came a boat and the heavy dipping of its oars was like a heron's flight. The old woman was sitting on the low stone wall outside her cottage.

"'Tis a lonesome place," said I.

"'Tis so," she agreed, "a lonesome place, but any place is lonesome without one you'd care for."

"Your own flock are gone from you, I suppose?" I asked.

"I never had but the one," she replied, "the one son only," and I knew because she did not add a prayer for his soul that he was still alive.

"Is it in America he is?" I asked. (It is to America all the boys of the locality go when they leave home.)

"No, then," she replied simply. "It is in the asylum in Cork he is on me these twelve years."

I had no fear of trespassing on her emotions. These lonesome people in the wild places, it is their nature to speak; they must cry out their sorrows like the wild birds.

"God help us!" I said, "Far enough!"

"Far enough," she sighed. "Too far for an old woman. There was a nice priest here one time brought me up in his car to see him. All the ways to this wild place he brought it, and he drove me into the city. It is a place I was never used to, but it eased my mind to see poor Denis well-cared-for and well-liked. It was a trouble to me before that, not knowing would they see what a good boy he was before his madness came on him. He knew me;

299

he saluted me, but he said nothing until the superintendent came to tell me the tea was ready for me. Then poor Denis raised his head and says: 'Leave ye not forget the toast. She was ever a great one for her bit of toast.' It seemed to give him ease and he cried after. A good boy he was and is. It was like him after seven long years to think of his old mother and her little bit of toast."

"God help us," I said for her voice was like the birds', hurrying high, immensely high, in the colored light, out to sea to the last islands where their nests were.

"Blessed be His holy will," the old woman added, "there is no turning aside what is in store. It was a teacher that was here at the time. Miss Regan her name was. She was a fine big jolly girl from the town. Her father had a shop there. They said she had three hundred pounds to her own cheek the day she set foot in the school, and—'tis hard to believe but 'tis what they all said: I will not belie her—'twasn't banished she was at all, but she came here of her own choice, for the great liking she had for the sea and the mountains. Now, that is the story, and with my own eyes I saw her, day in day out, coming down the little pathway you came yourself from the road and sitting beyond there in a hollow you can hardly see, out of the wind. The neighbors could make nothing of it, and she being a stranger, and with only the book Irish, they left her alone. It never seemed to take a peg out of her, only sitting in that hole in the rocks, as happy as the day is long, reading her little book or writing her letters. Of an odd time she might bring one of the little scholars along with her to be picking posies.

"That was where my Denis saw her. He'd go up to her of an evening and sit on the grass beside her, and off and on he might take her out in the boat with him. And she'd say with that big laugh of hers: 'Denis is my beau.' Those now were her words and she meant no more harm by it than the child unborn, and I knew it and Denis knew it, and it was a little joke we had, the three of us. It was the same way she used to joke about her little hollow. 'Mrs. Sullivan,' she'd say, 'leave no one near it. It is my nest and my cell and my little prayer-house, and maybe I would be like the birds and catch the smell of the stranger and then fly away from ye all.' It did me good to hear her laugh, and whenever I saw Denis moping or idle I would say it to him myself: 'Denis, why wouldn't you go out and pay your attentions to Miss Regan and all saying you are her intended?' It was only a joke. I would say the same thing to her face, for Denis was such a quiet boy, no way rough or accustomed to the girls at all—and how would he in this lonesome place?

"I will not belie her; it was she saw first that poor Denis was after more than company, and it was not to this cove she came at all then but to the little cove beyond the headland, and 'tis hardly she would go there itself without a little scholar along with her. 'Ah,' I says, for I missed her company, 'isn't it the great stranger Miss Regan is becoming?' and Denis would put on his coat and go hunting in the dusk till he came to whatever spot she was. Little ease that was to him, poor boy, for he lost his tongue entirely, and lying on his belly before her, chewing an old bit of grass, is all he would do till she got up and left him. He could not help himself, poor boy. The madness was on him, even then, and it was only when I saw the plunder done that I knew there was no cure for him only to put her out of his mind entirely. For 'twas madness in him and he knew it, and that was what made him lose his tongue—he that was maybe without the price of an ounce of 'baccy—I will not deny it: often enough he had to do without it when the hens would not be laying, and often enough stirabout and praties was all we had for days. And there was she with money to her name in the bank! And that wasn't all, for he was a good boy; a quiet, goodnatured boy, and another would take pity on him, knowing he would make her a fine steady husband, but she was not the sort, and well I knew it from the first day I laid eyes on her, that her hand would never rock the cradle. There was the madness out and out.

"So here was I, pulling and hauling, coaxing him to stop at home, and hiding whatever little thing was to be done till evening the way his hands would not be idle. But he had no heart in the work, only listening, always listening, or climbing the cnuceen to see would he catch a glimpse of her coming or going. And, oh, Mary, the heavy sigh he'd give when his bit of supper was over and I bolting the house for the night, and he with the long hours of darkness forninst him—my heart was broken thinking of it. It was the madness, you see. It was on him. He could hardly sleep or eat, and at night I would hear him, turning and groaning as loud as the sea on the rocks.

"It was then when the sleep was a fever to him that he took to walking in the night. I remember well the first night I heard him lift the latch. I put on my few things and went out after him. It was standing here I heard his feet on the stile. I went back and latched the door and hurried after him. What else could I do, and this place terrible after the fall of night with rocks and hills and water and streams, and he, poor soul, blinded with the dint of sleep. He travelled the road a piece, and then took to the hills, and I followed him with my legs all torn with briars and furze. It was over beyond by the new house that he gave up. He turned to me then the way a little child that is running away turns and clings to your knees; he turned to me and said: 'Mother, we'll go home now. It was the bad day for you ever you brought me into the world.' And as the day was breaking I got him back to bed and covered him up to sleep.

"I was hoping that in time he'd wear himself out, but it was worse he was getting. I was a strong woman then, a mayen-strong woman. I could cart a load of seaweed or dig a field with any man, but the nightwalking broke me. I knelt one night before the Blessed Virgin and prayed whatever was to happen, it would happen while the light of life was in me, the way I would not be leaving him lonesome like that in a wild place.

"And it happened the way I prayed. Blessed be God, he woke that night or the next night on me and he roaring. I went in to him but I couldn't hold him. He had the strength of five men. So I went out and locked the door behind me. It was down hill I faced in the starlight to the little house above the cove. The Donoghues came with me: I will not belie them; they were fine powerful men and good neighbors. The father and the two sons came with me and brought the rope from the boats. It was a hard struggle they had of it and a long time before they got him on the floor, and a longer time before they got the ropes on him. And when they had him tied they put him back into bed for me, and I covered him up, nice and decent, and put a hot stone to his feet to take the chill of the cold floor off him.

"Sean Donoghue spent the night sitting beside the fire with me, and in the morning he sent one of the boys off for the doctor. Then Denis called me in his own voice and I went into him. 'Mother,' says Denis, 'will you leave me this way against the time they come for me?' I hadn't the heart. God knows I hadn't. 'Don't do it, Peg,' says Sean. 'If 'twas a hard job trussing him before, it will be harder the next time, and I won't answer for it.'

"'You're a kind neighbor, Sean,' says I, 'and I would never make little of you, but he is the only son I ever reared and I'd sooner he'd kill me now than shame him at the last.'

"So I loosened the ropes on him and he lay there very quiet all day without breaking his fast. Coming on to evening he asked me for the sup of tea and he drank it, and soon after the doctor and another man came in the car. They said a few words to Denis but he made them no answer and the doctor gave me the bit of writing. 'It will be tomorrow before they come for him,' says he, 'and 'tisn't right for you to be alone in the house with the man.' But I said I would stop with him and Sean Donoghue said the same.

"When darkness came on there was a little bit of a wind blew up from the sea and Denis began to rave to himself, and it was her name he was calling all the time. 'Winnie,' that was her name, and it was the first time I heard it spoken. 'Who is that he is calling?' says Sean. 'It is the schoolmistress,' says I, 'for though I do not recognize the name, I know 'tis no one else he'd be asking for.' 'That is a bad sign,' says Sean. 'He'll get worse as the night goes on and the wind rises. 'Twould be better for me go down and get the boys to put the ropes on him again while he's quiet.' And it was then something struck me, and I said: 'Maybe if she came to him herself for a minute he would be quiet after.' 'We can try it anyway,'says Sean, 'and if the girl has a kind heart she will come.'

"It was Sean that went up for her. I would not have the courage to ask her. Her little house is there on the edge of the hill; you can see it as you go back the road with the bit of garden before it the new teacher left grow wild. And it was a true word Sean said for 'twas worse Denis was getting, shouting out against the wind for us to get Winnie for him. Sean was a long time away or maybe I felt it long, and I thought it might be the way she was afeared to come. There are many like that, small blame to them. Then I heard her step that I knew so well on the boreen beside the house and I ran to the door, meaning to say I was sorry for the trouble we were giving her, but when I opened the door Denis called out her name in a loud voice, and the crying fit came on me, thinking how lighthearted we used to be together.

"I couldn't help it, and she pushed in apast me into the bedroom with her face as white as that wall. The candle was lighting on the dresser. He turned to her roaring with the mad look in his eyes, and then went quiet all of a sudden, seeing her like that overright him with her hair all tumbled in the wind. I was coming behind her. I heard it. He put up his two poor hands and the red mark of the ropes on his wrists and whispered to her: 'Winnie, asthore, isn't it the long time you were away from me?'

"'It is, Denis, it is indeed,' says she, 'but you know I couldn't help it.'

"'Don't leave me anymore now, Winnie,' says he, and then he said no more, only the two eyes lighting out on her as she sat by the bed.

And Sean Donoghue brought in the little stooleen for me, and there we were, the three of us, talking, and Denis paying us no attention, only staring at her.

"'Winnie,' says he, 'lie down here beside me.'

"'Oye,' says Sean, humoring him, 'don't you know the poor girl is played out after her day's work? She must go home to bed.'

"'No, no, no,' says Denis and the terrible mad light in his eyes. 'There is a high wind blowing and 'tis no night for one like her to be out. Leave her sleep here beside me. Leave her creep in under the clothes to me the way I'll keep her warm.'

"'Oh, oh, oh, oh,' says I, 'indeed and indeed, Miss Regan, 'tis I'm sorry for bringing you here. 'Tisn't my son is talking at all but the madness in him. I'll go now,' says I, 'and bring Sean's boys to put the ropes on him again.'

"'No, Mrs. Sullivan,' says she in a quiet voice. 'Don't do that at all. I'll stop here with him and he'll go fast asleep. Won't you, Denis?'

"'I will, I will,' says he, 'but come under the clothes to me. There does a terrible draught blow under that door.'

"'I will indeed, Denis,' says she, 'if you'll promise me to go to sleep.'

"'Oye, whisht, girl,' says I. "Tis you that's mad. While you're here you're in my charge, and how would I answer to your father if you stopped in here by yourself?'

"'Never mind about me, Mrs. Sullivan,' she said. 'I'm not a bit in dread of Denis. I promise you there will no harm come to me. You and Mr. Donoghue can sit outside in the kitchen and I'll be all right here.'

"She had a worried look but there was something about her there was no mistaking. I wouldn't take it on myself to cross the girl. We went out to the kitchen, Sean and myself, and we heard every whisper that passed between them. She got into the bed beside him: I heard her. He was whispering into her ear the sort of foolish things boys do be saying at that age, and then we heard no more only the pair of them breathing. I went to the room door and looked in. He was lying with his arm about her and his head on her bosom, sleeping like a child, sleeping like he slept in his good days with no worry at all on his poor face. She did not look at me and I did not speak to her. My heart was too full. God help us, it was an old song of my father's that was going through my head: 'Lonely Rock is the one wife my children will know.'"

"Later on, the candle went out and I did not light another. I wasn't a bit afraid for her then. The storm blew up and he slept through it all, breathing nice and even. When it was light I made a cup of tea for her and beckoned her from the room door. She loosened his hold and slipped out of bed. Then he stirred and opened his eyes.

"'Winnie,' says he, 'where are you going?'

"'I'm going to work, Denis,' says she. 'Don't you know I must be at school early?'

"'But you'll come back to me tonight, Winnie?' says he.

"'I will, Denis,' says she. 'I'll come back, never fear.'

"And he turned on his side and went fast asleep again.

"When she walked into the kitchen I went on my two knees before her and kissed her hands. I did so. There would no words come to me, and we sat there, the three of us, over our tea, and I declare for the time being I felt 'twas worth it all, all the troubles of his birth and rearing and all the lonesome years ahead.

"It was a great ease to us. Poor Denis never stirred, and when the police came he went along with them without commotion or handcuffs or anything that would shame him, and all the words he said to me was: 'Mother, tell Winnie I'll be expecting her.'

"And isn't it a strange and wonderful thing? From that day to the day she left us there did no one speak a bad word about what she did, and the people couldn't do enough for her. Isn't it a strange thing and the world as wicked as it is, that no one would say the bad word about her?"

Darkness had fallen over the Atlantic, blank gray to its farthest reaches.

CYNTHIA OZICK

The Shawl

Stella, cold, cold, the coldness of hell. How they walked on the roads together, Rosa with Magda curled up between sore breasts, Magda wound up in the shawl. Sometimes Stella carried Magda. But she was jealous of Magda. A thin girl of fourteen, too small, with thin breasts of her own, Stella wanted to be wrapped in a shawl, hidden away, asleep, rocked by the march, a baby, a round infant in arms. Magda took Rosa's nipple, and Rosa never stopped walking, a walking cradle. There was not enough milk; sometimes Magda sucked air; then she screamed. Stella was ravenous. Her knees were tumors on sticks, her elbows chicken bones.

Rosa did not feel hunger; she felt light, not like someone walking but like someone in a faint, in trance, arrested in a fit, someone who is already a floating angel, alert and seeing everything, but in the air, not there, not touching the road. As if teetering on the tips of her fingernails. She looked into Magda's face through a gap in the shawl: a squirrel in a nest, safe, no one could reach her inside the little house of the shawl's windings. The face, very round, a pocket mirror of a face: but it was not Rosa's bleak complexion, dark like cholera, it was another kind of face altogether, eyes blue as air, smooth feathers of hair nearly as yellow as the Star sewn into Rosa's coat. You could think she was one of *their* babies.

Rosa, floating, dreamed of giving Magda away in one of the villages. She could leave the line for a minute and push Magda into the hands of any woman on the side of the road. But if she moved out of line they might shoot. And even if she fled the line for half a second and pushed the shawl-bundle at a stranger, would the woman take it? She might be surprised, or afraid; she might drop the shawl, and Magda would fall out and strike her head and die. The little round head. Such a good child, she gave up screaming, and sucked now only for the taste of the drying nipple itself. The neat grip of the tiny gums. One mite of a tooth tip sticking up in the bottom gum, how shining, an elfin tombstone of white marble gleaming there. Without complaining, Magda relinquished Rosa's teats, first the left, then the right; both were cracked, not a sniff of milk. The duct-crevice extinct, a dead volcano, blind eye, chill hole, so Magda took the corner of the shawl and milked it instead. She sucked and sucked, flooding the threads with wetness. The shawl's good flavor, milk of linen.

It was a magic shawl, it could nourish an infant for three days and three nights. Magda did not die, she stayed alive, although very quiet. A peculiar smell, of cinnamon and almonds, lifted out of her mouth. She held her eyes open every moment, forgetting how to blink or nap, and Rosa and sometimes Stella studied their blueness. On the road they raised one burden of a leg after another and studied Magda's face. "Aryan," Stella said, in a voice grown as thin as a string; and Rosa thought how Stella gazed at Magda like a young cannibal. And the time that Stella said "Aryan," it sounded to Rosa as if Stella had really said "Let us devour her."

But Magda lived to walk. She lived that long, but she did not walk very well, partly because she was only fifteen months old, and partly because the spindles of her legs could not hold up her fat belly. It was fat with air, full and round. Rosa gave almost all her food to Magda, Stella gave nothing; Stella was ravenous, a growing child herself, but not growing much. Stella did not menstruate. Rosa did not menstruate. Rosa was ravenous, but also not; she learned from Magda how to drink the taste of a finger in one's mouth. They were in a place without pity, all pity was annihilated in Rosa, she looked at Stella's bones without pity. She was sure that Stella was waiting for Magda to die so she could put her teeth into the little thighs.

Rosa knew Magda was going to die very soon; she should have been dead already, but she had been buried away deep inside the magic shawl, mistaken there for the shivering mound of Rosa's breasts; Rosa clung to the shawl as if it covered only herself. No one took it away from her. Magda was mute. She never cried. Rosa hid her in the barracks, under the shawl, but she knew that one day someone would inform; or one day someone, not even Stella, would steal Magda to eat her. When Magda began to walk Rosa knew that Magda was going to die very soon, something would happen. She was afraid to fall asleep; she slept with the weight of her thigh on Magda's body; she was afraid she would smother Magda under her thigh. The weight of Rosa was becoming less and less; Rosa and Stella were slowly turning into air.

Magda was quiet, but her eyes were horribly alive, like blue tigers. She watched. Sometimes she laughed—it seemed a laugh, but how could it be? Magda had never seen anyone laugh. Still, Magda laughed at her shawl when the wind blew its corners, the bad wind with pieces of black in it, that made Stella's and Rosa's eyes tear. Magda's eyes were always clear and tearless. She watched like a tiger. She guarded her shawl. No one could touch it;

only Rosa could touch it. Stella was not allowed. The shawl was Magda's own baby, her pet, her little sister. She tangled herself up in it and sucked on one of the corners when she wanted to be very still.

Then Stella took the shawl away and made Magda die.

Afterward Stella said: "I was cold."

And afterward she was always cold, always. The cold went into her heart: Rosa saw that Stella's heart was cold. Magda flopped onward with her little pencil legs scribbling this way and that, in search of the shawl; the pencils faltered at the barracks opening, where the light began. Rosa saw and pursued. But already Magda was in the square outside the barracks, in the jolly light. It was the roll-call arena. Every morning Rosa had to conceal Magda under the shawl against a wall of the barracks and go out and stand in the arena with Stella and hundreds of others, sometimes for hours, and Magda, deserted, was quiet under the shawl, sucking on her corner. Every day Magda was silent, and so she did not die. Rosa saw that today Magda was going to die, and at the same time a fearful joy ran in Rosa's two palms, her fingers were on fire, she was astonished, febrile: Magda, in the sunlight, swaying on her pencil legs, was howling. Ever since the drying up of Rosa's nipples, ever since Magda's last scream on the road, Magda had been devoid of any syllable; Magda was a mute. Rosa believed that something had gone wrong with her vocal cords, with her windpipe, with the cave of her larynx; Magda was defective, without a voice; perhaps she was deaf; there might be something amiss with her intelligence; Magda was dumb. Even the laugh that came when the ash-stippled wind made a clown out of Magda's shawl was only the air-blown showing of her teeth. Even when the lice, head lice and body lice, crazed her so that she became as wild as one of the big rats that plundered the barracks at daybreak looking for carrion, she rubbed and scratched and kicked and bit and rolled without a whimper. But now Magda's mouth was spilling a long viscous rope of clamor.

"Maaaa—"

It was the first noise Magda had ever sent out from her throat since the drying up of Rosa's nipples.

"Maaaa . . . aaa!"

Again! Magda was wavering in the perilous sunlight of the arena, scribbling on such pitiful little bent shins. Rosa saw. She saw that Magda was grieving for the loss of her shawl, she saw that Magda was going to die. A tide of commands hammered in Rosa's nipples: Fetch, get, bring! But she did not know which to go after first, Magda or the shawl. If she jumped out into the arena to snatch Magda up, the howling would not stop, because Magda would still not have the shawl; but if she ran back into the barracks to find the shawl, and if she found it, and if she came after Magda holding it and shaking it, then she would get Magda back, Magda would put the shawl in her mouth and turn dumb again.

Rosa entered the dark. It was easy to discover the shawl. Stella was heaped under it, asleep in her thin bones. Rosa tore the shawl free and flew —she could fly, she was only air—into the arena. The sunheat murmured of another life, of butterflies in summer. The light was placid, mellow. On the other side of the steel fence, far away, there were green meadows speckled with dandelions and deep-colored violets; beyond them, even farther, innocent tiger lilies, tall, lifting their orange bonnets. In the barracks they spoke of "flowers," of "rain": excrement, thick turd-braids, and the slow stinking maroon waterfall that slunk down from the upper bunks, the stink mixed with a bitter fatty floating smoke that greased Rosa's skin. She stood for an instant at the margin of the arena. Sometimes the electricity inside the fence would seem to hum; even Stella said it was only an imagining, but Rosa heard real sounds in the wire: grainy sad voices. The farther she was from the fence, the more clearly the voices crowded at her. The lamenting voices strummed so convincingly, so passionately, it was impossible to suspect them of being phantoms. The voices told her to hold up the shawl, high; the voices told her to shake it, to whip with it, to unfurl it like a flag. Rosa lifted, shook, whipped, unfurled. Far off, very far, Magda leaned across her air-fed belly, reaching out with the rods of her arms. She was high up, elevated, riding someone's shoulder. But the shoulder that carried Magda was not coming toward Rosa and the shawl, it was drifting away, the speck of Magda was moving more and more into the smoky distance. Above the shoulder a helmet glinted. The light tapped the helmet and sparkled it into a goblet. Below the helmet a black body like a domino and a pair of black boots hurled themselves in the direction of the electrified fence. The electric voices began to chatter wildly. "Maamaa, maaamaaa," they all hummed together. How far Magda was from Rosa now, across the whole square, past a dozen barracks, all the way on the other side! She was no bigger than a moth.

All at once Magda was swimming through the air. The whole of Magda traveled through loftiness. She looked like a butterfly touching a silver vine. And the moment Magda's feathered round head and her pencil legs and balloonish belly and zigzag arms splashed against the fence, the steel voices went mad in their growling, urging Rosa to run and run to the spot where Magda had fallen from her flight against the electrified fence; but of course Rosa did not obey them. She only stood, because if she ran they would shoot, and if she tried to pick up the sticks of Magda's body they would shoot, and if she let the wolf's screech ascending now through the ladder of her skeleton break out, they would shoot; so she took Magda's shawl and filled her own mouth with it, stuffed it in and stuffed it in, until she was swallowing up the wolf's screech and tasting the cinnamon and almond depth of Magda's saliva; and Rosa drank Magda's shawl until it dried.

A Conversation with My Father

My father is eighty-six years old and in bed. His heart, that bloody motor, is equally old and will not do certain jobs any more. It still floods his head with brainy light. But it won't let his legs carry the weight of his body around the house. Despite my metaphors, this muscle failure is not due to his old heart, he says, but to a potassium shortage. Sitting on one pillow, leaning on three, he offers last-minute advice and makes a request.

"I would like you to write a simple story just once more," he says, "the kind de Maupassant wrote, or Chekhov, the kind you used to write. Just recognizable people and then write down what happened to them next."

I say, "Yes, why not? That's possible." I want to please him, though I don't remember writing that way. I *would* like to try to tell such a story, if he means the kind that begins: "There was a woman . . ." followed by plot, the absolute line between two points which I've always despised. Not for literary reasons, but because it takes all hope away. Everyone, real or invented, deserves the open destiny of life.

Finally I thought of a story that had been happening for a couple of years right across the street. I wrote it down, then read it aloud. "Pa," I said, "how about this? Do you mean something like this?"

Once in my time there was a woman and she had a son. They lived nicely, in a small apartment in Manhattan. This boy at about fifteen became a junkie, which is not unusual in our neighborhood. In order to maintain her close friendship with him, she became a junkie too. She said it was part of the youth culture, with which she felt very much at home. After a while, for a number of reasons, the boy gave it all up and left the city and his mother in disgust. Hopeless and alone, she grieved. We all visit her.

"O.K., Pa, that's it," I said, "an unadorned and miserable tale."

"But that's not what I mean," my father said. "You misunderstood me on purpose. You know there's a lot more to it. You know that. You left everything out. Turgenev wouldn't do that. Chekhov wouldn't do that. There are in fact Russian writers you never heard of, you don't have an inkling of, as good as anyone, who can write a plain ordinary story, who would not leave out what you have left out. I object not to facts but to people sitting in trees talking senselessly, voices from who knows where. . . ."

"Forget that one, Pa, what have I left out now? In this one?"

"Her looks, for instance."

"Oh. Quite handsome, I think. Yes."

"Her hair?"

"Dark, with heavy braids, as though she were a girl or a foreigner."

"What were her parents like, her stock? That she became such a person. It's interesting, you know."

"From out of town. Professional people. The first to be divorced in their county. How's that? Enough?" I asked.

"With you, it's all a joke," he said. "What about the boy's father? Why didn't you mention him? Who was he? Or was the boy born out of wedlock?"

"Yes," I said. "He was born out of wedlock."

"For Godsakes, doesn't anyone in your stories get married? Doesn't anyone have the time to run down to City Hall before they jump into bed?"

"No," I said. "In real life, yes. But in my stories, no."

"Why do you answer me like that?"

"Oh, Pa, this is a simple story about a smart woman who came to N.Y.C. full of interest love trust excitement very up to date, and about her son, what a hard time she had in this world. Married or not, it's of small consequence."

"It is of great consequence," he said.

"O.K.," I said.

"O.K. O.K. yourself," he said, "but listen. I believe you that she's good-looking, but I don't think she was so smart."

"That's true," I said. "Actually that's the trouble with stories. People start out fantastic. You think they're extraordinary, but it turns out as the work goes along, they're just average with a good education. Sometimes the other way around, the person's a kind of dumb innocent, but he outwits you and you can't even think of an ending good enough."

"What do you do then?" he asked. He had been a doctor for a couple of decades and then an artist for a couple of decades and he's still interested in details, craft, technique.

"Well, you just have to let the story lie around till some agreement can be reached between you and the stubborn hero."

"Aren't you talking silly now?" he asked. "Start again," he said. "It so happens I'm not going out this evening. Tell the story again. See what you can do this time."

"O.K.," I said. "But it's not a five-minute job." Second attempt:

Once, across the street from us, there was a fine handsome woman, our neighbor. She had a son whom she loved because she'd known him since birth (in helpless chubby infancy, and in the wrestling, hugging ages, seven to ten, as well as earlier and later). This boy, when he fell into the fist of adolescence, became a junkie. He was not a hopeless one. He was in fact hopeful, an ideologue and successful converter. With his busy brilliance, he wrote persuasive articles for his high-school newspaper. Seeking a wider audience, using important connections, he drummed into Lower Manhattan newsstand distribution a periodical called *Oh! Golden Horse!*

In order to keep him from feeling guilty (because guilt is the stony heart of nine tenths of all clinically diagnosed cancers in America today, she said), and because she had always believed in giving bad habits room at home where one could keep an eye on them, she too became a junkie. Her kitchen was famous for a while—a center for intellectual addicts who knew what they were doing. A few felt artistic like Coleridge[1] and others were scientific and revolutionary like Leary.[2] Although she was often high herself, certain good mothering reflexes remained, and she saw to it that there was lots of orange juice around and honey and milk and vitamin pills. However, she never cooked anything but chili, and that no more than once a week. She explained, when we talked to her, seriously, with neighborly concern, that it was her part in the youth culture and she would rather be with the young, it was an honor, than with her own generation.

One week, while nodding through an Antonioni film, this boy was severely jabbed by the elbow of a stern and proselytizing girl, sitting beside him. She offered immediate apricots and nuts for his sugar level, spoke to him sharply, and took him home.

She had heard of him and his work and she herself published, edited, and wrote a competitive journal called *Man Does Live by Bread Alone.* In the organic heat of her continuous presence he could not help but become interested once more in his muscles, his arteries, and nerve connections. In fact he began to love them, treasure them, praise them with funny little songs in *Man Does Live. . . .*

[1] Samuel Taylor Coleridge (1772–1834), English Romantic poet, who was an opium addict.

[2] Timothy Leary (b. 1920), sometime Harvard professor of psychology and early advocate of the use of LSD.

the fingers of my flesh transcend
my transcendental soul
the tightness in my shoulders end
my teeth have made me whole

To the mouth of his head (that glory of will and determination) he brought hard apples, nuts, wheat germ, and soybean oil. He said to his old friends, From now on, I guess I'll keep my wits about me. I'm going on the natch. He said he was about to begin a spiritual deep-breathing journey. How about you too, Mom? he asked kindly.

His conversion was so radiant, splendid, that neighborhood kids his age began to say that he had never been a real addict at all, only a journalist along for the smell of the story. The mother tried several times to give up what had become without her son and his friends a lonely habit. This effort only brought it to supportable levels. The boy and his girl took their electronic mimeograph and moved to the bushy edge of another borough. They were very strict. They said they would not see her again until she had been off drugs for sixty days.

At home alone in the evening, weeping, the mother read and reread the seven issues of *Oh! Golden Horse!* They seemed to her as truthful as ever. We often crossed the street to visit and console. But if we mentioned any of our children who were at college or in the hospital or dropouts at home, she would cry out, My baby! My baby! and burst into terrible, face-scarring, time-consuming tears. The End.

First my father was silent, then he said, "Number One: You have a nice sense of humor. Number Two: I see you can't tell a plain story. So don't waste time." Then he said sadly, "Number Three: I suppose that means she was alone, she was left like that, his mother. Alone. Probably sick?"

I said, "Yes."

"Poor woman. Poor girl, to be born in a time of fools, to live among fools. The end. The end. You were right to put that down. The end."

I didn't want to argue, but I had to say, "Well, it is not necessarily the end, Pa."

"Yes," he said, "what a tragedy. The end of a person."

"No, Pa," I begged him. "It doesn't have to be. She's only about forty. She could be a hundred different things in this world as time goes on. A teacher or a social worker. An ex-junkie! Sometimes it's better than having a master's in education."

"Jokes," he said. "As a writer that's your main trouble. You don't want to recognize it. Tragedy! Plain tragedy! Historical tragedy! No hope. The end."

"Oh, Pa," I said. "She could change."

"In your own life, too, you have to look it in the face." He took a couple of nitroglycerin. "Turn to five," he said, pointing to the dial on the oxygen tank. He inserted the tubes into his nostrils and breathed deep. He closed his eyes and said, "No."

I had promised the family to always let him have the last word when arguing, but in this case I had a different responsibility. That woman lives across the street. She's my knowledge and my invention. I'm sorry for her. I'm not going to leave her there in that house crying. (Actually neither would Life, which unlike me has no pity.)

Therefore: She did change. Of course her son never came home again. But right now, she's the receptionist in a storefront community clinic in the East Village. Most of the customers are young people, some old friends. The head doctor has said to her, "If we only had three people in this clinic with your experiences.. . ."

"The doctor said that?" My father took the oxygen tubes out of his nostrils and said, "Jokes. Jokes again."

"No, Pa, it could really happen that way, it's a funny world nowadays."

"No," he said. "Truth first. She will slide back. A person must have character. She does not."

"No, Pa," I said. "That's it. She's got a job. Forget it. She's in that storefront working."

"How long will it be?" he asked. "Tragedy! You too. When will you look it in the face?"

Dorothy Parker

Soldiers of the Republic

That Sunday afternoon we sat with the Swedish girl in the big café in Valencia. We had vermouth in thick goblets, each with a cube of honeycombed gray ice in it. The waiter was so proud of that ice he could hardly bear to leave the glasses on the table, and thus part from it forever. He went to his duty—all over the room they were clapping their hands and hissing to draw his attention—but he looked back over his shoulder.

It was dark outside, the quick, new dark that leaps down without dusk on the day; but, because there were no lights in the streets, it seemed as set and as old as midnight. So you wondered that all the babies were still up. There were babies everywhere in the café, babies serious without solemnity and interested in a tolerant way in their surroundings.

At the table next ours, there was a notably small one; maybe six months old. Its father, a little man in a big uniform that dragged his shoulders down, held it carefully on his knee. It was doing nothing whatever, yet he and his thin young wife, whose belly was already big again under her sleazy dress, sat watching it in a sort of ecstasy of admiration, while their coffee cooled in front of them. The baby was in Sunday white; its dress was patched so delicately that you would have thought the fabric whole had not the patches varied in their shades of whiteness. In its hair was a bow of new blue ribbon, tied with absolute balance of loops and ends. The ribbon was of no use; there was not enough hair to require restraint. The bow was sheerly an adornment, a calculated bit of dash.

"Oh, for God's sake, stop that!" I said to myself. "All right, so it's got a piece of blue ribbon on its hair. All right, so its mother went without eating so it could look pretty when its father came home on leave. All right, so it's her business, and none of yours. All right, so what have you got to cry about?"

The big, dim room was crowded and lively. That morning there had been a bombing from the air, the more horrible for broad daylight. But nobody in the café sat tense and strained, nobody desperately forced forgetfulness. They drank coffee or bottled lemonade, in the pleasant, earned ease of Sunday afternoon, chatting of small, gay matters, all talking at once, all hearing and answering.

There were many soldiers in the room, in what appeared to be the uniforms of twenty different armies until you saw that the variety lay in the differing ways the cloth had worn or faded. Only a few of them had been wounded; here and there you saw one stepping gingerly, leaning on a crutch or two canes, but so far on toward recovery that his face had color. There were many men, too, in civilian clothes—some of them soldiers home on leave, some of them governmental workers, some of them anybody's guess. There were plump, comfortable wives, active with paper fans, and old women as quiet as their grandchildren. There were many pretty girls and some beauties, for whom you did not remark, "There's a charming Spanish type," but said, "What a beautiful girl!" The women's clothes were not new, and their material was too humble ever to have warranted skillful cutting.

"It's funny," I said to the Swedish girl, "how when nobody in a place is best-dressed, you don't notice that everybody isn't."

"Please?" the Swedish girl said.

No one, save an occasional soldier, wore a hat. When we had first come to Valencia, I lived in a state of puzzled pain as to why everybody on the streets laughed at me. It was not because "West End Avenue" was writ across my face as if left there by a customs officer's chalked scrawl. They like Americans in Valencia, where they have seen good ones—the doctors who left their practices and came to help, the calm young nurses, the men of the International Brigade. But when I walked forth, men and women courteously laid their hands across their splitting faces and little children, too innocent for dissembling, doubled with glee and pointed and cried, "*Olé!*" Then, pretty late, I made my discovery, and left my hat off; and there was laughter no longer. It was not one of those comic hats, either; it was just a hat.

The café filled to overflow, and I left our table to speak to a friend across the room. When I came back to the table, six soldiers were sitting there. They were crowded in, and I scraped past them to my chair. They looked tired and dusty and little, the way that the newly dead look little, and the first things you saw about them were the tendons in their necks. I felt like a prize sow.

They were all in conversation with the Swedish girl. She has Spanish, French, German, anything in Scandinavian, Italian, and English. When she has a moment for regret, she sighs that her Dutch is so rusty she can no longer speak it, only read it, and the same is true of her Rumanian.

They had told her, she told us, that they were at the end of forty-eight hours' leave from the trenches, and, for their holiday, they had all pooled their money for cigarettes, and something had gone wrong, and the cigarettes had never come through to them. I had a pack of American cigarettes—in Spain rubies are as nothing to them—and I brought it out, and by nods and smiles and a sort of breast stroke, made it understood that I was offering it to those six men yearning for tobacco. When they saw what I meant, each one of them rose and shook my hand. Darling of me to share my cigarettes with the men on their way back to the trenches. Little Lady Bountiful. The prize sow.

Each one lit his cigarette with a contrivance of yellow rope that stank when afire and was also used, the Swedish girl translated, for igniting grenades. Each one received what he had ordered, a glass of coffee, and each one murmured appreciatively over the tiny cornucopia of coarse sugar that accompanied it. Then they talked.

They talked through the Swedish girl, but they did to us that thing we all do when we speak our own language to one who has no knowledge of it. They looked us square in the face, and spoke slowly, and pronounced their words with elaborate movements of their lips. Then, as their stories came, they poured them at us so vehemently, so emphatically that they were sure we must understand. They were so convinced we would understand that we were ashamed for not understanding.

But the Swedish girl told us. They were all farmers and farmers' sons, from a district so poor that you try not to remember there is that kind of poverty. Their village was next that one where the old men and the sick men and the women and children had gone, on a holiday, to the bullring; and the planes had come over and dropped bombs on the bullring, and the old men and the sick men and the women and the children were more than two hundred.

They had all, the six of them, been in the war for over a year, and most of that time they had been in the trenches. Four of them were married. One had one child, two had three children, one had five. They had not had word from their families since they had left for the front. There had been no communication; two of them had learned to write from men fighting next them in the trench, but they had not dared to write home. They belonged to a union, and union men, of course, are put to death if taken. The village where their families lived had been captured, and if your wife gets a letter from a union man, who knows but they'll shoot her for the connection?

They told about how they had not heard from their families for more than a year. They did not tell it gallantly or whimsically or stoically. They told it as if—Well, look. You have been in the trenches, fighting, for a year. You have heard nothing of your wife and your children. They do not know if you are dead or alive or blinded. You do not know where they are, or if they are. You must talk to somebody. That is the way they told about it.

One of them, some six months before, had heard of his wife and his three children—they had such beautiful eyes, he said—from a brother-in-law in France. They were all alive then, he was told, and had a bowl of beans a day. But his wife had not complained of the food, he heard. What had troubled her was that she had no thread to mend the children's ragged clothes. So that troubled him, too.

"She has no thread," he kept telling us. "My wife has no thread to mend with. No thread."

We sat there, and listened to what the Swedish girl told us they were saying. Suddenly one of them looked at the clock, and then there was excitement. They jumped up, as a man, and there were calls for the waiter and rapid talk with him, and each of them shook the hand of each of us. We went through more swimming motions to explain to them that they were to take the rest of the cigarettes—fourteen cigarettes for six soldiers to take to war— and then they shook our hands again. Then all of us said "*Salud!*" as many times as could be for six of them and three of us, and then they filed out of the café, the six of them, tired and dusty and little, as men of a mighty horde are little.

Only the Swedish girl talked, after they had gone. The Swedish girl has been in Spain since the start of the war. She has nursed splintered men, and she has carried stretchers into the trenches and, heavier laden, back to the hospital. She has seen and heard too much to be knocked into silence.

Presently it was time to go, and the Swedish girl raised her hands above her head and clapped them twice together to summon the waiter. He came, but he only shook his head and his hand, and moved away.

The soldiers had paid for our drinks.

PETRONIUS

The Widow of Ephesus

Once upon a time there was a certain married woman in the city of Ephesus whose fidelity to her husband was so famous that the women from all the neighboring towns and villages used to troop into Ephesus merely to stare at this prodigy. It happened, however, that her husband one day died. Finding the normal custom of following the cortege with hair unbound and beating her breast in public quite inadequate to express her grief, the lady insisted on following the corpse right into the tomb, an underground vault of the Greek type, and there set herself to guard the body, weeping and wailing night and day. Although in her extremes of grief she was clearly courting death from starvation, her parents were utterly unable to persuade her to leave, and even the magistrates, after one last supreme attempt, were rebuffed and driven away. In short, all Ephesus had gone into mourning for this extraordinary woman, all the more since the lady was now passing her fifth consecutive day without once tasting food. Beside the failing woman sat her devoted maid, sharing her mistress's grief and relighting the lamp whenever it flickered out. The whole city could speak, in fact, of nothing else: here at last, all classes alike agreed, was the one true example of conjugal fidelity and love.

In the meantime, however, the governor of the province gave orders that several thieves should be crucified in a spot close by the vault where the lady was mourning her dead husband's corpse. So, on the following night, the soldier who had been assigned to keep watch on the crosses so that nobody could remove the thieves' bodies for burial suddenly noticed a light blazing among the tombs and heard the sounds of groaning. And prompted by a natural human curiosity to know who or what was making those sounds, he descended into the vault.

But at the sight of a strikingly beautiful woman, he stopped short in terror, thinking he must be seeing some ghostly apparition out of hell. Then, observing the corpse and seeing the tears on the lady's face and the scratches her fingernails had gashed in her cheeks, he realized what it was: a widow, in inconsolable grief. Promptly fetching his little supper back down to the tomb, he implored the lady not to persist in her sorrow or break her heart with useless mourning. All men alike, he reminded her, have the same end; the same resting place awaits us all. He used, in short, all those platitudes we use to comfort the suffering and bring them back to life. His consolations, being unwelcome, only exasperated the widow more; more violently than ever she beat her breast, and tearing out her hair by the roots, scattered it over the dead man's body. Undismayed, the soldier repeated his arguments and pressed her to take some food, until the little maid, quite overcome by the smell of the wine, succumbed and stretched out her hand to her tempter. Then, restored by the food and wine, she began herself to assail her mistress's obstinate refusal.

"How will it help you," she asked the lady, "if you faint from hunger? Why should you bury yourself alive, and go down to death before the Fates have called you? What does Vergil say?—

Do you suppose the shades and ashes of the dead are by such sorrow touched?

No, begin your life afresh. Shake off these woman's scruples; enjoy the light while you can. Look at that corpse of your poor husband: doesn't it tell you more eloquently than any words that you should live?"

None of us, of course, really dislikes being told that we must eat, that life is to be lived. And the lady was no exception. Weakened by her long days of fasting, her resistance crumbled at last, and she ate the food the soldier offered her as hungrily as the little maid had eaten earlier.

Well, you know what temptations are normally aroused in a man on a full stomach. So the soldier, mustering all those blandishments by means of which he had persuaded the lady to live, now laid determined siege to her virtue. And chaste though she was, the lady found him singularly attractive and his arguments persuasive. As for the maid, she did all she could to help the soldier's cause, repeating like a refrain the appropriate line of Vergil:

If love is pleasing, lady, yield yourself to love.

To make the matter short, the lady's body soon gave up the struggle; she yielded and our happy warrior enjoyed a total triumph on both counts. That very night their marriage was consummated, and they slept together the second and the third night too, carefully shutting the door of the tomb so that any passing friend or stranger would have thought the lady of famous chastity had at last expired over her dead husband's body.

As you can perhaps imagine, our soldier was a very happy man, utterly delighted with his lady's ample beauty and that special charm that a secret love confers. Every night, as soon as the sun had set, he bought what few provisions his slender pay permitted and smuggled them down to the tomb. One night, however, the parents of one of the crucified thieves, noticing that the watch was being badly kept, took advantage of our hero's absence to remove their son's body and bury it. The next morning, of course, the soldier was horror-struck to discover one of the bodies missing from its cross, and ran to tell his mistress of the horrible punishment which awaited him for neglecting his duty. In the circumstances, he told her, he would not wait to be tried and sentenced, but would punish himself then and there with his own sword. All he asked of her was that she make room for another corpse and allow the same gloomy tomb to enclose husband and lover together.

Our lady's heart, however, was no less tender than pure. "God forbid," she cried, "that I should have to see at one and the same time the dead bodies of the only two men I have ever loved. No, better far, I say, to hang the dead than kill the living." With these words, she gave orders that her husband's body should be taken from its bier and strung up on the empty cross. The soldier followed this good advice, and the next morning the whole city wondered by what miracle the dead man had climbed up on the cross.

JAYNE ANNE PHILLIPS

Sweethearts

We went to the movies every Friday and Sunday. On Friday nights the Colonial filled with an oily fragrance of teenagers while we hid in the back row of the balcony. An aura of light from the projection booth curved across our shoulders, round under cotton sweaters. Sacred grunts rose in black corners. The screen was far away and spilling color—big men sweating on their horses and women with powdered breasts floating under satin. Near the end the film smelled hot and twisted as boys shuddered and girls sank down in their seats. We ran to the lobby before the lights came up to stand by the big ash can and watch them walk slowly downstairs. Mouths swollen and ripe, they drifted down like a sigh of steam. The boys held their arms tense and shuffled from one foot to the other while the girls sniffed and combed their hair in the big mirror. Outside the neon lights on Main Street flashed stripes across asphalt in the rain. They tossed their heads and shivered like ponies.

On Sunday afternoons the theater was deserted, a church that smelled of something frying. Mrs. Causton stood at the door to tear tickets with her fat buttered fingers. During the movie she stood watching the traffic light change in the empty street, pushing her glasses up over her nose and squeezing a damp kleenex. Mr. Penny was her skinny yellow father. He stood by the office door with his big push broom, smoking cigarettes and coughing.

Walking down the slanted floor to our seats we heard the swish of her thighs behind the candy counter and our shoes sliding on the worn carpet. The heavy velvet curtain moved its folds. We waited, and a cavernous dark pressed close around us, its breath pulling at our faces.

After the last blast of sound it was Sunday afternoon, and Mr. Penny stood jingling his keys by the office door while we asked to use the phone. Before he turned the key he bent over and pulled us close with his bony arms. Stained fingers kneading our chests, he wrapped us in old tobacco and called us his little girls. I felt his wrinkled heart wheeze like a dog on a leash. Sweethearts, he whispered.

Luigi Pirandello

The Little Hut

Never before had anyone seen such a dawn.

A small girl came out of the little hut. Her dishevelled hair was straggling over her forehead, and she was wearing a faded red kerchief on her head. As she buttoned up her shabby little dress she yawned, still entangled in the net of sleep, and stared straight in front of her. Far into the distance she gazed, her eyes wide-open, just as if she could see nothing at all.

Far, far away, a long fire-red strip wove bizarrely in and out of the vast emerald green expanse of trees, which vanished at last in the distance.

The whole sky was strewn with little yellow clouds that flamed like crocuses.

The girl went on her way, heedless of it all. A little hill rose up on the right. Gradually its slope became gentler and gentler, until suddenly, there beneath her gaze lay displayed an immense flood of water, the sea.

The little girl seemed struck and deeply moved by that scene, and she stood there looking at the boats as they flew over the waves, dyed a pale yellow by the morning sun.

It was completely silent. The almost imperceptible gentle night breeze was still fluttering the air, and making the sea shudder. Slowly, very slowly, the air became perfumed with the delicate smell of earth.

After a short while the little girl turned away. She wandered off through the still uncertain light, reached the top of the cliff and sat down. Absent-mindedly she looked at the green valley, laughing there below her, and began to sing a little song softly to herself. Suddenly, however, as if something had just struck her, she stopped her sing-song, and shouted at the top of her voice, 'Zi' Jeli! Hey, Zi' Jee. . .!'

And a rough voice answered from the valley, 'Hey-ey!'
'Come up here. The boss wants you!'

Meanwhile, the little girl, her head lowered, was on her way back to the hut. Jeli had come up from down below, still not really awake, with his jacket over his left shoulder and his pipe stuck in his mouth—he always had that pipe clenched between his teeth.

The moment he got inside the hut, he said good morning to Papà Camillo. Malia, the land-agent's elder daughter, gazed intently into his face, her eyes like arrows, so penetrating that they would have pierced through stone.

Jeli returned her look.

Papà Camillo was a stub of a man, as huge in girth as a barrel. Malia this morning had the face of one of Paolo Veronese's women, and in her eyes you could clearly read the blessed simplicity of her heart.

'Listen, Jeli,' said Papà Camillo, 'I want you to get the fruit ready. We've got the gentry coming from the big city. Pick out some good stuff, eh? Because, if you don't—well, as sure as there's a living God . . .!'

'Huh, the usual old guff!' Jeli replied. 'You know very well that you've got no need to try that sort of thing on me! On *me!*'

'Meanwhile,' went on Papà Camillo, taking him by the arm and leading him out of the hut, 'Meanwhile, if you ever get the urge again to. . . . No, I won't say it. You know perfectly well what I'm talking about.'

Jeli just stood there, quite dumbfounded.

Papà Camillo went on down into the valley.

There was no getting the better of him in that argument, so the young man went back up to the hut.

'We're done for now!' said Malia.

'You're a fool!' said Jeli. 'If we can't get what we want by fair means.. . .'

'Oh, Jeli! What are you hinting at, Jeli?'

'*What?* Do you mean to say you don't understand? We'll run away together.'

'Run away together?' said the girl, surprised.

'Or . . .' added Jeli—and he put the shining crescent of the sickle about his neck.

'Oh, my God!' exclaimed Malia, and her shudder seemed to run right through her body.

'Till this evening, then. Seven o'clock. Be ready!' said Jeli, and disappeared.

The girl gave a cry.

It was getting dark.

The appointed hour was approaching and Malia, her face very, very pale and her lips like two dried rose-petals, was seated outside the door. She was watching the waves of darkness engulf the green plain and when, in the distance, the church bell in the village rang out the Ave Maria, she prayed too.

That solemn silence seemed like a divine prayer on the part of Nature.

She'd been waiting there a long time when Jeli came. He'd left his pipe behind this time. He was more passionate and very resolute.

'Is it time already?' asked Malia, trembling.

'A quarter of an hour either way. It's all time gained,' replied Jeli.

'But——'

'Hell's bells! Look, I think it's high time you stopped that *butting* of yours. Haven't you realized, dear heart, that it's a question of——?'

'Oh yes, I realize that. Yes, I know only too well that it's a question of ——!' Malia hastened to reply. She still couldn't reconcile herself to what he'd so ill-advisedly resolved to do. In the meantime, a distant whistle told Jeli that the carriage was ready.

'Come on! Let's get moving!' he said. 'Don't look so glum, Maliella! Out there there's a whole world of joy awaiting us.' Malia gave a cry. Jeli took her by the arm, rushed her along the path. The moment he set foot in the dog-cart he said, 'As fast as you can go!'

The two young people clasped one another very tightly and kissed one another for the first time in freedom.

At nine o'clock Papà Camillo came back up from the valley and gave a tremendously loud whistle. The little girl came rushing out, and before she'd got to where he was, he asked her, 'Where's Jeli? Have you seen Jeli?'

'Oh, Papà Camillo! Papà Camillo!' she panted, her voice sounding choked.

'What are you trying to tell me, you skinny little misery?' roared Papà Camillo.

'Jeli's . . . run away . . . with Maliella. . . .'

And a hoarse, savage sound burst from Papà Camillo's throat. He rushed on up the path, flew into the hut, picked up his shotgun, and fired into the air. The little girl looked at him, stunned.

It was a strange spectacle, the mad fury of that man. A frantic laugh burst shatteringly from his lips, and died away in a strangled rattle. He no longer knew what he was doing. Quite beside himself with rage, he set fire to the little hut, as if intent on destroying everything that reminded him of his daughter. Then off he dashed, furiously, shot-gun in hand, along the path. Perhaps he hoped to find the lovers somewhere along it.

The blood-red tongues of fire reached up to the sky through the gloom of the evening.

Smoke rose up from the little black hut. Smoke and a steady crackling—just as if the hut were saying good-bye to the little girl with that persistent crackle, as she stood there staring at it, pale and horrified. You got the impression that her every thought was following that column of smoke, as it mounted up from her modest home. Smoke rose up from the little black hut. Smoke and a steady crackling. And the little girl stood there, not saying a word, her gaze fixed on the sombre ashes.

EDGAR ALLAN POE

The Tell-Tale Heart

True!—nervous—very, very dreadfully nervous I had been and am; but why *will* you say that I am mad? The disease had sharpened my senses —not destroyed—not dulled them. Above all was the sense of hearing acute. I heard all things in the heaven and in the earth. I heard many things in hell. How, then, am I mad? Hearken! and observe how healthily—how calmly I can tell you the whole story.

It is impossible to say how first the idea entered my brain; but once conceived, it haunted me day and night. Object there was none. Passion there was none. I loved the old man. He had never wronged me. He had never given me insult. For his gold I had no desire. I think it was his eye! yes, it was this! One of his eyes resembled that of a vulture—a pale blue eye, with a film over it. Whenever it fell upon me, my blood ran cold; and so by degrees—very gradually—I made up my mind to take the life of the old man, and thus rid myself of the eye for ever.

Now this is the point. You fancy me mad. Madmen know nothing. But you should have seen *me*. You should have seen how wisely I proceeded— with what caution—with what foresight—with what dissimulation I went to work! I was never kinder to the old man than during the whole week before I killed him. And every night, about midnight, I turned the latch of his door and opened it—oh, so gently! And then, when I had made an opening sufficient for my head, I put in a dark lantern, all closed, closed, so that no light shone out, and then I thrust in my head. Oh, you would have laughed to see how cunningly I thrust it in! I moved it slowly—very, very slowly, so that I might not disturb the old man's sleep. It took me an hour to place my whole head within the opening so far that I could see him as he lay upon his bed.

Ha—would a madman have been so wise as this? And then, when my head was well in the room, I undid the lantern cautiously—oh, so cautiously—cautiously (for the hinges creaked)—I undid it just so much that a single thin ray fell upon the vulture eye. And this I did for seven long nights—every night just after midnight—but I found the eye always closed; and so it was impossible to do the work; for it was not the old man who vexed me, but his Evil Eye. And every morning, when the day broke, I went boldly into the chamber, and spoke courageously to him, calling him by name in a hearty tone, and inquiring how he had passed the night. So you see he would have been a very profound old man, indeed, to suspect that every night, just at twelve, I looked in upon him while he slept.

Upon the eighth night I was more than usually cautious in opening the door. A watch's minute hand moves more quickly than did mine. Never before that night had I *felt* the extent of my own powers—of my sagacity. I could scarcely contain my feelings of triumph. To think that there I was, opening the door, little by little, and he not even to dream of my secret deeds or thoughts. I fairly chuckled at the idea; and perhaps he heard me; for he moved on the bed suddenly, as if startled. Now you may think that I drew back—but no. His room was as black as pitch with the thick darkness (for the shutters were close fastened, through fear of robbers), and so I knew that he could not see the opening of the door, and I kept pushing it on steadily, steadily.

I had my head in, and was about to open the lantern, when my thumb slipped upon the tin fastening, and the old man sprang up in the bed, crying out—"Who's there?"

I kept quite still and said nothing. For a whole hour I did not move a muscle, and in the meantime I did not hear him lie down. He was still sitting up in the bed listening;—just as I have done, night after night, hearkening to the death watches in the wall.

Presently I heard a slight groan, and I knew it was the groan of mortal terror. It was not a groan of pain or of grief—oh, no!—it was the low stifled sound that arises from the bottom of the soul when overcharged with awe. I knew the sound well. Many a night, just at midnight, when all the world slept, it has welled up from my own bosom, deepening with its dreadful echo, the terrors that distracted me. I say I knew it well. I knew what the old man felt, and pitied him, although I chuckled at heart. I knew that he had been lying awake ever since the first slight noise, when he had turned in the bed. His fears had been ever since growing upon him. He had been trying to fancy them causeless, but could not. He had been saying to himself—"It is nothing but the wind in the chimney—it is only a mouse crossing the floor," or "it is merely a cricket which has made a single chirp." Yes, he has been trying to comfort himself with these suppositions; but he had found all in vain. *All in vain*; because Death, in approaching him, had stalked with his black shadow before him, and enveloped the victim. And it was the mournful influence of the unperceived shadow that caused him to feel—although he neither saw nor heard—to *feel* the presence of my head within the room.

When I had waited a long time, very patiently, without hearing him lie down, I resolved to open a little—a very, very little crevice in the lantern. So I opened it—you cannot imagine how stealthily, stealthily—until, at length, a single dim ray, like the thread of the spider, shot from out the crevice and full upon the vulture eye.

It was open—wide, wide open—and I grew furious as I gazed upon it. I saw it with perfect distinctness—all a dull blue, with a hideous veil over it that chilled the very marrow in my bones, but I could see nothing else of the old man's face or person: for I had directed the ray as if by instinct, precisely upon the damned spot.

And now have I not told you that what you mistake for madness is but over-acuteness of the senses?—now, I say, there came to my ears a low, dull, quick sound, such as a watch makes when enveloped in cotton. I knew *that* sound well too. It was the beating of the old man's heart. It increased my fury, as the beating of a drum stimulates the soldier into courage.

But even yet I refrained and kept still. I scarcely breathed. I held the lantern motionless. I tried how steadily I could maintain the ray upon the eye. Meantime the hellish tattoo of the heart increased. It grew quicker and quicker, and louder and louder every instant. The old man's terror *must* have been extreme! It grew louder, I say, louder every moment!—do you mark me well? I have told you that I am nervous: so I am. And now at the dead hour of the night, amid the dreadful silence of that old house, so strange a noise as this excited me to uncontrollable terror. Yet, for some minutes longer I refrained and stood still. But the beating grew louder, louder! I thought the heart must burst. And now a new anxiety seized me—the sound would be heard by a neighbor! The old man's hour had come! With a loud yell, I threw open the lantern and leaped into the room. He shrieked once—once only. In an instant I dragged him to the floor, and pulled the heavy bed over him. I then smiled gaily, to find the deed so far done. But, for many minutes, the heart beat on with a muffled sound. This, however, did not vex me; it would not be heard through the wall. At length it ceased. The old man was dead. I removed the bed and examined the corpse. Yes, he was stone, stone dead. I placed my hand upon the heart and held it there many minutes. There was no pulsation. He was stone dead. His eye would trouble me no more.

If still you think me mad, you will think so no longer when I describe the wise precautions I took for the concealment of the body. The night waned, and I worked hastily, but in silence. First of all I dismembered the corpse. I cut off the head and the arms and the legs.

I then took up three planks from the flooring of the chamber, and deposited all between the scantlings. I then replaced the boards so cleverly, so cunningly, that no human eye—not even *his*—could have detected anything wrong. There was nothing to wash out—no stain of any kind—no blood-spot whatever. I had been too wary for that. A tub had caught all—ha! ha!

When I had made an end of these labors, it was four o'clock—still dark as midnight. As the bell sounded the hour, there came a knocking at the street door. I went down to open it with a light heart—for what had I *now* to fear? There entered three men, who introduced themselves, with perfect suavity, as officers of the police. A shriek had been heard by a neighbor during the night; suspicion of foul play had been aroused; information had been lodged at the police office, and they (the officers) had been deputed to search the premises.

I smiled—for *what* had I to fear? I bade the gentlemen welcome. The shriek, I said, was my own in a dream. The old man, I mentioned, was absent in the country. I took my visitors all over the house. I bade them search— search *well*. I led them, at length, to *his* chamber. I showed them his treasures, secure, undisturbed. In the enthusiasm of my confidence, I brought chairs into the room, and desired them *here* to rest from their fatigues, while I myself; in the wild audacity of my perfect triumph, placed my own seat upon the very spot beneath which reposed the corpse of the victim.

The officers were satisfied. My *manner* had convinced them. I was singularly at ease. They sat, and while I answered cheerily, they chatted familiar things. But, ere long, I felt myself getting pale and wished them gone. My head ached, and I fancied a ringing in my ears: but still they sat and still chatted. The ringing became more distinct:—it continued and became more distinct: I talked more freely to get rid of the feeling: but it continued and gained definitiveness—until, at length, I found that the noise was *not* within my ears.

No doubt I now grew *very* pale;—but I talked more fluently, and with a heightened voice. Yet the sound increased—and what could I do? It was *a low, dull, quick sound—much such a sound as a watch makes when enveloped in cotton*. I gasped for breath—and yet the officers heard it not. I talked more quickly—more vehemently; but the noise steadily increased. I arose and argued about trifles, in a high key and with violent gesticulations, but the noise steadily increased. Why *would* they not be gone? I paced the floor to and fro with heavy strides, as if excited to fury by the observation of the men —but the noise steadily increased. Oh God! what *could* I do? I foamed— I raved—I swore! I swung the chair upon which I had been sitting, and grated it upon the boards, but the noise arose over all and continually increased. It grew louder—louder—*louder*! And still the men chatted pleasantly, and smiled. Was it possible they heard not? Almighty God!—no, no! They heard!—they suspected!—they *knew*!—they were making a mockery of my horror!—this I thought, and this I think. But any thing was better than this agony! Any thing was more tolerable than this derision! I could bear those hypocritical smiles no longer! I felt that I must scream or die!—and now—again!—hark! louder! louder! louder! *louder*!—

"Villains!" I shrieked, "dissemble no more! I admit the deed!—tear up the planks!—here, here!—it is the beating of his hideous heart!"

First Person: Edgar Allan Poe on "The Single Unifying Effect"

But it is of [Hawthorne's] tales that we desire principally to speak. The tale proper, in our opinion, affords unquestionably the fairest field for the exercise of the loftiest talent, which can be afforded by the wide domains of mere prose. Were we bidden to say how the highest genius could be most advantageously employed for the best display of its own powers, we should answer, without hesitation—in the composition of a rhymed poem, not to exceed in length what might be perused in an hour. Within this limit alone can the highest order of true poetry exist. We need only here say, upon this topic, that, in almost all classes of composition, the unity of effect or impression is a point of the greatest importance. It is clear, moreover, that this unity cannot be thoroughly preserved in productions whose perusal cannot be completed at one sitting. We may continue the reading of a prose composition, from the very nature of prose itself, much longer than we can persevere, to any good purpose, in the perusal of a poem. This latter, if truly fulfilling the demands of the poetic sentiment, induces an exaltation of the soul which cannot be long sustained. All high excitements are necessarily transient. Thus a long poem is a paradox. And, without unity of impression, the deepest effects cannot be brought about. Epics were the offspring of an imperfect sense of Art, and their reign is no more. A poem *too* brief may produce a vivid, but never an intense or *enduring impression*. Without a certain continuity of effort—without a certain duration or repetition of purpose—the soul is never deeply moved. There must be the dropping of the water upon the rock. . . .

Were we called upon, however, to designate that class of composition which, next to such a poem as we have suggested, should best fulfill the demands of high genius—should offer it the most advantageous field exertion —we should unhesitatingly speak of the prose tale, as Mr. Hawthorne has here exemplified it. We allude to the short prose narrative, requiring from a half-hour to one or two hours in its perusal. The ordinary novel is objectionable, from its length, for reasons already stated in substance. As it cannot be read at one sitting, it deprives itself, of course, of the immense force derivable from *totality*. Worldly interests intervening during the pauses of perusal, modify, annul, or counteract, in a greater or less degree, the impressions of the book. But simple cessation in reading would, of itself, be sufficient to destroy the true unity. In the brief tale, however, the author is enabled to carry out the fullness of his intention, be it what it may. During the hour of perusal the soul of the reader is at the writer's control. There are no external or extrinsic influences—resulting from weariness or interruption.

A skillful literary artist has constructed a tale. If wise, he has not fashioned his thoughts to accommodate his incidents; but having conceived, with deliberate care, a certain unique or single *effect* to be wrought out, he then invents such incidents—he then combines such events as may best aid him in establishing this preconceived effect. If his very initial sentence tend not to the outbringing of this effect, then he has failed in his first step. In the whole composition there should be no word written, of which the tendency, direct or indirect, is not to the one pre-established design. And by such means, with such care and skill, a picture is at length painted which leaves in the mind of him who contemplates it with a kindred art, a sense of the fullest satisfaction. The idea of the tale has been presented unblemished, because undisturbed; and this is an end unattainable by the novel. Undue brevity is just as exceptionable here as in the poem; but undue length is yet more to be avoided.

We have said that the tale has a point of superiority even over the poem. In fact, while the *rhythm* of this latter is an essential aid in the development of the poem's highest idea—the idea of the Beautiful—the artificialities of this rhythm are an inseparable bar to the development of all points of thought or expression which have their basis in *Truth*. But Truth is often, and in very great degree, the aim of the tale. Some of the finest tales are tales of ratiocination. Thus the field of this species of composition, if not in so elevated a region of the mountain of Mind, is a tableland of far vaster extent than the domain of the mere poem. Its products are never so rich, but infinitely more numerous, and more appreciable by the mass of mankind. The writer of the prose tale, in short, may bring to his theme a vast variety of modes or reflections of thought and expression—(the ratiocinative, for example, the sarcastic, or the humorous) which are not only antagonistical to the nature of the poem, but absolutely forbidden by one of its most peculiar and indispensable adjuncts; we allude, of course, to rhythm. It may be added, here, *par parenthèse*, that the author who aims at the purely beautiful in a prose tale is laboring at a great disadvantage. For Beauty can be better treated in the poem. Not so with terror, or passion, or horror, or a multitude of such other points. . . .

Of Mr. Hawthorne's "Tales" we would say, emphatically, that they belong to the highest region of Art—an Art subservient to genius of a very lofty order. We have supposed, with good reason for so supposing, that he had been thrust into his present position by one of the impudent cliques which beset our literature, and whose pretensions it is our full purpose to expose at the earliest opportunity; but we have been most agreeably mistaken. We know of few compositions which the critic can more honestly commend than these "Twice-Told Tales." As Americans, we feel proud of the book.

Mr. Hawthorne's distinctive trait is invention, creation, imagination, originality—a trait which, in the literature of fiction, is positively worth all the rest. But the nature of the originality, so far as regards its manifestation in letters, is but imperfectly understood. The inventive or original mind as frequently displays itself in novelty of *tone* as in novelty of matter. Mr. Hawthorne is original in *all* points.

It would be a matter of some difficulty to designate the best of these tales; we repeat that, without exception, they are beautiful. . . . In the way of objection we have scarcely a word to say of these tales. There is, perhaps, a somewhat too general or prevalent *tone* —a tone of melancholy and mysticism. The subjects are insufficiently varied. There is not so much of *versatility* evinced as we might well be warranted in expecting from the high powers of Mr. Hawthorne. But beyond these trivial exceptions we have really none to make. The style is purity itself. Force abounds. High imagination gleams from every page. Mr. Hawthorne is a man of the truest genius. . . .

V. S. PRITCHETT

A Story of Don Juan

One night of his life Don Juan slept alone. Returning to Seville in the spring, he was held up, some hours' ride from the city, by the floods of the Quadalquivir, a river as dirty as an old lion after the rains, and was obliged to stay at the finca of the Quintero family. The doorway, the walls, the windows of the house were hung with the black and violet draperies of mourning when he arrived there. Quintero's wife was dead. She had been dead a year. The young Quintero took him in and even smiled to see Don Juan spattered and drooping in the rain like a sodden cockerel. There was malice in his smile: Quintero was mad with loneliness and grief. The man who had possessed and discarded all women was received by a man demented because he had lost only one.

'My house is yours,' said Quintero, speaking the formula. There was bewilderment in his eyes; those who grieve do not find the world and its people either real or believable. Irony inflects the voices of mourners, and there was malice, too, in Quintero's further greetings; he could receive Don Juan now without that fear, that terror which he brought to the husbands of Seville. It was perfect, Quintero thought, that for once in his life Don Juan should have arrived at an empty house.

There was not even (as Don Juan quickly found out) a maid, for Quintero was served only by a manservant, being unable any longer to bear the sight of women. This servant dried the guest's clothes and in an hour or two brought in a bad dinner, food which stamped up and down in the stomach, like people waiting for a coach in the cold. Quintero was torturing his body as well as his mind, and as the familiar pains arrived they agonised him and set him off about his wife. Grief had also made Quintero an actor. His eyes had the hollow, taper-haunted dusk of the theatre as he spoke of the beautiful girl. He dwelled upon their courtship, on details of her beauty and temperament, and how he had rushed her from the church to the marriage bed like a man racing a tray of diamonds through the streets into the safety of a bank vault. The presence of Don Juan turned every man into an artist when he was telling his own love-story—one had to tantalise and surpass the great seducer—and Quintero, rolling it all off in the grand manner, could not resist telling that his bride had died on her marriage night.

'Man!' cried Don Juan. He started straight off on stories of his own. But Quintero hardly listened; he had returned to the state of exhaustion and emptiness which is natural to grief. As Don Juan talked, the madman followed his own thoughts like an actor preparing and mumbling his next entrance; and the thought he had had, when Don Juan first appeared at the door, returned to him: a man must be a monster to make a man feel triumphant that his own wife was dead. Half-listening, and indigestion aiding, Quintero felt within himself the total hatred of all the husbands of Seville for this diabolical man. And as Quintero brooded upon this it occurred to him that it was probably not by chance that he had a vengeance in his power.

The decision was made. The wine being finished, Quintero called for his manservant and gave orders to change Don Juan's room.

'For,' said Quintero dryly, 'His Excellency's visit is an honour and I cannot allow one who has slept in the most delicately scented rooms in Spain to pass the night in a chamber which stinks to heaven of goat.'

'The closed room?' said the manservant, astonished that the room which still held the great dynastic marriage bed and which had not been used more than half a dozen times by his master since the lady's death was to be given to a stranger.

Yet to this room Quintero led his guest and there parted from him with eyes so sparking with ill-intention that Don Juan, who was sensitive to this kind of point, understood perfectly that the cat was being let into the cage only because the bird had long ago flown out. The humiliation was unpleasant. Don Juan saw the night stretching before him like a desert.

What a bed to lie in: so wide, so unutterably vacant, so malignantly inopportune! He took off his clothes, snuffed the lamp wick. He lay down knowing that on either side of him lay wastes of sheet, draughty and uninhabited except by bugs. A desert. To move an arm one inch to the side, to push out a leg, however cautiously, was to enter desolation. For miles and miles the foot might probe, the fingers or the knee explore a friendless Antarctica. Yet to lie rigid and still was to have a foretaste of the grave. And here, too, he was frustrated; for though the wine kept him yawning, that awful food romped in his stomach, jolting him back from the edge of sleep the moment he got there.

There is an art in sleeping alone in a double bed, but this art was unknown to Don Juan. The difficulty is easily solved. If one cannot sleep on one side of the bed, one moves over and tries the other. Two hours or more must have passed before this occurred to him. Sullen-headed, he advanced into the desert, and the night air lying chill between the sheets flapped and made him shiver. He stretched out his arm and crawled towards the opposite pillow. The coldness, the more than virgin frigidity of linen! He put down his head and, drawing up his knees, he shivered. Soon, he supposed, he would be warm again, but, in the meantime, ice could not have been colder. It was unbelievable.

Ice was the word for that pillow and those sheets. Ice. Was he ill? Had the rain chilled him that his teeth must chatter like this and his legs tremble? Far from getting warmer, he found the cold growing. Now it was on his forehead and his cheeks, like arms of ice on his body, like legs of ice upon his legs. Suddenly in superstition he got up on his hands and stared down at the pillow in the darkness, threw back the bedclothes and looked down upon the sheet; his breath was hot, yet blowing against his cheeks was a breath colder than the grave, his shoulders and body were hot, yet limbs of snow were drawing him down; and just as he would have shouted his appalled suspicion, lips like wet ice unfolded upon his own and he sank down to a kiss, unmistakably a kiss, which froze him like a winter.

In his own room Quintero lay listening. His mad eyes were exalted and his ears were waiting. He was waiting for the scream of horror. He knew the apparition. There would be a scream, a tumble, hands fighting for the light, fists knocking at the door. And Quintero had locked the door. But when no scream came, Quintero lay talking to himself, remembering the night the apparition had first come to him and had made him speechless and left him choked and stiff. It would be even better if there were no scream! Quintero lay awake through the night, building castle after castle of triumphant revenge and receiving, as he did so, the ovations of the husbands of Seville. 'The stallion is gelded!' At an early hour Quintero unlocked the door and waited downstairs impatiently. He was a wreck after a night like that.

Don Juan came down at last. He was (Quintero observed) pale. Or was he pale?

'Did you sleep well?' Quintero asked furtively.

'Very well,' Don Juan replied.

'I do not sleep well in strange beds myself,' Quintero insinuated. Don Juan smiled and replied that he was more used to strange beds than his own. Quintero scowled.

'I reproach myself; the bed was large,' he said.

But the large, Don Juan said, were necessarily as familiar to him as the strange. Quintero bit his nails. Some noise had been heard in the night— something like a scream, a disturbance. The manservant had noticed it also. Don Juan answered him that disturbances in the night had indeed bothered him at the beginning of his career, but now he took them in his stride. Quintero dug his nails into the palms of his hands. He brought out the trump.

'I am afraid,' Quintero said, 'it was a cold bed. You must have *frozen*.'

'I am never cold for long,' Don Juan said, and, unconsciously anticipating the manner of a poem that was to be written in his memory two centuries later, declaimed: 'The blood of Don Juan is hot, for the sun is the blood of Don Juan.'

Quintero watched. His eyes jumped like flies to every movement of his guest. He watched him drink his coffee. He watched him tighten the stirrups of his horse. He watched Don Juan vault into the saddle. Don Juan was humming, and when he went off was singing, was singing in that intolerable tenor of his which was like a cock-crow in the olive groves.

Quintero went into the house and rubbed his unshaven chin. Then he went out again to the road where the figure of Don Juan was now only a small smoke of dust between the eucalyptus trees. Quintero went up to the room where Don Juan had slept and stared at it with accusations and suspicions. He called the manservant.

'I shall sleep here tonight,' Quintero said.

The manservant answered carefully. Quintero was mad again and the moon was still only in its first quarter. The man watched his master during the day looking towards Seville. It was too warm after the rains, the country steamed like a laundry.

And then, when the night came, Quintero laughed at his doubts. He went up to the room and as he undressed he thought of the assurance of those ice-cold lips, those icicle fingers and those icy arms. She had not come last night; oh, what fidelity! To think, he would say in his remorse to the ghost, that malice had so disordered him that he had been base and credulous enough to use the dead for a trick.

Tears were in his eyes as he lay down and for some time he dared not turn on his side and stretch out his hand to touch what, in his disorder, he had been willing to betray. He loathed his heart. He craved—yet how could he hope for it now?—that miracle of recognition and forgiveness. It was this craving which moved him at last. His hands went out. And they were met.

The hands, the arms, the lips moved out of their invisibility and soundlessness towards him. They touched him, they clasped him, they drew him down, but—what was this? He gave a shout, he fought to get away, kicked out and swore; and so the manservant found him wrestling with the sheets, striking out with fists and knees, roaring that he was in hell. Those hands, those lips, those limbs, he screamed, were *burning* him. They were of ice no more. They were of fire.

MARCEL PROUST

Before the Night

"Even though I'm still quite strong, you know" (she spoke with a more intimate sweetness, the way accentuation can mellow the overly harsh things that one must say to the people one loves), "you know I could die any day now—even though I may just as easily live another few months. So I can no longer wait to reveal to you something that has been weighing on my conscience; afterwards you will understand how painful it was to tell you." Her pupils, symbolic blue flowers, discolored as if they were fading. I thought she was about to cry, but she did nothing of the kind. "I'm quite sad about intentionally destroying my hope of still being esteemed by my best friend after my death, about tarnishing and shattering his memory of me, in terms of which I often imagine my own life in order to see it as more beautiful and more harmonious. But my concern about an aesthetic arrangement" (she smiled while pronouncing that epithet with the slightly ironic exaggeration accompanying her extremely rare use of such words in conversation) "cannot repress the imperious need for truth that forces me to speak. Listen, Leslie, I have to tell you this. But first, hand me my coat. This terrace is a bit chilly, and the doctor forbade me to get up if it's not necessary." I handed her the coat. The sun was already gone, and the sea, which could be spotted through the apple trees, was mauve. As airy as pale, withered wreaths and as persistent as regrets, blue and pink cloudlets floated on the horizon. A melancholy row of poplars sank into the darkness, leaving their submissive crowns in churchlike rosiness; the final rays, without grazing their trunks, stained their branches, hanging festoons of light on these balustrades of darkness. The breeze blended the three smells of sea, wet leaves, and milk. Never had the Norman countryside more voluptuously softened the melancholy of evening, but I barely savored it—deeply agitated as I was by my friend's mysterious words.

"I loved you very much, but I've given you little, my poor friend."

Forgive me for defying the rules of this literary genre by interrupting a *confession* to which I should listen in silence," I cried out, trying to use humor to calm her down, but in reality mortally sad. "What do you mean you've given me little? And the less I've asked for, the more you've given me, indeed far more than if our senses had played any part in our affection. You were as supernatural as a Madonna and as tender as a wet nurse; I worshiped you, and you nurtured me. I loved you with an affection whose tangible prudence was not disturbed by any hope for carnal pleasure. Did you not requite my feelings with incomparable friendship, exquisite tea, naturally embellished conversation, and how many bunches of fresh roses? You alone, with your maternal and expressive hands, could cool my feverish brow, drip honey between my withered lips, put noble images into my life. Dear friend, I do not want to hear that absurd confession. Give me your hands so I may kiss them: it's cold, why don't we go inside and talk about something else."

"Leslie, you must listen to me all the same, my poor dear. It's crucial. Have you never wondered whether I, after becoming a widow at twenty, have remained one . . .?"

"I'm certain of it, but it's none of my business. You are a creature so superior to anyone else that any weakness of yours would have a nobility and beauty that are not to be found in other people's good deeds. You've acted as you've seen fit, and I'm certain that you've never done anything that wasn't pure and delicate."

"Pure! Leslie, your trust grieves me like an anticipated reproach. Listen . . . I don't know how to tell you this. It's far worse than if I had loved you, say, or someone else, yes, truly, anyone else."

I turned as white as a sheet, as white as she, alas, and, terrified that she might notice it, I tried to laugh and I repeated without really knowing what I was saying: "Ah! Ah! Anyone else—how strange you are."

"I said far worse, Leslie, I can't decide at this moment, however luminous it may be. In the evening one sees things more calmly, but I don't see this clearly, and there are enormous shadows on my life. Still, if, in the depths of my conscience, I believe that it was not worse, why be ashamed to tell you?"

"Was it worse?" I did not understand; but, prey to a horrible agitation that was impossible to disguise, I started trembling in terror as in a nightmare. I did not dare look at the garden path, which, now filled with night and dread, opened before us, nor did I dare to close my eyes. Her voice, which, broken by deeper and deeper sadness, had faded, suddenly grew louder, and, in a clear and natural tone, she said to me:

"Do you remember when my poor friend Dorothy was caught with a soprano, whose name I've forgotten?" (I was delighted with this diversion, which, I hoped, would definitively lead us away from the tale of her sufferings.) "Do you recall explaining to me that we could not despise her?

I remember your exact words: 'How can we wax indignant about habits that Socrates (it involved men, but isn't that the same thing?), who drank the hemlock rather than commit an injustice, cheerfully approved of among his closest friends? If fruitful love, meant to perpetuate the race, noble as a familial, social, human duty, is superior to purely sensual love, then there is no hierarchy of sterile loves, and such a love is no less moral—or, rather, it is no more immoral for a woman to find pleasure with another woman than with a person of the opposite sex. The cause of such love is a nervous impairment which is too exclusively nervous to have any moral content. One cannot say that, because most people see as red the objects qualified as red, those people who see them as violet are mistaken. Furthermore,' you added, 'if we refine sensuality to the point of making it aesthetic, then, just as male and female bodies can be equally beautiful, there is no reason why a truly artistic woman might not fall in love with another woman. In a truly artistic nature, physical attraction and repulsion are modified by the contemplation of beauty. Most people are repelled by a jellyfish. Michelet, who appreciated the delicacy of their hues, gathered them with delight. I was revolted by oysters, but after musing' (you went on) 'about their voyages through the sea, which their taste would now evoke for me, they have become a suggestive treat, especially when I am far from the sea. Thus, physical aptitudes, the pleasure of contact, the enjoyment of food, the pleasures of the senses are all grafted to where our taste for beauty has taken root.'

"Don't you think that these arguments could help a woman physically predisposed to this kind of love to come to terms with her vague curiosity, particularly if, for example, certain statuettes of Rodin's have triumphed—artistically—over her repugnance; don't you think that these arguments would excuse her in her own eyes, appease her conscience—and that this might be a great misfortune?"

I don't know how I managed to stifle my cry: a sudden flash of lightning illuminated the drift of her confession, and I simultaneously felt the brunt of my dreadful responsibility. But, letting myself be blindly led by one of those loftier inspirations that tear off our masks and recite our roles extempore when we fail to do justice to ourselves, when we are too inadequate to play our roles in life, I calmly said: "I can assure you that I would have no remorse whatsoever, for I truly feel no scorn, not even pity, for those women."

She said mysteriously, with an infinite sweetness of gratitude: "You are generous." She then quickly murmured with an air of boredom, the way one disdains commonplace details even while expressing them: "You know, despite everyone's secrecy, it dawned on me that you've all been anxiously trying to determine who fired the bullet, which couldn't be extracted and which brought on my illness. I've always hoped that this bullet wouldn't be discovered. Fine, now that the doctor appears certain, and you might suspect innocent people, I'll make a clean breast of it. Indeed, I prefer to tell you the truth." With the tenderness she had shown when starting to speak about her imminent death, so that her tone of voice might ease the pain that her words would cause, she added: "In one of those moments of despair that are quite natural in any truly *living* person, it was I who . . . wounded myself."

I wanted to go over and embrace her, but much as I tried to control myself, when I reached her, my throat felt strangled by an irresistible force, my eyes filled with tears, and I began sobbing. She, at first, dried my tears, laughed a bit, consoled me gently as in the past with a thousand lovely words and gestures. But from deep inside her an immense pity for herself and for me came welling up, spurting toward her eyes—and flowed down in burning tears. We wept together. The accord of a sad and vast harmony. Her pity and mine, blending into one, now had a larger object than ourselves, and we wept about it, voluntarily, unrestrainedly. I tried to drink her poor tears from her hands. But more tears kept streaming, and she let them benumb her. Her hand froze through like the pale leaves that have fallen into the basins of fountains. And never had we known so much grief and so much joy.

ALFIA RIFAAT

Distant View of a Minaret

Through half-closed eyes she looked at her husband. Lying on his right side, his body was intertwined with hers and his head bent over her right shoulder. As usual at such times she felt that he inhabited a world utterly different from hers, a world from which she had been excluded. Only half-aware of the movements of his body, she turned her head to one side and stared up at the ceiling, where she noticed a spider's web. She told herself she'd have to get out the long broom and brush it down.

When they were first married she had tried to will her husband into sensing the desire that burned within her and so continuing the act longer; she had been too shy and conscious of the conventions to express such wishes openly. Later on, feeling herself sometimes to be on the brink of the experience some of her married women friends talked of in hushed terms, she had found the courage to be explicit about what she wanted. At such moments it had seemed to her that all she needed was just one more movement and her body and soul would be quenched, that once achieved they would between them know how to repeat the experience. But on each occasion, when breathlessly imploring him to continue, he would—as though purposely to deprive her—quicken his movements and bring the act to an abrupt end. Sometimes she had tried in vain to maintain the rhythmic movements a little longer, but always he would stop her. The last time she had made such an attempt, so desperate was she at this critical moment, that she had dug her fingernails into his back, compelling him to remain inside her. He had given a shout as he pushed her away and slipped from her:

'Are you mad, woman? Do you want to kill me?'

It was as though he had made an indelible tattoo mark of shame deep inside her, so that whenever she thought of the incident she felt a flush coming to her face. Thenceforth she had submitted to her passive role, sometimes asking herself: 'Perhaps it's me who's at fault. Perhaps I'm unreasonable in my demands and don't know how to react to him properly.'

There had been occasions when he had indicated that he had had relationships with other women, and sometimes she had suspicions that maybe he still had affairs, and she was surprised that the idea no longer upset her.

She was suddenly aroused from her thoughts by his more urgent movements. She turned to him and watched him struggling in the world he occupied on his own. His eyes were tight closed, his lips drawn down in an ugly contortion, and the veins in his neck stood out. She felt his hand on her leg, seizing it above the knee and thrusting it sideways as his movements became more frenzied. She stared up at her foot that now pointed towards the spider's web and noted her toenails needed cutting.

As often happened at this moment she heard the call to afternoon prayers filtering through the shutters of the closed window and bringing her back to reality. With a groan he let go of her thigh and immediately withdrew. He took a small towel from under the pillow, wrapped it round himself, turned his back to her and went to sleep.

She rose and hobbled to the bathroom where she seated herself on the bidet and washed herself. No longer did she feel any desire to complete the act with herself as she used to do in the first years of marriage. Under the shower she gave her right side to the warm water, then her left, repeating the formula of faith as the water coursed down her body. She wrapped her soaking hair in a towel and wound a large second one under her armpits. Returning to the bedroom, she put on a long house-gown, then took up the prayer carpet from on top of the wardrobe and shut the door behind her.

As she passed through the living-room, the sounds of pop music came to her from the room of her son Mahmoud. She smiled as she imagined him stretched out on his bed, a school book held in front of him; she was amazed at his ability to concentrate in the face of such noise. She closed the living-room door, spread the rug and began her prayers. When she had performed the four *rak'as* she seated herself on the edge of the prayer carpet and counted off her glorifications of the almighty, three at a time on the joints of each finger. It was late autumn and the time for the sunset prayer would soon come and she enjoyed the thought that she would soon be praying again. Her five daily prayers were like punctuation marks that divided up and gave meaning to her life. Each prayer had for her a distinct quality, just as different foods had their own flavours. She folded up the carpet and went out on to the small balcony.

Dusting off the cane chair that stood there, she seated herself and looked down at the street from the sixth floor. She was assailed by the din of buses, the hooting of cars, the cries of street vendors and the raucous noise of competing radios from nearby flats. Clouds of smoke rose up from the outpourings of car exhausts veiling the view of the tall solitary minaret that could be seen between two towering blocks of flats. This single minaret, one of the twin minarets of the Mosque of Sultan Hasan, with above it a thin slice of the Citadel, was all that was now left of the panoramic view she had once had of old Cairo, with its countless mosques and minarets against a background of the Mokattam Hills and Mohamed Ali's Citadel.

Before marriage she had dreamed of having a house with a small garden in a quiet suburb such as Maadi or Helwan. On finding that it would be a long journey for her husband to his work in the centre of the city, she had settled for this flat because of its views. But with the passing of the years, buildings had risen on all sides, gradually narrowing the view. In time this single minaret would also be obscured by some new building.

Aware of the approach of the call to sunset prayers, she left the balcony and went to the kitchen to prepare her husband's coffee. She filled the brass *kanaka* with water and added a spoonful of coffee and a spoonful of sugar. Just as it was about to boil over she removed it from the stove and placed it on the tray with the coffee cup, for he liked to have the coffee poured out in front of him. She expected to find him sitting up in bed smoking a cigarette. The strange way his body was twisted immediately told her that something was wrong. She approached the bed and looked into the eyes that stared into space and suddenly she was aware of the odour of death in the room. She left and placed the tray in the living-room before passing through to her son's room. He looked up as she entered and immediately switched off the radio and stood up:

'What's wrong, mother?'

'It's your father . . .'

'He's had another attack?'

She nodded. 'Go downstairs to the neighbours and ring Dr. Ramzi. Ask him to come right away.'

She returned to the living room and poured out the coffee for herself. She was surprised at how calm she was.

MARY ROBISON

Yours

Allison struggled away from her white Renault, limping with the weight
of the last of the pumpkins. She found Clark in the twilight on the twig-and-
leaf-littered porch behind the house.

He wore a wool shawl. He was moving up and back in a padded glider,
pushed by the ball of his slippered foot.

Allison lowered a big pumpkin, let it rest on the wide floor boards.

Clark was much older—seventy-eight to Allison's thirty-five. They were
married. They were both quite tall and looked something alike in their facial
features. Allison wore a natural-hair wig. It was a thick blonde hood around
her face. She was dressed in bright-dyed denims today. She wore durable
clothes, usually, for she volunteered afternoons at a children's day-care center.

She put one of the smaller pumpkins on Clark's long lap. "Now, nothing surreal," she told him. "Carve just a *regular* face. These are for kids."

In the foyer, on the Hepplewhite desk, Allison found the maid's chore
list with its cross-offs, which included Clark's supper. Allison went quickly
through the day's mail: a garish coupon packet, a bill from Jamestown
Liquors, November's pay-TV program guide, and the worst thing, the fun-
niest, an already opened, extremely unkind letter from Clark's relations up
North. "You're an old fool," Allison read, and, "You're being cruelly de-
ceived." There was a gift check for Clark enclosed, but it was uncashable,
signed, as it was, "Jesus H. Christ."

Late, late into this night, Allison and Clark gutted and carved the
pumpkins together, at an old table set on the back porch, over newspaper
after soggy newspaper, with paring knives and with spoons and with a

343

Swiss Army knife Clark used for exact shaping of tooth and eye and nostril. Clark had been a doctor, an internist, but also a Sunday watercolorist. His four pumpkins were expressive and artful. Their carved features were suited to the sizes and shapes of the pumpkins. Two looked ferocious and jagged. One registered surprise. The last was serene and beaming.

Allison's four faces were less deftly drawn, with slits and areas of distortion. She had cut triangles for noses and eyes. The mouths she had made were just wedges—two turned up and two turned down.

By one in the morning they were finished. Clark, who had bent his long torso forward to work, moved back over to the glider and looked out sleepily at nothing. All the lights were out across the ravine.

Clark stayed. For the season and time, the Virginia night was warm. Most leaves had been blown away already, and the trees stood unbothered. The moon was round above them.

Allison cleaned up the mess.

"Your jack-o'-lanterns are much, much better than mine," Clark said to her.

"Like hell," Allison said.

"Look at me," Clark said, and Allison did.

She was holding a squishy bundle of newspapers. The papers reeked sweetly with the smell of pumpkin guts.

"Yours are *far* better," he said.

"You're wrong. You'll see when they're lit," Allison said.

She went inside, came back with yellow vigil candles. It took her a while to get each candle settled, and then to line up the results in a row on the porch railing. She went along and lit each candle and fixed the pumpkin lids over the little flames.

"See?" she said.

They sat together a moment and looked at the orange faces.

"We're exhausted. It's good-night time," Allison said. "Don't blow out the candles. I'll put in new ones tomorrow."

That night, in their bedroom, a few weeks earlier in her life than had been predicted, Allison began to die. "Don't look at me if my wig comes off," she told Clark. "Please."

Her pulse cords were fluttering under his fingers. She raised her knees and kicked away the comforter. She said something to Clark about the garage being locked.

At the telephone, Clark had a clear view out back and down to the porch. He wanted to get drunk with his wife once more. He wanted to tell her, from the greater perspective he had, that to own only a little talent, like his, was an awful, plaguing thing; that being only a little special meant you expected too much, most of the time, and liked yourself too little. He wanted to assure her that she had missed nothing.

He was speaking into the phone now. He watched the jack-o'-lanterns. The jack-o'-lanterns watched him.

NATSUME SOSEKI

The Third Night

Such was my dream:—A boy, six years of age, was riding on my back. Doubtless it was my son. The only thing I could not account for was that all unknown to me his eyesight had been lost and his head cleanly shaven. When I asked him when he lost his eyesight, he replied, "Well, it was a long time ago." His voice was unmistakably that of a boy, but his manner of speaking was exactly that of a grown-up man, and my equal as a man at that. On either side of the narrow row road were green paddy-fields. From time to time, the fleeting figures of herons could be seen in the gathering darkness.

"Now we are come to the rice-fields, aren't we?" said the rider on my back.

"How can you tell that?" I asked, turning my face backward.

"Why, we can hear herons screaming," he replied.

And thereupon, herons were really heard crying, twice or so.

My son being as he was, I began to dread him a little. With such a boy on my back, I thought, some ill will befall me. Thinking where I should desert him, I looked far into the night and saw a large grove. It was just at the very moment when I thought the grove would be an ideal place to abandon him, that from my back I heard a sound of gentle mockery.

"What are you laughing at?"

The boy did not reply, but merely asked,

"Am I heavy, Father?"

"No," I replied.

"Ere long you will find me heavy," he said.

In silence I walked on, heading for the grove. The road through the rice-fields meandered irregularly and I could not reach the destination as I wished. After a while I came where the road forked off. I stood at the junction of the forked road and took a rest.

"There must be a stone standing here," cried the boy.

Sure enough, there was a stone with equal sides, of eight inches, standing as high as my waist. On the face of it there were inscriptions—"Left-Higa-Kubo" and "Right-Hotta-Hara." It was all dark, but the words inscribed were distinctly seen. The red inscriptions were seemingly of a colour like that of the water-lizard. (A Japanese water-lizard or eft is usually dark all over its body, except for its belly having red mottles.)

"To the left is better, I suppose," the boy advised. I looked to the left and there the grove was casting its dark shadow over our heads from the high sky. I hesitated.

"You need not hesitate," said he. I began to walk towards the grove. Wondering in the recesses of my heart how he knew so well in his blindness, I continued to walk along the straight road, and as I approached the grove, the voice from my back said, "How sorely my blindness tries me!"

"That's why I am carrying you on my back," I replied.

"I must thank you for carrying me, but everybody makes a fool of me. Even Father makes a fool of me. That's what I hate."

I felt a strange distress. Thinking I would go fast to the grove and abandon him, I hurried on.

"When you go a little further, you will come to understand—It was on just such a night as this," said he on my back, as if he had been talking to himself. "What?" I asked in a sharp tone. "What? You ought to know all about it," said the boy scornfully. Then, I began to feel I had known, but could not remember exactly. Only I felt it must have been on such a night. And I felt that all would become clear to me when I had gone a little further. If, however, I should remember, the memory might prove to be an awful thing for me. So before summoning my memory I felt I must relieve myself of his presence, and I quickened my pace the more.

Rain had been falling for some time. Gradually the road became dark. Practically I did not know where I was. Only on my back a little boy clung closely to me, and the little boy, reflecting all my past, present and future, gleamed like the most relentless of mirrors that searches out the smallest facts. And he was my boy at that. And he was blind. I was in infinite distress.

"Just here, it was just here. Just at the root of that cedar."

Amidst the sound of the falling rain the boy's voice was distinctly heard. Involuntarily I stopped. Without my knowing it, we were already in the grove. About six feet ahead there was something black which, as the boy said, seemed to be a cedar-tree.

"Father, it was at the root of the cedar, was it not?"

"Yes, it was," unconsciously I replied.

"The fifth year of the Bunka era, the year of the Dragon, I suppose."

Perfectly naturally I felt that it had been the fifth year of the Bunka era, the year of the Dragon.

"It was just a hundred years ago that you killed me, was it not?"

As soon as I heard him say this, the consciousness that a hundred years back in the fifth year of the Bunka era, the year of the Dragon, on a dark night like this, at the root of the cedar I had killed a blind man, suddenly came to me. And just then, when I realized I had been a murderer, the boy on my back became all of a sudden as heavy as a stone image of *Jizo.*°

°*Jizo*, a guardian deity of children. His images, usually of stone, are frequently used as symbols of heaviness in Japanese literature.

John Steinbeck

Breakfast

This thing fills me with pleasure. I don't know why, I can see it in the smallest detail. I find myself recalling it again and again, each time bringing more detail out of a sunken memory, remembering brings the curious warm pleasure.

It was very early in the morning. The eastern mountains were black-blue, but behind them the light stood up faintly colored at the mountain rims with a washed red, growing colder, grayer and darker as it went up and overhead until, at a place near the west, it merged with pure night.

And it was cold, not painfully so, but cold enough so that I rubbed my hands and shoved them deep into my pockets, and I hunched my shoulders up and scuffled my feet on the ground. Down in the valley where I was, the earth was that lavender gray of dawn. I walked along a country road and ahead of me I saw a tent that was only a little lighter gray than the ground. Beside the tent there was a flash of orange fire seeping out of the cracks of an old rusty iron stove. Gray smoke spurted up out of the stubby stovepipe, spurted up a long way before it spread out and dissipated.

I saw a young woman beside the stove, really a girl. She was dressed in a faded cotton skirt and waist. As I came close I saw that she carried a baby in a crooked arm and the baby was nursing, its head under her waist out of the cold. The mother moved about, poking the fire, shifting the rusty lids of the stove to make a greater draft, opening the oven door; and all the time the baby was nursing, but that didn't interfere with the mother's work, nor with the light quick gracefulness of her movements. There was something very precise and practiced in her movements. The orange fire flicked out of the cracks in the stove and threw dancing reflections on the tent.

I was close now and I could smell frying bacon and baking bread, the warmest, pleasantest odors I know. From the east the light grew swiftly. I came near to the stove and stretched my hands out to it and shivered all over when the warmth struck me. Then the tent flap jerked up and a young man came out and an older man followed him. They were dressed in new blue dungarees and in new dungaree coats with the brass buttons shining. They were sharp-faced men, and they looked much alike.

The younger had a dark stubble beard and the older had a gray stubble beard. Their heads and faces were wet, their hair dripped with water, and water stood out on their stiff beards and their cheeks shone with water. Together they stood looking quietly at the lightening east; they yawned together and looked at the light on the hill rims. They turned and saw me.

"Morning," said the older man. His face was neither friendly nor unfriendly.

"Morning, sir," I said.

"Morning," said the young man.

The water was slowly drying on their faces. They came to the stove and warmed their hands at it.

The girl kept to her work, her face averted and her eyes on what she was doing. Her hair was tied back out of her eyes with a string and it hung down her back and swayed as she worked. She set tin cups on a big packing box, set tin plates and knives and forks out too. Then she scooped fried bacon out of the deep grease and laid it on a big tin platter, and the bacon cricked and rustled as it grew crisp. She opened the rusty oven door and took out a square pan full of high big biscuits.

When the smell of that hot bread came out, both of the men inhaled deeply. The young man said softly, "Kee-rist!"

The elder man turned to me, "Had your breakfast?"

"No."

"Well, sit down with us, then."

That was the signal. We went to the packing case and squatted on the ground about it. The young man asked, "Picking cotton?"

"No."

"We had twelve days' work so far," the young man said.

The girl spoke from the stove. "They even got new clothes."

The two men looked down at their new dungarees and they both smiled a little.

The girl set out the platter of bacon, the brown high biscuits, a bowl of bacon gravy and a pot of coffee, and then she squatted down by the box too. The baby was still nursing, its head up under her waist out of the cold. I could hear the sucking noises it made.

We filled our plates, poured bacon gravy over our biscuits and sugared our coffee. The older man filled his mouth full and he chewed and chewed and swallowed. Then he said, "God Almighty, it's good," and he filled his mouth again.

The young man said, "We been eating good for twelve days."

We all ate quickly, frantically, and refilled our plates and ate quickly again until we were full and warm. The hot bitter coffee scalded our throats. We threw the last little bit with the grounds in it on the earth and refilled our cups.

There was color in the light now, a reddish gleam that made the air seem colder. The two men faced the east and their faces were lighted by the dawn, and I looked up for a moment and saw the image of the mountain and the light coming over it reflected in the older man's eyes.

Then the two men threw the grounds from their cups on the earth and they stood up together. "Got to get going," the older man said.

The younger turned to me. "'Fyou want to pick cotton, we could maybe get you on."

"No. I got to go along. Thanks for breakfast."

The older man waved his hand in a negative. "O. K. Glad to have you." They walked away together. The air was blazing with light at the eastern skyline. And I walked away down the country road.

That's all. I know, of course, some of the reasons why it was pleasant. But there was some element of great beauty there that makes the rush of warmth when I think of it.

P'U SUNG-LING

The Young Lady of the Tung T'ing Lake

The spirits of the Tung-t'ing lake are very much in the habit of borrow-
ing boats. Sometimes the cable of an empty junk will cast itself off, and away
goes the vessel over the waves to the sound of music in the air above. The
boatmen crouch down in one corner and hide their faces, not daring to look
up until the trip is over and they are once more at their old anchorage.

Now a certain Mr. Lin, returning home after having failed at the exam-
ination for Master's degree, was lying down very tipsy on the deck of his
boat, when suddenly strains of music and singing began to be heard. The
boatmen shook Mr. Lin, but failing to rouse him, ran down and hid themselves in the hold below. Then someone came and lifted him up, letting
him drop again on to the deck, where he was allowed to remain in the same
drunken sleep as before. By-and-by the noise of the various instruments
became almost deafening, and Lin, partially waking up, smelt a delicious
odour of perfumes filling the air around him. Opening his eyes, he saw that
the boat was crowded with a number of beautiful girls; and knowing that
something strange was going on, he pretended to be fast asleep. There was
then a call for Chih-ch'êng, upon which a young waiting-maid came forward
and stood quite close to Mr. Lin's head. Her stockings were the colour of the
kingfisher's wing, and her feet encased in tiny purple shoes, no bigger than
one's finger. Much smitten with this young lady, he took hold of her stocking
with his teeth, causing her, the next time she moved, to fall forward flat on
her face. Someone, evidently in authority, asked what was the matter; and
when he heard the explanation, was very angry, and gave orders to take off
Mr. Lin's head. Soldiers now came and bound Lin, and on getting up he beheld a man sitting with his face to the south, and dressed in the garments of

351

a king. "Sire," cried Lin, as he was being led away, "the king of the Tung-t'ing lake was a mortal named Lin; your servant's name is Lin also. His Majesty was a disappointed candidate; your servant is one too. His Majesty met the Dragon Lady, and was made immortal; your servant has played a trick upon this girl, and he is to die. Why this inequality of fortunes?" When the king heard this, he bade them bring him back, and asked him, saying, "Are you, then, a disappointed candidate?" Lin said he was; whereupon the king handed him writing materials, and ordered him to compose an ode upon a lady's headdress. Some time passed before Lin, who was a scholar of some repute in his own neighbourhood, had done more than sit thinking about what he should write; and at length the king upbraided him, saying, "Come, come, a man of your reputation should not take so long." "Sire," replied Lin, laying down his pen, "it took ten years to complete the Songs of the Three Kingdoms; whereby it may be known that the value of compositions depends more upon the labour given to them than the speed with which they are written." The king laughed, and waited patiently from early morning till noon, when a copy of the verses was put into his hand, with which he declared himself very pleased. He now commanded that Lin should be served with wine; and shortly after there followed a collation of all kinds of curious dishes, in the middle of which an officer came in and reported that the register of people to be drowned had been made up. "How many in all?" asked the king. "Two hundred and twenty-eight," was the reply; and then the king inquired who had been deputed to carry it out; whereupon he was informed that the generals Mao and Nan had been appointed to do the work. Lin here rose to take leave, and the king presented him with ten ounces of pure gold and a crystal square, telling him that it would preserve him from any danger he might encounter on the lake. At this moment the king's retinue and horses ranged themselves in proper order upon the surface of the lake; and His Majesty, stepping from the boat into his sedan-chair, disappeared from view.

When everything had been quiet for a long time, the boatmen emerged from the hold and proceeded to shape their course northwards. The wind, however, was against them, and they were unable to make any headway; when all of a sudden an iron cat appeared floating on the top of the water. "General Mao has come," cried the boatmen, in great alarm; and they and all the passengers on board fell down on their faces. Immediately afterwards a great wooden beam stood up from the lake, nodding itself backwards and forwards, which the boatmen, more frightened than ever, said was General Nan. Before long a tremendous sea was raging, the sun was darkened in the heavens, and every vessel in sight was capsized. But Mr. Lin sat in the middle of the boat, with the crystal square in his hand, and the mighty waves broke around without doing them any harm. Thus were they saved, and Lin returned home; and whenever he told his wonderful story, he would assert that, although unable to speak positively as to the facial beauty of the young lady he had seen, he dared say that she had the most exquisite pair of feet in the world.

Subsequently, having occasion to visit the city of Wu-ch'ang, he heard of an old woman who wished to sell her daughter, but was unwilling to accept money, giving out that any one who had the fellow of a certain crystal square in her possession should be at liberty to take the girl. Lin thought this very strange; and taking his square with him sought out the old woman, who was delighted to see him, and told her daughter to come in. The young lady was about fifteen years of age, and possessed of surpassing beauty; and after saying a few words of greeting, she turned round and went within again. Lin's reason had almost fled at the sight of this peerless girl, and he straightway informed the old woman that he had such an article as she required, but could not say whether it would match hers or not. So they compared their squares together, and there was not a fraction of difference between them, either in length or breadth. The old woman was overjoyed, and inquiring where Lin lived, bade him go home and get a bridal chair, leaving his square behind him as a pledge of his good faith. This he refused to do; but the old woman laughed, and said, "You are too cautious, Sir; do you think I should run away for a square?" Lin was thus constrained to leave it behind him, and hurrying away for a chair, made the best of his way back. When, however, he got there, the old woman was gone. In great alarm he inquired of the people who lived near as to her whereabouts; no one, however, knew; and it being already late he returned disconsolately to his boat. On the way, he met a chair coming towards him, and immediately the screen was drawn aside, and a voice cried out, "Mr. Lin! why so late?" Looking closely, he saw that it was the old woman, who, after asking him if he hadn't suspected her of playing him false, told him that just after he left she had had the offer of a chair; and knowing that he, being only a stranger in the place, would have some trouble in obtaining one, she had sent her daughter on to his boat. Lin then begged she would return with him, to which she would not consent; and accordingly, not fully trusting what she said, he hurried on himself as fast as he could, and, jumping into the boat, found the young lady already there. She rose to meet him with a smile, and then he was astonished to see that her stockings were the colour of a kingfisher's wing, her shoes purple, and her appearance generally like that of the girl he had met on the Tung-t'ing lake. While he was still confused, the young lady remarked, "You stare, Sir, as if you had never seen me before!" but just then Lin noticed the tear in her stocking made by his own teeth, and cried out in amazement, "What! are you Chih-ch'êng?" The young lady laughed at this; whereupon Lin rose, and, making her a profound bow, said, "If you are that divine creature, I pray you tell me at once, and set my anxiety at rest." "Sir," replied she, "I will tell you all. That personage you met on the boat was actually the king of the Tung-t'ing lake. He was so pleased with your talent that he wished to bestow me upon you; but, because I was a great favourite with Her Majesty the Queen, he went back to consult with her. I have now come at the Queen's own command." Lin was highly pleased; and washing his hands, burnt incense, with his face towards the lake, as if it were the Imperial Court, and then they went home together.

Subsequently, when Lin had occasion to go to Wu-ch'ang, his wife asked to be allowed to avail herself of the opportunity to visit her parents; and when they reached the lake, she drew a hairpin from her hair, and threw it into the water. Immediately a boat rose from the lake, and Lin's wife, stepping into it, vanished from sight like a bird on the wing. Lin remained waiting for her on the prow of his vessel, at the spot where she had disappeared; and by-and-by, he beheld a houseboat approach, from the window of which there flew a beautiful bird, which was no other than Chih-ch'êng. Then some one handed out from the same window gold and silk, and precious things in great abundance, all presents to them from the Queen. After this, Chih-ch'êng went home regularly twice every year, and Lin soon became a very rich man, the things he had being such as no one had ever before seen or heard of.

PAUL THEROUX

Neighbors

I had two neighbors at Overstrand Mansions—we shared the same landing. In America 'neighbor' has a friendly connotation; in England it is a chilly word, nearly always a stranger, a map reference more than anything else. One of my neighbors was called R. Wigley; the other had no nameplate.

It did not surprise me at all that Corner Door had no nameplate. He owned a motorcycle and kept late nights. He wore leather—I heard it squeak; and boots—they hit the stairs like hammers on an anvil. His motorcycle was a Kawasaki—Japanese of course. The British are patriotic only in the abstract, and they can be traitorously frugal—tax havens are full of Brits. They want value for money, even when they are grease monkeys, bikers with skinny faces and sideburns and teeth missing, wearing jackboots and swastikas. That was how I imagined Corner Door, the man in 4C.

I had never seen his face, though I had heard him often enough. His hours were odd; he was always rushing off at night and returning in the early morning—waking me when he left and waking me again when he came back. He was selfish and unfriendly, scatterbrained, thoughtless—no conversation but plenty of bike noise. I pictured him wearing one of those German helmets that look like kettles, and I took him to be a coward at heart, who sneaked around whining until he had his leather suit and his boots on, until he mounted his too-big Japanese motorcycle, which he kept in the entryway of Overstrand Mansions, practically blocking it. When he was suited up and mounted on his bike he was a Storm Trooper with blood in his eye.

It also struck me that this awful man might be a woman, an awful woman. But even after several months there I never saw the person from 4C face to face. I saw him—or her—riding away, his back, the chrome studs patterned on his jacket. But women didn't behave like this. It was a man.

R. Wigley was quite different—he was a civil servant: Post Office, Welsh I think, very methodical. He wrote leaflets. The Post Office issued all sorts of leaflets—explaining pensions, television licenses, road tax, driving permits, their savings bank, and everything else, including of course stamps. The leaflets were full of directions and advice. In this complicated literate country you were expected to read your way out of difficulty.

When I told Wigley I wouldn't be in London much longer than a couple of years, he became hospitable. No risk, you see. If I had been staying for a long time he wouldn't have been friendly—wouldn't have dared. Neighbors are a worry: they stare, they presume, they borrow things, they ask you to forgive them their trespasses. In the most privacy-conscious country in the world neighbors are a problem. But I was leaving in a year or so, and I was an American diplomat—maybe I was a spy! He suggested I call him Reg.

We met at the Prince Albert for a drink. A month later, I had him over with the Scadutos, Vic and Marietta, and it was then that talk turned to our neighbors. Wigley said there was an actor on the ground floor and that several country Members of Parliament lived in Overstrand Mansions when the Commons was in session. Scaduto asked him blunt questions I would not have dared to ask, but I was glad to hear his answers. Rent? Thirty-seven pounds a week. Married? Had been—no longer. University? Bristol. And when he asked Wigley about his job, Scaduto listened with fascination and then said, 'It's funny, but I never actually imagined anyone writing those things. It doesn't seem like real writing.'

Good old Skiddoo.

Wigley said, 'I assure you, it's quite real.'

Scaduto went on interrogating him—Americans are tremendous questioners—but Wigley's discomfort made me reticent. The British confined conversation to neutral impersonal subjects, resisting any effort to be trapped into friendship. They got to know each other by allowing details to slip out, little mentions that, gathered together, became revelations. The British liked having secrets—they had lost so much else—and that was one of their secrets.

Scaduto asked, 'What are your other neighbors like?'

I looked at Wigley. I wondered what he would say. I would not have dared to put the question to him.

He said, 'Some of them are incredibly noisy and others downright frightening.'

This encouraged me. I said, 'Our Nazi friend with the motorcycle, for one.'

Had I gone too far?

'I was thinking of that prig, Hurst,' Wigley said, 'who has the senile Labrador that drools and squitters all over the stairs.'

'I've never seen our motorcyclist,' I said. 'But I've heard him. The bike. The squeaky leather shoulders. The boots.' I caught Wigley's eye. 'It's just the three of us on this floor, I guess.'

I had lived there just over two months without seeing anyone else.

Wigley looked uncertain, but said, 'I suppose so.'

'My kids would love to have a motorcycle,' Marietta Scaduto said. 'I've got three hulking boys, Mr Wigley.'

I said, 'Don't let them bully you into buying one.'

'Don't you worry,' Marietta said. 'I think those things are a menace.'

'Some of them aren't so bad,' Wigley said. 'Very economical.' He glanced at me. 'So I've heard.'

'It's kind of an image-thing, really. Your psychologists will tell you all about it.' Skiddoo was pleased with himself: he liked analyzing human behavior—'deviants' were his favorites, he said. 'It's classic textbook-case stuff. The simp plays big tough guy on his motorcycle. Walter Mitty turns into Marlon Brando. It's an aggression thing. Castration complex. What do you for laughs, Reg?'

Wigley said, 'I'm not certain what you mean by laughs.'

'Fun,' Scaduto said. 'For example, we've got one of these home computers. About six thousand bucks, including some accessories—hardware, software. Christ, we've had hours of fun with it. The kids love it.'

'I used to be pretty keen on aircraft,' Wigley said, and looked very embarrassed saying so, as if he were revealing an aberration in his boyhood.

Scaduto said, 'Keen in what way?'

'Taking snaps of them,' Wigley said.

'Snaps?' Marietta Scaduto said. She was smiling.

'Yes,' Wigley said. 'I had one of those huge Japanese cameras that can do anything. They're absolutely idiot-proof and fiendishly expensive.'

'I never thought anyone taking dinky little pictures of planes could be described as "keen."' Scaduto said the word like a brand name for ladies' underwear.

'Some of them were big pictures,' Wigley said coldly.

'Even big pictures,' Scaduto said. 'I could understand flying in the planes, though. Getting inside, being airborne, and doing the loop-the-loop.'

Wigley said, 'They were bombers.'

'Now you're talking, Reg!' Scaduto's sudden enthusiasm warmed the atmosphere a bit, and they continued to talk about airplanes.

'My father had an encyclopedia,' Wigley said. 'You looked up "aeroplane." It said, "Aeroplane: See Flying-Machine."'

Later, Marietta said, 'These guys on their motorcycles, I was just thinking. They really have a problem. Women never do stupid things like that.'

Vic Scaduto said, 'Women put on long gowns, high heels, padded bras. They pile their hair up, they pretend they're princesses. That's worse, fantasy-wise. Or they get into really tight provocative clothes, all tits and ass, swinging and bouncing, lipstick, the whole bit, cleavage hanging down. And then—I'm not exaggerating—and then they say, "Don't touch me or I'll scream."'

Good old Skiddoo.

'You've got a big problem if you think that,' Marietta said. She spoke then to Wigley. 'Sometimes the things he says are sick.'

Wigley smiled and said nothing.

'And he works for the government,' Marietta said. 'You wouldn't think so, would you?'

That was it. The Scadutos went out arguing, and Wigley left. A highly successful evening, I thought.

Thanks to Scaduto's pesterings I knew much more about Wigley. He was decent, he was reticent, and I respected him for the way he handled Good Old Skiddoo. And we were no more friendly than before. That was all right with me: I didn't want to be burdened with his friendship any more than he wanted to be lumbered with mine. I only wished that the third tenant on the floor was as gracious a neighbor as Wigley.

Would Wigley join me in making a complaint? He said he'd rather not. That was the British way—don't make a fuss, Reggie.

He said, 'To be perfectly frank, he doesn't actually bother me.'

This was the first indication I'd had that it was definitely a man, not a woman.

'He drives me up the wall sometimes. He keeps the craziest hours. I've never laid eyes on him, but I know he's weird.'

Wigley smiled at me and I immediately regretted saying *He's weird*, because, saying so, I had revealed something of myself.

I said, 'I can't make a complaint unless you back me up.'

'I know.'

I could tell that he thought I was being unfair. It created a little distance, this annoyance of mine, which looked to him like intolerance. I knew this because Wigley had a girl friend and didn't introduce me. A dozen times I heard them on the stairs. People who live alone are authorities on noises. I knew their laughs. I got to recognize the music, the bed-springs, the bath water. He did not invite me over.

And of course there was my other subject, the Storm Trooper from 4C with his thumping jackboots at the oddest hours. I decided at last that wimpy little Wigley (as I now thought of him) had become friendly with him, perhaps ratted on me and told him that I disliked him.

Wigley worked at Post Office Headquarters, at St Martin's-le-Grand, taking the train to Victoria and then the tube to St Paul's. I sometimes saw him entering or leaving Battersea Park Station while I was at the bus stop. Occasionally, we walked together to or from Overstrand Mansions, speaking of the weather.

One day, he said, 'I might be moving soon.'

I felt certain he was getting married. I did not ask.

'Are you sick of Overstrand Mansions?'

'I need a bigger place.'

He was definitely getting married.

I had the large balcony apartment in front. Wigley had a two-room apartment just behind me. The motorcyclist's place I had never seen.

'I wish it were the Storm Trooper who was leaving, and not you.'

He was familiar with my name for the motorcyclist.

'Oh, well,' he said, and walked away.

Might be moving, he had said. It sounded pretty vague. But the following Friday he was gone. I heard noise and saw the moving van in front on Prince of Wales Drive. Bumps and curses echoed on the stairs. I didn't stir—too embarrassing to put him on the spot, especially as I had knocked on his door that morning, hoping for the last time to get him to join me in a protest against the Storm Trooper. I'm sure he saw me through his spy-hole in the door—Wigley, I mean. But he didn't open. So he didn't care about the awful racket the previous night—boots, bangs, several screams. Wigley was bailing out and leaving me to deal with it.

He went without a word. Then I realized he had sneaked away. He had not said good-bye; I had never met his girl friend; he was getting married—maybe already married. British neighbors!

I wasn't angry with him, but I was furious with the Storm Trooper, who had created a misunderstanding between Wigley and me. Wigley had tolerated the noise and I had hated it and said so. The Storm Trooper had made me seem like a brute!

But I no longer needed Wigley's signature on a complaint. Now there were only two of us here. I could go in and tell him exactly what I thought of him. I could play the obnoxious American. Wigley's going gave me unexpected courage. I banged on his door and shook it, hoping that I was waking him up. There was no answer that day or any day. And there was no more noise, no Storm Trooper, no motorcycle, from the day Wigley left.

JAMES THURBER

The Secret Life of Walter Mitty

"We're going through!" The Commander's voice was like thin ice breaking. He wore his full-dress uniform, with the heavily braided white cap pulled down rakishly over one cold gray eye. "We can't make it, sir. It's spoiling for a hurricane, if you ask me." "I'm not asking you, Lieutenant Berg," said the Commander. "Throw on the power lights! Rev her up to 8,500! We're going through!" The pounding of the cylinders increased: ta-pocketa-pocketa-pocketa-*pocketa-pocketa*. The Commander stared at the ice forming on the pilot window. He walked over and twisted a row of complicated dials. "Switch on No. 8 auxiliary!" he shouted. "Switch on No. 8 auxiliary!" repeated Lieutenant Berg. "Full strength in No. 3 turret!" shouted the Commander. "Full strength in No. 3 turret!" The crew, bending to their various tasks in the huge, hurtling eight-engined Navy hydroplane, looked at each other and grinned. "The Old Man'll get us through," they said to one another. "The Old Man ain't afraid of Hell!" . . .

"Not so fast! You're driving too fast!" said Mrs. Mitty. "What are you driving so fast for?"

"Hmm?" said Walter Mitty. He looked at his wife, in the seat beside him, with shocked astonishment. She seemed grossly unfamiliar, like a strange woman who had yelled at him in a crowd. "You were up to fifty-five," she said. "You know I don't like to go more than forty. You were up to fifty-five." Walter Mitty drove on toward Waterbury in silence, the roaring of the SN202 through the worst storm in twenty years of Navy flying fading in the remote, intimate airways of his mind. "You're tensed up again," said Mrs. Mitty. "It's one of your days. I wish you'd let Dr. Renshaw look you over."

Walter Mitty stopped the car in front of the building where his wife went to have her hair done. "Remember to get those overshoes while I'm having my hair done," she said. "I don't need overshoes," said Mitty. She put her mirror back into her bag. "We've been all through that," she said, getting out of the car. "You're not a young man any longer." He raced the engine a little. "Why don't you wear your gloves? Have you lost your gloves?" Walter Mitty reached in a pocket and brought out the gloves. He put them on, but after she had turned and gone into the building and he had driven on to a red light, he took them off again. "Pick it up, brother!" snapped a cop as the light changed, and Mitty hastily pulled on his gloves and lurched ahead. He drove around the streets aimlessly for a time, and then he drove past the hospital on his way to the parking lot.

. . . "It's the millionaire banker, Wellington McMillan," said the pretty nurse. "Yes?" said Walter Mitty, removing his gloves slowly. "Who has the case?" "Dr. Renshaw and Dr. Benbow, but there are two specialists here, Dr. Remington from New York and Mr. Pritchard-Mitford from London. He flew over." A door opened down a long, cool corridor and Dr. Renshaw came out. He looked distraught and haggard. "Hello, Mitty," he said. "We're having the devil's own time with McMillan, the millionaire banker and close personal friend of Roosevelt. Obstreosis of the ductal tract. Tertiary. Wish you'd take a look at him." "Glad to," said Mitty.

In the operating room there were whispered introductions: "Dr. Remington, Dr. Mitty, Mr. Pritchard-Mitford, Dr. Mitty." "I've read your book on streptothricosis," said Pritchard-Mitford, shaking hands. "A brilliant performance, sir." "Thank you," said Walter Mitty. "Didn't know you were in the States, Mitty," grumbled Remington. "Coals to Newcastle, bring Mitford and me up here for a tertiary." "You are very kind," said Mitty. A huge, complicated machine, connected to the operating table, with many tubes and wires, began at this moment to go pocketa-pocketa-pocketa. "The new anesthetizer is giving way!" shouted an interne. "There is no one in the East who knows how to fix it!" "Quiet, man!" said Mitty, in a low, cool voice. He sprang to the machine, which was now going pocketa-pocketa-queep-pocketa-queep. He began fingering delicately a row of glistening dials. "Give me a fountain pen!" he snapped. Someone handed him a fountain pen. He pulled a faulty piston out of the machine and inserted the pen in its place. "That will hold for ten minutes," he said. "Get on with the operation." A nurse hurried over and whispered to Renshaw, and Mitty saw the man turn pale. "Coreopsis has set in," said Renshaw nervously. "If you would take over, Mitty?" Mitty looked at him and at the craven figure of Benbow, who drank, and at the grave, uncertain faces of the two great specialists. "If you wish," he said. They slipped a white gown on him; he adjusted a mask and drew on thin gloves; nurses handed him shining. . . .

"Back it up, Mac! Look out for that Buick!" Walter Mitty jammed on the brakes. "Wrong lane, Mac," said the parking-lot attendant, looking at Mitty closely. "Gee. Yeh," muttered Mitty. He began cautiously to back out of the lane marked "Exit Only." "Leave her sit there," said the attendant. "I'll put her away." Mitty got out of the car. "Hey, better leave the key." "Oh," said Mitty, handing the man the ignition key. The attendant vaulted into the car, backed it up with insolent skill, and put it where it belonged.

They're so damn cocky, thought Walter Mitty, walking along Main Street; they think they know everything. Once he had tried to take his chains off, outside New Milford, and he had got them wound around the axles. A man had had to come out in a wrecking car and unwind them, a young, grinning garageman. Since then Mrs. Mitty always made him drive to the garage to have the chains taken off. The next time, he thought, I'll wear my right arm in a sling; they won't grin at me then. I'll have my right arm in a sling and they'll see I couldn't possibly take the chains off myself. He kicked at the slush on the sidewalk. "Overshoes," he said to himself, and he began looking for a shoe store.

When he came out into the street again, with the overshoes in a box under his arm, Walter Mitty began to wonder what the other thing was his wife had told him to get. She had told him, twice, before they set out from these weekly trips to town—he was always getting something wrong. Kleenex, he thought, Squibb's, razor blades? No. Toothpaste, toothbrush, bicarbonate, carborundum, initiative and referendum? He gave it up. But she would remember it. "Where's the what's-its-name?" she would ask. "Don't tell me you forgot the what's-its-name." A newsboy went by shouting something about the Waterbury trial.

. . . "Perhaps this will refresh your memory." The District Attorney suddenly thrust a heavy automatic at the quiet figure on the witness stand. "Have you ever seen this before?" Walter Mitty took the gun and examined it expertly. "This is my Webley-Vickers 50.80," he said calmly. An excited buzz ran around the courtroom. The Judge rapped for order. "You are a crack shot with any sort of firearms, I believe?" said the District Attorney, insinuatingly. "Objection!" shouted Mitty's attorney. "We have shown that the defendant could not have fired the shot. We have shown that he wore his right arm in a sling on the night of the fourteenth of July." Walter Mitty raised his hand briefly and the bickering attorneys were stilled. "With any known make of gun," he said evenly, "I could have killed Gregory Fitzhurst at three hundred feet *with my left hand*." Pandemonium broke loose in the courtroom. A woman's scream rose above the bedlam and suddenly a lovely, dark-haired girl was in Walter Mitty's arms. The District Attorney struck at her savagely. Without rising from his chair, Mitty let the man have it on the point of the chin. "You miserable cur!" . . .

"Puppy biscuit," said Walter Mitty. He stopped walking and the buildings of Waterbury rose up out of the misty courtroom and surrounded him again. A woman who was passing laughed. "He said 'Puppy biscuit,'" she said to her companion. "That man said 'Puppy biscuit' to himself." Walter Mitty hurried on. He went into an A. & P., not the first one he came to but a smaller one farther up the street. "I want some biscuit for small, young dogs," he said to the clerk. "Any special brand, sir?" The greatest pistol shot in the world thought a moment. "It says 'Puppies Bark for It' on the box," said Walter Mitty.

His wife would be through at the hairdresser's in fifteen minutes, Mitty saw in looking at his watch, unless they had trouble drying it; sometimes they had trouble drying it. She didn't like to get to the hotel first; she would want him to be there waiting for her as usual. He found a big leather chair in the lobby, facing a window, and he put the overshoes and the puppy biscuit on the floor beside it. He picked up an old copy of *Liberty* and sank down into the chair. "Can Germany Conquer the World through the Air?" Walter Mitty looked at the pictures of bombing planes and of ruined streets. . . . "The cannonading has got the wind up in young Raleigh, sir," said the sergeant. Captain Mitty looked up at him through tousled hair. "Get him to bed," he said wearily. "With the others. I'll fly alone." "But you can't, sir," said the sergeant anxiously. "It takes two men to handle that bomber and the Archies are pounding hell out of the air. Von Richtman's circus is between here and Saulier." "Somebody's got to get that ammunition dump." said Mitty. "I'm going over. Spot of brandy?" He poured a drink for the sergeant and one for himself. War thundered and whined around the dugout and battered at the door. There was a rending of wood and splinters flew through the room. "A bit of a near thing," said Captain Mitty carelessly. "The box barrage is closing in," said the sergeant. "We only live once, Sergeant," said Mitty, with his faint, fleeting smile. "Or do we?" He poured another brandy and tossed it off. "I never see a man could hold his brandy like you, sir," said the sergeant. "Begging your pardon, sir." Captain Mitty stood up and strapped on his huge Webley-Vickers automatic. "It's forty kilometers through hell, sir," said the sergeant. Mitty finished one last brandy. "After all," he said softly, "what isn't?" The pounding of the cannon increased; there was the rat-tat-tatting of machine guns, and from somewhere came the menacing pocket-pocketa-pocketa of the new flame-throwers. Walter Mitty walked to the door of the dugout humming "Auprès de Ma Blonde." He turned and waved to the sergeant. "Cheerio!" he said. . . .

Something struck his shoulder. "I've been looking all over this hotel for you," said Mrs. Mitty. "Why do you have to hide in this old chair? How did you expect me to find you?" "Things close in," said Walter Mitty vaguely. "What?" Mrs. Mitty said. "Did you get the what's-its-name? The puppy biscuit? What's in that box?" "Overshoes," said Mitty. "Couldn't you have put them on in the store?" "I was thinking," said Walter Mitty. "Does it ever occur to you that I am sometimes thinking?" She looked at him. "I'm going to take your temperature when I get you home," she said.

They went out through the revolving doors that made a faintly derisive whistling sound when you pushed them. It was two blocks to the parking lot. At the drugstore on the corner she said, "Wait here for me. I forgot something. I won't be a minute." She was more than a minute. Walter Mitty lighted a cigarette. It began to rain, rain with sleet in it. He stood up against the wall of the drugstore, smoking. . . . He put his shoulders back and his heels together. "To hell with the handkerchief," said Walter Mitty scornfully. He took one last drag on his cigarette and snapped it away. Then with that faint, fleeting smile playing about his lips, he faced the firing squad; erect and motionless, proud and disdainful, Walter Mitty the Undefeated, inscrutable to the last.

Wilmar N. Tognazzini

Love of His Life

When I saw the bearded lady at the carnival, I was determined to woo her. Such was my fetish, yet my relatives were supportive.

"Your name?" the minister asked of me.

"Robert Cedric Foster," I said. It all seemed too good to be true.

"And yours?" he asked of my bearded bride.

"William Angelo Duvani."

Leo Tolstoy

The Three Hermits

Translated by *AYLMML MAUIH*

*"But when ye pray, use not vain repetitions, as the heathen do:
for they think that they shall be heard for their much speaking.
Be ye not therefore like unto them: for your Father knoweth what
things ye have need of, before ye ask him."*

—MATT VI. 6, 7.

A bishop set sail in a ship from the city of Archangelsk to Solovki.° In the same ship sailed some pilgrims to the saints.

The wind was propitious, the weather was clear, the sea was not rough. The pilgrims, some of whom were lying down, some lunching, some sitting in little groups, conversed together.

The bishop also came on deck and began to walk up and down on the bridge. As he approached the bow, he saw a knot of people crowded together. A little muzhik was pointing his hand at something in the sea, and talking; and the people were listening.

The bishop stood still, and looked where the little muzhik was pointing; nothing was to be seen, except the sea glittering in the sun.

The bishop came closer and began to listen. When the little muzhik saw the bishop, he took off his cap, and stopped speaking. The people also, when they saw the bishop, took off their hats, and paid their respects.

°Solovki: The Slovetsky Monastery, at the mouth of the Dvina River.

"Don't mind me, brothers," said the bishop. "I have also come to listen to what you are saying, my good friend."

"This fisherman was telling us about some hermits," said a merchant, who was bolder than the rest.

"What about the hermits?" asked the bishop, as he came to the gunwale, and sat down on a box. "Tell me too; I should like to hear. What were you pointing at?"

"Well, then, yonder's the little island just heaving in sight," said the little peasant; and he pointed toward the port side. "On that very islet, three hermits live, working out their salvation."

"Where is the little island?" asked the bishop.

"Here, look along my arm, if you please. You see that little cloud? Well, just below it to the left it shows like a streak."

The bishop looked and looked; the water gleamed in the sun, but from lack of practice he could not see anything.

"I don't see it," says he. "What sort of hermits are they who live on the little island?"

"God's people," replied the peasant. "For a long time I had heard tell of them, but I never chanced to see them until last summer."

And the fisherman again began to relate how he had been out fishing, and how he was driven to that island, and knew not where he was. In the morning he started to look around, and stumbled upon a little earthen hut; and he found in the hut one hermit, and then two others came in. They fed him, and dried him, and helped him repair his boat.

"What sort of men were they?" asked the bishop.

"One was rather small, humpbacked, very, very old; he was dressed in well-worn stole; he must have been more than a hundred years old; the gray hairs in his beard were already turning green; but he always had a smile ready, and he was as serene as an angel of heaven. The second was taller, also old, in a torn kaftan; his long beard was growing a little yellowish, but he was a strong man; he turned my boat over as if it had been a tub,—and I didn't even have to help him: he was also a jolly man. But the third was tall, with a long beard reaching to his knee, and white as the moon; but he was gloomy; his eyes glared out from under beetling brows; and he was naked, all save a plaited belt."

"What did they say to you?" asked the bishop.

"They did everything mostly without speaking, and they talked very little among themselves; one had only to look, and the other understood. I began to ask the tall one if they had lived there long. He frowned, muttered something, grew almost angry: then the little old man instantly seized him by the hand, smiled, and the large man said nothing. But the old man said, 'Excuse us,' and smiled."

While the peasant was speaking, the ship had been sailing nearer and nearer to the islands.

"There, now you can see plainly," said the merchant. "Now please look, your reverence," said he, pointing.

The bishop tried to look, and he barely managed to make out a black speck—the little island.

The bishop gazed and gazed; and he went from the bow to the stern, and he approached the helmsman.

"What is that little island," says he, "that you see over yonder?"

"As far as I know, it has no name; there are a good many of them here."

"Is it true as they say, that some monks are winning their salvation there?"

"They say so, your reverence, but I don't rightly know. Fishermen, they say, have seen them. Still, folks talk a good deal of nonsense."

"I should like to land on the little island, and see the hermits," said the bishop. "How can I manage it?"

"It is impossible to go there in the ship," said the helmsman. "You might do it in a boat, but you will have to ask the captain."

They summoned the captain.

"I should like to have a sight of those hermits," said the bishop. "Is it out of the question to take me there?"

The captain tried to dissuade him.

"It is possible, quite possible, but we should waste much time; and I take the liberty of assuring your reverence, they are not worth looking at. I have heard from people that those old men are perfectly stupid; they don't understand anything, and can't say anything, just like some sort of sea-fish."

"I wish it," said the bishop. "I will pay for the trouble, if you will take me there."

There was nothing else to be done: the sailors arranged it; they shifted sail. The helmsman put the ship about and they sailed toward the island. A chair was set for the bishop on the bow. He sat down and looked. And all the people gathered on the bow, all looked at the little island. And those who had trustworthy eyes already began to see rocks on the island, and point out the hut. And one even saw the three hermits. The captain got out a spy-glass, gazed through it, handed it to the bishop.

"He is quite right," said the captain; "there on the shore at the right, standing on a great rock, are three men."

The bishop also looked through the glass; he pointed it in the right direction and plainly saw the three men standing there,—one tall, the second shorter, but the third very short. They were standing on the shore, hand in hand.

The captain came to the bishop:—

"Here, your reverence, the ship must come to anchor; if it suit you, you can be put ashore in a yawl, and we will anchor out here and wait for you."

Immediately they got the tackle ready, cast anchor, and furled the sails; the vessel brought up, began to roll. They lowered a boat, the rowers manned it, and the bishop started to climb down by the companionway. The bishop climbed down, took his seat on the thwart; the rowers lifted their oars; they sped away to the island. They sped away like a stone from a sling; they could see the three old men standing,—the tall one naked, with his plaited belt; the shorter one in his torn kaftan; and the little old humpbacked one, in his old stole,—all three were standing there, hand in hand.

The sailors reached shore and caught hold with the boat-hook. The bishop got out.

The hermits bowed before him; he blessed them; they bowed still lower. And the bishop began to speak to them:—

"I heard," says he, "that you hermits were here, working out your salvation, that you pray Christ our God for your fellow-men; and I am here by God's grace, an unworthy servant of Christ, called to be a shepherd to His flock; and so I desired also, if I might, to give instruction to you, who are the servants of God."

The hermits made no reply; they smiled, they exchanged glances.

"Tell me how you are working out your salvation, and how you serve God," said the bishop.

The middle hermit sighed, and looked at the aged one, at the venerable one; the tall hermit frowned, and looked at the aged one, at the venerable one. And the venerable old hermit smiled, and said:—

"Servant of God, we have not the skill to serve God; we only serve ourselves, getting something to eat."

"How do you pray to God?" asked the bishop.

And the venerable hermit said:—

"We pray thus: 'You three, have mercy on us three.' "

And as soon as the venerable hermit said this, all three of the hermits raised their eyes to heaven, and all three said, "*Troe vas, troe nas, pomiluĭ nas!*"

The bishop smiled, and said:—

"You have heard this about the Holy Trinity, but you should not pray so. I have taken a fancy to you, men of God. I see that you desire to please God, but you know not how to serve Him. You should not pray so; but listen to me, I will teach you. I shall not teach you my own words, but shall teach you from God's scriptures how God commanded all people to pray to God."

And the bishop began to explain to the hermits how God revealed Himself to men. He taught them about God the Father, God the Son, and God the Holy Spirit, and said:—

"God the Son came upon earth to save men, and this is the way He taught all men to pray; listen, and repeat after me"—

And the bishop began to say:—

"*Our Father.*"

And one hermit repeated:—

"*Our Father.*"

And then the second repeated:—

"*Our Father.*"

And the third also repeated:—

"*Our Father.*"

"*Who art in heaven;*" and the hermits tried to repeat, "*Who art in heaven.*"

But the middle hermit mixed the words up, he could not repeat them so; and the tall, naked hermit could not repeat them,—his mustache had grown so as to cover his mouth, he could not speak distinctly; and the venerable, toothless hermit could not stammer the words intelligibly.

The bishop said it a second time; the hermits repeated it again. And the bishop sat down on a little boulder, and the hermits stood about him; and they looked at his lips, and they repeated it after him until they knew it. And all that day till evening the bishop labored with them; and ten times, and twenty times, and a hundred times, he repeated each word, and the hermits learned it by rote. And when they got mixed up, he set them right, and made them begin all over again.

And the bishop did not leave the hermits until he had taught them the whole of the Lord's Prayer. They repeated it after him, and then by themselves.

First of all, the middle hermit learned it, and he repeated it from beginning to end; and the bishop bade him say it again and again, and still again to repeat it; and the others also learned the whole prayer.

It was already beginning to grow dark, and the moon was just coming up out of the sea, when the bishop arose to go back to the ship.

The bishop said farewell to the hermits; they all bowed very low before him. He raised them to their feet and kissed each of them, bade them pray as he had taught them; and he took his seat in the boat, and returned to the ship.

And while the bishop was rowed back to the ship, he heard all the time how the hermits were repeating the Lord's Prayer at the top of their voices.

They returned to the ship, and here the voices of the hermits could no longer be heard; but they could still see, in the light on the moon, the three old men standing in the very same place on the shore,—one shorter than the rest in the middle, with the tall one on the right, and the other on the left hand.

The bishop returned to the ship, climbed up on deck; the anchor was hoisted; the sails were spread, and bellied with wind; the ship began to move, and they sailed away.

The bishop came to the stern, and took a seat there, and kept looking at the little island. At first the hermits were to be seen; then they were hidden from sight, and only the island was visible; and then the island went out of sight, and only the sea was left playing in the moonlight.

The pilgrims lay down to sleep, and all was quiet on deck. But the bishop cared not to sleep; he sat by himself in the stern, looked out over the sea in the direction where the island had faded from sight, and thought about the good hermits.

He thought of how they had rejoiced in what they had learned in the prayer; and he thanked God because He had led him to the help of the hermits, in teaching them the word of God.

Thus the bishop was sitting and thinking, looking at the sea in the direction where the little island lay hidden. And his eyes were filled with the moonlight, as it danced here and there on the waves. Suddenly he saw something shining and gleaming white in the track of the moon. Was it a bird, a gull, or a boat-sail gleaming white? The bishop strained his sight.

"A sail-boat," he said to himself, "is chasing us. Yes, it is catching up with us very rapidly. It was far, far off, but now it is close to us. But, after all, it is not much like a sail-boat. Anyway, something is chasing us, and catching up with us."

And the bishop could not decide what it was,—a boat, or not a boat; a bird, or not a bird; a fish, or not a fish. It was like a man, but very great; but a man could not be in the midst of the sea.

The bishop got up and went to the helmsman.

"Look!" says he, "what is that? what is that, brother? what is it?" said the bishop.

But by this time he himself saw. It was the hermits running over the sea. Their gray beards gleamed white, and shone; and they drew near the ship as if it were stationary.

The helmsman looked. He was scared, dropped the tiller, and cried with a loud voice:—

"Lord! the hermits are running over the sea as if it were dry land!"

The people heard and sprang up; all rushed aft. All beheld the hermits running, hand in hand. The end ones swung their arms; they signaled the ship to come to. All three ran over the water as if it were dry land, and did not move their feet.

It was not possible to bring the ship to before the hermits overtook it, came on board, raised their heads, and said with one voice:—

"We have forgotten, servant of God, we have forgotten what thou didst teach us. While we were learning it, we remembered it; but when we ceased for an hour to repeat it, one word slipped away; we have forgotten it: the whole was lost. We remembered none of it; teach it to us again."

The bishop crossed himself, bowed low to the hermits, and said:—

"Acceptable to God is your prayer, ye hermits. It is not for me to teach you. Pray for us sinners."

And the bishop bowed before the feet of the hermits. And the hermits paused, turned about, and went back over the sea. And until the morning, there was something seen shining in the direction where the hermits had gone.

First Person: Leo Tolstoy, "What is Art?"

Artistic (and also scientific) creation is such mental activity as brings dimly-perceived feelings (or thoughts) to such a degree of clearness that these feelings (or thoughts) are transmitted to other people.

The process of "creation"—one common to all men and therefore known to each of us by inner experience—occurs as follows: a man surmises or dimly feels something that is perfectly new to him, which he has never heard of from anybody. This something new impresses him, and in ordinary conversation he points out to others what he perceives, and to his surprise finds that what is apparent to him is quite unseen by them. They do not see or do not feel what he tells them of. This isolation, discord, disunion from others, at first disturbs him, and verifying his own perception the man tries in different ways to communicate to others what he has seen, felt, or understood; but these others still do not understand what he communicates to them, or do not understand it as he understands or feels it. And the man begins to be troubled by a doubt as to whether be imagines and dimly feels something that does not really exist, or whether others do not see and do not feel something that does exist. And to solve this doubt he directs his whole strength to the task of making his discovery so clear that there cannot be the smallest doubt, either for himself or for other people, as to the existence of that which he perceives; and as soon as this elucidation is completed and the man himself no longer doubts the existence of what he has seen, understood, or felt, others at once see, understand, and feel as he does, and it is this effort to make clear and indubitable to himself and to others what both to others and to him had been dim and obscure, that is the source from which flows the production of man's spiritual activity in general, or what we call works of art—which widen man's horizon and oblige him to see what had not been perceived before.*

It is in this that the activity of an artist consists; and also to this activity is related the feeling of the recipient. This feeling has its source in imitativeness, or rather in a capacity to be infected, and in a certain hypnotism—that is to say in the fact that the artist's stress of spirit elucidating to himself the subject that had been doubtful to him, communicates itself, through the artistic production, to the recipients. A work of art is then finished when it has been brought to such clearness that it communicates itself to others and evokes in them the same feeling that the artist experienced while creating it.

What was formerly unperceived, unfelt, and uncomprehended by them, is by intensity of feeling brought to such a degree of clearness that it becomes acceptable to all, and the production is a work of art.

The satisfaction of the intense feeling of the artist who has achieved his aim gives pleasure to him. Participation in this same stress of feeling and in its satisfaction, a yielding to this feeling, the imitation of it and infection by it (as by a yawn), the experiencing in brief moments what the artist has lived through while creating his work, is the enjoyment those who assimilate a work of art obtain.

Such in my opinion is the peculiarity that distinguishes art from any other activity.

---

*The division of the results of man's mental activity into scientific, philosophic, theological, artistic, and other groups, is made for convenience of observation. But such divisions do not exist in reality; just as the divisions of the River Vólga into the Tver, Nizlmigórod, Simbirsk and Sarátov sections, are not divisions of the river itself, but divisions we make for our own convenience.

According to this division, all that imparts to mankind something new, achieved by an artist's stress of feeling and thought, is a work of art. But that this mental activity should really have the importance people attach to it, it is necessary that it should contribute what is good to humanity, for it is evident that to a new evil, to a new temptation leading people into evil, we cannot attribute the value given to art as to something that benefits mankind. The importance, the value, of art consists in widening man's outlook, in increasing the spiritual wealth that is humanity's capital.

Therefore, though a work of art must always include something new, yet the revelation of something new will not always be a work of art. That it should be a work of art, it is necessary:

1. That the new idea, content of the work, should be of importance to mankind.
2. That this content should be expressed so clearly that people may understand it.
3. That what incites the author to work at his production should be an inner need and not an external inducement.

And therefore that in which no new thing is disclosed will not be a work of art; and that which has for its content what is insignificant and therefore unimportant to man will not be a work of art however intelligibly it may be expressed, and even if the author has worked at it sincerely from an inner impulse. Nor will that be a work of art which is so expressed as to be unintelligible, however sincere may be the author's relation to it; nor that which has been produced by its author not from an inner impulse but for an external aim, however important may be its content and however intelligible its expression.

That is a work of art which discloses something new and at the same time in some degree satisfies the three conditions: content, form, and sincerity.

And here we come to the problem of how to define that lowest degree of content, beauty, and sincerity, which a production must possess to be a work of art.

To be a work of art it must, in the first place, be a thing which has for its content something hitherto unknown but of which man has need; secondly, it must show this so intelligibly that it becomes generally accessible; and thirdly, it must result from the author's need to solve an inner doubt.

A work in which all three conditions are present even to a slight degree, will be a work of art; but a production from which even one of them is absent will not be a work of art.

But it will be said that every work contains something needed by man, and every work will be to some extent intelligible, and that an author's relation to every work has some degree of sincerity. Where is the limit of needful content, intelligible expression, and sincerity of treatment? A reply to this question will be given us by a clear perception of the highest limit to which art may attain: the opposite of the highest limit will show the lowest limit, dividing all that cannot be accounted art from what is art. The highest limit of content is such as is always necessary to all men. That which is always necessary to all men is what is good or moral.* The lowest limit of content, consequently, will be such as is not needed by men, and is a bad and immoral content. The highest limit of expression will be such as is always intelligible to all men. What is thus intelligible is that which has nothing in it obscure, superfluous, or indefinite, but only what is clear, concise, and definite—what is called beautiful. Conversely, the lowest limit of expression will be such as is obscure, diffuse, and indefinite—that is to say formless. The highest limit of the artist's relation to his subject will be such as evokes in the soul of all men an impression of reality—the reality not so much of what exists, as of what goes on in the soul of the artist. This impression of reality is produced by truth only, and therefore the highest relation of an author to his subject is *sincerity*. The lowest limit, conversely, will be that in which the author's relation to his subject is not genuine but false. All works of art lie between these two limits.

A perfect work of art will be one in which the content is important and significant to all men, and therefore it will be *moral*. The expression will be quite clear, intelligible to all, and therefore *beautiful*; the author's relation to his work will be altogether sincere and heartfelt, and therefore true. Imperfect works, but still works of art, will be such productions as satisfy all three conditions though it be but in unequal degree. That alone will be no work of art, in which either the content is quite insignificant and unnecessary to man, or the expression quite unintelligible, or the relation of the author to the work quite insincere. In the degree of perfection attained in each of these respects lies the difference in quality between all true works of art. Sometimes the first predominates, sometimes the second, and sometimes the third.

All the remaining imperfect productions fall naturally, according to the three fundamental conditions of art, into three chief kinds: (1) those which stand out by the importance of their content, (2) those which stand out by their beauty of form, and (3) those which stand out by their heartfelt sincerity. These three kinds all yield approximations to perfect art, and are inevitably produced wherever there is art.

Thus among young artists heartfelt sincerity chiefly prevails, coupled with insignificance of content and more or less beauty of form. Among older artists, on the contrary, the importance of the content often predominates

---

*Half-a-century ago no explanation would have been needed of the words "important," "good," and "moral," but in our time nine out of ten educated people, at these words, will ask with a triumphant air: "What is important, good or moral?" assuming that these words express something conditional and not admitting of definition, and therefore I must answer this anticipated objection. That which unites people not by violence but by love: that which serves to disclose the joy of the union of men with one another, is "important," "good," or "moral." "Evil" and "immoral" is that which divides them, that leads men to the suffering produced by disunion. "Important" is that which causes people to understand and to love what they previously did not understand or love.

over beauty of form and sincerity. Among laborious artists beauty of form predominates over content and sincerity.

All works of art may be appraised by the prevalence in them of the first, the second, or the third quality, and they may all be subdivided into (1) those that have content and are beautiful, but have little sincerity; (2) those that have content, but little beauty and little sincerity; (3) those that have little content, but are beautiful and sincere, and so on, in all possible combinations and permutations.

All works of art, and in general all the mental activities of man, can be appraised on the basis of these three fundamental qualities; and they have been and are so appraised.

The differences in valuation have resulted, and do result, from the extent of the demand presented to art by certain people at a certain time in regard to these three conditions.

So for instance in classical times the demand for significance of content was much higher, and the demand for clearness and sincerity much lower than they subsequently became, especially in our time. The demand for beauty became greater in the Middle Ages, but on the other hand the demand for significance and sincerity became lower; and in our time the demand for sincerity and truthfulness has become much greater, but on the other hand the demand for beauty, and especially for significance, has been lowered.

The evaluation of works of art is necessarily correct when all three conditions are taken into account, and inevitably incorrect when works are valued not on the basis of all three conditions but only of one or two of them.

And yet such evaluation of works of art on the basis of only one of the three conditions is an error particularly prevalent in our time, lowering the general level of what is demanded from art to what can be reached by a mere imitation of it, and confusing the minds of critics, and of the public, and of artists themselves, as to what is really art and as to where its boundary lies—the line that divides it from craftsmanship and from mere amusement.

This confusion arises from the fact that people who lack the capacity to understand true art, judge of works of art from one side only, and according to their own characters and training observe in them the first, the second, or the third side only, imagining and assuming that this one side perceptible to them—and the significance of art based on this one condition—defines the whole of art. Some see only the importance of the content, others only the beauty of form, and others again only the artist's sincerity and therefore truthfulness. And according to what they see they define the nature of art itself, construct their theories, and praise and encourage those who, like themselves, not understanding wherein a work of art consists, turn them out like pancakes and inundate our world with foul floods of all kinds of follies and abominations which they call "works of art."

Such are the majority of people, and, as representatives of that majority, such were the originators of the three aesthetic theories already alluded to, which meet the perceptions and demands of that majority.

All these theories are based on a misunderstanding of the whole importance of art and on severing its three fundamental conditions; and therefore these three false theories of art clash, as a result of the fact that real art has three fundamental conditions of which each of those theories accepts but one.

The first theory, of so-called "tendencious" art, accepts as a work of art one that has for its subject something which, though it be not new, is important to all men by its moral content, independently of its beauty and spiritual depth.

The second ("art for art's sake") recognizes as a work of art only that which has beauty of form, independently of its novelty, the importance of its content, or its sincerity.

The third theory, the "realistic," recognizes as a work of art only that in which the author's relation to his subject is sincere, and which is therefore truthful. The last theory says that however insignificant or even foul may be the content, with a more or less beautiful form the work will be good, if the author's relation to what he depicts is sincere and therefore truthful.

All these theories forget one chief thing—that neither importance, nor beauty, nor sincerity, provides the requisite for works of art, but that the basic condition of the production of such works is that the artist should be conscious of something new and important; and that therefore, just as it always has been, so it always will be, necessary for a true artist to be able to perceive something quite new and important. For the artist to see what is new, it is necessary that he should observe and think, and not occupy his life with trifles which hinder his attentive penetration into, and meditation on, life's phenomena. In order that the new things he sees may be important ones, the artist must be a morally enlightened man, and he must not live a selfish life but must share the common life of humanity.

If only he sees what is new and important he will be sure to find a form which will express it, and the sincerity which is an essential content of artistic production will be present. He must be able to express the new subject so that all may understand it. For this he must have such mastery of his craft that when working he will think as little about the rules of that craft as a man when walking thinks of the laws of motion. And in order to attain this, the artist must not look round on his work and admire it, must not make technique his aim—as one who is walking should not contemplate and admire his gait—but should be concerned only to express his subject clearly, and in such a way as to be intelligible to all.

Finally, to work at his subject not for external ends but to satisfy his inner need, the artist must rise superior to motives of avarice and vanity. He must love with his own heart and not with another's, and not pretend that he loves what others love or consider worthy of love.

And to attain all this the artist must do as Balaam did when the messengers came to him and he went apart awaiting God so as to say only what God commanded; and he must not do as that same Balaam afterwards did when, tempted by gifts, he went to the king against God's command, as was evident even to the ass on which he rode, though not perceived by him while blinded by avarice and vanity.

In our time nothing of that kind is demanded. A man who wishes to follow art need not wait for some important and new perception to arise in his soul, which he can sincerely love and having loved can clothe in suitable form. In our time a man who wishes to follow art either takes a subject current at the time and praised by people who in his opinion are clever, and clothes it as best he can in what is called "artistic form"; or he chooses a subject which gives him most opportunity to display his technical skill, and with toil and patience produces what he considers to be a work of art; or having received some chance impression he takes what caused that impression for his subject, imagining that it will yield a work of art since it happened to produce an impression on him.

And so there appear an innumerable quantity of so-called works of art which, as in every mechanical craft, can be produced without the least intermission. There are always current fashionable notions in society, and with patience a technique can always be learnt, and something or other will always seem interesting to some one. Having separated the conditions that should be united in a true work of art, people have produced so many works of pseudo-art that the public, the critics, and the pseudo-artists themselves, are left quite without any definition of what they themselves hold to be art.

The people of to-day have, as it were, said to themselves: "Works of art are good and useful; so it is necessary to produce more of them." It would indeed be a very good thing if there were more; but the trouble is that you can only produce to order works which are no better than works of mere craftsmanship because of their lack of the essential conditions of art.

A really artistic production cannot be made to order, for a true work of art is the revelation (by laws beyond our grasp) of a new conception of life arising in the artist's soul, which, when expressed, lights up the path along which humanity progresses.

Jean Toomer

Fern

Face flowed into her eyes. Flowed in soft cream foam and plaintive ripples, in such a way that wherever your glance may momentarily have rested, it immediately thereafter wavered in the direction of her eyes. The soft suggestion of down slightly darkened, like the shadow of a bird's wing might, the creamy brown color of her upper lip. Why, after noticing it, you sought her eyes, I cannot tell you. Her nose was aquiline, Semitic. If you have heard a Jewish cantor sing, if he has touched you and made your own sorrow seem trivial when compared with his, you will know my feeling when I follow the curves of her profile, like mobile rivers, to their common delta. They were strange eyes. In this, that they sought nothing—that is, nothing that was obvious and tangible and that one could see, and they gave the impression that nothing was to be denied. When a woman seeks, you will have observed, her eyes deny. Fern's eyes desired nothing that you could give her; there was no reason why they should withhold. Men saw her eyes and fooled themselves. Fern's eyes said to them that she was easy. When she was young, a few men took her, but got no joy from it. And then, once done, they felt bound to her (quite unlike their hit and run with other girls), felt as though it would take them a lifetime to fulfill an obligation which they could find no name for. They became attached to her, and hungered after finding the barest trace of what she might desire. As she grew up, new men who came to town felt as almost everyone did who ever saw her: that they would not be denied. Men were everlastingly bringing her their bodies. Something inside of her got tired of them, I guess, for I am certain that for the life of her she could not tell why or how she began to turn them off. A man in fever is no trifling thing to send away. They began to leave her, baffled and ashamed, yet vowing to themselves that some day they would do some fine thing for her: send her candy every week and not let her know whom it came from, watch out for her wedding-day and give her a magnificent something with no name on it, buy a house and deed it to her, rescue her from some unworthy fellow who had tricked her into marrying him. As you know, men are apt to idolize or fear that which they cannot understand, especially if it be a woman. She did not deny them, yet the fact was that they were denied. A sort of superstition crept into their consciousness of her being somehow above them. Being above them meant that she was not to be approached by anyone. She became a virgin. Now a virgin in a small southern town is by no means the usual thing, if you will believe me. That the sexes were made to mate is the practice of the South. Particularly, black folks were made to mate. And it is black folks whom I have been talking about thus far. What white men thought of Fern I can arrive at only by analogy. They let her alone.

Anyone, of course, could see her, could see her eyes. If you walked up the Dixie Pike most any time of day, you'd be most likely to see her resting listless-like on the railing of her porch, back propped against a post, head tilted a little forward because there was a nail in the porch post just where her head came which for some reason or other she never took the trouble to pull out. Her eyes, if it were sunset, rested idly where the sun, molten and glorious, was pouring down between the fringe of pines. Or maybe they gazed at the gray cabin on the knoll from which an evening folk-song was coming. Perhaps they followed a cow that had been turned loose to roam and feed on cotton-stalks and corn leaves. Like as not they'd settle on some vague spot above the horizon, though hardly a trace of wistfulness would come to them. If it were dusk, then they'd wait for the search-light of the evening train which you could see miles up the track before it flared across the Dixie Pike, close to her home. Wherever they looked, you'd follow them and then waver back. Like her face, the whole countryside seemed to flow into her eyes. Flowed into them with the soft listless cadence of Georgia's South. A young Negro, once, was looking at her, spellbound, from the road. A white man passing in a buggy had to flick him with his whip if he was to get by without running him over. I first saw her on her porch. I was passing with a fellow whose crusty numbness (I was from the North and suspected of being prejudiced and stuck-up) was melting as he found me warm. I asked him who she was. "That's Fern," was all that I could get from him. Some folks already thought that I was given to nosing around; I let it go at that, so far as questions were concerned. But at first sight of her I felt as if I heard a Jewish cantor sing. As if his singing rose above the unheard chorus of a folk-song. And I felt bound to her. I too had my dreams: something I would do for her. I have knocked about from town to town too much not to know the futility of mere change of place. Besides, picture if you can, this cream-colored solitary girl sitting at a tenement window looking down on the indifferent throngs of Harlem. Better that she listen to folk-songs at dusk in Georgia, you would say, and so would I. Or, suppose she came up North and married. Even a doctor or a lawyer, say, one who would be sure to get along—that is, make money. You and I know, who have had experience in such things, that love is not a thing like prejudice which can be bettered by changes of town. Could men in Washington, Chicago, or New York, more than the men of Georgia, bring her something left vacant by the bestowal of their bodies? You and I who know men in these cities will have to say, they could not. See her out and out a prostitute along State Street in Chicago. See her move into a southern town where white men are more aggressive. See her become a white man's concubine. . . . Something I must do for her. There was myself. What could I do for her? Talk, of course. Push back the fringe of pines upon new horizons. To what purpose? and what for? Her? Myself? Men in her case seem to lose their selfishness. I lost mine before I touched her. I ask you, friend (it makes no difference if you sit in the Pullman or the Jim Crow as the train crosses her road), what thoughts would come to you—that is, after you'd finished with the thoughts that leap into men's minds at the sight of a pretty woman who will not deny them; what thoughts would come to you, had you seen her in a quick flash, keen and intuitively, as she sat there on her porch when your train thundered by? Would you have got off at the next station and come back for her to take her where? Would you have completely forgotten her as soon as you reached Macon, Atlanta, Augusta, Pasadena, Madison, Chicago, Boston, or New Orleans? Would you tell your wife or sweetheart about a girl you saw? Your thoughts can help me, and I would like to know. Something I would do for her . . .

One evening I walked up the Pike on purpose, and stopped to say hello. Some of her family were about, but they moved away to make room for me. Damn if I knew how to begin. Would you? Mr. and Miss So-and-So, people, the weather, the crops, the new preacher, the frolic, the church benefit, rabbit and possum hunting, the new soft drink they had at old Pap's store, the schedule of the trains, what kind of town Macon was, Negro's migration north, bollweevils, syrup, the Bible—to all these things she gave a yassur or nassur, without further comment. I began to wonder if perhaps my own emotional sensibility had played one of its tricks on me. "Lets take a walk," I at last ventured. The suggestion, coming after so long an isolation, was novel enough, I guess, to surprise. But it wasnt that. Something told me that men before me had said just that as a prelude to the offering of their bodies. I tried to tell her with my eyes. I think she understood. The thing from her that made my throat catch, vanished. Its passing left her visible in a way I'd thought, but never seen. We walked down the Pike with people on all the porches gaping at us. "Doesnt it make you mad?" She meant the row of petty gossiping people. She meant the world. Through a canebrake that was ripe for cutting, the branch was reached. Under a sweet-gum tree, and where reddish leaves had dammed the creek a little, we sat down. Dusk, suggesting the almost imperceptible procession of giant trees, settled with a purple haze about the cane. I felt strange, as I always do in Georgia, particularly at dusk. I felt that things unseen to men were tangibly immediate. It would not have surprised me had I had vision. People have them in Georgia more often than you would suppose. A black woman once saw the mother of Christ and drew her in charcoal on the courthouse wall . . . When one is on the soil of one's ancestors, most anything can come to one . . . From force of habit, I suppose, I held Fern in my arms—that is, without at first noticing it. Then my mind came back to her. Her eyes, unusually weird and open, held me. Held God. He flowed in as I've seen the countryside flow in. Seen men. I must have done something—what, I dont know, in the confusion of my emotion. She sprang up. Rushed some distance from me. Fell to her knees, and began swaying, swaying. Her body was tortured with something it could not let out. Like boiling sap it flooded arms and fingers till she shook them as if they burned her. It found her throat, and spattered inarticulately in plaintive, convulsive sounds, mingled with calls to Christ Jesus. And then she sang, brokenly. A Jewish cantor singing with a broken voice. A child's voice, uncertain, or an old man's. Dusk hid her; I could hear only her song. It seemed to me as though she were pounding her head in anguish upon the ground. I rushed to her. She fainted in my arms.

There was talk about her fainting with me in the canefield. And I got one or two ugly looks from town men who'd set themselves up to protect her. In fact, there was talk of making me leave town. But they never did. They kept a watch-out for me, though. Shortly after, I came back North. From the train window I saw her as I crossed her road. Saw her on her porch, head tilted a little forward where the nail was, eyes vaguely focused on the sunset. Saw her face flow into them, the countryside and something that I call God, flowing into them . . . Nothing ever really happened. Nothing ever came to Fern, not even I. Something I would do for her. Some fine unnamed thing . . . And, friend, you? She is still living, I have reason to know. Her name, against the chance that you might happen down that way, is Fernie May Rosen.

John Updike

Lifeguard

Beyond doubt, I am a splendid fellow. In the autumn, winter, and spring, I execute the duties of a student of divinity; in the summer I disguise myself in my skin and become a lifeguard. My slightly narrow and gingerly hirsute but not necessarily unmanly chest becomes brown. My smooth back turns the color of caramel, which, in conjunction with the whipped cream of my white pith helmet, gives me, some of my teenage satellites assure me, a delightfully edible appearance. My legs, which I myself can study, cocked as they are before me while I repose on my elevated wooden throne, are dyed a lustreless maple walnut that accentuates their articulate strength. Correspondingly, the hairs of my body are bleached blond, so that my legs have the pointed elegance of, within the flower, umber anthers dusted with pollen.

For nine months of the year, I pace my pale hands and burning eyes through immense pages of biblical text barnacled with fudging commentary; through multi-volumed apologetics couched in a falsely friendly Victorian voice and bound in subtly abrasive boards of finely ridged, pre-faded red; through handbooks of liturgy and histories of dogma; through the bewildering duplicities of Tillich's divine politicking; through the suave table talk of Father D'Arcy, Etienne Gilson, Jacques Maritain, and other such moderns mistakenly put at their ease by the exquisite antique furniture and overstuffed larder of the hospitable St Thomas; through the terrifying attempts of Kierkegaard, Berdyaev, and Barth to scourge God into being. I sway appalled on the ladder of minus signs by which theologians would surmount the void. I tiptoe like a burglar into the house of naturalism to steal the silver. An acrobat, I swing from wisp to wisp. Newman's iridescent cobwebs crush in my hands. Pascal's blackboard mathematics are erased by a passing shoulder. The cave drawings, astoundingly vital by candlelight, of those aboriginal magicians, Paul and Augustine, in daylight fade into mere anthropology. The diverting productions of literary flirts like Chesterton, Eliot, Auden, and Greene—whether they regard Christianity as a pastel forest designed for a fairyland romp or a deliciously miasmic pit from which chiaroscuro can be mined with mechanical buckets—in the end all infallibly strike, despite the comic variety of gongs and mallets, the note of the rich young man who on the coast of Judaea refused in dismay to sell all that he had.

Then, for the remaining quarter of the solar revolution, I rest my eyes on a sheet of brilliant sand printed with the runes of naked human bodies. That there is no discrepancy between my studies, that the texts of the flesh complement those of the mind, is the easy burden of my sermon.

On the back rest of my lifeguard's chair is painted a cross—true, a red cross, signifying bandages, splints, spirits of ammonia, and sunburn unguents. Nevertheless, it comforts me. Each morning, as I mount into my chair, my athletic and youthfully fuzzy toes expertly gripping the slats that make a ladder, it is as if I am climbing into an immense, rigid, loosely fitting vestment.

Again, in each of my roles I sit attentively perched on the edge of an immensity. That the sea, with its multiform and mysterious hosts, its savage and senseless rages, no longer comfortably serves as a divine metaphor indicates how severely humanism has corrupted the apples of our creed. We seek God now in flowers and good deeds, and the immensities of blue that surround the little scabs of land upon which we draw our lives to their unsatisfactory conclusions are suffused by science with vacuous horror. I myself can hardly bear the thought of stars, or begin to count the mortalities of coral. But from my chair the sea, slightly distended by my higher perspective, seems a misty old gentleman stretched at his ease in an immense armchair which has for arms the arms of this bay and for an antimacassar the freshly laundered sky. Sailboats float on his surface like idle and unrelated but benevolent thoughts. The soughing of the surf is the rhythmic lifting of his ripple-stitched vest as he breathes. Consider. We enter the sea with a shock; our skin and blood shout in protest. But, that instant, that leap, past, what do we find? Ecstasy and buoyance. Swimming offers a parable. We struggle and thrash, and drown; we succumb, even in despair, and float, and are saved.

With what timidity, with what a sense of trespass, do I set forward even this obliquely a thought so official! Forgive me. I am not yet ordained; I am too disordered to deal with the main text. My competence is marginal, and I will confine myself to the gloss of flesh with which this particular margin, this one beach, is annotated each day.

Here the cinema of life is run backwards. The old are the first to arrive. They are idle, and have lost the gift of sleep. Each of our bodies is a clock that loses time. Young as I am, I can hear in myself the protein acids ticking; I wake at odd hours and in the shuddering darkness and silence feel my death rushing towards me like an express train. The older we get, and the fewer the mornings left to us, the more deeply dawn stabs us awake. The old ladies wear wide straw hats and, in their hats' shadows, smiles as wide, which they bestow upon each other, upon salty shells they discover in the morning-smooth sand, and even upon me, downy-eyed from my night of dissipation. The gentlemen are often incongruous; withered white legs support brazen barrel chests, absurdly potent, bustling with white froth. How these old roosters preen on their 'condition'! With what fatuous expertness they swim in the icy water—always, however, prudently parallel to the shore, at a depth no greater than their height.

Then come the middle-aged, burdened with children and aluminum chairs. The men are scarred with the marks of their vocation—the red fore-arms of the gasoline-station attendant, the pale X on the back of the overall-wearing mason or carpenter, the clammer's nicked ankles. The hair on their bodies has as many patterns as matted grass. The women are wrinkled but fertile, like the Iraqi rivers that cradled the seeds of our civilization. Their children are odious. From their gaunt faces leer all the vices, the greeds, the grating urgencies of the adult, unsoftened by maturity's reticence and fa-tigue. Except that here and there, a girl, the eldest daughter, wearing a knit suit striped horizontally with green, purple, and brown, walks slowly, care-fully, puzzled by the dawn enveloping her thick smooth body, her waist not yet nipped but her throat elongated.

Finally come the young. The young matrons bring fat and fussing in-fants who gobble the sand like sugar, who toddle blissfully into the surf and bring me bolt upright on my throne. My whistle tweets. The mothers rouse. Many of these women are pregnant again, and sluggishly lie in their loose suits like cows tranced in a meadow. They gossip politics, and smoke inces-santly, and lift their troubled eyes in wonder as a trio of flat-stomached nymphs parades past. These maidens take all our eyes. The vivacious red-head, freckled and white-footed, pushing against her boy and begging to be ducked; the solemn brunette, transporting the vase of herself with held breath; the dimpled blonde in the bib and diapers of her bikini, the lambent fuzz of her midriff shimmering like a cat's belly. Lust stuns me like the sun.

You are offended that a divinity student lusts? What prigs the unchurched are. Are not our assaults on the supernatural lascivious, a kind of indecency? If only you knew what de Sadian degradations, what frightful psychological spelunking, our gentle transcendentalist professors set us to, as preparation for our work, which is to shine in the darkness.

I feel that my lust makes me glow; I grow cold in my chair, like a torch of ice, as I study beauty. I have studied much of it, wearing all styles of bathing suit and facial expression, and have come to this conclusion: a woman's beauty lies, not in any exaggeration of the specialized zones, nor in any general harmony that could be worked out by means of the *sectio aurea* or a similar aesthetic superstition; but in the arabesque of the spine. The curve by which the back modulates into the buttocks. It is here that grace sits and rides a woman's body.

I watch from my white throne and pity women, deplore the demented judgement that drives them towards the braggart muscularity of the mesomorph and the prosperous complacence of the endomorph when it is we ectomorphs who pack in our scrawny sinews and exacerbated nerves the most intense gift, the most generous shelter, of love. To desire a woman is to desire to save her. Anyone who has endured intercourse that was neither predatory nor hurried knows how through it we descend, with a partner, into the grotesque and delicate shadows that until then have remained locked in the most guarded recess of our soul: into this harbor we bring her. A vague and twisted terrain becomes inhabited; each shadow, touched by the exploration, blooms into a flower of act. As if we are an island upon which a woman, tossed by her laboring vanity and blind self-seeking, is blown, and there finds security, until, an instant before the anticlimax, Nature with a smile thumps down her trump, and the island sinks beneath the sea.

There is great truth in those motion pictures which are slandered as true neither to the Bible nor to life. They are—written though they are by demons and drunks—true to both. We are all Solomons lusting for Sheba's salvation. The God-filled man is filled with a wilderness that cries to be populated. The stony chambers need jewels, furs, tints of cloth and flesh, even though, as in Samson's case, the temple comes tumbling. Women are an alien race of pagans set down among us. Every seduction is a conversion.

Who has loved and not experienced that sense of rescue? It is not true that our biological impulses are tricked out with ribands of chivalry; rather, our chivalric impulses go clanking in encumbering biological armor. Eunuchs love. Children love. I would love.

My chief exercise, as I sit above the crowds, is to lift the whole mass into immortality. It is not a light task; the throng is so huge, and its members so individually unworthy. No *memento mori* is so clinching as a photograph of a vanished crowd. Cheering Roosevelt, celebrating the Armistice, there it is, wearing its ten thousand straw hats and stiff collars, a fearless and wooden-faced bustle of life: it is gone. A crowd dies in the street like a derelict; it leaves no heir, no trace, no name. My own persistence beyond the last rim of time is easy to imagine; indeed, the effort of imagination lies the other way— to conceive of my ceasing. But when I study the vast tangle of humanity that blackens the beach as far as the sand stretches, absurdities crowd in on me. Is it as maiden, matron, or crone that the females will be eternalized? What will they do without children to watch and gossip to exchange? What of the thousand deaths of memory and bodily change we endure—can each be redeemed at a final Adjustments Counter? The sheer numbers involved make the mind scream. The race is no longer a tiny clan of simian aristocrats lording it over an ocean of grass; mankind is a plague racing like fire across the exhausted continents. This immense clot gathered on the beach, a fraction of a fraction—can we not say that this breeding swarm is its own immortality and end the suspense? The beehive in a sense survives; and is each of us not proved to be a hive, a galaxy of cells each of whom is doubtless praying, from its pew in our thumbnail or oesophagus, for personal resurrection? Indeed, to the cells themselves cancer may seem a revival of faith. No, in relation to other people oblivion is sensible and sanitary.

This sea of others exasperates and fatigues me most on Sunday mornings. I don't know why people no longer go to church—whether they have lost the ability to sing or the willingness to listen. From eight-thirty onwards they crowd in from the parking lot, ants each carrying its crumb of baggage, until by noon, when the remote churches are releasing their gallant and gaily dressed minority, the sea itself is jammed with hollow heads and thrashing arms like a great bobbing backwash of rubbish. A transistor radio somewhere in the sand releases in a thin, apologetic gust the closing peal of a transcribed service. And right here, here at the very height of torpor and confusion, I slump, my eyes slit, and the blurred forms of Protestantism's errant herd seem gathered by the water's edge in impassioned poses of devotion. I seem to be lying dreaming in the infinite rock of space before Creation, and the actual scene I see is a vision of impossibility: a Paradise. For had we existed before the gesture that split the firmament, could we have conceived of our most obvious possession, our most platitudinous blessing, the moment, the single ever-present moment that we perpetually bring to our lips brimful?

So: be joyful. Be Joyful is my commandment. It is the message I read in your jiggle. Stretch your skins like pegged hides curing in the miracle of the sun's moment. Exult in your legs' scissoring, your waist's swivel. Romp; eat the froth; be children. I am here above you; I have given my youth that you may do this. I wait. The tides of time have treacherous undercurrents. You are borne continually towards the horizon. I have prepared myself; my muscles are instilled with everything that must be done. Someday my alertness will bear fruit; from near the horizon there will arise, delicious, translucent, like a green bell above the water, the call for help, the call, a call, it saddens me to confess, that I have yet to hear.

Luisa Valenzuela

I'm Your Horse in the Night

Translated from the Spanish by Deborah Bonner

The doorbell rang: three short rings and one long one. That was the signal, and I got up, annoyed and a little frightened; it could be them, and then again, maybe not; at these ungodly hours of the night it could be a trap. I opened the door expecting anything except him, face to face, at last.

He came in quickly and locked the door behind him before embracing me. So much in character, so cautious, first and foremost checking his—our—rear guard. Then he took me in his arms without saying a word, not even holding me too tight but letting all the emotions of our new encounter overflow, telling me so much by merely holding me in his arms and kissing me slowly. I think he never had much faith in words, and there he was, as silent as ever, sending me messages in the form of caresses.

We finally stepped back to look at one another from head to foot, not eye to eye, out of focus. And I was able to say Hello showing scarcely any surprise despite all those months when I had no idea where he could have been, and I was able to say

I thought you were fighting up north
I thought you'd been caught
I thought you were in hiding
I thought you'd been tortured and killed
I thought you were theorizing about the revolution in another country

Just one of many ways to tell him I'd been thinking of him, I hadn't stopped thinking of him or felt as if I'd been betrayed. And there he was, always so goddamn cautious, so much the master of his actions.

"Quiet, Chiquita. You're much better off not knowing what I've been up to."

Then he pulled out his treasures, potential clues that at the time eluded me: a bottle of cachaça and a Gal Costa record. What had he been up to in Brazil? What was he planning to do next? What had brought him back, risking his life, knowing they were after him? Then I stopped asking myself questions (quiet, Chiquita, he'd say). Come here, Chiquita, he was saying, and I chose to let myself sink into the joy of having him back again, trying not to worry. What would happen to us tomorrow, and the days that followed?

Cachaça's a good drink. It goes down and up and down all the right tracks, and then stops to warm up the corners that need it most. Gal Costa's voice is hot, she envelops us in its sound and half-dancing, half-floating, we reach the bed. We lie down and keep on staring deep into each other's eyes, continue caressing each other without allowing ourselves to give into the pure senses just yet. We continue recognizing, rediscovering each other.

Beto, I say, looking at him. I know that isn't his real name, but it's the only one I can call him out loud. He replies:

"We'll make it someday, Chiquita. but let's not talk now."

It's better that way. Better if he doesn't start talking about how we'll make it someday and ruin the wonder of what we're about to attain right now, the two of us, all alone.

"A noite eu so teu cavalo," Gal Costa suddenly sings from the record player.

"I'm your horse in the night," I translate slowly. And so as to bind him in a spell and stop him from thinking about other things:

"It's a saint's song, like in the *macumba*. Someone who's in a trance says she's the horse of the spirit who's riding her, she's his mount."

"Chiquita, you're always getting carried away with esoteric meanings and witchcraft. You know perfectly well that she isn't talking about spirits. If you're my horse in the night it's because I ride you, like this, see? . . . Like this . . . That's all."

It was so long, so deep and so insistent, so charged with affection that we ended up exhausted. I fell asleep with him still on top of me.

I'm your horse in the night.

The goddamn phone pulled me out in waves from a deep well. Making an enormous effort to wake up, I walked over to the receiver, thinking it could be Beto, sure, who was no longer by my side, sure, following his inveterate habit of running away while I'm asleep without a word about where he's gone. To protect me, he says.

From the other end of the line, a voice I thought belonged to Andrés— the one we call Andrés—began to tell me:

"They found Beto dead, floating down the river near the other bank. It looks as if they threw him alive out of a chopper. He's all bloated and decomposed after six days in the water, but I'm almost sure it's him."

"No, it can't be Beto," I shouted carelessly. Suddenly the voice no longer sounded like Andrés: it felt foreign, impersonal.

"You think so?"

"Who is this?" Only then did I think to ask. But that very moment they hung up.

Ten, fifteen minutes? How long must I have stayed there staring at the phone like an idiot until the police arrived? I didn't expect them. But, then again, how could I not? Their hands feeling me, their voices insulting and threatening, the house searched, turned inside out. But I already knew. So what did I care if they broke every breakable object and tore apart my dresser?

They wouldn't find a thing. My only real possession was a dream and they can't deprive me of my dreams just like that. My dream the night before, when Beto was there with me and we loved each other. I'd dreamed it, dreamed every bit of it, I was deeply convinced that I'd dreamed it all in the richest detail, even in full color. And dreams are none of the cops' business.

They want reality, tangible facts, the kind I couldn't even begin to give them.

Where is he, you saw him, he was here with you, where did he go? Speak up, or you'll be sorry. Let's hear you sing, bitch, we know he came to see you, where is he, where is he holed up? He's in the city, come on, spill it, we know he came to get you.

I haven't heard a word from him in months. He abandoned me, I haven't heard from him in months. He ran away, went underground. What do I know, he ran off with someone else, he's in another country. What do I know, he abandoned me, I hate him, I know nothing.

(Go ahead, burn me with your cigarettes, kick me all you wish, threaten, go ahead, stick a mouse in me so it'll eat my insides out, pull my nails out, do as you please. Would I make something up for that? Would I tell you he was here when a thousand years ago he left me forever?)

I'm not about to tell them my dreams. Why should they care? I haven't seen that so-called Beto in more than six months, and I loved him. The man simply vanished. I only run into him in my dreams, and they're bad dreams that often become nightmares.

Beto, you know now, if it's true that they killed you, or wherever you may be, Beto, I'm your horse in the night and you can inhabit me whenever you wish, even if I'm behind bars. Beto, now that I'm in jail I know that I dreamed you that night; it was just a dream. And if by some wild chance there's a Gal Costa record and a half-empty bottle of cachaça in my house, I hope they'll forgive me: I will them out of existence.

VILLIERS DE L'ISLE-ADAM

The Doctor's Heroism

To kill in order to cure!

—OFFICIAL MOTTO OF THE BROUSSAIS HOSPITAL

The extraordinary case of Doctor Hallidonhill is soon to be tried in London. The facts in the matter are these:

On the 20th of last May, the two great waiting rooms of the illustrious specialist were thronged with patients, holding their tickets in their hands.

At the entrance stood the cashier, wearing a long black frock coat; he took the indispensable fee of two guineas from each patient, tested the gold with a sharp tap of the hammer, and cried automatically, "All right."

In his glassed-in office, around which were ranged great tropical shrubs, each growing in a huge Japanese pot, sat the stiff little Doctor Hallidonhill. Beside him, at a little round table, his secretary kept writing out brief prescriptions. At the swinging doors, covered with red velvet studded with gold-headed nails, stood a giant valet whose duty it was to carry the feeble consumptives to the lobby whence they were lowered in a luxurious elevator as soon as the official signal, "Next!" had been given.

The patients entered with dim and glassy eyes, stripped to the waist, with their clothes thrown over their arms. As soon as they entered they received the application of the plessimeter and the tube on back and chest.

"Tick! tick! plaff! Breathe now! . . . Plaff . . . Good . . ."

Then followed a prescription dictated in a second or two; then the well-known "Next!"

Every morning for three years, between nine o'clock and noon, this procession of sufferers filed past.

On this particular day, May 20th, just at the stroke of nine, a sort of long skeleton, with wild, wandering eyes, cavernous cheeks, and nude torso that looked like a parchment-covered cage lifted occasionally by a racking cough—in short a being so wasted that it seemed impossible for him to live—came in with a blue-fox skin mantle thrown over his arm, and tried to keep himself from falling by catching at the long leaves of the shrubs.

"Tick, tick, plaff! Oh, the devil Can't do anything for you!" grumbled Doctor Hallidonhill. "What do you think I am—a coroner? In less than a week you will spit up the last cell of this left lung—the right is already riddled like a sieve! Next!"

The valet was just about to carry out the client, when the eminent therapeutist suddenly slapped himself on the forehead, and brusquely asked, with a dubious smile:

"Are you rich?"

"I'm a millionaire—much more than a millionaire," sobbed the unhappy being whom Hallidonhill thus peremptorily had dismissed from the world of the living.

"Very well, then. Go at once to Victoria Station. Take the eleven-o'clock express for Dover! Then the steamer for Calais. Then take the train from Calais to Marseilles—secure a sleeping car with steam in it! And then to Nice. There try to live on watercress for six months—nothing but watercress—no bread, no fruit, no wine, nor meats of any kind. One teaspoonful of iodized rainwater every two days. And watercress, watercress, watercress—pounded and brayed in its own juice . . . that is your only chance—and still, let me tell you this: this supposed cure I know of only through hearsay; it is being dinned into my ears all the time; I don't believe in it the least bit. I suggest it only because yours seems to be a hopeless case, yet I think it is worse than absurd. Still, anything is possible.. . . Next!"

The consumptive Croesus was carefully deposited in the cushioned car of the elevator; and the regular procession commenced through the office.

Six months later, the 3rd of November, just at the stroke of nine o'clock, a sort of giant, with a terrifying yet jovial voice whose tones shook every pane of glass in the doctor's office and set all the leaves of all the tropical plants a-tremble, a great chubby-cheeked colossus, clothed in rich furs —burst like a human bombshell through the sorrowful ranks of Doctor Hallidonhill's clients, and rushed, without ticket, into the sanctum of the Prince of Science, who had just come to sit down before his desk. He seized him round the body, and, bathing the wan and worn cheeks of the doctor in tears, kissed him noisily again and again. Then he set him down in his green armchair in an almost suffocated state.

"Two million francs—if you want," shouted the giant. "Or three million. I owe my breath to you—the sun, resistless passions, life—everything. Ask me for anything—anything at all."

"Who is this madman? Put him out of here," feebly protested the doctor, after a moment's prostration.

"Oh, no you don't," growled the giant, with a glance at the valet that made him recoil as from a blow. "The fact is," he continued, "I understand now, that even you, you my savior, cannot recognize me. I am the watercress man, the hopeless skeleton, the helpless patient. Nice. Watercress, watercress, watercress! Well, I've done my six months of watercress diet—look at your work now! See here—listen to that!"

And he began to drum upon his chest with two huge fists solid enough to shatter the skull of an ox.

"What!" cried the doctor, leaping to his feet, "you are—my gracious, are you the dying man whom I . . ."

"Yes, yes, a thousand times yes!" yelled the giant. "I am the very man. The moment I landed yesterday evening I ordered a bronze statue of you; and I will secure you a monument in Westminster when you die."

Then dropping himself upon an immense sofa, whose springs creaked and groaned beneath his weight, he continued with a sigh of delight, and a beatific smile:

"Ah, what a good thing life is!"

The doctor said something in a whisper, and the secretary and the valet left the room. Once alone with his resuscitated patient, Hallidonhill, stiff, wan and glacial as ever, stared at the giant's face in silence for a minute or two. Then, suddenly:

"Allow me, if you please, to take that fly off your forehead!"

And rushing forward as he spoke, the doctor pulled a short "Bulldog revolver" from his pocket, and quick as a flash fired into the left temple of the visitor.

The giant fell with his skull shattered, scattering his grateful brains over the carpet of the room. His hands thrashed automatically for a few moments.

In ten cuts of the doctor's scissors, through cloak, garments, and underwear, the dead man's breast was laid bare. The grave surgeon cut open the chest lengthwise, with a single stroke of his broad scalpel.

When, about a quarter of an hour later, a policeman entered the office to request Doctor Hallidonhill to go with him, he found him sitting calmly at his bloody desk, examining with a strong magnifying glass, an enormous pair of lungs that lay spread out before him. The Genius of Science was trying to find, from the case of the deceased, some satisfactory explanation of the more than miraculous action of watercress.

"Constable," he said as he rose to his feet, "I felt it necessary to kill that man, as an immediate autopsy of his case might, I thought, reveal to me a secret of the gravest importance, regarding the now degenerating vitality of the human species. That is why I did not hesitate, let me confess, *to sacrifice my conscience to my duty.*"

Needless to add that the illustrious doctor was almost immediately released upon a nominal bond, his liberty being of far more importance than his detention. This strange case, as I have said, is shortly to come up before the British Assizes.

We believe that this sublime crime will not bring its hero to the gallows; for the English, as well as ourselves, are fully able to comprehend *that the exclusive love of the Humanity of the Future without any regard for the individual of the Present is, in our own time, the one sole motive that ought to justify the acquittal under any circumstances, of the magnanimous Extremists of Science.*

HELENA VIVIEN VIRAMONTES

The Moths

I was fourteen years old when Abuelita° requested my help. And it seemed only fair. Abuelita had pulled me through the rages of scarlet fever by placing, removing and replacing potato slices on the temples of my fore-head; she had seen me through several whippings, an arm broken by a dare jump off Tío Enrique's° toolshed, puberty, and my first lie. Really, I told Amá,° it was only fair.

Not that I was her favorite granddaughter or anything special. I wasn't even pretty or nice like my older sisters and I just couldn't do the girl things they could do. My hands were too big to handle the fineries of crocheting or embroidery and I always pricked my fingers or knotted my colored threads time and time again while my sisters laughed and called me bull hands with their cute waterlike voices. So I began keeping a piece of jagged brick in my sock to bash my sisters or anyone who called me bull hands. Once, while we all sat in the bedroom, I hit Teresa on the forehead, right above her eyebrow and she ran to Amá with her mouth open, her hand over her eye while blood seeped between her fingers. I was used to the whippings by then.

I wasn't respectful either. I even went so far as to doubt the power of Abuelita's slices, the slices she said absorbed my fever. "You're still alive, aren't you?" Abuelita snapped back, her pasty gray eye beaming at me and burning holes in my suspicions. Regretful that I had let secret questions drop out of my mouth, I couldn't look into her eyes. My hands began to fan out, grow like a liar's nose until they hung by my side like low weights. Abuelita

°*Abuelita:* Grandmother
°*Tío Enrique:* Uncle Henry
°*Amá:* Mama

made a balm out of dried moth wings and Vicks and rubbed my hands, shaped them back to size and it was the strangest feeling. Like bones melting. Like sun shining through the darkness of your eyelids. I didn't mind helping Abuelita after that, so Amá would always send me over to her.

In the early afternoon Amá would push her hair back, hand me my sweater and shoes, and tell me to go to Mama Luna's. This was to avoid another fight and another whipping, I knew. I would deliver one last direct shot on Marisela's arm and jump out of our house, the slam of the screen door burying her cries of anger, and I'd gladly go help Abuelita plant her wild lilies or jasmine or heliotrope or cilantro or hierbabuena in red Hills Brothers coffee cans. Abuelita would wait for me at the top step of her porch holding a hammer and nail and empty coffee cans. And although we hardly spoke, hardly looked at each other as we worked over root transplants, I always felt her gray eye on me. It made me feel, in a strange sort of way, safe and guarded and not alone. Like God was supposed to make you feel.

On Abuelita's porch, I would puncture holes in the bottom of the coffee cans with a nail and a precise hit of a hammer. This completed, my job was to fill them with red clay mud from beneath her rose bushes, packing it softly, then making a perfect hole, four fingers round, to nest a sprouting avocado pit, or the spidery sweet potatoes that Abuelita rooted in mayonnaise jars with toothpicks and daily water, or prickly chayotes that produced vines that twisted and wound all over her porch pillars, crawling to the roof, up and over the roof, and down the other side, making her small brick house look like it was cradled within the vines that grew pear-shaped squashes ready for the pick, ready to be steamed with onions and cheese and butter. The roots would burst out of the rusted coffee cans and search for a place to connect. I would then feed the seedlings with water.

But this was a different kind of help, Amá said, because Abuelita was dying. Looking into her gray eye, then into her brown one, the doctor said it was just a matter of days. And so it seemed only fair that these hands she had melted and formed found use in rubbing her caving body with alcohol and marihuana, rubbing her arms and legs, turning her face to the window so that she could watch the Bird of Paradise blooming or smell the scent of clove in the air. I toweled her face frequently and held her hand for hours. Her gray wiry hair hung over the mattress. Since I could remember, she'd kept her long hair in braids. Her mouth was vacant and when she slept, her eyelids never closed all the way. Up close, you could see her gray eye beaming out the window, staring hard as if to remember everything. I never kissed her. I left the window open when I went to the market.

Across the street from Jay's Market there was a chapel. I never knew its denomination, but I went in just the same to search for candles. I sat down on one of the pews because there were none. After I cleaned my fingernails, I looked up at the high ceiling. I had forgotten the vastness of these places, the coolness of the marble pillars and the frozen statues with blank eyes. I was alone. I knew why I had never returned.

That was one of Apá's° biggest complaints. He would pound his hands on the table, rocking the sugar dish or spilling a cup of coffee and scream that if I didn't go to mass every Sunday to save my god-damn sinning soul, then I had no reason to go out of the house, period. Punto final. He would grab my arm and dig his nails into me to make sure I understood the importance of catechism. Did he make himself clear? Then he strategically directed his anger at Amá for her lousy ways of bringing up daughters, being disrespectful and unbelieving, and my older sisters would pull me aside and tell me if I didn't get to mass right this minute, they were all going to kick the holy shit out of me. Why am I so selfish? Can't you see what it's doing to Amá, you idiot? So I would wash my feet and stuff them in my black Easter shoes that shone with Vaseline, grab a missal and veil, and wave good-bye to Amá.

I would walk slowly down Lorena to First to Evergreen, counting the cracks on the cement. On Evergreen I would turn left and walk to Abuelita's. I liked her porch because it was shielded by the vines of the chayotes and I could get a good look at the people and car traffic on Evergreen without them knowing. I would jump up the porch steps, knock on the screen door as I wiped my feet and call Abuelita? mi Abuelita? As I opened the door and stuck my head in, I would catch the gagging scent of toasting chile on the placa. When I entered the sala, she would greet me from the kitchen, wringing her hands in her apron. I'd sit at the corner of the table to keep from being in her way. The chiles made my eyes water. Am I crying? No, Mama Luna, I'm sure not crying. I don't like going to mass, but my eyes watered anyway, the tears dropping on the tablecloth like candle wax. Abuelita lifted the burnt chiles from the fire and sprinkled water on them until the skins began to separate. Placing them in front of me, she turned to check the menudo. I peeled the skins off and put the flimsy, limp looking green and yellow chiles in the molcajete and began to crush and crush and twist and crush the heart out of the tomato, the clove of garlic, the stupid chiles that made me cry, crushed them until they turned into liquid under my bull hand. With a wooden spoon, I scraped hard to destroy the guilt, and my tears were gone. I put the bowl of chile next to a vase filled with freshly cut roses. Abuelita touched my hand and pointed to the bowl of menudo that steamed in front of me. I spooned some chile into the menudo and rolled a corn tortilla thin with the palms of my hands. As I ate, a fine Sunday breeze entered the kitchen and a rose petal calmly feathered down to the table.

I left the chapel without blessing myself and walked to Jay's. Most of the time Jay didn't have much of anything. The tomatoes were always soft and the cans of Campbell soups had rusted spots on them. There was dust on the tops of cereal boxes. I picked up what I needed: rubbing alcohol, five cans of chicken broth, a big bottle of Pine Sol. At first Jay got mad because I thought I had forgotten the money. But it was there all the time, in my back pocket.

°*Apá*: Papa, Daddy (baby's word for father).

When I returned from the market, I heard Amá crying in Abuelita's kitchen. She looked up at me with puffy eyes. I placed the bags of groceries on the table and began putting the cans of soup away. Amá sobbed quietly. I never kissed her. After a while, I patted her on the back for comfort. Finally: "¿Y mi Amá?" she asked in a whisper, then choked again and cried into her apron.

Abuelita fell off the bed twice yesterday, I said, knowing that I shouldn't have said it and wondering why I wanted to say it because it only made Amá cry harder. I guess I became angry and just so tired of the quarrels and beatings and unanswered prayers and my hands just there hanging helplessly by my side. Amá looked at me again, confused, angry, and her eyes were filled with sorrow. I went outside and sat on the porch swing and watched the people pass. I sat there until she left. I dozed off repeating the words to myself like rosary prayers: when do you stop giving when do you start giving when do you . . . and when my hands fell from my lap, I awoke to catch them. The sun was setting, an orange glow, and I knew Abuelita was hungry.

There comes a time when the sun is defiant. Just about the time when moods change, inevitable seasons of a day, transitions from one color to another, that hour or minute or second when the sun is finally defeated, finally sinks into the realization that it cannot with all its power to heal or burn, exist forever, there comes an illumination where the sun and earth meet, a final burst of burning red orange fury reminding us that although endings are inevitable, they are necessary for rebirths, and when that time came, just when I switched on the light in the kitchen to open Abuelita's can of soup, it was probably then that she died.

The room smelled of Pine Sol and vomit and Abuelita had defecated the remains of her cancerous stomach. She had turned to the window and tried to speak, but her mouth remained open and speechless. I heard you, Abuelita, I said, stroking her cheek, I heard you. I opened the windows of the house and let the soup simmer and overboil on the stove. I turned the stove off and poured the soup down the sink. From the cabinet I got a tin basin, filled it with lukewarm water and carried it carefully to the room. I went to the linen closet and took out some modest bleached white towels. With the sacredness of a priest preparing his vestments, I unfolded the towels one by one on my shoulders. I removed the sheets and blankets from her bed and peeled off her thick flannel nightgown. I toweled her puzzled face, stretching out the wrinkles, removing the coils of her neck, toweled her shoulders and breasts. Then I changed the water. I returned to towel the creases of her stretch-marked stomach, her sporadic vaginal hairs, and her sagging thighs. I removed the lint from between her toes and noticed a mapped birthmark on the fold of her buttock. The scars on her back which were as thin as the life lines on the palms of her hands made me realize how little I really knew of Abuelita. I covered her with a thin blanket and went into the bathroom. I washed my hands, and turned on the tub faucets and watched the water pour into the tub with vitality and steam. When it was full, I turned off the water and undressed. Then, I went to get Abuelita.

She was not as heavy as I thought and when I carried her in my arms, her body fell into a V, and yet my legs were tired, shaky, and I felt as if the distance between the bedroom and bathroom was miles and years away. Amá, where are you?

I stepped into the bathtub one leg first, then the other. I bent my knees slowly to descend into the water slowly so I wouldn't scald her skin. There, there, Abuelita, I said, cradling her, smoothing her as we descended, I heard you. Her hair fell back and spread across the water like eagle's wings. The water in the tub overflowed and poured onto the tile of the floor. Then the moths came. Small, gray ones that came from her soul and out through her mouth fluttering to light, circling the single dull light bulb of the bathroom. Dying is lonely and I wanted to go to where the moths were, stay with her and plant chayotes whose vines would crawl up her fingers and into the clouds; I wanted to rest my head on her chest with her stroking my hair, telling me about the moths that lay within the soul and slowly eat the spirit up; I wanted to return to the waters of the womb with her so that we would never be alone again. I wanted. I wanted my Amá. I removed a few strands of hair from Abuelita's face and held her small light head within the hollow of my neck. The bathroom was filled with moths, and for the first time in a long time I cried, rocking us, crying for her, for me, for Amá, the sobs emerging from the depths of anguish, the misery of feeling half born, sobbing until finally the sobs rippled into circles and circles of sadness and relief. There, there, I said to Abuelita, rocking us gently, there, there.

VOLTAIRE

Plato's Dream

Plato dreamed a lot, and people have dreamed no less since. It had seemed to him that human nature was once double, and that as a punishment for its faults it was divided into male and female.

He had proved that there can be only five perfect worlds, because there are only five regular bodies in mathematics. His *Republic* was one of his great dreams. He had also dreamed that sleep is born out of waking and waking out of sleep, and that we are sure to lose our eyesight if we look at an eclipse elsewhere than in a pool of water. In those days dreams gave a man a great reputation.

Here is one of his dreams, which is not one of the least interesting. It seemed to him that the great Demiurge, the eternal Geometrician, having populated infinite space with innumerable globes, decided to test the knowledge of the genii who had been witnesses of his works. He gave each of them a little piece of matter to arrange, much as Phidias and Zeuxis might have given their disciples statues and pictures to make, if it is permissible to compare small things with great.

Demogorgon° had as his share the bit of mud that is called *Earth;* and, having arranged it in the manner that we see today, he claimed to have made a masterpiece. He thought he had triumphed over envy, and was expecting praise, even from his colleagues; he was quite surprised to be received by them with hoots.

One of them, who was a very bad joker, said to him:

°Demogorgon: A mysterious, terrible, and evil divinity.

"Truly, you have worked very well: you have separated your world in two, and you have put a great space of water between the two hemispheres, so that there should be no communication between the two. They will freeze with cold at your two poles, they will die of heat at your equinoctial line. You have prudently established great deserts of sand, so that those who cross them may die of hunger and thirst. I am fairly content with your sheep, cows, and hens; but frankly I am none too much so with your snakes and spiders. Your onions and artichokes are very good things; but I don't see what your idea was in covering the earth with so many venomous plants, unless you had the intention of poisoning the inhabitants. Moreover it seems to me that you have formed about thirty kinds of monkeys, many more kinds of dogs, and only four or five kinds of men: it is true that you have given this last animal what you call reason; but in all conscience, that reason of his is too ridiculous and comes too close to madness. Moreover it appears to me that you set no great store by that two-footed animal, since you have given him so many enemies and so little defense, so many maladies and so few remedies, so many passions and so little wisdom. Apparently you do not want many of those animals to remain on earth; for, without counting the dangers to which you expose them, you have done your calculating so well that someday the smallpox will carry off regularly every year the tenth part of this species, and the sister of this smallpox° will poison the source of life in the remaining nine-tenths; and as if that were still not enough, you have so arranged things that half the survivors will be occupied in pleading suits, the other half in killing each other; no doubt they will be very much obliged to you, and that's a fine masterpiece you have made."

Demogorgon blushed: he fully sensed that there was moral evil and physical evil in the work he had done, but he maintained that there was more good than evil.

"It is easy to criticize," said he; "but do you think it is so easy to make an animal that is always reasonable, that is free, and that never abuses its liberty? Do you think that when a person has nine or ten thousand plants to cause to multiply, he can so easily keep some of these plants from having harmful qualities? Do you imagine that with a certain quantity of water, sand, mud, and fire, one can have neither sea nor desert? You, sir, who like to laugh, you have just arranged the planet Mars; we shall see how you made out with your two great bands, and what a fine effect your moonless nights make; we shall see whether among your people there is neither madness nor illness."

Indeed, the genii examined Mars, and they fell roughly upon the mocker. The serious genie who had molded Saturn was not spared; his colleagues, the makers of Jupiter, Mercury, Venus, each had reproaches to take.

They wrote fat volumes and pamphlets; they said witty things; they composed songs; they made each other look ridiculous; the factions grew bitter; finally the eternal Demiurge imposed silence on them all:

°smallpox: The pox, or syphilis.

"You have made," he said to them, "some things good and some bad, because you have much intelligence and because you are imperfect; your works will last only a few hundreds of millions of years, after which, having learned more, you will do better: it belongs to me alone to make things perfect and immortal."

That is what Plato was teaching his disciples. When he had finished speaking, one of them said to him: "And then you awoke."

ALICE WALKER

Roselily

Dearly Beloved,

She dreams; dragging herself across the world. A small girl in her mother's white robe and veil, knee raised waist high through a bowl of quicksand soup. The man who stands beside her is against this standing on the front porch of her house, being married to the sound of cars whizzing by on highway 61.

we are gathered here

Like cotton to be weighed. Her fingers at the last minute busily removing dry leaves and twigs. Aware it is a superficial sweep. She knows he blames Mississippi for the respectful way the men turn their heads up in the yard, the women stand waiting and knowledgeable, their children held from mischief by teachings from the wrong God. He glares beyond them to the occupants of the cars, white faces glued to promises beyond a country wedding, noses thrust forward like dogs on a track. For him they usurp the wedding.

in the sight of God

Yes, open house. That is what country black folks like. She dreams she does not already have three children. A squeeze around the flowers in her hands chokes off three and four and five years of breath. Instantly she is ashamed and frightened in her superstition. She looks for the first time at the preacher, forces humility into her eyes, as if she believes he is, in fact, a man of God. She can imagine God, a small black boy, timidly pulling the preacher's coattail.

to join this man and this woman

She thinks of ropes, chains, handcuffs, his religion. His place of worship. Where she will be required to sit apart with covered head. In Chicago, a word she hears when thinking of smoke, from his description of what a cinder was, which they never had in Panther Burn. She sees hovering over the heads of the clean neighbors in her front yard black specks falling, clinging, from the sky. But in Chicago. Respect, a chance to build. Her children at last from underneath the detrimental wheel. A chance to be on top. What a relief, she thinks. What a vision, a view, from up so high.

in holy matrimony.

Her fourth child she gave away to the child's father who had some money. Certainly a good job. Had gone to Harvard. Was a good man but weak because good language meant so much to him he could not live with Roselily. Could not abide TV in the living room, five beds in three rooms, no Bach except from four to six on Sunday afternoons. No chess at all. She does not forget to worry about her son among his father's people. She wonders if the New England climate will agree with him. If he will ever come down to Mississippi, as his father did, to try to right the country's wrongs. She wonders if he will be stronger than his father. His father cried off and on throughout her pregnancy. Went to skin and bones. Suffered nightmares, retching and falling out of bed. Tried to kill himself. Later told his wife he found the right baby through friends. Vouched for, the sterling qualities that would make up his character.

It is not her nature to blame. Still, she is not entirely thankful. She supposes New England, the North, to be quite different from what she knows. It seems right somehow to her that people who move there to live return home completely changed. She thinks of the air, the smoke, the cinders. Imagines cinders big as hailstones; heavy, weighing on the people. Wonders how this pressure finds its way into the veins, roping the springs of laughter.

If there's anybody here that knows a reason why

But of course they know no reason why beyond what they daily have come to know. She thinks of the man who will be her husband, feels shut away from him because of the stiff severity of his plain black suit. His religion. A lifetime of black and white. Of veils. Covered head. It is as if her children are already gone from her. Not dead, but exalted on a pedestal, a stalk that has no roots. She wonders how to make new roots. It is beyond her. She wonders what one does with memories in a brand-new life. This had seemed easy, until she thought of it. "The reasons why . . . the people who" . . . she thinks, and does not wonder where the thought is from.

these two should not be joined

She thinks of her mother, who is dead. Dead, but still her mother. Joined. This is confusing. Of her father. A gray old man who sold wild mink, rabbit, fox skins to Sears, Roebuck. He stands in the yard, like a man waiting for a train. Her young sisters stand behind her in smooth green dresses, with flowers in their hands and hair. They giggle, she feels, at the absurdity of the wedding. They are ready for something new. She thinks the man beside her should marry one of them. She feels old. Yoked. An arm seems to reach out from behind her and snatch her backward. She thinks of cemeteries and the long sleep of grandparents mingling in the dirt. She believes that she believes in ghosts. In the soil giving back what it takes.

together,

In the city. He sees her in a new way. This she knows, and is grateful. But is it new enough? She cannot always be a bride and virgin, wearing robes and veil. Even now her body itches to be free of satin and voile, organdy and lily of the valley. Memories crash against her. Memories of being bare to the sun. She wonders what it will be like. Not to have to go to a job. Not to work in a sewing plant. Not to worry about learning to sew straight seams in workingmen's overalls, jeans, and dress pants. Her place will be in the home, he has said, repeatedly, promising her rest she had prayed for. But now she wonders. When she is rested, what will she do? They will make babies—she thinks practically about her fine brown body, his strong black one. They will be inevitable. Her hands will be full. Full of what? Babies. She is not comforted.

let him speak

She wishes she had asked him to explain more of what he meant. But she was impatient. Impatient to be done with sewing. With doing everything for three children, alone. Impatient to leave the girls she had known since childhood, their children growing up, their husbands hanging around her, already old, seedy. Nothing about them that she wanted, or needed. The fathers of her children driving by, waving, not waving; reminders of times she would just as soon forget. Impatient to see the South Side, where they would live and build and be respectable and respected and free. Her husband would free her. A romantic hush. Proposal. Promises. A new life! Respectable, reclaimed, renewed. Free! In robe and veil.

or forever hold

She does not even know if she loves him. She loves his sobriety. His refusal to sing just because he knows the tune. She loves his pride. His blackness and his gray car. She loves his understanding of her *condition*. She thinks she loves the effort he will make to redo her into what he truly wants. His love of her makes her completely conscious of how unloved she was before. This is something; though it makes her unbearably sad. Melancholy. She blinks her eyes. Remembers she is finally being married, like other girls. Like other girls, women? Something strains upward behind her eyes. She thinks of the something as a rat trapped, cornered, scurrying to and fro in her head, peering through the windows of her eyes. She wants to live for once. But doesn't know quite what that means. Wonders if she has ever done it. If she ever will. The preacher is odious to her. She wants to strike him out of the way, out of her light, with the back of her hand. It seems to her he has always been standing in front of her, barring her way.

his peace.

The rest she does not hear. She feels a kiss, passionate, rousing, within the general pandemonium. Cars drive up blowing their horns. Firecrackers go off. Dogs come from under the house and begin to yelp and bark. Her husband's hand is like the clasp of an iron gate. People congratulate. Her children press against her. They look with awe and distaste mixed with hope at their new father. He stands curiously apart, in spite of the people crowding about to grasp his free hand. He smiles at them all but his eyes are as if turned inward. He knows they cannot understand that he is not a Christian. He will not explain himself. He feels different, he looks it. The old women thought he was like one of their sons except that he had somehow got away from them. Still a son, not a son. Changed.

She thinks how it will be later in the night in the silvery gray car. How they will spin through the darkness of Mississippi and in the morning be in Chicago, Illinois. She thinks of Lincoln, the president. That is all she knows about the place. She feels ignorant, *wrong*, backward. She presses her worried fingers into his palm. He is standing in front of her. In the crush of well-wishing people, he does not look back.

Commentary: Edwidge Danticat on "Crafting 'Roselily'"

Alice Walker's "Roselily" is one of my favorite short stories of all time. I first read it in college, at a moment when I was trying to make some important decision about my life. Was I going to be a teacher, or a writer? Once I graduated, would I remain in New York, where my family was also living, or would I start over somewhere else?

As these questions came to mind, I realized that while planning my future, I was struggling with the idea of doing whatever I wanted or considering what would ultimately be best for me. Perhaps this is why this story struck such a strong chord with me then, and still does now, as there are always moments in my life—and indeed in all our lives—when we must make extremely difficult choices, and even after the pros and cons have been weighed, it is no easier to tell whether or what we have chosen the right path.

"Roselily" details a young woman's reflections as she is being married. Often at weddings, we comment on the bride's appearance, how beautiful her face, her hair, her dress looks; however, we rarely stop to wonder what the bride, or the groom for that matter, is thinking. We simply assume that they are happy. If they seem the slightest bit hesitant, we dismiss their reservations by saying they have "cold feet." This story forces us to reconsider the notion that weddings are always fairy tale moments in women's lives. It encourages us to search beyond this bride's outer expressions and look deeper, into her thoughts. Rather than having the wedding guests, and curious passersby, examine the bride, it is she who examines them, even as she probes her own uncertainties about the marriage.

Through Roselily's recollections, we learn that she, by her own definition, is not a typical bride. A "stalk that has no roots," she feels that the wedding ceremony would be better suited for her young sisters who are part of the bridal party. She has four children, one of whom was conceived with a married man and given away to him and his wife. She is not certain that she loves the groom, just that she admires many things about him, among them his sobriety and his pride. The groom's religion—the story hints that he is a member of the Chicago-based Nation of Islam—is also a source of trepidation for her, as it requires her to wear a veil and sit apart from him during the service. This is obviously not the marriage of her dreams, but one she feels she cannot pass up because it will mean no longer having to work at a sewing plant and building a better life for her children and herself.

"Roselily" is written in a stream of consciousness style, a method of writing in which a character's emotions are presented as they occur. Since this story is told in third person, that is, we are reading the character's thoughts in the author's voice rather than in the character's own voice, the author weaves in the opening lines of the wedding ceremony and shows how they trigger different "streams" of thought in Roselily's mind.

There are two ways to read the story. One to follow the lines down the page and use the italicized fragments as headings for each section that follows. The other way is to first read the italicized lines together as one section and then the subsequent blocks of text without interruption. Either way you are in for a rich literary experience.

Writing teachers often tell their students that God is in the details. I have taken this to mean that a writer can create an extremely vivid and convincing world for the reader as he or she chooses evocative, dramatic details and successfully brings them together like patches in a quilt, or fragments in a puzzle.

This story is built around a string of magnificent details. Take for example Roselily's name. One might say that she is doubly a flower, one who failed to blossom in the way that she might have desired. Images of others flowers abound throughout the story. To mirror Roselily's own conflicted mind, in each instance, the flowers represent sadness rather than joy. Wearing her dead mother's "White robe and veil," Roselily feels like "cotton to be weighted." Her marriage is a trade, a barter of one kind of "quicksand soup" for another.

A writer who uses dramatic detail as masterfully as Alice Walker does here puts a great deal of trust in the reader. In other words, it is up to each of us to gather the pieces and put the puzzle together. Just as we do every day in our own lives.

MONICA WARE

Mislaid Plans

A rash of new bills came that morning. The letter from their insurance company announced the cancellation of their policies.

She sighed and rose wearily to tell her husband. The kitchen smelled of gas. On his desk she found the note.

"... the money from my life insurance will be enough for you and the children ..."

EUDORA WELTY

A Visit of Charity

It was mid-morning—a very cold, bright day. Holding a potted plant before her, a girl of fourteen jumped off the bus in front of the Old Ladies' Home, on the outskirts of town. She wore a red coat, and her straight yellow hair was hanging down loose from the pointed white cap all the little girls were wearing that year. She stopped for a moment beside one of the prickly dark shrubs with which the city had beautified the Home, and then proceeded slowly toward the building, which was of whitewashed brick and reflected the winter sunlight like a block of ice. As she walked vaguely up the steps she shifted the small pot from hand to hand; then she had to set it down and remove her mittens before she could open the heavy door.

"I'm a Campfire Girl. . . . I have to pay a visit to some old lady," she told the nurse at the desk. This was a woman in a white uniform who looked as if she were cold; she had close-cut hair which stood up on the very top of her head exactly like a sea-wave. Marian, the little girl, did not tell her that this visit would give her a minimum of only three points in her score.

"Acquainted with any of our residents?" asked the nurse. She lifted one eyebrow and spoke like a man.

"With any old ladies? No—but—that is, any of them will do," Marian stammered. With her free hand she pushed her hair behind her ears, as she did when it was time to study Science.

The nurse shrugged and rose. "You have a nice *multiflora cineraria* there," she remarked as she walked ahead down the hall of closed doors to pick out an old lady.

There was loose, bulging linoleum on the floor. Marian felt as if she were walking on the waves, but the nurse paid no attention to it. There was a smell in the hall like the interior of a clock. Everything was silent until, behind one of the doors, an old lady of some kind cleared her throat like a sheep bleating. This decided the nurse. Stopping in her tracks, she first extended her arm, bent her elbow, and leaned forward from the hips—all to examine the watch strapped to her wrist; then she gave a loud double-rap on the door.

"There are two in each room," the nurse remarked over her shoulder.

"Two what?" asked Marian without thinking. The sound like a sheep's bleating almost made her turn around and run back.

One old woman was pulling the door open in short, gradual jerks, and when she saw the nurse a strange smile forced her old face dangerously awry. Marian, suddenly propelled by the strong, impatient arm of the nurse, saw next the side-face of another old woman, even older, who was lying flat in bed with a cap on and a counterpane drawn up to her chin.

"Visitor," said the nurse, and after one more shove she was off up the hall.

Marian stood tongue-tied; both hands held the potted plant. The old woman, still with that terrible, square smile (which was a smile of welcome) stamped on her bony face, was waiting. . . . Perhaps she said something. The old woman in bed said nothing at all, and she did not look around.

Suddenly Marian saw a hand, quick as a bird claw, reach up in the air and pluck the white cap off her head. At the same time, another claw to match drew her all the way into the room, and the next moment the door closed behind her.

"My, my, my," said the old lady at her side.

Marian stood enclosed by a bed, a washstand and a chair; the tiny room had altogether too much furniture. Everything smelled wet—even the bare floor. She held on to the back of the chair, which was wicker and felt soft and damp. Her heart beat more and more slowly, her hands got colder and colder, and she could not hear whether the old women were saying anything or not. She could not see them very clearly. How dark it was! The window shade was down, and the only door was shut. Marian looked at the ceiling. . . . It was like being caught in a robbers' cave, just before one was murdered.

"Did you come to be our little girl for a while?" the first robber asked.

Then something was snatched from Marian's hand—the little potted plant.

"Flowers!" screamed the old woman. She stood holding the pot in an undecided way. "Pretty flowers," she added.

Then the old woman in bed cleared her throat and spoke. "They are not pretty," she said, still without looking around, but very distinctly.

Marian suddenly pitched against the chair and sat down in it.

"Pretty flowers," the first old woman insisted. "Pretty—pretty . . ."

Marian wished she had the little pot back for just a moment—she had forgotten to look at the plant herself before giving it away. What did it look like?

"Stinkweeds," said the other old woman sharply. She had a bunchy white forehead and red eyes like a sheep. Now she turned them toward Marian. The fogginess seemed to rise in her throat again, and she bleated, "Who—are—you?"

To her surprise, Marian could not remember her name. "I'm a Camp-fire Girl," she said finally.

"Watch out for the germs," said the old woman like a sheep, not addressing anyone.

"One came out last month to see us," said the first old woman.

A sheep or a germ? wondered Marian dreamily, holding on to the chair.

"Did not!" cried the other old woman.

"Did so! Read to us out of the Bible, and we enjoyed it!" screamed the first.

"Who enjoyed it!" said the woman in bed. Her mouth was unexpectedly small and sorrowful, like a pet's.

"We enjoyed it," insisted the other. "You enjoyed it—I enjoyed it."

"We all enjoyed it," said Marian, without realizing that she had said a word.

The first old woman had just finished putting the potted plant high, high on the top of the wardrobe, where it could hardly be seen from below. Marian wondered how she had ever succeeded in placing it there, how she could ever have reached so high.

"You mustn't pay any attention to old Addie," she now said to the little girl. "She's ailing today."

"Will you shut your mouth?" said the woman in bed. "I am not."

"You're a story."

"I can't stay but a minute—really, I can't," said Marian suddenly. She looked down at the wet floor and thought that if she were sick in here they would have to let her go.

With much to-do the first old woman sat down in a rocking chair—still another piece of furniture!—and began to rock. With the fingers of one hand she touched a very dirty cameo pin on her chest. "What do you do at school?" she asked.

"I don't know . . ." said Marian. She tried to think but she could not.

"Oh, but the flowers are beautiful," the old woman whispered. She seemed to rock faster and faster; Marian did not see how anyone could rock so fast.

"Ugly," said the woman in bed.

"If we bring flowers—" Marian began, and then fell silent. She had almost said that if Campfire Girls brought flowers to the Old Ladies' Home, the visit would count one extra point, and if they took a Bible with them on the bus and read it to the old ladies, it counted double. But the old woman had not listened, anyway; she was rocking and watching the other one, who watched back from the bed.

"Poor Addie is ailing. She has to take medicine—see?" she said, pointing a horny finger at a row of bottles on the table, and rocking so high that her black comfort shoes lifted off the floor like a little child's.

"I am no more sick than you are," said the woman in bed.

"Oh, yes you are!"

"I just got more sense than you have, that's all," said the other old woman, nodding her head.

"That's only the contrary way she talks when *you all* come," said the first old lady with sudden intimacy. She stopped the rocker with a neat pat of her feet and leaned toward Marian. Her hand reached over—it felt like a petunia leaf, clinging and just a little sticky.

"Will you hush! Will you hush!" cried the other one.

Marian leaned back rigidly in her chair.

"When I was a little girl like you, I went to school and all," said the old woman in the same intimate, menacing voice. "Not here—another town . . ."

"Hush!" said the sick woman. "You never went to school. You never came and you never went. You never were anything—only here. You never were born! You don't know anything. Your head is empty, your heart and hands and your old black purse are all empty, even that little old box that you brought with you you brought empty—you showed it to me. And yet you talk, talk, talk, talk, talk all the time until I think I'm losing my mind! Who are you? You're a stranger—a perfect stranger! Don't you know you're a stranger? Is it possible that they have actually done a thing like this to anyone—sent them in a stranger to talk, and rock, and tell away her whole long rigmarole? Do they seriously suppose that I'll be able to keep it up, day in, day out, night in, night out, living in the same room with a terrible old woman—forever?"

Marian saw the old woman's eyes grow bright and turn toward her. This old woman was looking at her with despair and calculation in her face. Her small lips suddenly dropped apart, and exposed a half circle of false teeth with tan gums.

"Come here, I want to tell you something," she whispered. "Come here!"

Marian was trembling, and her heart nearly stopped beating altogether for a moment.

"Now, now, Addie," said the first old woman. "That's not polite. Do you know what's really the matter with old Addie today?" She, too looked at Marian; one of her eyelids dropped low.

"The matter?" the child repeated stupidly. "What's the matter with her?"

"Why, she's mad because it's her birthday!" said the first old woman beginning to rock again and giving a little crow as though she had answered her own riddle.

"It is not, it is not!" screamed the old woman in bed. "It is not my birthday, no one knows when that is but myself, and will you please be quiet and say nothing more, or I'll go straight out of my mind!" She turned her eyes toward Marian again, and presently she said in the soft, foggy voice, "When the worst comes to the worst, I ring this bell, and the nurse comes." One of her hands was drawn out from under the patched counterpane—a thin little hand with enormous black freckles. With a finger which would not hold still she pointed to a little bell on the table among the bottles.

"How old are you?" Marian breathed. Now she could see the old woman in bed very closely and plainly, and very abruptly, from all sides, as in dreams. She wondered about her—she wondered for a moment as though there was nothing else in the world to wonder about. It was the first time such a thing had happened to Marian.

"I won't tell!"

The old face on the pillow, where Marian was bending over it, slowly gathered and collapsed. Soft whimpers came out of the small open mouth. It was a sheep that she sounded like—a little lamb. Marian's face drew very close, the yellow hair hung forward.

"She's crying!" She turned a bright, burning face up to the first old woman.

"That's Addie for you," the old woman said spitefully.

Marian jumped up and moved toward the door. For the second time, the claw almost touched her hair, but it was not quick enough. The little girl put her cap on.

"Well, it was a real visit," said the old woman, following Marian through the doorway and all the way out into the hall. Then from behind she suddenly clutched the child with her sharp little fingers. In an affected, high-pitched whine she cried, "Oh, little girl, have you a penny to spare for a poor old woman that's not got anything of her own? We don't have a thing in the world—not a penny for candy—not a thing! Little girl, just a nickel—a penny—"

Marian pulled violently against the old hands for a moment before she was free. Then she ran down the hall, without looking behind her and without looking at the nurse, who was reading *Field & Stream* at her desk. The nurse, after another triple motion to consult her wrist watch, asked automatically the question put to visitors in all institutions: "Won't you stay and have dinner with *us*?"

Marian never replied. She pushed the heavy door open into the cold air and ran down the steps.

Under the prickly shrub she stooped and quickly, without being seen, retrieved a red apple she had hidden there.

Her yellow hair under the white cap, her scarlet coat, her bare knees all flashed in the sunlight as she ran to meet the big bus rocketing through the street.

"Wait for me!" she shouted. As though at an imperial command, the bus ground to a stop.

She jumped on and took a big bite out of the apple.

First Person: Eudora Welty on Setting: "Place in Fiction"

Place is one of the lesser angels that watch over the racing hand of fiction, perhaps the one that gazes benignly enough from off to one side, while others, like character, plot, symbolic meaning, and so on, are doing a good deal of wing-beating about her chair, and feeling, who in my eyes carries the crown, soars highest of them all and rightly relegates place into the shade. Nevertheless, it is this lowlier angel that concerns us here. There have been signs that she has been rather neglected of late; maybe she could do with a little petitioning.

What place has place in fiction? It might be thought so modest a one that it can be taken for granted: the location of a novel; to use a term of the day, it may make the novel "regional." The term, like most terms used to pin down a novel, means little; and Henry James said there isn't any difference between "the English novel" and "the American novel," since there are only two kinds of novels at all, the good and the bad. Of course Henry James didn't stop there, and we all hate generalities, and so does place. Yet as soon as we step down from the general view to the close and particular, as writers must and readers may and teachers well know how to, and consider what good writing may be, place can be seen, in her own way, to have a great deal to do with that goodness, if not to be responsible for it. How so?

First, with the goodness—validity—in the raw material of writing. Second, with the goodness in the writing itself—the achieved world of appearance, through which the novelist has his whole say and puts his whole case. There will still be the lady, always, who dismissed *The Ancient Mariner* on grounds of implausibility. Third, with the goodness—the worth—in the writer himself: place is where he has his roots, place is where he stands; in his experience out of which he writes, it provides the base of reference; in his work, the point of view. Let us consider place in fiction in these three wide aspects.

Wide, but of course connected—vitally so. And if in some present-day novels the connection has apparently slipped, that makes a fresh reason for us to ponder the subject of place. For novels, besides being the pleasantest things imaginable, are powerful forces on the side. Mutual understanding in the world being nearly always, as now, at low ebb, it is comforting to remember that it is through art that one country can nearly always speak reliably to another, if the other can hear at all. Art, though, is never the voice of a country; it is an even more precious thing, the voice of the individual, doing its best to speak, not comfort of any sort, indeed, but truth. And the art that speaks it most unmistakably, most directly, most variously, most fully, is fiction; in particular, the novel.

Why? Because the novel from the start has been bound up in the local, the "real," the present, the ordinary day-to-day of human experience. Where the imagination comes in is in directing the use of all this. That use is endless, and there are only four words, of all the millions we've hatched, that a novel rules out: "Once upon a time." They make a story a fairy tale by the simple sweep of the remove—by abolishing the present and the place where we are instead of conveying them to us. Of course we shall have some sort of fairy tale with us always—just now it is the historical novel. Fiction is properly at work on the here and now, or the past made here and now; for in novels *we* have to be there. Fiction provides the ideal texture through which the feeling and meaning that permeate our own personal, present lives will best show through. For in his theme—the most vital and important part of the work at hand—the novelist has the blessing of the inexhaustible subject: you and me. You and me, here. Inside that generous scope and circumference—who could ask for anything more?—the novel can accommodate practically anything on earth; and has abundantly done so. The novel so long as it be *alive* gives pleasure, and must always give pleasure, enough to stave off the departure of the Wedding Guest forever, except for that one lady.

It is by the nature of itself that fiction is all bound up in the local. The internal reason for that is surely that *feelings* are bound up in place. The human mind is a mass of associations—associations more poetic even than actual. I say, "The Yorkshire Moors," and you will say, "*Wuthering Heights*," and I have only to murmur, "If Father were only alive—" for you to come back with "We could go to Moscow," which certainly is not even so. The truth is, fiction depends for its life on place. Location is the crossroads of circumstance, the proving ground of "What happened? Who's here? Who's coming?"—and that is the heart's field.

Unpredictable as the future of any art must be, one condition we may hazard about writing: of all the arts, it is the one least likely to cut the cord that binds it to its source. Music and dancing, while originating out of place—groves!—and perhaps invoking it still to minds pure or childlike, are no longer bound to dwell there. Sculpture exists out in empty space: that is what it commands and replies to. Toward painting, place, to be so highly visible, has had a curious and changing relationship. Indeed, wasn't it when landscape invaded painting, and painting was given, with the profane content, a narrative content, that this worked to bring on a revolution to the art? Impressionism brought not the likeness-to-life but the mystery of place onto canvas; it was the method, not the subject, that told this. Painting and writing, always the closest two of the sister arts (and in ancient Chinese days only the blink of an eye seems to have separated them), have each a still closer connection with place than they have with each other; but a difference lies in their respective requirements of it, and even further in the way they use it— the written word being ultimately as different from the pigment as the note of the scale is from the chisel.

One element, which has just been mentioned, is surely the underlying bond that connects all the arts with place. All of them celebrate its mystery. Where does this mystery lie? Is it in the fact that place has a more lasting identity than we have, and we unswervingly tend to attach ourselves to identity? Might the magic lie partly, too, in the *name* of the place—since that is what *we* gave it? Surely, once we have it named, we have put a kind of poetic claim on its existence; the claim works even out of sight—may work forever sight unseen. The Seven Wonders of the World still give us this poetic kind of gratification. And notice we do not say simply "The Hanging Gardens"—that would leave them dangling out of reach and dubious in nature; we say "The Hanging Gardens of Babylon," and there they are, before our eyes, shimmering and garlanded and exactly elevated to the Babylonian measurement.

DOROTHY WEST

The Richer, the Poorer

Over the years Lottie had urged Bess to prepare for her old age. Over the years Bess had lived each day as if there were no other. Now they were both past sixty, the time for summing up. Lottie had a bank account that had never grown lean. Bess had the clothes on her back, and the rest of her worldly possessions in a battered suitcase.

Lottie had hated being a child, hearing her parents' skimping and scraping. Bess had never seemed to notice. All she ever wanted was to go outside and play. She learned to skate on borrowed skates. She rode a borrowed bicycle. Lottie couldn't wait to grow up and buy herself the best of everything.

As soon as anyone would hire her, Lottie put herself to work. She minded babies, she ran errands for the old.

She never touched a penny of her money, though her child's mouth watered for ice cream and candy. But she could not bear to share with Bess, who never had anything to share with her. When the dimes began to add up to dollars, she lost her taste for sweets.

By the time she was twelve, she was clerking after school in a small variety store. Saturdays she worked as long as she was wanted. She decided to keep her money for clothes. When she entered high school, she would wear a wardrobe that neither she nor anyone else would be able to match.

But her freshman year found her unable to indulge so frivolous a whim, particularly when her admiring instructors advised her to think seriously of college. No one in her family had ever gone to college, and certainly Bess would never get there. She would show them all what she could do, if she put her mind to it.

She began to bank her money, and her bankbook became her most private and precious possession.

In her third year of high school she found a job in a small but expanding restaurant, where she cashiered from the busy hour until closing. In her last year of high school the business increased so rapidly that Lottie was faced with the choice of staying in school or working full time.

She made her choice easily. A job in hand was worth two in the future.

Bess had a beau in the school band, who had no other ambition except to play a horn. Lottie expected to be settled with a home and family while Bess was still waiting for Harry to earn enough to buy a marriage license.

That Bess married Harry straight out of high school was not surprising. That Lottie never married at all was not really surprising either. Two or three times she was halfway persuaded, but to give up a job that paid well for a homemaking job that paid nothing was a risk she was incapable of taking.

Bess's married life was nothing for Lottie to envy. She and Harry lived like gypsies, Harry playing in second-rate bands all over the country, even getting himself and Bess stranded in Europe. They were often in rags and never in riches.

Bess grieved because she had no child, not having sense enough to know she was better off without one. Lottie was certainly better off without nieces and nephews to feel sorry for. Very likely Bess would have dumped them on her doorstep.

That Lottie had a doorstep they might have been left on was only because her boss, having bought a second house, offered Lottie his first house at a price so low and terms so reasonable that it would have been like losing money to refuse.

She shut off the rooms she didn't use, letting them go to rack and ruin. Since she ate her meals out, she had no food at home, and did not encourage callers, who always expected a cup of tea.

Her way of life was mean and miserly, but she did not know it. She thought she lived frugally in her middle years so that she could live in comfort and ease when she most needed peace of mind.

The years, after forty, began to race. Suddenly Lottie was sixty, and retired from her job by her boss's son, who had no sentimental feeling about keeping her on until she was ready to quit.

She made several attempts to find other employment, but her dowdy appearance made her look old and inefficient. For the first time in her life Lottie would gladly have worked for nothing, to have some place to go, something to do with her day.

Harry died abroad, in a third-rate hotel, with Bess weeping as hard as if he had left her a fortune. He had left her nothing but his horn. There wasn't even money for her passage home.

Lottie, trapped by the blood tie, knew she would not only have to send for her sister, but take her in when she returned. It didn't seem fair that Bess should reap the harvest of Lottie's lifetime of self-denial.

It took Lottie a week to get a bedroom ready, a week of hard work and hard cash. There was everything to do, everything to replace or paint. When she was through the room looked so fresh and new that Lottie felt she deserved it more than Bess.

She would let Bess have her room, but the mattress was so lumpy, the carpet so worn, the curtains so threadbare that Lottie's conscience pricked her. She supposed she would have to redo that room, too, and went about doing it with an eagerness that she mistook for haste.

When she was through upstairs, she was shocked to see how dismal downstairs looked by comparison. She tried to ignore it, but with nowhere to go to escape it, the contrast grew more intolerable.

She worked her way from kitchen to parlor, persuading herself she was only putting the rooms to rights to give herself something to do. At night she slept like a child after a long and happy day of playing house. She was having more fun than she had ever had in her life. She was living each hour for itself.

There was only a day now before Bess would arrive. Passing her gleaming mirrors, at first with vague awareness, then with painful clarity, Lottie saw herself as others saw her, and could not stand the sight.

She went on a spending spree from the specialty shops to beauty salon, emerging transformed into a woman who believed in miracles.

She was in the kitchen basting a turkey when Bess rang the bell. Her heart raced, and she wondered if the heat from the oven was responsible.

She went to the door, and Bess stood before her. Stiffly she suffered Bess's embrace, her heart racing harder, her eyes suddenly smarting from the onrush of cold air.

"Oh, Lottie, it's good to see you," Bess said, but saying nothing about Lottie's splendid appearance. Upstairs Bess, putting down her shabby suitcase, said, "I'll sleep like a rock tonight," without a word of praise for her lovely room. At the lavish table, top-heavy with turkey, Bess said, "I'll take light and dark, both," with no marveling at the size of the bird, or that there was turkey for two elderly women, one of them too poor to buy her own bread.

With the glow of good food in her stomach, Bess began to spin stories. They were rich with places and people, most of them lowly, all of them magnificent. Her face reflected her telling, the joys and sorrows of her remembering, and above all, the love she lived by that enhanced the poorest place, the humblest person.

Then it was that Lottie knew why Bess had made no mention of her finery, or the shining room, or the twelve-pound turkey. She had not even seen them. Tomorrow she would see the room as it really looked, and Lottie as she really looked, and the warmed-over turkey in its second-day glory. Tonight she saw only what she had come seeking, a place in her sister's home and heart.

She said, "That's enough about me. How have the years used you?"

"It was me who didn't use them," said Lottie wistfully. "I saved for them. I saved for them. I forgot the best of them would go without my ever spending a day or a dollar enjoying them. That's my life story in those few words, a life never lived.

"Now it's too near the end to try."

Bess said, "To know how much there is to know is the beginning of learning to live. Don't count the years that are left us. At our time of life it's the days that count. You've too much catching up to do to waste a minute of a waking hour feeling sorry for yourself."

Lottie grinned, a real wide-open grin, "Well to tell the truth, I felt sorry for you. Maybe if I had any sense I'd feel sorry for myself, after all. I know I'm too old to kick up my heels, but I'm going to let you show me how. If I land on my head, I guess it won't matter, I feel giddy already, and I like it."

Oscar Wilde

The Artist

One evening there came into his soul the desire to fashion an image of *The Pleasure that abideth for a Moment*. And he went forth into the world to look for bronze. For he could only think in bronze.

But all the bronze of the whole world had disappeared, nor anywhere in the whole world was there any bronze to be found, save only the bronze of the image of *The Sorrow that endureth for Ever*.

Now this image he had himself, and with his own hands, fashioned, and had set it on the tomb of the one thing he had loved in life. On the tomb of the dead thing he had most loved had he set this image of his own fashioning, that it might serve as a sign of the love of man that dieth not, and a symbol of the sorrow of man that endureth for ever. And in the whole world there was no other bronze save the bronze of this image.

And he took the image he had fashioned, and set it in a great furnace, and gave it to the fire.

And out of the bronze of the image of *The Sorrow that endureth for Ever* he fashioned an image of *The Pleasure that abideth for a Moment*.

TENNESSEE WILLIAMS

Tent Worms

Billy Foxworth had been grumbling for days about the tent worms that were building great, sagging canopies of transparent gray tissue among the thickly grown berry trees that surrounded their summer cottage on the cape. His wife, Clara, had dreams and preoccupations of her own, and had listened without attention to these grumblings. Once in a while she had looked at him darkly and thought, If he but knew! He has more to worry about than those tent worms! "Tent worms? What are tent worms?" she once murmured dreamily, but her mind wandered off while he defined them to her. He must have gone on talking about them for quite a while, for her mind described a wide orbit among her private reflections before he brought her back to momentary attention by slamming his coffee cup down on the saucer and exclaiming irritably, "Stop saying 'Yes, yes, yes' when you're not listening to a goddamn word I say!"

"I heard you," she protested crossly. "You were maundering like an old woman about those worms! Am I supposed to sit here starry-eyed with excitement while you—"

"All right," he said. "You asked me what they were, and I was trying to tell you."

"I don't care what they are," she said. "Maybe they bother you, but they don't bother me."

"Stop being childish!" he snapped.

They had a sun terrace on the back of their cottage where Clara reclined in a deck chair all afternoon, enjoying her private reflections while Billy worked at his typewriter on the screened porch just within. For five years Clara had not thought about the future. She was thinking about it now.

It had become a tangible thing once more, owing to the information she had, to which Billy did not have access, in spite of the fact that it concerned Billy even more than herself, because it concerned what was happening to Billy that Billy did not or was not supposed to know about. No, he did not know about it, she was practically sure that he didn't, or if he did, it was only in his unconscious, kept back there because he refused to accept it or didn't even dare to suspect it. That was why he had become so childish this summer, maundering like an idiot about those worms when it was August and they would be leaving here soon, going back to New York, and certainly Billy would never come back here again and she, God knows—let the worms eat the whole place up, let them eat the trees and the house and the beach and the ocean itself as far as she was concerned!

But about three o'clock one afternoon she smelled smoke. She looked around and there was Billy with a torch of old newspapers, setting fire to the tent worms' canopies of webby gray stuff. There he was in his khaki shorts holding up a flaming torch of newspapers to the topmost branches of the little stunted trees where the tent worms had built their houses.

He was burning them out, childishly, senselessly, in spite of the fact that there were thousands of them. Yes, looking over the trees from the sun terrace she could see that the tent worms had spread their dominion from tree to tree till now, finally, near the end of the summer, there was hardly a tree that did not support one or more of the gray tissue canopies that devoured their leaves. Still Billy was attempting to combat them single-handed with his silly torches of paper.

Clara got up and let out a loud cry of derision.

"What in hell do you think you are doing!"

"I am burning out the tent worms," he answered gravely.

"Are you out of your mind? There are millions of them!"

"That's all right. I'm going to burn them all out before we leave here!"

She gave up. Turned away and sank back in her deck chair.

All that afternoon the burning continued. It was no good protesting, although the smoke and odor were quite irritating. The best that Clara could do was drink, and so she did. She made herself a thermos of Tom Collinses, and she drank them all afternoon while her husband attacked the insects with his paper torches. Along about five o'clock Clara Foxworth began to feel happy and carefree. Her dreams took a sanguine turn. She saw herself that winter in expensive mourning, in handsomely tailored black suits with a little severe jewelry and a cape of black furs, and she saw herself with various escorts, whose features were still indistinguishable, in limousines that purred comfortably through icy streets from a restaurant to a theater, from a theater to an apartment, not yet going to nightclubs so soon after—

Ah! Her attitude was healthy, she was not being insincere and pretending to feel what she didn't. Pity? Yes, she felt sorry for him but when love had ceased being five or six years ago, why make an effort to think it would be a loss?

Toward sundown the phone rang.

It rang so rarely now that the sound surprised her. Not only she but their whole intimate circle—of friends?—had drawn back from them into their own concerns, as actors disperse to their offstage lives when a curtain has fallen and they're released from performance.

She took her time about answering, having already surmised that the caller would be their doctor, and it was.

Professional cheer is uncheering.

"How's it going, sweetie?"

"How's what going?"

"Your escape from the poisonous vapors of the metropolis?"

"If that's a serious question, Doc, I'll give you a serious answer. Your patient is nostalgic for the poisonous vapors and so is creating some here."

"What, what?"

"Is the connection bad?"

"No, just wondered what you meant."

"I will enlighten you gladly. Billy, your patient, is polluting the air of our summer retreat by burning out something called tent worms. The smoke is suffocating, worse than carbon monoxide in a traffic jam in a tunnel. I'm coughing and choking and still he keeps at it."

"Well, at least he's still active."

"Oh, that he is. Would you like me to call him to the phone?"

"No, just tell him I—no, don't tell him I called, he might wonder why."

"Why in hell didn't you tell him so he'd know and—"

She didn't know how to complete her protestation so she cried into the phone: "I can't bear it, it's more than I can bear. My mind is full of awful, awful thoughts, speculations about how long I'll have to endure it, when will it be finished."

"Easy, sweetie."

"Easy for you, not me. And don't call me sweetie. I'm not a sweetie, there's nothing sweet about me. I've turned savage. Unless he stops burning those tent worms, I'm going to go, alone, back to the city, at least no diseased vegetation and paper torches, and him staggering out there. Got to hang up. He's coming toward the house."

"Clara, it's hard to be human, but for God's sake try."

"Can you tell me how to? Write me a prescription so that I can?"

She glanced out the picture window between the phone and the slow, exhausted return of Billy toward the sun deck, which the sun was deserting.

"Clara, love takes disguises. Your mind is probably full of fantasies that you'll dismiss with shame when this ordeal is over."

"You scored a point there. I'm full of fantasies of a bit of a future."

"You mentioned a prescription."

"Yes. What?"

"Recollection of how it was before."

"Seems totally unreal."

"Right now, yes, but try to."

"Thanks. I'll try to breathe. If only the sea wind would blow the smoke away. . . ."

When she returned to the sun deck he had completed his exhausted return. He had a defeated look and he had burned himself in several places and applied poultices of wet baking soda, which smelled disagreeably. He took the other sun chair and pulled it a little away from where his wife was reclining and turned it so that she wouldn't look at his face.

"Giving it up?" she murmured.

"Ran out of paper and matches," he answered faintly.

There was no more talk between them. The tide was returning shoreward, and now the smooth water was lapping quietly near them.

Tent worms, she said to herself.

Then she said it out loud: "Tent worms!"

"Why are you shouting about it, it's nothing to shout about. A blight on vegetation is like a blight on your body."

"This is just a place rented for summer and we'll never come back."

"A man in his youth is like a summer place," he said in such a soft, exhausted voice that she didn't catch it.

"What was that?"

He repeated it to her a little louder.

Then she knew that he knew. Their chairs remained apart on the sun deck as the sun disappeared altogether.

As dark falls, a pair of long companions respond to the instinct of drawing closer together.

Unsteadily she rose from her deck chair and hauled it closer to his. His scorched hand rested on his chair arm. After a while, the sentimental moon risen from the horizon to replace the sun's vigil, she placed her hand over his.

A chill wind of shared apprehension swept over the moonlit sun deck and their fingers wound together. She thought of their early passion for each other and how time had burned it down as he attempted to burn the tent worms away from their summer place to which they, no, would never return, separately or together.

S. L. WISENBERG

Big Ruthie Imagines
Sex without Pain

Ruthie imagines sex without pain. She imagines it the way she tries to reconstruct dreams, really reconstruct. Or builds an image while she is praying. She imagines a blue castle somewhere on high, many steps, a private room, fur rug, long mattress, white stucco walls, tiny windows. She imagines leaving her body. It frightens her. If she leaves her body, leaves it cavorting on the bed/fur rug/kitchen table (all is possible when there is sex without pain), she may not get it back. Her body may just get up and walk away, without her, wash itself, apply blusher mascara lipstick, draw up her clothes around it, take her purse and go out to dinner. Big Ruthie herself will be left on the ceiling, staring down at the indentations on the mattress and rug, wishing she could reach down and take a book from a shelf. She does not now nor has she ever owned a fur rug. But when Big Ruthie achieves sex without pain, she will have a fluffy fur rug. Maybe two. White, which she'll send to the cleaners, when needed.

She imagines sex without pain: an end to feeling Ruben tear at her on his way inside, scuffing his feet so harshly at her door, unwitting, can't help himself, poor husband of hers.

She knows there is a name for it. She has looked it up in various books and knows it is her fault. All she must do is relax. It was always this way, since the honeymoon. Of course the first months she told herself it was the newness. She is so big on the outside, so wide of hip, ample of waist, how could this be—a cosmic joke?—this one smallness where large, extra large would have smoothed out the wrinkles in her marriage bed? When all her clothes are size 18 plus elastic, why does this one part of her refuse to grow along with her? At first she thought, The membranes will stretch. Childbirth

426

will widen. Heal and stretch, heal and stretch. But no. She has never healed, never quite healed. From anything. She carries all her scars from two child-hood dog bites, from a particularly awful bee sting. I am marked, she thinks.

Ruben is the only lover she has ever had. "OK, God," Big Ruthie says, well into her thirty-fifth year, "I'm not asking for sex without ambivalence or sex without tiny splinters of anger/resentment. I am not even asking, as per usual, for a new body, a trade-in allowance for my ever-larger and -larger layers of light cream mounds. I am not asking you to withdraw my name-sake candy bar from the market, to wipe its red-and-white wrapper from the face of the earth. I have grown used to the teasing. It's become second na-ture, in fact. And I am not asking you to cause my avoirdupois, my spare tire and trunk, to melt in one great heavenly glide from my home to yours. I am only asking for a slight adjustment. One that I cannot change by diet alone. As if I have ever changed any part or shape of my body through diet. For once I am not asking you to give me something that just looks nice. Make me, O Lord, more internally accommodating." Big Ruthie, turning thirty-five, prays. Alone, in bed.

She is afraid.

She is afraid she will lose herself, her body will siphon out into Ruben's, the way the ancient Egyptians removed the brains of their dead through the nose. Ruthie wants to carve out an inner largeness, yet fears she will become ghostlike, as see-through as a negligee, an amoeba, one of those floaters you get in your eye that's the size of an inchworm. A transparent cell. Mitosis, meiosis. She will be divided and conquered. She imagines her skin as nothing more than a bag, a vacuum-cleaner bag, collapsing when you turn off the control. No sound, no motion, no commotion, all the wind sucked out of her. Still. A fat polar bear lying on the rug. Hibernating with-out end. No one will be able to wake Big Ruthie or move her in order to vac-uum. No one.

She mentioned it once, timidly, to the ob/gyn man. He patted her on the knee. Mumbled about lubrication. Maybe the pain didn't really exist, Big Ruthie thought. Maybe it was her imagination and this was the intensity of feeling they talked about. But it is pain. It combines with that other feeling so that she wants it and doesn't want it, can't push this word away from her brain: *invaded*. My husband is invading me. He makes her feel rough and red down there. As if he's made of sandpaper. Even with the lubricant they bought. It makes her want to cry and sometimes she does, afterward, turning her head away. How could her Ellen and Cecilia fit through there and not her Ruben?

Still Big Ruthie imagines sex without pain, imagines freedom: f——ing out of doors. In picnic groves. She imagines longing for it during the day, as she vacuums, sweeps, wipes dishes, changes diapers, slices cheese for sand-wiches, bathes her daughters, reads them stories. She imagines it like a tune from the radio trapped in her mind. It will overtake her, this sex without pain, this wanting, this sweet insistence. A rope will pull her to bed. Beds. Fur rugs. Rooftops. Forests, tree houses. She imagines doing it without thinking. Her family does nothing without thinking, worrying, wringing, twisting hands, with a spit and glance over the shoulder at the evil eye. At Lilith, strangler of children, Adam's first wife, who wanted to be on top. Who wanted sex without pain. Whenever she wanted.

Sometimes Ruthie begins. She might tickle Ruben. She might hope: This time, this time, because I started it, we will share one pure, smooth sweep, one glide, a note a tune a long song, as sweet as pleasant as a kiss. She thinks, if she can conquer this, get over this obstacle, she of two children, a house, and a husband—if she, Big Ruthie, can find her way to this sex without pain—then Ruben would be able to rope her, he would be able to lasso her from the next room, from across the house. She would begin to rely on him, and on sex, on sex without pain. Then any man would be able, with a nod of his head, a wink of his eye, to pull her to him. Ruthie and Anyman with a fur rug, without a fur rug. Big Ruthie will advertise herself: a woman who has sex without pain. She will become a woman in a doorway, a large woman blocking a large doorway, foot behind her, against the door, a thrust to her head, a toss, a wafting of her cigarette. Big Ruthie will start to smoke, before, after, and during.

Nothing will stop her. She will be expert. Till she can do it in her sleep. With her capable hands, with her ever-so-flexible back, front, sides, mouth. With the mailman, roofer, plumber; she could become the plumber's assistant, he, hers. She will go at it. She will not be ladylike. She will be a bad girl. She will swing on a swing in a goodtime bar. She will become a goodtime girl, wearing garters that show, no girdle at all, black lace stockings rounded by her thighs and calves, brassy perfume that trails her down the street. People will know: That is Big Ruthie's scent. She will have a trademark, a signature.

Big Ruthie, the goodtime girl.

Fleshy Ruthie, the goodtime girl.

Bigtime Ruthie. Twobit Ruthie.

Ruthie knows that other people have sex without pain. Men, for instance. Ruben. She has watched his eyes squint in concentrated delight. She herself sometimes cries out, the way he does, but she knows his is a pure kind of white kind of pleasure, while hers is dark, gray, troubled. It hurts on the outside just as he begins and moments later when he moves inside her. This was Eve's curse—not bleeding or cramps, not childbirth, but this— hurts as much as what? As the times Ruben doesn't shave and he kisses her and leaves her cheeks and chin pink and rough for days. But this is worse.

If she could have sex without pain, she would have sex without fear, and without fear of sex without pain.

Then the thought of no sex at all would make her afraid, more than she is now of sex with pain, more than she is afraid of losing her body, more than she is afraid of never losing it, never being light.

Ruben said once she was insatiable. This is because she squirmed and writhed, wanting to savor everything, all the moments that led to the act; she wanted to forestall the act of sex with pain. When she has sex without pain, she will go on forever, single-minded of purpose. One-track mind. She is afraid she will forget everything—will forget the multiplication table, the rule for *i* before *e*, to take her vitamins, when to add bleach, how to can fruit, drive, run a Hadassah meeting using *Robert's Rules of Order*, bind newspapers for the Scouts' paper drives, change diapers, speak Yiddish, follow along in the Hebrew, sing the Adon Olam, make round ground balls of things: gefilte fish, matzah balls. Ruthie will become a performer, a one-note gal, one-trick pony, performing this sex without pain, her back arcing like a circus artist on a trapeze, a girl in a bar in the French Quarter. "You cannot contain yourself," Ruben will say, turning aside. She will feel as if she is overflowing the cups of her bra. Her body will fill the streets. People will say, "That Ruthie sure wants it."

She tries to avoid it. So does Ruben. They are sleepy. Or the children keep them awake, worrying. There is less and less time for it. When they travel and stay in hotels, the girls stay in the room with them, to save money for sightseeing. Ruben still kisses her, in the morning and when he comes home from work, after he removes his hat.

But if she and Ruben could have sex without pain, there would be no dinner for him waiting hot and ready at the table. Big Ruthie would ignore all her duties. She would become captive to it. Body twitching. Wet. Rivulets. She would no longer be in control. No longer in the driver's seat, but in back, necking, petting, dress up, flounces up, panties down or on the dash, devil-maycare, a hand on her——. "Sorry, officer, we had just stopped to look for—." "We were on our way home, must have fallen asleep—."

Sex would become like chocolate fudge. Like lemon-meringue pie. Like pearls shimmering under a chandelier. Or van Gogh close enough to see the paint lines. Blue-gray clouds after a rainstorm. Loveliness. Would Big Ruthie ever sleep?

> *Big Ruthie's life will become a dream, a dream of those blue castles with long mattresses she will lie across, will f——k in, far away, will never ever come back from, the place high on the improbable hill of sex without pain, the impossible land of sex without pain.*
>
> *There in the castle she will find the Messiah himself. He too is insatiable. She will welcome him inside her. She will long for him, miss his rhythms, when he departs her body. Up there in his castle, she will keep him from descending to do his duty for at least another forty years. In his land of sex without pain, she and he will tarry.*

Tobias Wolff

Powder

Just before Christmas my father took me skiing at Mount Baker. He'd had to fight for the privilege of my company, because my mother was still angry with him for sneaking me into a nightclub during his last visit, to see Thelonious Monk.

He wouldn't give up. He promised, hand on heart, to take good care of me and have me home for dinner on Christmas Eve, and she relented. But as we were checking out of the lodge that morning it began to snow, and in this snow he observed some rare quality that made it necessary for us to get in one last run. We got in several last runs. He was indifferent to my fretting. Snow whirled around us in bitter, blinding squalls, hissing like sand, and still we skied. As the lift bore us to the peak yet again, my father looked at his watch and said, "Criminy. This'll have to be a fast one."

By now I couldn't see the trail. There was no point in trying. I stuck to him like white on rice and did what he did and somehow made it to the bottom without sailing off a cliff. We returned our skis and my father put chains on the Austin-Healey while I swayed from foot to foot, clapping my mittens and wishing I was home. I could see everything. The green tablecloth, the plates with the holly pattern, the red candles waiting to be lit.

We passed a diner on our way out. "You want some soup?" my father asked. I shook my head. "Buck up," he said. "I'll get you there. Right, doctor?"

I was supposed to say, "Right, doctor," but I didn't say anything.

A state trooper waved us down outside the resort. A pair of sawhorses were blocking the road. The trooper came up to our car and bent down to my father's window. His face was bleached by the cold. Snowflakes clung to his eyebrows and to the fur trim of his jacket and cap.

"Don't tell me," my father said.

The trooper told him. The road was closed. It might get cleared, it might not. Storm took everyone by surprise. So much, so fast. Hard to get people moving. Christmas Eve. What can you do.

My father said, "Look. We're talking about five, six inches. I've taken this car through worse than that."

The trooper straightened up. His face was out of sight but I could hear him. "The road is closed."

My father sat with both hands on the wheel, rubbing the wood with his thumbs. He looked at the barricade for a long time. He seemed to be trying to master the idea of it. Then he thanked the trooper, and with a weird, old-maidy show of caution turned the car around. "Your mother will never forgive me for this," he said.

"We should have left before," I said. "Doctor."

He didn't speak to me again until we were in a booth at the diner, waiting for our burgers. "She won't forgive me," he said. "Do you understand? Never."

"I guess," I said, but no guesswork was required; she wouldn't forgive him.

"I can't let that happen." He bent toward me. "I'll tell you what I want. I want us all to be together again. Is that what you want?"

"Yes, sir."

He bumped my chin with his knuckles. "That's all I needed to hear."

When we finished eating he went to the pay phone in the back of the diner, then joined me in the booth again. I figured he'd called my mother, but he didn't give a report. He sipped at his coffee and stared out the window at the empty road. "Come on, come on," he said, though not to me. A little while later he said it again. When the trooper's car went past, lights flashing, he got up and dropped some money on the check. "Okay. Vamanos."

The wind had died. The snow was falling straight down, less of it now and lighter. We drove away from the resort, right up to the barricade. "Move it," my father told me. When I looked at him he said, "What are you waiting for?" I got out and dragged one of the sawhorses aside, then put it back after he drove through. He pushed the door open for me. "Now you're an accomplice," he said. "We go down together." He put the car into gear and gave me a look. "Joke, son."

Down the first long stretch I watched the road behind us, to see if the trooper was on our tail. The barricade vanished. Then there was nothing but snow: snow on the road, snow kicking up from the chains, snow on the trees, snow in the sky; and our trail in the snow. Then I faced forward and had a shock. The lay of the road behind us had been marked by our own tracks, but there were no tracks ahead of us. My father was breaking virgin snow between a line of tall trees. He was humming "Stars Fell on Alabama." I felt snow brush along the floorboards under my feet. To keep my hands from shaking I clamped them between my knees.

My father grunted in a thoughtful way and said, "Don't ever try this yourself."

"I won't."

"That's what you say now, but someday you'll get your license and then you'll think you can do anything. Only you won't be able to do this. You need, I don't know—a certain instinct."

"Maybe I have it."

"You don't. You have your strong points, but not this. I only mention it because I don't want you to get the idea this is something just anybody can do. I'm a great driver. That's not a virtue, okay? It's just a fact, and one you should be aware of. Of course you have to give the old heap some credit, too. There aren't many cars I'd try this with. Listen!"

I did listen. I heard the slap of the chains, the stiff, jerky rasp of the wipers, the purr of the engine. It really did purr. The old heap was almost new. My father couldn't afford it, and kept promising to sell it, but here it was.

I said, "Where do you think that policeman went to?"

"Are you warm enough?" He reached over and cranked up the blower. Then he turned off the wipers. We didn't need them. The clouds had brightened. A few sparse, feathery flakes drifted into our slipstream and were swept away. We left the trees and entered a broad field of snow that ran level for a while and then tilted sharply downward. Orange stakes had been planted at intervals in two parallel lines and my father steered a course between them, though they were far enough apart to leave considerable doubt in my mind as to exactly where the road lay. He was humming again, doing little scat riffs around the melody.

"Okay then. What are my strong points?"

"Don't get me started," he said. "It'd take all day."

"Oh, right. Name one."

"Easy. You always think ahead."

True. I always thought ahead. I was a boy who kept his clothes on numbered hangers to insure proper rotation. I bothered my teachers for homework assignments far ahead of their due dates so I could draw up schedules. I thought ahead, and that was why I knew that there would be other troopers waiting for us at the end of our ride, if we even got there. What I did not know was that my father would wheedle and plead his way past them—he didn't sing "O Tannenbaum," but just about—and get me home for dinner, buying a little more time before my mother decided to make the split final. I knew we'd get caught; I was resigned to it. And maybe for this reason I stopped moping and began to enjoy myself.

Why not? This was one for the books. Like being in a speedboat, only better. You can't go downhill in a boat. And it was all ours. And it kept coming, the laden trees, the unbroken surface of snow, the sudden white vistas. Here and there I saw hints of the road, ditches, fences, stakes, but not so many that I could have found my way. But then I didn't have to. My father was driving. My father in his forty-eighth year, rumpled, kind, bankrupt of honor, flushed with certainty. He was a great driver. All persuasion, no coercion. Such subtlety at the wheel, such tactful pedalwork. I actually trusted him. And the best was yet to come—switchbacks and hairpins impossible to describe. Except maybe to say this: if you haven't driven fresh powder, you haven't driven.

Virginia Woolf

A Haunted House

Whatever hour you woke there was a door shutting. From room to room they went, hand in hand, lifting here, opening there, making sure—a ghostly couple.

"Here we left it," she said. And he added, "Oh, but here too!" "It's upstairs," she murmured. "And in the garden," he whispered. "Quietly," they said, "or we shall wake them."

But it wasn't that you woke us. Oh, no. "They're looking for it; they're drawing the curtain," one might say, and so read on a page or two. "Now they've found it," one would be certain, stopping the pencil on the margin. And then, tired of reading, one might rise and see for oneself, the house all empty, the doors standing open, only the wood pigeons bubbling with content and the hum of the threshing machine sounding from the farm. "What did I come in here for? What did I want to find?" My hands were empty. "Perhaps it's upstairs then?" The apples were in the loft. And so down again, the garden still as ever, only the book had slipped into the grass.

But they had found it in the drawing-room. Not that one could ever see them. The window panes reflected apples, reflected roses; all the leaves were green in the glass. If they moved in the drawing-room, the apple only turned its yellow side. Yet, the moment after, if the door was opened, spread about the floor, hung upon the walls, pendant from the ceiling—what? My hands were empty. The shadow of a thrush crossed the carpet; from the deepest wells of silence the wood pigeon drew its bubble of sound. "Safe, safe, safe," the pulse of the house beat softly. "The treasure buried; the room . . ." the pulse stopped short. Oh, was that the buried treasure?

A moment later the light had faded. Out in the garden then? But the trees spun darkness for a wandering beam of sun. So fine, so rare, coolly sunk beneath the surface the beam I sought always burnt behind the glass. Death was the glass; death was between us; coming to the woman first, hundreds of years ago, leaving the house, sealing all the windows; the rooms were darkened. He left it, left her, went North, went East, saw the stars turned in the Southern sky; sought the house, found it dropped beneath the Downs. "Safe, safe, safe," the pulse of the house beat gladly. "The Treasure yours."

The wind roars up the avenue. Trees stoop and bend this way and that. Moonbeams splash and spill wildly in the rain. But the beam of the lamp falls straight from the window. The candle burns stiff and still. Wandering through the house, opening the windows, whispering not to wake us, the ghostly couple seek their joy.

"Here we slept," she says. And he adds, "Kisses without number." "Waking in the morning—" "Silver between the trees—" "Upstairs—" "In the garden—" "When summer came—" "In winter snowtime—" The doors go shutting far in the distance, gently knocking like the pulse of a heart.

Nearer they come; cease at the doorway. The wind falls, the rain slides silver down the glass. Our eyes darken; we hear no steps beside us; we see no lady spread her ghostly cloak. His hands shield the lantern. "Look," he breathes. "Sound asleep. Love upon their lips."

Stooping, holding their silver lamp above us, long they look and deeply. Long they pause. The wind drives straightly; the flame stoops slightly. Wild beams of moonlight cross both floor and wall, and, meeting, stain the faces bent; the faces pondering; the faces that search the sleepers and seek their hidden joy.

"Safe, safe, safe," the heart of the house beats proudly. "Long years—" he sighs. "Again you found me." "Here," she murmurs, "sleeping; in the garden reading; laughing, rolling apples in the loft. Here we left our treasure—" Stooping, their light lifts the lids upon my eyes. "Safe! safe! safe!" the pulse of the house beats wildly. Waking, I cry "Oh, is this *your* buried treasure? The light in the heart."

Instructions for Crafting
Very Short Stories

1. Determine what you are trying to show the reader about the world or human beings. What you decide will be your predetermined goal, and every stylistic element in your story must work toward that end or be discarded, regardless of brilliance.
2. Develop the story's structure, and, if applicable, consider the best ways in which to dramatize the forces in opposition, the major problem and how the major problem is resolved.
3. Based on your predetermined goal, choose your voice, point of view, and setting, as well as the additional tools you will employ to achieve your objective, such as symbolism, dialogue, or perhaps dramatic monologue: The choice is entirely up to you.
4. Write a rough draft without worrying about getting anything right the first time. Hemingway once said all writing is revision.
5. Edit your draft for logic, clarity, and plausibility. If you must read a sentence twice to understand it, consider recasting it. You may want to experiment with structure, point of view, and voice until you feel you are closer to your desired effect. Give your work time to breathe between edit sessions. The goal is to come back to it with fresh eyes and an objective perspective. Part of your editing process should include, if at all possible, constructive criticism from an objective and knowledgeable source. Listen to the critique without rebuttal and thank the person for taking the time to read your work. Keep in mind that very short stories can be intense. You have to focus and control the material. If you can't control it and there are inconsistencies in technique, such as voice, you are probably still too close to the material to write about it effectively.
6. Have compassion for all of your characters.

7. Write down everything related to your story, wherever you may be. You may discard 95 percent of what you jot down, but the balance may prove quite helpful to your story.

8. Continually read excellent fiction. Analyze the devices used and ascertain why they succeed.

9. Continually write fiction, nonfiction, and poetry. They all serve to improve your communication skills, which may prove beneficial later in life when you must write succinct, cogent, and clear e-mails, memos, or reports.

10. Consider creating a subtle and symmetrical conclusion by echoing a critical detail appearing earlier in your story.

Exercises

Write a very short story (55 to 1,500 words) about one of the following:
1. A wedding
2. A funeral
3. A religious rite-of-passage ceremony, such as a first communion or a bar mitzvah
4. A traumatic incident
5. A family gathering
6. Someone you noticed but did not know at a social event
7. Two voters arguing outside a polling booth
8. A humorous incident
9. Someone who you do not know, but who lives in your dorm, apartment, or neighborhood. Imagine that he or she is grappling with a major life issue, such as losing a scholarship or being downsized.
10. A romantic relationship that went well or poorly
11. A college student who is considering dropping out, or worse
12. A parent and sibling embattled in a test of wills
13. Two siblings who constantly fight with each other or compete for their parents' affection
14. A fictitious doctor or actor whose life is spiraling out of control
15. A religious day or time of year, like Ramadan, Christmas or Hanukkah
16. A friendship that blossoms as a result of trust or fades as a result of deceit
17. A ghost
18. Courage
19. Love
20. Perseverance

Glossary

Allegory   Narrative that symbolizes a second and often higher meaning.

A Very Short Story   Fictional narrative typically ranging from one paragraph to six book-length pages; or between 30 and 1,500 words. The very short story's primary stylistic features are voice, point of view and setting.

Diction   Word choice. For example, standard English, regional vernacular, flowery language or slang.

Dialogue   Conversation between two or more people that propels a story forward and reveals character.

Dramatic Monologue   Story in which a character speaks directly to the reader about a crisis.

Fable   Story, often with animals that have human characteristics, that provides a moral lesson.

Folktale   Very short story that is a rich part of a culture's literary tradition, such as a fairy tale.

Imagery   Figurative language that summons in the reader's mind a picture related to one of the five senses, such as the aroma from a steaming cup of hot chocolate.

Naturalism   Stories that show characters lives determined by forces beyond their control.

Parable   Short narrative constructed to convey a moral principle.

Point of View   The perspective of the story's narrator. First-person point of view ("I lifted his bullet-riddled body and.. . .") typically conveys a sense of urgency, and its narrator lacks comprehensive knowledge of the characters and events in the story. Third-person point of view

("They didn't realize he was still alive because.. ..") is usually objective and omniscient (see LeGuin's detailed essay on the topic).

Prose Poem   Story with a lyrical voice that is not in verse form.

Realism   Story reflective of verisimilitude or the truth found in everyday life.

Satire   Story that augments humor, irony and wit to illustrate human or institutional frailties.

Setting   This device refers to time and place and how they influence the story, in much the same way that cultural environment and heritage impacts one's personality (see Welty's essay on setting). Setting also relates to macro considerations, such as the social and political ethos of the time and place.

Stream of Consciousness   The continual flowing of thoughts through the mind of a character. For example, Alice Walker uses this device to great effect in "Roselily."

Structure   The specific placement of events and details to achieve the writer's predetermined effect, which in this genre, may deviate from the standard construction of crisis, climax and resolution. A crisis is the problem; a climax, or the high point of the story, is where a major change transpires; and a resolution is the end result of the story's main dramatic complication. It is important to note that character in the very short story is typically only a glanced symbol, and plot—the sequence of what happens in a story—is a slim shadow of the larger and more important overall structure.

Suspense   Feeling of anxiousness in the reader that makes her want to know what is going to occur in a story or how the story is going to end.

Symbolism   Detail that underscores a story's theme. For example, the title of Ann Beattie's story "Janus," or, more simply, an image of a worm-riddled apple in a narrative whose theme is lost innocence.

Syntax   The way the sentence is constructed. For example, it can be simple, and brief like Hemingway's or longer and more complex, like Nabokov's.

Tone   The emotional mood, which can be anything from sad and depressed to optimistic and joyous, and anything in between, e.g., sarcastic, resigned, lyrical, etc.

Voice   The writer's voice comprises sentence construction (syntax), word choice (diction), and tone. It acts as a musical instrument in the fine art of crafting the very short story. It bears the primary responsibility of seducing the reader, and in this genre, doing so from the very first sentence. Its rhythm and emotion function in much the same way as a ballad's melody and mood (see Baraka and LeGuin's essays on this feature of form).

Credits

"Cata 1., 2., and 3" from A .38 Special and a Broken Heart by Jonis Agee. Reprinted with the permission of Coffee House Press from Jonis Agee, A .38 SPECIAL AND A BROKEN HEART.

"Hands," from WINSEBERG, OHIO by Sherwood Anderson. "Hands," from WINESBURG, OHIO by Sherwood Anderson, copyright © 1919 by B.W. Huebsch; Copyright © 1947 by Eleanor Copenhaven Anderson. Used by permission of Viking Penguin, a division of Penguin Putnam, Inc.

"Writing Stories," from SHERWOOD ANDERSON'S MEMOIRS, Vol. 19 of THE COMPLETE WORKS OF SHERWOOD ANDERSON by ed. Kiehinosuke Ohashi. Reprinted by permission of Harold Ober Associates, Incorporated. Copyright © 1942 by Eleanor Anderson. Copyright renewed 1969 by Eleanor Copenhaven Anderson.

Robert Allen Papinchak on "Anderson's Prose Style" by Robert Allen Papinchak. Reprinted by permission of Robert Allen Papinchak.

"Happy Endings," from MURDER IN THE DARK AND SIMPLE MURDERS by Margaret Atwood. "Happy Endings," from GOOD BONES AND SIMPLE MURDERS by Margaret Atwood, copyright © 1983, 1992, 1994 by O.W. Toad, Ltd. A Nan A. Talese Book. Used by permission of Doubleday, a division of Random House, Inc.

"My First Goose," from THE COLLECTED STORIES OF ISAAC BABEL by Isaac Babel. Reprinted by permission of S.G. Phillips, Inc.

"Words" from TALES, published by Grove Press, Inc. Copyright © 1967 LeRoi Jones by Amiri Baraka. "Words," from TALES by Amiri Baraka. Copyright © 1967 LeRoi Jones.

Amiri Baraka on "Voice and Beginnings," by Amiri Baraka. "Beginnings," by Amiri Baraka, from THREE MINUTES OR LESS. Copyright © 2000.

"Janus" from WHERE YOU'LL FIND ME by Ann Beattie. Reprinted with the permission of Simon & Schuster from WHERE YOU'LL FIND ME AND OTHER STORIES by Ann Beattie. Copyright © 1986 by Irony & Pity, Inc.

"Fifth Story-The Pot of Basil" from THE DECAMERON by Giovanni Boccaccio. Reprinted with permission from THE DECAMERON by Boccaccio, translated by G.H. McWilliam (Penguin Classics, 1986), copyright © G.H. McWilliam, 1986.

"The Astronomer's Wife" by Kay Boyle. Reprinted by permission of the Estate of Kay Boyle and the Watkins/Loomis Agency.

"The Book of Sand," from THE BOOK OF SAND by Jorge Luis Borges. "The Book of Sand," from COLLECTED FICTIONS by Jorge Luis Borges, translated by Andrew Hurley, copyright © 1998 by Maria Kodama; translation copyright © 1998 by Penguin Putnam, Inc. Used by permission of Viking Penguin, a division of Penguin Putnam, I

"The Monster," from BERTOLT BRECHT, SHORT STORIES, 1921–1946 by Bertolt Brecht. Copyright © 1949, copyright renewed © 1983 Stefan S. Brecht.

"My Madness," from BETTING ON THE MUSE: POEMS & STORIES BY CHARLES BUKOWSKI. Copyright © 1996 by Linda Lee Bukowski. Reprinted from BETTING ON THE MUSE: POEMS AND STORIES with the permission of Black Sparrow Press.

"The Tale of the Cats" from ITALIAN FOLKTALES by Italo Calvino. "The Tale of the Cats," from ITALIAN FOLKTALES: SELECTED AND RETOLD by Italo Calvino, copyright © 1956 by Giulio Einaudi editore, s.p.a., English translation by George Martin copyright © 1980 by Harcourt, Inc., reprinted by permission of Harcourt, Inc.

Italo Calvino on 'Economy of Expression' from SIX MEMOS FROM THE NEXT MILLENNIUM, translated by Patrick Creagh. Italo Calvino on 'Quickness' in Narrative," translated by Patrick Creagh, from SIX MEMOS FROM THE NEXT MILLENNIUM. English translation copyright © 1992 by Patrick Creagh.

"The Werewolf," from BURNING YOUR BOATS by Angela Carter. Copyright © The Estate of Angela Carter, 1995. Reproduced by permission of the Estate of Angela Carter c/o Rogers, Coleridge & White Ltd., 20 Powis Mews, Londons W11 1JN.

"Popular Mechanics," from WHAT WE TALK ABOUT WHEN WE TALK ABOUT LOVE by Raymond Carver. Copyright © 1981 by Raymond Carver. Used by permission of Alfred A. Knopf, a division of Random House, Inc.

Raymond Carver, "On Writing" from FIRES. Reprinted by permission of International Creative Management, Inc. Copyright © 1983 by Tess Gallagher.

"The Physician's Tale," from THE CANTERBURY TALES by Geoffrey Chaucer. Reprinted with the permission of Simon & Schuster from THE CANTERBURY TALES OF GEOFFREY CHAUCER by Geoffrey Chaucer. Copyright © 1948 by Simon & Schuster. Copyright renewed © 1975 by Simon and Schuster.

"The Worm in the Apple," from THE STORIES OF JOHN CHEEVER. Copyright © 1978 by John Cheever. Used by permission of Alfred A. Knopf, a division of Random House, Inc.

"The Huntsman," from ANTON CHEKHOV EARLY STORIES. Translation copyright © 1982 Patrick Miles and Harvey Pitcher. Reprinted with permission.

Vladimir Nabokov on 'Chekhov's Prose' from LECTURES ON RUSSIAN LITERATURE. Excerpt from, "Anton Checkhov (1860–1904)," in LECTURES ON RUSSIAN LITERATURE, copyright © 1981 by the Estate of Vladimir Nabokov, reprinted by permission of Harcourt, Inc.

"Caline," from THE COMPLETE WORKS OF KATE CHOPIN. Reprinted by permission of Louisiana State University Press from THE COMPLETE WORKS OF KATE CHOPIN, by Kate Chopin. Copyright © 1969 by Louisiana State University Press.

"My Name," from THE HOUSE ON MANGO STREET by Sandra Cisneros. Copyright © 1984 by Sandra Cisneros. Published by Vintage Books, a division of Random House, Inc., and in hardcover by Alfred A. Knopf in 1994. Reprinted by permission of Susan Bergholz Literary Services, New York.

"Bygone Spring," from THE COLLECTED STORIES OF COLETTE by Colette, edited by Robert Phelps, and translated by Matthew Ward. Translation copyright © 1983 by Farrar, Straus & Giroux, Inc.

"Continuity of Parks," from END OF THE GAME AND OTHER STORIES by Julio Cortazar, translated by Paul Blackburn. Copyright © 1967 by Random House, Inc. Used by permission of Pantheon Books, a division of Random House, Inc.

"Night Women" from KRIK? KRAK! by Edwidge Danticat. Reprinted by permission of Soho Press. Copyright © 1991, 1992, 1993, 1994, 1995 by Edwidge Danticat.

Index